To Samuel and Nathaniel, my grandchildren,
who make life such fun

CONTENTS

CHAPTER 1

A Chelsea Childhood

The earliest event I can remember is falling on my head from a swing on to the worn grass of the Chelsea Babies' Club playground sometime in 1933. I was three years old. I don't recall now whether it hurt or not, but I do remember the hours my mother spent trying to get the blood clots out of my hair.

The Chelsea Babies' Club was a determinedly progressive nursery school at the end of our road, Glebe Place. On the short way to school was a menacing poster nailed to a pole. 'If you don't like cats, don't have kittens,' it read. 'If you don't like kittens, don't keep cats.' The Club's founders believed in healthy exercise, year round, in the open air. In the winters, we skipped and frolicked, reddened and blued by the cold, in sturdy knickers and liberty bodices, an odd kind of vest with rubber buttons at the bottom end, presumably to link it to the knickers. The presiding enthusiast for this Spartan regime was a Miss Bunn, around whom glowing infants flourished like buttercups.

I must have been an irritating infant. Apart from falling off swings and trying to climb perilous objects, according to one member of staff, at three years old I talked incessantly. Since my family were all given to talking, nursery school was probably my best chance of being heard.

My parents named me Shirley, not after the celebrated child filmstar of the time, Shirley Temple, but after Charlotte Brontë's 'gallant little cavalier' in her novel of that name, a champion of social justice. I never cared for the name, nor for the book, which I have never managed to read all through. Perhaps that was why my father called me 'Poppy', and 'Poppy' became my childhood name.

My brother, John Edward, two and a half years older than me, was a sensitive, gentle boy with dark-brown eyes and long eye-lashes. As a small child, he closely resembled my mother's beloved younger brother Edward, killed in the First World War. She doted upon John. He was physically delicate, and had been born with slightly bowed legs, in consequence of which he was obliged to wear leg irons as a small child. He was protective and loving towards me, and I basked in his affection, while striving to outdo him. We were friends as well as rivals. Together we invented a private language and a virtual family, called the Dears, around whom we wove stories told late into the night until we finally fell asleep. John was a thoughtful, well-behaved child. He read a lot, and liked listening to music. He disliked sports, and tried to avoid the team games that took up at least two afternoons a week at his traditional Chelsea preparatory school. But he enjoyed swimming and climbing trees, an activity we enjoyed together when our parents bought a cottage in the New Forest just before the outbreak of the Second World War. When he grew into his teen years, he spent a lot of time painting and composing.

My parents, my brother and I, and my mother's dear friend Winifred Holtby lived in a long, thin house with a long, thin garden at 19 Glebe Place, Chelsea. Our street was much favoured by artists, actors and other Chelsea characters. It was an exciting place to grow up in, not just because of the jungle gyms and rope walks at the nursery school, and the muttering bereted painters setting up easels in the street, but because our house presented all sorts of challenges. The house itself was four cramped storeys high, plus a cellar and an attic. There were lots of stairs to climb or to slide down. A favourite game was to see how many stairs my brother and I could jump down; four were easy, six daunting. Then there were my parents' bookcases, which ran from floor to ceiling like climbing-frames, with the added zest of forbidden books on the top shelf. Soon after I could read, I sneaked Havelock Ellis and Marie Stopes from that top shelf. I had learned from my brother that these were naughty books. They turned out to be very boring, but I was amazed by one illustration, a blurred spot underneath which was written: 'This photograph of a human egg is several times life-size.'

George Catlin, my father, was a slim, handsome, scholarly man and physically a little awkward. An only child, he had spent his lonely boyhood reading prodigiously. His erudition ran deep. He had studied the Greek classics, and also substantial parts of the works of the Christian fathers, from St Augustine to St Anselm and Thomas Aquinas, read in Latin. He was not, however, a man at ease in an ivory tower. He longed to be involved in public affairs, in the world of happenings and events.

My father gave me the single greatest gift with which a child can be endowed, self-confidence. Diffident though he was, he loved me from babyhood, perhaps because I resembled his own mother who had died prematurely when he was only twenty-two. He and I conspired together. I climbed his bookshelves, right up to the ceiling, clinging grubbily to the dusty ledges. He never tried to stop me, and both of us knew he wouldn't tell my mother, who would immediately anticipate cracked skulls and broken arms. That I was a girl was irrelevant to his ambitions for me. I could be anything I wanted to be. His feminism was not an intellectual construct. Quite simply, he saw no reason to think that women were lesser beings than men. Until I was sixteen or so, it never occurred to me that this was a rare attitude for a man born in the nineteenth century to take.

Intelligent, ambitious and shy, my father so closely resembled the film actor Leslie Howard, renowned for the role of Ashley in the film *Gone with the Wind*, that people stopped him in the street to ask for his autograph. He longed to be a politician, a career he was in no way cut out for. He disdained the career that the circumstance of having to make a living thrust upon him – for his father, an Anglican priest, was painfully poor – that of university lecturer. All his life long, he wanted to be what he wasn't. At Oxford University he had established something of a record, winning the Chancellor's English Essay Prize, the Gladstone and the Matthew Arnold Memorial Prizes, all in the space of two years. He was later awarded a Ph.D. for his thesis on Thomas Hobbes's *Leviathan*, at a time when doctorates in philosophy were extremely rare. But he had no great respect for his own considerable academic achievements. He slipped into sycophancy when encountering notable public figures. When I was old enough to notice, I wept inwardly for him, but could never persuade him to see these men for what many of them were – pompous, pushy or self-obsessed.

My father had adored his mother, Edith Kate, who married when she was only twenty-two a considerably older man, George Catlin, who was an ordained minister in the Church of England. Before long, she rebelled against the constraints of being a vicar's wife. She was widely read, and her commonplace book reveals the intensity of her commitment to educate herself. The carefully copied quotations range from George Meredith to William Wilberforce, and are decorated with pen-and-ink drawings of local churches and villages. She came to resent the exclusion of women from civic life. She supported the National Union of Women's Suffrage Societies, organisations that campaigned for women to have a vote, though they eschewed violent methods towards that end.

This brought her into conflict with many members of the Church her husband served. Parish councillors and patrons of Anglican livings were disinclined to appoint curates with radical wives. The marriage became strained, and Edith Catlin left her husband and son in 1915 to work in a charity settlement in the East End of London. Her son, who had won an Exhibition to New College, Oxford, was broken-hearted. Two years later, she died of uraemia after a failed operation. His understanding of the cause that had driven her shaped the rest of his life. It was a significant reason for his attraction to my mother.

My mother, Vera Brittain, was a conscientious but rather remote parent. She was small, dark-haired, intense, serious and single-minded. My brother and I were brought up to respect her work; she was the family's main breadwinner. She was also intensely ambitious. She once wrote of the unhappy years she spent at Oxford immediately after the First World War, 'Only Ambition held me to life.' As a child, I realised that her deepest commitment was to writing, then to my brother and only after them, to me. I don't recall resenting this at all, but it taught me to be independent. My mother was not widely liked. Her candour, which she did little to modify, left behind a trail of offended acquaintances, often fellow authors. At least two of her friend-ships with well-known contemporaries, the writers Phyllis Bentley and Storm Jameson, broke up eventually on the rocks of my mother's criticisms and convictions.

My mother's memories of the First World War were never far away, and were haunted by the men she had lost, men she was determined to make immortal by her writing. By my teens, I had a rounded image of Roland Leighton, the fiancé killed in France just before Christmas 1915, and of Edward, the sensitive, music-loving brother who survived until June 1918 when he was killed in the final Austrian offensive against Italy. Victor Richardson and Geoffrey Thurlow, the two other dear friends of Edward, who died in 1917, were less clearly defined in my mind. But I had a feeling that both had been in love with Vera too, probably the only young woman they had come to know well with whom they could share the horrors of the war. My mother kept their letters, books and poems, charting the change from the romantic heroism of the early months, best captured in Rupert Brooke's poetry, to the disillusion and despair of the trenches, and the legacy of devastated towns and villages.

Soon after he volunteered for military service, my mother sent her fiancé Roland a copy of Rupert Brooke's war sonnets, *1914*. At Christmas 1917, from Étaples in northern France, she sent her brother Edward, inscribed to 'my bien-aimé', Gilbert Frankau's *City of Fear*, a brutal description of the murdered town of Ypres. Edward sent her, a few days later, Robert Nichols's poems, *Ardours and Endurances*. Under the inscription, she later wrote the date of Edward's death in Italy, 15 June 1918, and Nichols's words 'I, too, take leave of all I ever had.'

The legacy of the war cast a permanent shadow over her life which nothing could quite dispel. Four years of war had accentuated her natural trait of anxiety. As I wrote in a 1978 preface to her famous autobiography, *Testament of Youth*, 'it was hard for her to laugh unconstrainedly; at the back of her mind, the row upon row of wooden crosses were planted too deeply'. But she did allow herself some moments of frivolity. She loved clothes, and used to take me with her while she tried on the elegant polka-dotted silk dresses and emphatic hats of the 1930s. A new hat or pair of gloves could lift her spirits for days. It was a pleasure I did not share. After the first ten minutes of each encounter with a supercilious sales lady, I began to think about ponies and tricycles, and to resent the waste of my time. These early experiences immunised me against both shopping and fashion. For years I bought the first thing I saw that looked even vaguely as if it might suit me, though often it didn't.

Our disciplined, hard-working and peripatetic household was completed by Amy Francis, who was recruited at the age of eighteen to help look after the children, and became, as cook and housekeeper, central to the enterprise.

One floor of our house was the domain of my mother's beloved friend Auntie Winifred. Winifred Holtby, who had met my mother in the autumn of 1919 when both were students at Somerville College, Oxford, was, like her, a writer. The two young women had shared flats, first in Doughty Street, Bloomsbury, and then in Maida Vale, after leaving university, and together tried to break into the world of journalism and writing books. Both were regarded as progressive writers, addressing topics like feminism and equal rights not much discussed in conventional society. They were also both passionate protagonists of the League of Nations, forerunner to today's United Nations, and lectured for the League of Nations Union up and down the country.

After my mother married in 1925, she and my father shared their home with Winifred. That seemed to some of their friends and acquaintances an odd arrangement. But my father held a professorship at Cornell University in New York State and was away a lot of the time. He recognised that my mother needed the loyal friendship and support Winifred unstintingly gave her. With eyes the colour of cornflowers and hair the pale gold of the summer wheat in her native Yorkshire wolds, Winifred couldn't easily be overlooked. Indeed she might have been a descendant of the Vikings who had ravaged and occupied so much of the east coast of Lincolnshire and Yorkshire centuries before. Tall – nearly six feet – and slim, she was incandescent with the radiance of her short and concentrated life. For she died, aged thirty-seven, when I was only five.

The fashions of the 1930s added drama to Winifred's striking appearance. She often wore a dark cloak, black or purple, with a wide-brimmed felt hat. Her favourite dress was a slim black shift decorated with sequins, which caught and reflected light in all the colours of the spectrum. It seemed to sum up her being, one that elicited radiance in others. 'My existence,' she once wrote, 'seems to me like a clear stream which has simply reflected other people's stories and problems.'* Those lives came from a wide spectrum of Yorkshire society. Brought up in the village of Rudston in the East Riding, Winifred as a little girl had accompanied her father David to agricultural events and around his farm. Her mother Alice, the first woman to become an alderman in Yorkshire, took her to meet her constituents, many of them struggling with the agricultural depression of the turn of the twentieth century. Their experiences became the material for Winifred's most ambitious book, *South Riding*, in which she explored the story of local government in her imaginary part of the county. For Winifred, local government, far from being lacklustre, involved itself in the deepest hopes and fears of its community.

Winifred was by nature a mediator, a peacemaker who tried to reconcile the powerful people who jostled for her affection: her mother Alderman Mrs Holtby; Lady Rhondda, proprietor and editor of the feminist journal *Time and Tide*; my mother and many more. Like many a peacemaker, she sometimes evoked contempt and cruelty in others. Virginia Woolf, aloof and disdainful of other women writers, dismissed her as 'poor, gaping Winifred', a savage allusion to her wide, toothy smile.

Lady Rhondda, daughter of the Welsh industrialist and politician David Thomas, later Lord Rhondda, was a friend of Winifred and an occasional visitor to our house. She used to travel with a carefully packed suitcase of medicines. I may have sensed that my mother disliked her, for I certainly did. She was fussy, domineering and unbending. She was also single-minded in her devotion to the women's cause, but I came to appreciate her contribution to that cause only much later in my life, when I got to know something about the work of the equal-rights organisation the Six Point Group, founded in 1918.

* Marion Shaw, *The Clear Stream: A Life of Winifred Holtby*, Virago, 1999.

For my brother and me, Winifred was the source of unending pleasure: stories, games, wild fantasies, exotic visitors and carved wooden crocodiles from South Africa, the country she had come to love after her visit there in 1926. Sometimes she looked after us in my parents' absence abroad. Our favourite game was 'elephants'. We would pile cushions high up on Winifred's back, and issue orders from our rickety howdah as she crawled carefully across the floor. Ordinary things became extraordinary, and occasionally frightening. When, in an absent-minded moment, she gave me undiluted antiseptic to gargle away a sore throat, I thought I had swallowed fire.

John and I loved Auntie Winifred. We were also aware how much her friendship meant to our mother. For Winifred was life-affirming, one of those blessed people who find the world a constant source of delight, excitement and laughter. She radiated gaiety. That gaiety helped to dispel the sadness that permeated my mother's life after her losses in the First World War.

Some critics and commentators, both at the time and since, have suggested that the relationship between Vera and Winifred must have been a lesbian one. The fact that Winifred continued to live in our household after my mother's marriage to George Catlin confirmed them in that belief. My mother deeply resented this. She felt that it was inspired by a subtle anti-feminism to the effect that women could never be real friends unless there was a sexual motivation, while the friendships of men had been celebrated in literature from classical times. Her book *Testament of Friendship* (1940), which told the story of her relationship with Winifred, was in part motivated by her determination to refute that assumption. But as a famous woman author holding progressive opinions about the position women should occupy, and one whose writing was readily accessible to a wide range of readers, my mother became an icon to feminists and in particular to lesbian feminists. She herself was instinctively heterosexual. She had inherited a Victorian legacy of prejudice but had largely overcome it through her own friendships with lesbian women. When I was fifteen, she explained to me that some men and women were homosexual. She sometimes asked me to accompany her when she met lesbian women who were besotted with her, to indicate her own commitment to a conventional marriage and family.

A generation later, my friend Val Mitchison, daughter of the Scottish writer and broadcaster Naomi Mitchison, and I were summoned to meet the President of the Junior Common Room at Somerville, and asked not to make public show of what was assumed to be a lesbian relationship. I was shocked because I knew it was not. Val, with her usual robustness, insisted on walking around Somerville's gardens hand in hand with me for the next few days, just to show the authorities they could go to hell. It took another generation before the myth that women who were heterosexual could not have close female friendships was dispelled.

While Auntie Winifred was a source of delight to John and me, our blood relatives were less appealing. We had no uncles or aunts, since my father was an only child and my mother had lost her brother in the First World War, but both maternal grandparents came from large families. My maternal grandmother, Edith Brittain, was the daughter of an impoverished organist and music teacher, Inglis Bervon, and was one of four sisters. Two of them married, the two others remained single. The eldest, Florence Bervon, a tall woman with piercing brown eyes, made herself into a headmistress despite having no teaching qualifications. She, together with her friend Louise Heath-Jones, shared the headship of St Monica's at Kingswood in Surrey, the private girls' school my mother attended. The third sister, Aunt Lillie, was cheerful and rather fussy. She married a thin, elegant businessman called Arthur Bentley-Carr, and they had one son, Robin, who later became a wartime squadron-leader in RAF Bomber Command. The youngest sister, Aunt Belle, was also the jolliest – funny and

candid. After working as a governess, the respectable profession
for unqualified young middle-class women, she had bought a teashop in Deal that she called 'The Golden Hinde'. John and I used
to stay with her, riding ponies over the South Downs, spending
long afternoons on the shingle beach, and retiring to a beach hut
for tea whenever it got too rainy or too cold.

My grandmother Edith had married into a much better-off
family than her own, and was conscious of the status this conferred upon her. I remember her as being very proper, punctual
and tidy, and well dressed in a rather elaborate way. I was transfixed by the fox furs she wore, with the fox perpetually eating its
own feet where the fastenings were. She was a good cook and a
careful housekeeper, keeping a close eye on the Welsh maids who
lived in the Brittain grandparents' extensive Kensington flat.

My grandfather, Thomas Arthur Brittain, had been overtaken
by melancholia following Edward's loss in battle and his own early
retirement. He had nothing to do, beyond getting dressed, about
which he was fastidious, going to Harrods and reading the newspapers. He lived a life of comfort and emptiness, occasionally
lightened by visits from my mother, who was punctilious about
visiting, and on Sundays by us two grandchildren. Sunday tea was
an important occasion, for which we were dressed in party
clothes. It did not disappoint us, for there was always an array of
rock cakes and Victoria sandwiches made by my grandmother, bis-
cuits and cherry sponge.

The Brittains, my grandfather's family, were a quarrelsome lot.
There were eleven children, of whom my grandfather was the
eldest, and they rarely met except at weddings and funerals. By
the time John and I were born, most of them were lost to us.
There were rumours of one who had gone to the Klondike to hunt
for gold. Just one, the youngest, Aunt Muriel, remained closely in
touch. She had 'married well', to use the phrase much in fashion
at the time, a young man called Henry Leigh Groves, the only
son of a successful Manchester businessman, William Grimble

Groves, who had made his money from a thriving brewery. In 1897 he had bought an impressive Victorian mansion, Holehird, in the Patterdale valley in the Lake District, designed by the renowned architect J. S. Crowther and commanding a panoramic view of Lake Windermere and the Langdale fells beyond.

Henry Leigh Groves trained as a water engineer and worked on the construction of reservoirs, but his real dedication was to public service. 'Service,' he once wrote sententiously, 'is the rent we pay for our room on earth.' Elected to the Westmorland County Council as representative for Bowness, he remained on it for forty-seven years and was its chairman from 1925 to 1927. He meant exactly what he said, and the rent he paid for his room on earth was indeed munificent. Becoming High Sheriff in 1938, he celebrated his office by donating the bed of Lake Windermere, 3642 acres in all, to the Westmorland County Council. The gift enabled the local authority to control development and commercial exploitation of the lake. He and Muriel also devoted themselves to creating a work of art out of the already extensive gardens he had inherited. There were large heated greenhouses in which a remarkable range of orchids flourished. Great-aunt Muriel used to enjoy taking guests between the rows of flesh-eating orchids, their exotic flowers moving to follow the warm scent of living beings.

Aunt Muriel was not particularly keen on her Brittain relatives, but fortunately for me, my mother was among the exceptions. Muriel liked my mother, who had been a bridesmaid at her wedding to Leigh in 1906. Muriel and Leigh never had any children, but they were generous hosts to John and me, encouraging us to row on the pond and scramble up the surrounding fells. I came to love the Lake District, and after the war quite often went to visit.

Aunt Muriel was an unpredictable lady, much given to practical jokes. I was disconcerted by her habit of wearing felt hats in bed, and by her occasionally putting wet sponges on the tops of doors, which would fall on unsuspecting maids carrying trays. My strangest moment was when, as a teenager, I met an unknown woman guest waiting outside the bathroom carrying a towel. Aunt Muriel denied her existence. Later that morning, as we waited outside the mansion for Uncle Leigh in his elegant 1920s Lancia to drive us to church, I saw the same person coming around the edge of the long façade of Holehird. Again, Aunt Muriel claimed she was unable to see anybody. To this day, I do not know whether I was seeing a ghost, or the real presence of my great-aunt's niece, a lady called Philippa Hole, an aspiring poet, who suffered from delusions and lived in a mental hospital. Her main delusion was that she was the wife of T. S. Eliot.

John intermittently dreamed of inheriting the house, but true to his lifelong commitment to Westmorland, Uncle Leigh gave Holehird and 550 acres of adjoining land to the County Council in 1945. Years later, the mansion was rented for a nominal amount to the Cheshire Homes, and for thirty years housed patients with incurable illnesses. The marvellous gardens were handed over to the Cumbrian Horticultural Society, and are still a joy to see.

In the years shortly before the Second World War, my mother enjoyed a period of fame as a best-selling writer. Her most renowned book, *Testament of Youth*, an autobiography of her wartime experience as a nurse and her personal agony in losing all the young men she most loved, had attracted enthusiastic reviews on both sides of the Atlantic. After it was published in 1933, she was invited to undertake prestigious lecture tours in North America, the apotheosis of a best-selling author.

We children once or twice travelled down with her to Southampton on the boat train, set apart from all the other trains at Waterloo by the romance and mystery of its destination. Uniformed porters manhandled huge belted trunks and handsome leather suitcases pasted with coloured stickers announcing their owners' previous voyages, to Paris, Delhi or Cape Town. Inside the carriages, each polished table boasted its complement of shaded orange lamps. Southampton docks were dominated by the haughty liners of the Atlantic, their row upon row of white cabins crowned by three or four red and black funnels towering above the piers. My mother's stateroom would be filled with flowers and yellow telegrams, heralds of the adventures to come. We children had only a notional idea of North America, a vast, vigorous continent on the other side of a huge blue ocean which commanded a large slice of the toy globe in our nursery.

My father adored meeting the great, and the great poseurs, of the political world, and could rarely distinguish between them. He was the instigator of the cocktail parties that brought all kinds of visitors to our house, though my mother's fame was the reason they came. Some of their guests were fashionable authors of the time. The guest my brother and I liked best was the actress Sybil Thorndike, a woman whose radiant and generous presence warmed all those she met. She was rare in acknowledging and liking children – most of my parents' guests loftily ignored our presence. Dressed in our nightclothes, we used to watch the arrivals through the banisters. Most thrilling of all to us were the Africans, for we had never before met anyone with a black skin. Among them was Clements Kadalie, the founder in 1919 of one of the first African trades unions, the Industrial and Commercial Union. He had met Auntie Winifred on the visit she had made to South Africa in 1926.

Persuaded that trades union organisation was the first vital step to the liberation of the African majority, Winifred raised the money to send out to South Africa an experienced union organiser, William Ballinger. He and his wife Margaret threw themselves into the cause of the Africans. Margaret became, in 1937, one of the three representatives of Africans in the House of Assembly, following the removal of all African voters from the electoral roll the year before. Sixteen years after entering the Assembly,

Margaret Ballinger became the first leader of the Liberal Party of South Africa. Seven years later, in 1960, she retired from Parliament when the Nationalist government of Hendrik Verwoerd abolished even this indirect form of representation of the African majority. To the Nationalist government, Africans were a different species, for whom democracy was inappropriate.

Just as Winifred had become committed to righting the injustices suffered by the African majority in South Africa, so my father had thrown himself into the cause of the independence of India. He had become an enthusiastic supporter of the Free India Movement, and Vice-Chairman of the Council for Indian Independence. One day in January 1936, a slim young visitor with dark rings under haunted brown eyes came to tea to meet fellow socialists in Britain. Jawaharlal Nehru had just got out of prison. His sister, Lakshmi Pandit, herself an activist in the struggle for Indian independence, a commanding and handsome woman who combined grace with intellect, became my parents' lifelong friend. Among the other visitors to my parents' house was H. G. Wells, with his high, squeaky voice; another, the renowned young author Rebecca West, intense, dark and powerful. According to my mother, who told me long afterwards, she overheard Wells declare to West, as she passed by offering drinks, 'I could take you between the tram lines!'

After the last guest had gone and the hum of conversation had ceased, my brother and I would slip into the drawing-room to finish off the dregs in the bottoms of the glasses, returning to bed in a warm and muzzy haze.

Despite the visitors and the occasional parties, ours was a highly disciplined household. My mother was a methodical, tidy person, characteristics that had served her well as a VAD nurse during the war. Her manuscripts were always well organised, her correspondence carefully filed. My father and I were both untidy. He had piles of newspapers, articles and books in his study, waiting to be read; I had toys and clothes scattered about the nursery.

Determinedly professional, my mother was at work in her study by 10 a.m., after reading the newspapers and the morning's letters, sorting out the shopping lists and paying the bills. At least an hour every day was devoted to replying to letters, often by hand, which the Royal Mail delivered that afternoon or at latest the following morning. Her correspondence was enormous, amounting to hundreds of letters and cards every month. Everyone who wrote to her was answered with the same conscientious and personal concern. She built up an extensive network of people from all over the world who felt, through letters, that she was a close friend. Her study was a sacred place, of blotters and pens in black-and-gold stands, of carefully ranged notepaper and envelopes, and of manuscripts composed in her neat, rounded script. Every member of the household well understood that only death, war or a serious accident would justify interrupting her there. It was many weary stairs away from ground level, where milkmen clinked the bottles in their horse-drawn floats, and pedlars bellowed their wares.

My brother and I had our own territory, a brightly painted yellow nursery on the third floor with wooden bars over the windows to stop us falling out. When we were very young, the room was shared with various nannies in starched white aprons, stern figures who were not to be disobeyed. Once left on our own to play, we spent long happy hours with our lead soldiers and farm animals, each piece carefully made and painted. Our soldiers were rarely engaged in battle. My brother liked to line them up on a linoleum parade ground, while I held elections and organised them into voting for the king, who wore a gold-and-white uniform and a cocked hat and was invariably elected. On occasion, when we were out of sorts with one another, one of us would bombard the other's soldiers with small pellets from tiny cannons, but we preferred setting up a cavalry charge. The hurtling horses of the Light Brigade flung themselves ceaselessly at the merciless guns of the Russians on our nursery floor.

At night, the nursery became a place of menace and mystery. My father had presented us with a bronze bust of Dante, one of his many attempts to insinuate into his children a love of history and literature. The bust had an uncompromisingly sharp profile, a beaky Roman nose, hollow cheeks, heavy-lidded bronze eyes and hair concealed under a tight hood. The headlights of passing taxis would momentarily gild the bust, then it would sink back into the shadows of the room, ever watchful, ever present. Dante had something to do with Hades, I believed, a ferryman of dead souls like Charon. I would lie motionless in bed, believing that any sudden movement might stir the bust into appalling life.

Every afternoon, after an austere lunch, my mother went walking around the regimented flowers in the parade-ground beds that studded the Embankment Gardens. At weekends, when I didn't have to go to my local school, she and I sometimes extended her customary expedition to a circuit of Battersea Park, by way of the handsome bridges spanning the brown and rolling Thames. Battersea Park had a couple of tennis courts where flannelled and pullovered young bloods disported themselves, and an aviary in which melancholy dusty birds plucked petulantly at their feathers. Saddest was an owl, which blinked desolately at the grey world outside his barred cage.

My childhood was enriched by meeting the children of my parents' friends, some of whom were to become my own. Robert Bruce was one of a large family of children whose lives straddled London and Scotland. His father, Lord Balfour of Burleigh, was Chairman of Lloyds Bank and owned a large estate near Stirling. A remarkably handsome man with a Roman profile, he and his impressive, intimidating wife had radical opinions which marked them out from other members of the Scottish aristocracy. Robert was to become a lifelong friend, who married my sister-in-law Jennifer some years after she and my brother John were divorced. He taught me whatever I know about climbing mountains. We spent hours practising belays and rock-holds on the big boulders of the escarpment south of Sheffield and then trying them out in Snowdonia or Scotland.

Every year my parents were invited to watch the Boat Race from the Chiswick home of Naomi Mitchison and her husband Dick, a successful lawyer. Both were strong supporters of the Labour Party, like my own parents. Naomi, an extraordinary woman whose bohemian style and forthright opinions shook conventional society, was already a well-known writer. She had five children, the youngest of whom, Valentine, was the same age as me. We would circle around each other at these parties, the way young children do. Ten years later, we were to become the closest of friends.

My parents spent the mornings in their separate studies, but meals were sociable occasions. Politics invaded our conversations. Mussolini stalked through our soup and Franco smirked in our puddings. Hitler's relentless ascent to power became an ever-darkening shadow over our ordered lives. My parents had heard him speak in Cologne in March 1936, the day before his reoccupation of the Rhineland, and had shuddered at his extraordinary capacity to shape men and women to his will. I, of course, understood little of all this, though I was addicted to the political cartoons of David Low, a great friend of my parents, which graphically illustrated these events. What I did understand was that no one would pay me any attention unless I engaged in political conversation too. 'You're only interested in Hitler, not me,' I informed them at the age of five. I confused the Reichstag fire in February 1933 with that of the Crystal Palace in November 1936; they all became one great awful conflagration in my mind.

That politics was the most exciting of all the exciting things in the world I never doubted. At age one, in 1931, I had been pushed in a pram along the high streets of Brentford and Chiswick, in the first of my father's unsuccessful forays as a Labour candidate in a general election. At five, I was told about his campaign in Sunderland. A stranger to luck, the first time since 1931 that he failed to fight an election as a Labour candidate was in 1945, when Clement Attlee led the Party to its first outright victory with a majority over all other parties of 146.

The politics of the dictators was the politics of intimidation and revenge. The politics of Britain was the politics of misery. It was the era of the Great Depression. Shabby men wearing the tarnished medals of the Great War for Civilisation stood in the gutters selling matches and shoelaces. Unable to pass the stooped seller of violets, my mother found a shilling for him. But we knew he wanted not a shilling but a job. The violets, hanging their small heads over the glass we put them in, seemed to sense our shame. The despair of the unemployed was captured in the powerful, bitter drawings of Arthur Wragg, another friend of my parents, in his book *Jesus Wept*, as telling as the photographs by Margaret Bourke-White of the sharecroppers in the American South.

I left the Babies' Club when I was four years old for the more demanding atmosphere of Mrs Spencer's Academy at Brechin Place, South Kensington, a small school of scrubbed, rosy, neatly uniformed boys and girls emulating their parents' image of the well-disciplined middle-class child. At home, the era of nannies had ended. Instead, John and I had a governess, a gentle German girl called Agnes, whose job was to teach us French and German. My affection for Agnes, who returned home to Germany when war broke out, tempered any xenophobic feelings I might have had. She retained her fondness for England, and after the war married a British serviceman. Another more formidable governess came to stay with us for a few months, Suzanne Piaget, daughter of the famous Swiss child psychologist, but whether she had any impact on me I do not remember.

When our family moved from Glebe Place in 1937 to the grander surroundings of Cheyne Walk, nearly two years after Winifred Holtby's early death from Bright's disease, I pleaded with my parents to let me attend the local school, Christ Church (Church of England) Elementary. Christ Church school was a mid-Victorian building with classrooms of high brown wooden walls topped by yellowing glass. Some of the classrooms had folding doors dividing them. When a teacher was ill or absent, the doors were pushed back so that the children could share the other class's lessons. Between the two classrooms, each of thirty or so children, would sit the teacher on a high wooden stool with a cane across her lap. Chatting among the children, let alone the throwing of paper darts, led to immediate and painful punishment.

Many of my fellow pupils were pasty-faced and skinny; some had the bowed legs of rickets. Their lifeless woollen jerseys had holes in the elbows, and they wore skirts and shorts cut down after long use by older brothers and sisters. Every other morning, all of us had to go through the indignity of having our heads searched for lice. Children who harboured them were shampooed with Lysol. The rest of us gave them a wide berth. One family in my class took turns to come to school. I asked one of them why. Between them, they had only two pairs of boots and the children had to share them. I asked my mother why I had four pairs of shoes and two pairs of sandals while they had only half of one.

At Christmas, the London County Council gave every child a bag of sweets and either a paper doll or a set of crayons. For many it was all the Christmas presents they ever received. I had a set of farm animals and a tricycle as well. I didn't understand why I had done so much better than my friends. But I did understand that social divisions were abysses it was dangerous to cross. Fearful of having my head banged on the tarmac of the school playground, I quickly learned to speak in a cockney accent and to leave and enter my house by the basement. I never said anything about it. My classmates simply assumed I was the cook's daughter. And I nearly was, for I adored our young cook-housekeeper Amy and her warm-hearted husband, Charles Burnett. They were my other parents, in some ways closer to me than my own. I felt I was their daughter too.

Education mirrored class and class mirrored education. At eight years old, I was too young to think through the ethos of the two very different schools I had attended, Mrs Spencer's Academy and Christ Church Elementary, but the comparison was so stark I cannot believe it had no effect on me. It wasn't just the differences in the classrooms and the teachers. It was the differences in the life experiences of the children, their housing, their parents and their aspirations. Comfortable middle-class England was unaware of these differences, and that was why having evacuee children from the big cities bivouacked upon them in the first two years of the war came as such a great shock. I suspect evacuation had a lot to do with the radical change in public attitudes between pre- and postwar society.

Because my family was so closely entwined with Amy's, I learned early on how unjust the education system was. She had been a clever little girl, whose hopes were pinned on the scholarship examination taken at the age of eleven. There were not many scholarships (this was well before the Butler Act of 1944) but Amy got one. The doors to paradise opened just a little, only to be slammed shut when her parents were unable to afford the school uniform required for grammar school. So Amy, like the rest of the girls in her family, 'went into service', the destination of many working-class girls.

Amy came from a large family who lived in Battersea, across the river, in a cramped Victorian terraced house. Her father was a small, wizened coalman, who delivered sacks of coal carried on a big green cart pulled by a solid, sweating horse. The sacks of coal were heavy, and over the years they bent Mr Francis into a bowed shape. His wife Lillian was a large, heavy woman, prematurely old after giving birth to nine children. Her body slumped from its bones, as if it had been hung up by the shoulders, the baggy bosom and stomach suspended below. She suffered the dragging physical miseries common to poor women of her generation and borne with stoicism.

The Francises' eldest son died when he was sixteen, of meningitis. They had buried three other children as well. Amy, the eldest daughter, serious and responsible, helped to bring up her surviving siblings. She became the model for Lydia Holly, the clever girl in Winifred Holtby's most famous novel, *South Riding*, deprived of a secondary education despite passing the eleven-plus examination because her family couldn't afford the grammar school uniform.

There was not much joy in Amy's life, only a great deal of responsibility, until in 1933 she met Charlie, a young man from Newcastle upon Tyne with a mysterious past. His mother was believed to have been a teacher, his father a successful businessman, but it was never clear whether they had married, and Charlie would not talk about it, even to Amy. Charlie was a hugely generous and sweet-natured person, sunny in temperament, funny and gregarious, and his love for Amy, who was shy and pretty, lightened her life and indeed the lives of all the members of my family. They were married in 1934. Our two families intertwined and became mutually dependent. The surviving children all worked for our family at one time or another, in the years before or after the war: vivacious red-haired Lily, reserved and quiet Renée, bouncy wild Sheila, dapper Ronnie. My mother could not have managed to become and remain a professional writer without their support. While she had been taught how to embroider, knit and sew as a child, she never learned more than the simplest cooking.

Amy and Charlie were both Roman Catholics. Charlie had studied as a boy at Salesian College, a respected south London Catholic school. His interest in music and international affairs had been sparked there, and he sympathised with my parents' preoccupations. He brought to our rather formal household a warmth and humour that swept barriers away. Yet, to the end of her life, my mother, who loved and relied on him, called him 'Burnett'. He called her 'Mrs Catlin'. Only Amy, as a younger woman, could be addressed by her Christian name, though she never called my mother 'Vera'.

My father was converted to Catholicism through his exploration of the works of John Henry Newman while he was a student at Oxford University after the First World War. His was an intellectual conversion, for there were no recent Catholic antecedents in his family. He married my mother in July 1925 at St James's, Spanish Place, a fashionable London Catholic church. Although herself a questioning member of the Church of England, she did not object. The wartime conversion of her first fiancé, Roland Leighton, had already aroused her interest, even empathy, for the Roman Catholic Church. Both my parents were of a sufficiently radical disposition to reject infant baptism. John and I were left free to decide what religion we wanted to belong to once we became adults.

Amy and Charlie had a different set of priorities. They took me to church with them most Sundays. I became familiar with the detached grandeur of the traditional Mass, recited in Latin by a priest whose beautifully robed back was turned to the congregation, and whose movements at the altar were obscure. The insistent rise and fall of Gregorian chant and the smell of incense infused my being, and became the sensual context of the Sabbath.

My father did not have an untroubled relationship with his Church. The Spanish Civil War pitched his deepest values, social democracy and Catholicism, into conflict with one another. He was a strong supporter of Spain's socialist government, and he spent several weeks in Catalonia helping its relief services to identify humanitarian needs. But he was a Catholic too. He identified with the radical priests of Catalonia against the unbending, merciless Castilian hierarchy. Early in 1937, he escaped from the siege of Barcelona shortly before the city fell to Franco's army by disguising himself in a soutane borrowed from a local priest. He was horrified by the concordat the Pope signed after the Civil War with General Franco, burying Spanish socialism for the foreseeable future. For a while he lapsed from any active involvement with the Church.

It is hard to recollect now how great was the dependence of middle-class families on their servants. There were no supermarkets and no convenience foods, no freezers and only rather primitive refrigerators and washing machines. So shopping, cooking and laundry made huge demands on people's time. Kitchen artefacts, like cutlery and serving dishes, were often beautifully crafted, but hours had to be devoted to cleaning and polishing them. Meals were fairly formal, though they rarely offered any satisfaction to gourmets. Overcooked vegetables and lots of mashed potato accompanied shepherd's pie or a piece of cod. Only rarely, on Sundays or birthdays, did we enjoy roast chicken or roast beef, and wine only appeared on auspicious occasions.

Class and domestic service reinforced one another. Employing a servant was as much a badge of class as owning a Bentley or Alfa-Romeo is today a badge of affluence. The maid in the middle-class household did the grungy jobs, cleaning out fireplaces, bringing up the coal, polishing furniture, endlessly brushing and dusting in a world where vacuum cleaners were still a novelty. If the household had several servants, hierarchy was strict: housekeeper and butler at the top, then the lady's maid, and at the bottom the scullery maid and garden boy. Live-in servants had attic bedrooms at the top of the house, and worked at the bottom, in semi-basements with light filtering in through the railings from the garden or street halfway up the window. The concealed world of servants operated beyond the staircase or green baize door that separated it from the world of sirs and madams who lived above, whose goings-on were part of the staple conversational diet of the servant world. Occasionally their conflicts and passions erupted into the floors above. Similarly, 'coping with the servants' was one of the preoccupations of well-off women, though not for my mother, always protective of her private time and space. For my grandmother, it was a staple of her conversation.

The house we had moved into in 1937, in Cheyne Walk, was a fine Georgian terrace house, distanced from the river only by the municipal gardens. It was light and elegant on its first and second floors, cramped on the third floor, mean and squashed in the attic rooms and in the dark basement. My room was in the attic under the roof, a tiny room but with unauthorised access to a lead-covered flat roof by way of a brick pediment. From that high perch I could see the whole of south London laid out before me, the glistening Thames, the warehouses and power stations of Lots Road and Battersea, the endless terraces of little redbrick Victorian houses snaking over the low hills on the opposite side of the river. I found scrambling up to the roof exciting, but I do not remember feeling particularly scared. Indeed, for most of my life, especially when I was young, I have hardly ever been frightened (except by Dante's bust when I was an infant). I make a sharp distinction between courage and fearlessness. Courage, like that of my sensitive Uncle Edward, who won the Military Cross for his bravery on the first day of the Battle of the Somme, was needed to overcome the fear he felt. Fearlessness is simply that – to be without fear, possibly through lack of imagination. It is much less impressive.

My family's brief trips to the continent of Europe before the war were limited to the chilly beaches of Normandy, misleadingly called 'the Opal Coast'. We children spent a holiday at Wimereux in the summer of 1935 with Auntie Winifred and Edith de Coundouroff, the young widow of the Holtbys' unofficially adopted Georgian son, missing and never found during the battles between White Russians and Reds after the Revolution. It was to be Winifred's last summer. Snapshots of the time show her drawn and gaunt, in the final stages of the Bright's disease which killed her that September. I remember her sitting on the beach wrapped in a cloak, watching us doing gymnastics led by an eager French instructor. She had, as usual, stepped into the breach when my grandfather, Thomas Arthur Brittain, disappeared from his home in west London, necessitating my mother's immediate return to England. His body was later discovered in the Thames at Isleworth, for on 2 August he had thrown himself into the river at Hammersmith Bridge. He had never recovered from the loss of his only son Edward on the Italian front very late in the Great War, his melancholia made worse by his early retirement from the paper mill that had been his working life. John and I would spend hours at his home in Edwardes Square looking at the cartoons in old copies of *Punch* and bringing a little brightness into his otherwise grey life. But it was not enough.

In the spring of 1939, my mother, conscious that war might be coming, decided to buy a cottage in the country with her earnings from *Testament of Youth*, where she could write and we children would be reasonably safe. It had to be near a station, since neither of my parents, then or later, was able to drive. They owned a small car, an Austin Seven, that, on the relatively rare occasions it was allowed out, was driven by by Charles Burnett. It was so under-powered that we all had to get out on steep hills. We enjoyed ourselves rocking back and forth to give it extra momentum.

The cottage eventually chosen was the former groom's house on an extensive estate near Lyndhurst in the New Forest. The owner, Mrs Drury Lowe, who lived in the big mock-Tudor mansion next door, still kept a carriage for her outings. She rode side-saddle to hounds, perching like a small bird on the back of a big thoroughbred hunter. The cottage became a treasured haven for my mother. She would sit in the little wooden shed, with her papers and her typewriter, protected from the wind but open to the small country garden she cherished, with its hollyhocks, bright-blue delphiniums, delicate Canterbury bells and borders of forget-me-nots. Amy would weed the flowerbeds, and John and I would climb the surrounding trees or play games on the grass.

The late summer of 1939 was a golden, tranquil season. My brother and I had discovered a large fallen beech tree that we called, for some unknown reason, 'the Submarine'. We spent hours climbing on it, exploring its majestic branches and trunk. In our garden, red admiral and tortoiseshell butterflies flitted around the buddleia and the early Michaelmas daisies.

It was on one buzzing warm morning that September that we children were summoned to listen to the family wireless with its bland, meshed face, crackling and whining in its effort to relay the news. In the broken voice of an old man terminally tired, Neville Chamberlain told us that we were at war with Germany. And my mother, my disciplined, professional mother, wept.

For me, however, war was heroism, adventure, excitement. I had just been moved from Christ Church Elementary to a boarding school at Swanage on the Dorset coast, where I was absorbed into the culture of bullying that makes a nightmare of the lives of so many English children. Every night in our dormitories we played fearsome games of 'truth or dare'. Children my friends and I disliked, because they were homesick or cried easily, were asked horrendous questions about their families or themselves. If they jibbed at replying, insistence on truth gave way to the relentless command of the dare. Dare to knock on matron's door, now, at midnight. Dare to carry a full potty of urine from bed to bed around the dormitory without once setting foot on the floor. Dare to perch on the window ledge for one whole minute until we haul you in.

Air raids offered a diversion from all this. On a few occasions, we watched dogfights between Spitfires and Messerschmitts from the slit trenches carved in the green downs. The victorious pilot would dip his wings to his downed opponent before flying away.

Neither Dorset nor the New Forest could escape the war, once the nine-month phoney war was over. The surroundings of our woodland hamlet were turned into a replica of the Maginot Line: trenches, gun emplacements, hardened bunkers, spikes for tanks. This was where the German invasion, if it came by way of the

Solent, was to be stopped. At the beginning, it all seemed more like theatre than reality. Next door, the manor house, requisitioned by the army, provided a backdrop for some twenty soldiers assembling mortars and machine-guns on the greensward, heedless of danger under a sunny sky. But one cloudy afternoon in November 1940 a low-flying German plane dropped a bomb on them, killing several men and leaving this tranquil place gashed and burned.

In late May 1940, German Panzer divisions had seized Amiens, Arras and Abbeville, three French towns my mother knew painfully well from the First World War. Attending the memorial service for George Lansbury, leader of the Labour Party and a pacifist of saintly disposition, my mother wrote in her daily diary, 'It seemed like a memorial for the human race.' Five days after that service, Belgium sued for peace and the dramatic evacuation of 338,000 soldiers of the British Expeditionary Force, trapped between the German army and the sea, began. 'Feel sick at heart,' my mother wrote, 'when I think of John and Shirley, and can only pray that the tide of war will roll over their heads without harming them.' On 31 May, with much of the BEF dramatically rescued from the beaches of Dunkirk by the most motley fleet ever assembled, she reported, 'Tens of thousands from BEF getting back across the Channel, hungry, half-clad and in any kind of boat that will take them, bombed all the time.' Even Swanage, where I was at school, experienced an air raid in early June.

Worse was to come, in the bombing and flooding of Holland, whose government refused to surrender, and then, on 14 June 1940, the fall of Paris to its traditional enemy. Nothing now stood between the German military machine and the British Isles except the choppy, grey twenty miles of the Channel, Shakespeare's 'moat'.

The speed of France's collapse and the over-running of her neighbours brought the prospect of a German invasion of Britain frighteningly close. My parents were driven by fear for our safety.

Invasion was expected imminently as the desperate preparations around our cottage made plain. Having seen and heard Hitler, they knew better than most what that would mean. But they were never worried about German bombing – indeed, they would bring us back from the United States as soon as they could after the threat of an invasion faded.* They wanted us to share the experience of the war that would shape our country's future. But the consequences of an invasion for us were different. My parents had reason to believe – which was later justified by the fact that their names appeared on the Gestapo blacklist – that if the Germans conquered Britain they would both be among the earliest people to be eliminated. *Testament of Youth* was anathema to the Nazis because of its message of peace. In the case of my father, the reasons were less clear, but he had gone with my mother to tour Germany for three weeks during Hitler's rise to power, collecting background material for a series of articles my mother wrote on the subject. In addition, by 1940 my father had become a prominent advocate for the United States joining the war.

A Minnesota couple who were acquaintances of my mother, Ruth and Woodard Colby, whom she had met in 1934 on the first of her lecture tours of the United States, volunteered to take us. We had never met them, but they sent her a telegram saying simply, 'Send us your children.' My mother was coincidentally wrestling with the moral dilemma of whether she had any right to risk us being orphaned in Britain, should the Germans invade.

The Colbys begged her to accompany us there. Long, agonised conversations between my parents followed. My father was by now heavily engaged in trying to obtain the support of the United States for Britain's war effort. It seemed likely that he would be making fairly frequent trips to the US, and that we children would see him there. For my mother, the agony of the decision

---

* Because the Atlantic Ocean was itself a battleground, it was 1943 before they found a neutral ship willing to take me (John having already gone back to England).

must have been acute. A worrier, she would spend many anxious hours wondering about our well-being in a situation where letters could take weeks to cross the Atlantic, and telephone conversations were difficult and very expensive. She was faced with yet another of the moral dilemmas that haunted her all through the wartime years.

In the end, she decided she had to refuse the offer for herself. As a leading pacifist, a sponsor of the Peace Pledge Union since 1937, she believed her evacuation to the United States would be an abandonment of her country, and would be presented by her critics as an act of cowardice. She felt she could not go. It was her duty to stay in England and to mobilise her fellow pacifists for whatever aid they could provide for the victims of the war. (She believed she would be able to visit us in Minnesota from time to time, but she was wrong. The government would refuse to allow her to travel abroad.) She concluded she had no right to risk our lives as well as her own. We would have to travel, unaccompanied by any adult family member, to the home in Minnesota we had never seen. During the Blitzkrieg, which began in London on 7 September and raged intensely for a month, and in the months afterwards, she was to experience scores of air raids. The Cheyne Walk house was badly damaged, and her diaries of the time record walking through streets filled with broken glass and remnants of bombed houses.

On 26 June 1940, our blazers labelled with our names, my brother and I, aged twelve and nearly ten, accompanied by our anxious parents, travelled by train to Liverpool. The ship that was to take us first to Canada, painted grey to baffle submarines, was hidden by a huge black tarpaulin screen. We did not even know its name. Leaving our parents on the quayside, we walked through the slit in the screen and into another world.

CHAPTER 2

Discovering the New World

The *Duchess of Atholl*, the ship on which we sailed to Canada, was known among seamen as 'the Drunken Duchess'. This nickname may have reflected the colourful life of the person the ship was named after, for the Red Duchess, as she was also known, was notorious in pre-war Britain for her strong radical views. Alternatively, it may have been a forewarning, since the ship heaved and pitched its way across the Atlantic, creaking at every joint.

The Battle of the Atlantic was moving into high gear in the summer of 1940. Some of the ship's older passengers, with their lively memories of the First World War, were haunted by the dread of German U-boats, the hyenas of the ocean. Sailing from Britain only a few days before us, the *Arandora Star* with its cargo of fifteen hundred refugees and evacuees, most of them Germans and Italians interned in Britain at the outset of the war, was torpedoed on 3 July. Two months later, on 17 September, the *City of Benares* was destroyed with the loss of 260 people, seventy-nine of them children. The overseas evacuation scheme was brought to an end.

The *Duchess of Atholl* ploughed northwards, skirting the shores of Greenland and then threading her way through the ice floes of Labrador. One morning I woke in my crowded little cabin to see through the porthole a huge iceberg only a few hundred feet away, sparkling in the early sun and radiantly white, apart from the deep blue of the crevasses that hinted at the mysterious depths beneath. The icebergs were at once menacing and protective, for the captain hoped to avoid the U-boats in these ice-bound northern seas.

Most of the children on the ship were accompanied by their mothers. My brother and I were among the very few who were not. Like other ten-year-olds, I was not apprehensive. I had only the dimmest idea about the hazards of the voyage. I enjoyed playing deck quoits with John, and board games in the cabins downstairs. Indeed, I don't think I had any sense of fear at all, only a sense of excitement. For me the Second World War was a tremendously exciting time. We were to experience a completely new culture in the United States. We would watch the country change from being strongly against the war to being strongly in favour of it, particularly where we were, in Minnesota, an isolationist state to begin with.

The mood of the ship's adult passengers, however, was sombre. They knew far more than we did about the dangers of crossing the Atlantic as the great naval war in that ocean proceeded. They also had little idea how they would make out in this new land, and many had left husbands and fathers behind in Britain. Their mood lifted as we entered the vast estuary of the Saint Lawrence River, so wide we could not see both shores simultaneously. We sailed up to Quebec, where the quayside was overflowing with people waving flags: Red Ensigns, Union Jacks and anything else they could get their hands on. The cheers swelled like a hallelujah chorus. It was a welcome not to be forgotten.

My brother and I were met by a Canadian admirer of my mother. We spent a couple of days at her house, visited by friendly neighbours full of admiration for 'gallant little England', and were then taken to the station for the long journey to the Twin Cities, St Paul and Minneapolis, in Minnesota. The journey became an extended feast of food and friendship as the other passengers heard about the two English evacuees in their midst. Budding politician that I was, I made the most of recounting my few encounters with air raids and dogfights between fighter pilots over the Dorset downs. One after another, the passengers came up the corridor with cakes, ice-cream, lemonade, candy, comics and conversation. In our strict English schools, we had never come across anything like it. Even at home, the rules had decreed austerity: a maximum of two boiled sweets a day, four on Sundays.

North America, I discovered, as we sped across the great plains of southern Ontario and past the Great Lakes on our two-day train journey, was all about space. Here were the huge skies, the cornfields running to the horizon, the massed evergreens of the forests. Working with so large a canvas, God had created a landscape of bold colours and massive shapes. The intricate cat's-cradle of lanes and hedges, streams and secret gardens, the English landscape I knew, did not belong here. Never had I experienced so strong a feeling of freedom and independence as on that train. Everything seemed possible. 'America', as Archibald MacLeish wrote, 'was promises', certainly for me.

Our new family met us at the station in Minneapolis, the larger of the Twin Cities. We were to live in the older city, St Paul. Our host, Dr Woodard Colby, was a respected paediatrician; his wife, Ruth, a forerunner of today's army of dedicated women community leaders. Dr Colby had been a naval surgeon in the First World War. A quiet, rigidly disciplined man, his reserve melted when he encountered sick children. He rarely expressed any political views, but he was an old-fashioned patriot, and probably somewhat conservative.

Conventionally brought up on a southern Minnesota farm, Ruth Colby yearned to widen her mental horizons. She was active in the Farmer-Labor movement, one of the rare blooms of social democracy to be found in the United States. Her hero was the radical Wisconsin progressive Robert La Follette, among whose disciples was a bright and talkative young Minnesota politician called Hubert Humphrey. Passionately internationalist, Ruth toiled for every relief or humanitarian campaign there was, among them China Relief, the American Jewish Joint Distribution Committee and later the unfortunately named Bundles for Britain.* In a cagily isolationist state, many of whose residents had German forebears, Ruth paraded the banners of her causes. It was not surprising that she had at once taken to my mother, who had stayed in her house for a few nights during her 1934 lecture tour.

Our new home was a rambling detached wooden house, three storeys high, set in a rolling lawn studded with occasional pine trees and paths. No fences or bushes were there to mark out each person's property, as there would have been in England. Back gardens were yards rather than gardens, scuffed grass with practice basketball nets hanging on the garage door, where neighbourhood kids left bicycles and roller skates casually in the corners. America may be a very property-conscious country, but it clings less determinedly to privacy than the British do.

Our schools, St Paul's Academy for John and Summit School for me, both single-sex, were half-an-hour's bike ride away, through streets of large, handsome wooden houses much like ours, with wide porches screened from mosquitoes. My junior high school was a big brick building with vaguely Gothic windows and arches, a form of architecture closely associated with the highest values of learning in American minds. It was surrounded by lawns and trees.

Summit School was unlike anything I imagined a school to be, apart from its long corridors and classrooms. The teachers were

---

* Bundles for Britain was an American organisation established in December 1939, which raised money to send clothes and medical supplies to wartime Britain.

informal and friendly, and cared more about our emotional and social development than about our ability to master multiplication tables or recite chunks of memorised poetry. We studied no history, apart from a quick skim through the epic of American independence, no Latin, no algebra. Instead there was social science, and science too, but at a level less demanding than in my English school. So I coasted through school and concentrated instead on all the other delights St Paul had to offer.

In my three years as an evacuee in Minnesota, I lived in a class-less society, whose members all shared the same accent and the same values. That perception, of course, was not quite accurate. St Paul had fine gradations between 'old money' (at least two generations back) and new money. Substantial amounts of old money gave the person who commanded it a special status. Whatever methods had been used to accumulate the money originally had been laundered by the passage of time. The possessor of old money was expected to donate to the arts and the local charities, possibly even to finance a theatre or a public hall bearing his or her name. Many wealthy families were staunchly loyal to the school or university they had attended, and poured money into alumni funds or special appeals for their graduating year. But the walls between social classes were porous (unlike the walls between different races). Money and talent would enable one to traverse them. The absence of accent as a defining feature enabled Americans to present themselves as whatever they wanted to be.

My new abode was a place of strong simplicities. There were clear rules. One was expected to be polite, punctual and reasonably tidy. The sitting-room, elaborate with its heavy standard lamps and hard sofas, was treated with respect. It boasted drapes, long heavy curtains moved by silk cords. Ruth changed for the evening meal, and her husband pulled out the dining-room chair for her to sit down. Theirs was a correct and somewhat formal relationship, as befitted a senior naval family. They did not share a bedroom. One of my few regrets was that I had no room of my own. I shared Ruth's room with her and with two beautiful but ill-tempered Siamese cats, one of whom, Prajadhipok, was inclined to bite me if I offended him. He resented my presence in what had been his domain, occasionally scolding me in the rasping tones of his breed.

I was accorded a good deal of freedom, as the youngest child in the family, and a girl. More was expected of boys: sporting prowess, dedication to service, academic attainment. The only child of the family, a good-looking young man called Gage, was already a naval ensign training in medicine. I thought him very handsome, especially in uniform, but in an abstract sort of way. My brother John, whose two passions in life were painting and composing music, was later on dispatched to Pillsbury Academy, where all the boys wore uniform and a good deal of time was taken up in drill. It seemed an inappropriate school for him, but he claimed to quite enjoy it.

I was far luckier. My joyous life revolved around a group of schoolmates, with whom I learned drama and dancing and played sports. Sometimes we stayed overnight in each other's houses, sleeping on eiderdowns under the dining-room table and raiding the refrigerator late at night. Best of all was my friendship with Pondie Ordway, a long skinny girl with velvet-brown eyes and a touch of wildness about her. As the autumn turned the leaves gold and crimson, Pondie and I explored the old Indian trails that twisted perilously down the steep banks of the Mississippi, a river so huge that even near its source it must have been a quarter-mile of turbulent water wide. We built rafts and tree houses, careered through the undergrowth down to the river edge, tried out the fringes of ice decorating the water as autumn turned to winter. And when winter settled in, we skied on the local golf course, coming home through thick, ink-blue evenings, or through nights sparkling with silvered snow. I had found, if not paradise, then certainly a wonderful new world.

Once in a while, the war impinged. There were the weekly

letters to my parents, whose images slowly faded into those of photographs rather than of real people. My new life was so exciting that I cannot remember feeling homesick after the first week or two. My parents' letters to John and me seemed like echoes from a distant place, visited a long time ago. There was the command performance at which, now aged ten, I was obliged to present a bouquet of flowers to Lady Halifax, wife of the British Ambassador, when she and her husband visited the Twin Cities on 9 May 1941 to support Bundles for Britain. It was a task I resented, a resentment not lessened by her stately appearance, complete with pearls and a fox fur. She was, however, graciousness itself, and the Twin Cities responded with yet more bundles for Britain, despite their deep uneasiness about a war in which the United States might yet be embroiled.

At first, back in the summer of 1940, although we were hospitably greeted, we were treated by some as the forerunners of an attempt to involve the United States in the war. The view in Minnesota among the parents of my friends – not all of them, but quite a lot of them – was that Europe was a wily, deceitful old bird. That certainly included Britain, which was trying to drag this clean, decent, innocent country into war and should be resisted at any price. On the left many Minnesotans belonged to the Farmer-Labor Party, which was progressive and pacifist. On the right there was deep suspicion of Franklin Delano Roosevelt. So in Minnesota there was no substantial group – as on the East Coast, and to some extent on the West Coast – who favoured the idea of America entering the war.

In December 1941, after we had been in St Paul for eighteen months, the situation changed completely, almost overnight. I remember the newspapers being full of the story of the Japanese attack on Pearl Harbor – 7 December 1941. All of a sudden we, the British, were America's brave allies. Of course the brilliant broadcaster Ed Murrow and other commentators had much earlier told, and celebrated, the story of the Battle of Britain. But in

Minnesota the effect of that was limited. What changed every-thing was the dramatic entry into the war of Japan.

So we British became the heroes of the hour, and I became the local hero because I was one of the very few British children in the Twin Cities. Indeed I did not know of any others besides my brother and me. The newspapers were covering what I did, among them my amateur efforts in school drama, and that was what led to my moment of fame. The producer of a film called *National Velvet*, based on Enid Bagnold's story of a girl who disguised her-self as a male jockey and then competed in the Grand National, the most formidable steeplechase in Britain, announced a com-petition for the part of this heroine. The requirements were that the girl should be fair-haired, a good horse-rider, about twelve years old, and should speak with an English accent. I had all these attributes, and my name was proposed by one of the leading film reviewers in the Middle West. Other names were suggested by film writers in other regions. All of us were given screen tests, and the list was whittled down to a few finalists. I was among them. For a short while it looked as if I might be launched on a career as a child star. But I was beaten by a beautiful English child living with her mother in California. Her name was Elizabeth Taylor.

What did the Minnesotans think of Hitler as a political leader? I don't recall him being seen as an embodiment of evil. There was no knowledge of the Holocaust yet, and little was known about Nazi persecution of the Jews. In Minnesota and in the states to the west of it the real enemy was Japan. It was when Japan attacked Pearl Harbor that the American West and the American Middle West – where Minnesota is – suddenly became enthusiasts for the conflict. It was fine to fight the Japanese – they were detested. Thousands of Japanese Americans were interned throughout the war – this was one of the darker pages of American history. But the Germans were seen differently. After all, many Minnesotans were descended from Germans, many others from Scandinavians, very few from the British. So there was quite a strong sense of

Germany being, at most, deluded; there was no sense of the Germans as evil people – in contrast to attitudes towards the Japanese, who were often called 'yellow bellies'. I was in that part of the United States that looked west rather than east in the war years.

Pearl Harbor taught Americans that they could not distance themselves entirely from the troubles of the rest of the world. There was a real feeling of shock that they could be assailed in this way. Americans continued, however, to assume that their homeland was invulnerable, with friendly and relatively weak neighbours to the south and to the north. It was to be another sixty years before that assumption was seriously shaken, by the events of 11 September 2001. Until December 1941, Americans thought about the Second World War as they had about the First, as something that happened 'over there'.

I remember that popular song of the First World War, 'Over There', which was now enthusiastically revived. America, it proclaimed, was once again gallantly coming to the rescue of its stumbling allies. But there was no real appreciation of the extraordinary sacrifice of the people of the Soviet Union. The Soviet Union was somehow beyond the bounds of people's knowledge. It wasn't that they hated it in the way that they later came to under McCarthy – it was simply that it wasn't there, it wasn't part of the spectrum. Where I was, the war was seen from beginning to end as almost completely an Anglo-American war, with the Americans becoming more and more important and Russia being written out of the script.

The moment when the war really struck home for me personally had come a year before Pearl Harbor. Winston Churchill had been begging Washington for months to lend the wartime British government fifty old destroyers, to replace those torpedoed in the Battle of the Atlantic, in exchange for access to bases on British-controlled soil. My imperturbable father, always eager to engage in high politics, crossed the Atlantic once again, this time to campaign for a deal. As a young political scientist at Cornell University where he had taught in the twenties and thirties, he had come to know a number of American politicians. One of them was Wendell Willkie, in 1940 Republican candidate for the presidency. My father was invited to join Willkie's campaign train that autumn, as an adviser on the war, and spent three days in September travelling with the candidate. President Franklin Roosevelt had approved the destroyers–bases deal by executive order on 2 September 1940, but had been opposed by the Republicans. The issue became significant in the election campaign, and my father lobbied Willkie to come out on Roosevelt's side.

After his campaign interlude, my father telephoned us. I had ardently followed the 1940 presidential election alongside my foster-mother Ruth, and was longing to hear a first-hand account from him. He was still a very familiar figure; little more than two months had elapsed since we had left England. I was also eagerly anticipating reports of my mother, Amy and Charlie, and looking forward to giving him presents for the family for Christmas. John and I had gone to some trouble to buy things we had heard couldn't be obtained in England. Furthermore, we knew my father's accounts of life in 'gallant little England' would give a new resonance to our own tales – further enhancing our special status among our schoolfriends. Few Minnesotan children had been overseas, and none had ever encountered war. My father arrived for a few days in St Paul on 18 September, and picked up the Christmas presents. We told him excitedly what we had been doing and he described the air raids and rationing Britain was now undergoing, before returning to Willkie's campaign trail. In early December, he embarked for Britain on the inevitably anonymous liner that would take him home. We didn't hear from him for several days, but during the war, that was to be expected. Nobody knew anything. We didn't know the name of his ship or when it was due to arrive.

Ruth was, like me, a news junkie. Every morning she devoured the local newspaper, the St Paul Pioneer Press; every evening, I did the same. For several days after my father's visit, the paper failed to come. I asked her, 'Where is the newspaper?' and she said, 'I don't know. It doesn't seem to have been delivered.' So I borrowed one from a schoolfriend. The headline leapt out at me: 'A British liner, the Western Prince, sailing from New York, has been torpedoed between Iceland and Ireland.' I remember thinking, That has to be my father's ship. Yet I couldn't believe he had been drowned.

For nearly a week, we had no idea what had happened to him. But then we got a telegram. The liner had been torpedoed just before dawn. With the other survivors he had spent a midwinter day on the Atlantic, some four hundred miles off the coast of Ireland, in an open lifeboat, bailing out the sea water that threatened to inundate it. He and most of his fellow passengers had been rescued, on 14 December. That was followed by four days in a little cargo ship carrying coal, which somehow managed to crowd into every inch of the remaining space over a hundred shipwrecked passengers and crewmen. One of them was the Canadian politician C. D. Howe, at that time Minister for Munitions and Supply in Ottawa. The little ship had taken them all to Gourock, near Glasgow. From there they made their way back to London by train. Five days after the ship sank, my father appeared at King's Cross, still in his pyjamas but with his overcoat over them. I don't recall ever doubting that he would survive. His imperturbable savoir-faire was contagious. And he felt it was all worth it. Against the isolationists in his own party, Wendell Willkie came out in support of the deal to exchange destroyers for bases.

A year after the Japanese attack on Pearl Harbor, in December 1941, few people in St Paul any longer supported isolationism, and no one talked any more about being sucked into war by Britain's ancient cunning. St Paul blossomed with white silk flags bearing a blue star for each son, brother or husband gone to war, a gold star for those who had lost their lives. Always hospitably treated, I was now more than ever the town's very own war baby, the personification of 'our gallant little ally'. Of course I made the most of my few wartime experiences, and of my father's Atlantic adventure (he was to be torpedoed again, and to be sunk a third time when the ship he was travelling on was rammed accidentally by an American destroyer). My classmates elected me captain of the form. And my cup ran over.

At least it did until sex raised its unsummoned head, sometime in 1942. Relations between boys and girls in the St Paul of the 1940s were channelled into a rite of passage. Up to the age of eleven, boys and girls played together unselfconsciously, but at twelve or thirteen everything became a ritual. It all began with a dance – 'the First Formal'. The First Formal meant being invited to the dance by a suitable lad, himself thirteen or fourteen; buying one's first ball dress; being sent a creamy-white gardenia in a ribboned box to pin on to the ball dress; and being taken in his parents' car to the dance. Everyone who was anyone in St Paul knew about the First Formal. To receive no invitation was devastating, the beginning of the end. The First Formal was the gateway to adulthood, and to all the rumoured joys of sex and romance.

After this rite of passage there would be several years of controlled courtship, known as 'necking'. Only a reckless few 'went all the way'. By nineteen or twenty, many of my schoolmates would marry, in a soft-focus haze of flowers, white wedding dresses and tasteful advertisements for cutlery, intoning 'This is For Keeps'. It often wasn't. But not to be married by twenty-five was as great a disaster for Twin Cities debutantes as for Jane Austen's a hundred and fifty years before.

I received the invitation most prized by almost every girl in the class – from none other than Johnny Driscoll, the boys' junior high school football captain. I was furious. Dancing was a sissy occupation, and who wanted to waste a whole evening on some pink-faced boy? I refused, to the consternation of my school, whose counsellors concluded that I must be emotionally troubled, perhaps a consequence of being so far from home. I wasn't. I was a flat-chested twelve-year-old English tomboy, but of course they'd never met one before. In classic pre-teen style, my passion, a crush my friend Pondie shared, was for Anne Lovering, a disdainful blonde senior-year student. Pondie and I left boxes of nicely wrapped candy and single red carnations on her school locker. At Commencement, the school's summer graduation ceremony, we were struck dumb with adoration as Anne Lovering swept up the school hall in a long white dress, to the strains of the great march from *Aida*.

Minnesota was not just St Paul. For part of the three long summer holidays I would go to a camp near the Lake of the Woods in the north of the state for a couple of weeks, living in a wooden cabin in the pinewoods with thirty or forty other girls. I didn't much care for the counsellors who accompanied us, older teenage girls on hand to discuss the younger girls' problems and preoccupations, and I never consulted them. But I did enjoy learning to sail small sailboats and to paddle canoes. Canoes are companions of silence, slicing through the water and leaving only a few glistening drops on the surface to mark their passage. No moose or bear was disturbed by them, and from the lakes one could observe their world. At night we would light a campfire and sing songs to which loons would respond in their eerie whooping tones, the sound of far-off places.

Nor was my America confined to the Middle West. For part of the long summer vacation in 1941, my brother and I travelled east, to stay with my mother's publisher George Brett and his family in Connecticut, and with the wife of one of Macmillan's editors, a fine sculptor called Marion (Mannie) Putnam. Connecticut seemed familiar territory. It had woods, fields separated by fences and hedges, fine old trees, an echo of the England I was fast forgetting.

The Bretts I was in awe of. First of all, they were rich, and second, Isobel Brett was a woman of elegance and presence, to a child rather forbidding. George Brett, a man of emphatic and vigorous personality with strong right-wing views, I could not decide how to relate to. My mother was infatuated with him, though his opinions and hers could hardly have been more different. I did not know about her feelings for him until much later in my life, and I did not share them. I was amazed at his habit of wearing only a G-string while swimming in his own swimming pool, for no adult, male or female, had ever flaunted buttocks in my presence before. But then I had never met anyone who owned a swimming pool before either. I wasn't at all sure how to behave in this opulent society.

Mannie Putnam and her tall blond son Christopher, my own age but nearly one and a half times my height, I adored. She combined style and flair with the softest heart imaginable. When I arrived at her house, she was weeping over a kitten killed by the block of ice she had accidentally dropped on it. Christopher was the handsome, graceful young man any girl would be proud to claim as her boyfriend. Balancing tentatively between childhood and adolescence, I was not yet ready to make any such claim. My few snapshots of those holidays show us building sandcastles together on the seashore.

America became my other country, an aspiration if not a motherland. It was, in that simple and heroic time, a country undivided by class, united by the war effort, a country of flourishing and vibrant communities with a shared sense of its exceptional destiny. Each morning, I recited with my classmates the secular American equivalent of the Lord's Prayer that used to start the English schoolday: 'I pledge allegiance to the Flag of the United States of America, and to the Republic for which it stands; one Nation, indivisible, with Liberty and Justice for all' (President Eisenhower, years later, was to add 'under God' after 'one Nation'). The United States was indeed exceptional, the world's only country (with the possible exception of Israel) to which most of its citizens had volunteered to go, or at least their forefathers had so chosen. The flag was a religious symbol, patriotism a form of faith. Many evenings, I lay on the floor in the dark listening on the gramophone to Dvořák's *New World* symphony, inundated by the sound and the images it evoked. I had found, I thought, the country where, in the words of Wordsworth I once learned by heart, 'Bliss was it in that dawn to be alive/But to be young was very heaven!'*

* *The Prelude*, Book xi.

CHAPTER 3

A Land Fit for Heroes

It was difficult to get back to England in the middle of the war unless the traveller was approaching sixteen and capable of National Service, or was in other ways necessary to the war effort. My brother had returned to England in a naval convoy in June 1943, and was already back at school. My parents, and particularly my mother, were anxious to reunite the family by bringing me home. They feared I might be lost to an American future if I knew nothing of wartime England and failed to put down roots there. Since John and I had left, we had had no contact with my mother except through letters and rare telephone calls. All her applications for an exit visa to enable her to visit us in the United States had been rejected, presumably on the grounds that she was a prominent pacifist, though she was never given a reason.

I was longing to share the experience of war in England with my family there. Minnesota seemed far away from what was happening. My American foster-mother Ruth loved travelling and I was sure I would see her once the war was over. She had been immensely generous, but I had never lost my loyalty to my mother whom I saw as an exceptional human being. As for my schoolfriends, I looked forward to sending them reports from the front line.

Looking for a ship that would carry noncombatants across the Atlantic, my parents discovered the *Serpa Pinto*, a Portuguese liner whose home port was neutral Lisbon. In August 1943, after three years as an evacuee in the United States, I set off on what should have been an eight-day crossing from Philadelphia to Lisbon. My parents had arranged for a fellow passenger and acquaintance, the great patron of music Sir Robert Mayer, to keep an eye on me. I spent almost all my time, however, with the only other unaccompanied girl of my own age, thirteen, a lively doctor's daughter from Cambridge called Rosemary Roughton. Four days out of Philadelphia, the *Serpa Pinto* ran into the worst cyclone its captain had encountered in twenty-five years at sea. The storm howled around the ship, which at times was awash in the raging waves. Clinging to our bunks, crashing against the walls or flung into the bed rails, Rosemary and I were overcome at times with wrenching seasickness, at others with the weakness of hunger. It was impossible to make one's way up the gangways and ladders to the dining-room, and in any case there could be no service, with cutlery and crockery cascading off the tables.

Desperate to escape the cyclone – for the lifeboats, already swung out on their davits, would not last long in the boiling sea – the captain turned south to the Azores. The Azores offered us the relief of solid earth, banana and orange trees, and the spectacle of little boys diving for coins from the top decks of the *Serpa Pinto*, cleaving through the bright-blue waters of the bay. On to our ship crowded a company of Portuguese troops bound for Lisbon. They enjoyed teasing us and making remarks about us that, fortunately, we could not understand. We sailed on to Madeira, for urgent repairs to the ship. The island was enchanting, orange and red bougainvillea rioting over old stone walls, and a pervasive smell of jasmine and donkeys. We spent three days there, long enough to try out the wooden sleds on which people careered down the cobblestoned streets from the top of the hill to the port, and to discover the honeyed delights of the local wine. With all its markets inaccessible, Madeira wine cost almost nothing to buy.

Back on the ship, Rosemary and I now faced a new hazard. We were the youngest of the unaccompanied children, most of whom were sophisticated adolescents, and we shared a cabin on our own. One day out of Madeira, our door was forced open by half a dozen sailors, who announced that they had come to cure our seasickness, a cure supposed to start with massaging bare stomachs. Words, whether pleading or shouted, failed to persuade them that we wanted no such cure. So we fought, kicking and scratching our way to the cabin door, and fled along the companionway, looking for some – any – bolthole. Mercifully, one appeared, the gentlemen's lavatory. As we hid together in one of the stalls, we heard the sailors go thundering by. Bound by the child's law of *omertà*, silence, we told none of the adults what had happened, and what – much worse – might yet happen. We recognised that the chances of a vengeful return visit were high. For two nights we hid in one of the lifeboats on the deck, under the thick canvas awning, sometimes soaked with salt water, always cold.

Arrived safely in Lisbon on 23 September, we found ourselves stranded. I had expected, like my brother John, to fly direct to England on a civilian plane that went from Lisbon roughly once a week. Both sides in the war had agreed not to attack it, providing it carried no passengers of military value. But on 1 June that year the plane had been attacked and shot down by a Junkers Ju 88 with the loss of all its passengers, including the man my father so closely resembled, the filmstar Leslie Howard.* The Germans, it was said later, had convinced themselves that the plane was carrying Winston Churchill. By the time Rosemary

---

* Jessica Mann, *Out of Harm's Way*, Headline, 2005.

and I got to Lisbon, all the British transport planes had been diverted to the Allied offensive in Italy. Children from the *Serpa Pinto*'s previous voyage and the new arrivals, 370 in all, were queuing up in Portugal until suitable aircraft could be found.

For the time being, since there was no plane to take us back to England, the *Serpa Pinto*'s returning evacuees were interned as enemy aliens. Day after day we were confined to the faded and dusty splendours of the Palace Hotel in Estoril, a resort once much favoured by exiled monarchs and their entourages. Forbidden to leave the hotel, or even to visit the beach except down a path edged with barbed wire in the company of a hotel porter, Rosemary and I comforted ourselves by sharing a daily bottle of Madeira. After a week or so, our state of muzzy cheeriness began to pall. We were bored. Even climbing on to the hotel's roofs and balconies ceased to divert us, though we managed one or two spectacular crawls along the fourth-floor ledges. So we ran away. We managed to find our way out of the hotel early one morning, and from there to the local railway station. We hid in the luggage van until the next stop, and then climbed into a third-class carriage, mingling with passengers carrying fruit, vegetables and live hens.

Lisbon was just as we had supposed from the spy films we had seen. There were well-dressed, sinister-looking men with umbrellas, even monocles. We could hear fragments of German, as well as French and Portuguese. There were brightly lit restaurants and shadowed alleyways. Rosemary and I were lucky enough to meet a group of students as we wandered around close to the station. They talked to us, and showed us their local haunts. But they were frightened of being apprehended by the PIDE, the fearsome security police of Salazar's dictatorship, so later that morning they left us on the doorstep of a leading Portuguese newspaper editor, Senhor Lowndes Marques, whose address my parents had sent me when they thought the *Serpa Pinto* might dock in Lisbon, and whose wife had kindly offered to keep an eye on us.

Irritated by our escapades, no doubt reported to them by the hotel, the Portuguese authorities informed their British counter-parts that we had to be removed immediately. So a couple of days later, I found myself at a rainy RAF airport near Bristol, having been brought back by a military plane. My father met me there. Although he was a man of deep emotions, his upbringing as an only child in a country vicarage, with an irritable, short-tempered father, had instilled in him a very English reserve. He loved to talk about political events, and about the people who shaped them; he was an avid collector of what one might call serious gossip; but he did not take much pleasure in the usual chatter about personal and financial peccadilloes. So on the slow train journey to London we talked about the war, the United States, John's return and my voyage home, but not about our feelings at this reunion.

For me this was a relief. I knew I was supposed to be ecstatic at being home again, but I didn't actually know how I felt. I was excited to be back in England. I wanted to feel personally the experience of the war. But I had not yet committed myself to this drab, class-bound, crowded island. It was to take two more years of war, the magic loveliness of the New Forest and the renais-sance of the 1945 election to bring that about.

On our arrival back in London, in the run-down elegance of Cheyne Walk, my father hid me behind a long velvet curtain when he heard my mother's key in the front-door lock. She had been speaking at a meeting in the Midlands, unaware of my return. My father knew the intense strain on my mother of the years of her children's absence and her fear that we might never reconnect with her and our father after the heady excitement of the United States. He knew too that my mother's anxieties had been deepened by her own vivid imagination. None of that did I understand, nor, at thirteen, sympathise with. I had learned to be independent, in charge of myself. I didn't want to be fussed over or protected. I revelled in my freedom. So I was wary of my mother's love for me.

My father called her into the living-room and I emerged from behind the curtain and twirled around in the firelight warming the grey autumn evening. My mother, only half-believing I was really there, held me close to her. She was soaked by the rain she had walked through, and I could not distinguish the raindrops from her tears. She must have felt the resistance in me. It was to take several years for me to learn to love her, and then it was to love her as an adult, a beloved friend, rather than as a child loves its mother.

The biggest cultural shock I encountered after my return to England was not the country's obvious shabbiness nor the austerity of most people's lifestyles, but the formality and exam-orientation of the schools. My determination to be autonomous and free collided with the English system. English schools were much stricter than their Minnesotan equivalents. True, the war had changed them. Meritocracy was beginning to replace, or at least supplement, class. The coalition government's Minister of Education, the impeccably educated R. A. Butler, had responded to the wartime-born demand for much better educational opportunities with a far-reaching advance, the 1944 Education Bill, the first significant legislation for forty years. Under this bill, which both the main parties supported, all children sat a public examination at eleven which divided them into three streams – grammar, technical and 'modern'. The number of grammar schools was expanded to accommodate between a sixth and a quarter of the child population, the proportion being determined by each local authority and, later, by the extra year of compulsory education to fifteen required by the Attlee government in 1947, mainly as the result of a relentless campaign by the then Education Minister, Ellen Wilkinson. The technical stream in the 1944 Act was intended to aim at advanced technical and other vocational qualifications. The modern school was to be a secondary, not just an extended elementary school, offering its pupils work-oriented training, for instance in commercial and service occupations.

The Butler Act, as it came to be known, took the concept of an academically segregated education system as far as it could go, and did so with dedication and determination. There were, however, two flaws which meant that it was still unsatisfactory. The technical stream never really got off the ground. Parents preferred their child to go to a grammar school if he or she passed the eleven-plus, and without the necessary public support, the money that technical schools needed for qualified teachers and good equipment was not forthcoming. Underlying that stinginess was the old cultural distinction, moulded by the great public schools and the ancient universities, that technical and vocational achievements were simply not on a par with the elegance of classical scholarship.

So the Butler Act was at once enlightened and obsolete. Given the four decades that had passed between 1902, which saw the establishment of local education authorities, and 1944 – years during which there had been little progress or change in publicly funded education – it had leapt a generation to bring English and Welsh education up to date. But by 1944, educational aspirations were running ahead of what the Butler Act laid down. The parents of the war generation wanted something different for their children than an impermeable ceiling at fourteen.

The eleven-plus system was too rigid to allow for variations in children's intellectual development, and this was its other great flaw. In theory a child who did well could transfer from a secondary modern to a grammar school. In practice less than 2 per cent of children ever did so. That in turn meant that parents insisted on courses in the modern schools that would enable their pupils to sit public examinations at fifteen or sixteen, leading on to professional and vocational qualifications. Some secondary modern schools developed sixth forms, but it was an expensive enterprise where only a small number of pupils stayed on at school to take exams. More often, they left school and pursued their studies at a further education college.

Furthermore, the Churches were not about to relinquish their longstanding stake in education. R. A. Butler's negotiations with them established a range of relationships in which control over the governance of schools was directly related to the state's financial contribution to them. Controlled Church schools were wholly financed by the state, though the Churches retained a voice in religious education. 'Aided' schools, as the word implies, depended upon contributions from the state, but retained an element of Church funding – at the time of the Butler Act, 25 per cent of the capital cost. New Church schools could only be built with state money if there was evidence of a demand for them. Hence most of them were built in new or expanded towns, or to meet the exploding birth rate of the late 1940s. For education planners, 'roofs over heads' trumped ideology when it came to building new schools.

Education policy is necessarily driven to a great extent by population trends. In the immediate postwar period, for the local education authorities that meant racing ahead of the tide of new births, as the birth rate rose to 1.05 million in 1947. (It then gradually declined to 800,000 in 1952, a fall of 20 per cent.) Necessity was as ever the mother of invention. Prefabricated classrooms were added to existing schools. Architects began to design new school buildings, some of them revolutionary in opening up schools to the outside world, bright, light and welcoming. Intensive short teacher-training courses were devised to attract ex-servicemen and women into teaching. They became some of the best teachers the schools had ever had.

Butler's Act had never sought to change the administration of schools, which remained in the hands of the local authorities. Education was their most important responsibility, and they exercised a great deal of discretion in establishing their own structures within the broad framework of the selective system.

This was paralleled by the discretion teachers enjoyed in framing the curriculum and teaching methods of their particular school, again within the broad framework established by the school inspectorate, the HMIs. At the national level, the Department of Education did not interfere directly in the curriculum, though it was inevitably shaped by the requirements of public examinations such as the School Certificate. At this time, the late 1940s and early 1950s, only a minority of children took any public examination after the eleven-plus.

Clement Attlee's 1945 Labour government was content to work within the bounds of the Butler Act, to which it had made its own substantial contribution. Political controversy centred on the issue of the school-leaving age. Given that most children in the state system left school at the age of fourteen, it was simply impracticable for schools to prepare them for the public examinations that were the gateways to higher education and to most professional jobs. That was left to the private system and to the grammar schools. So raising the school-leaving age – a national responsibility – was seen as the key to offering a proper secondary education to all children, one that would open the door to much greater opportunities.

The difficulty, as ever, was public expenditure. Already the rise in the birth rate was putting huge pressure on the education budget. Many more teachers had to be trained, many more schools built, to accommodate the additional children. To add to this another year of compulsory schooling for all children was simply beyond the government's capacity. After the school-leaving age was raised to fifteen, in 1947, it was to be twenty-five more years before it reached sixteen, the usual age for taking the School Certificate or the GCE, as it became.

In the 1940s the grammar schools, the elite of the English and Welsh schools system, were geared to a rigid regime of public examinations: the eleven-plus, the School Certificate at sixteen and (for a small minority) the Higher School Certificate, leading on to university and college entrance at eighteen. The school syllabus narrowed down in the two years of the sixth form to two or three specialist subjects, and standards were high. But rigorous though it was, more emphasis was put on personal essays and interviews than is the case today. There was room – indeed, a welcome – for the unconventional, the innovative, and the gifted eccentric.

For several weeks after my return home, I felt that I did not belong to my rather formal, preoccupied household, nor to the school to which my parents had consigned me. The uniform – navy-blue gym slip, white shirt and felt hat – seemed constricting, and clearly my new school had neither heard of, nor would have approved of, a First Formal. It was going to take time to adjust to Rab Butler's England. But I was pleased to be so evidently wanted by my parents and by Amy, now the mother of a little daughter, Marian, born on 17 July 1940. I was also excited by the unpredictable air raids.

Gradually the war, politics and my new schoolfriends made up for the delights of my life in St Paul. So too did my relationship with my father. Amy and Charlie had laid the foundations of my Catholicism in the late 1930s when they had taken me regularly to church, at the Holy Redeemer, close to our home in Glebe Place. Now I resumed my Sunday attendances, not only with the Burnetts but also with my father. His wartime experiences, among them being torpedoed on the *Western Prince*, had made him aware of life's fragility, and turned his mind towards eternal truths. After church, often itself a plunge into deep intellectual waters given the profundity of our priest Mgr Alfonso de Zulueta, my father and I would repair to the Pier Hotel, a once grand but now rather dog-eared establishment at the bottom of Oakley Street in Chelsea, where we would discuss philosophy and religion for an hour or so over a muddy brown liquid called coffee. He would regale me with comments on doctrines like infallibility, and whether there could be such a thing as a Just War. It was this latter doctrine that persuaded me that the war against Nazism was morally right, though not some of its instruments, such as the saturation bombing of civilians. So I never became a pacifist, like my mother. I was, rather, an internationalist and someone who remained deeply sceptical about the efficacy or morality of most wars.

I had gone back to school right away, to St Paul's Girls' School in Hammersmith. I was determined not to go to a boarding school, and on this I fiercely opposed the wishes of my parents. Academically, St Paul's was outstanding. It encouraged its pupils to engage in discussion with the teachers and with one another, not a common phenomenon in girls' schools sixty years ago. The emphasis was on academic and artistic excellence. The school yielded nothing to conventional views about the limited capacity of girls to master science and mathematics.

School discipline, however, was strict. My private adventures were curtailed, my tendency to show off disapproved of. Routine and order reasserted themselves – above all, authority in the shape of the dreaded High Mistress, the redoubtable Miss Ethel Strudwick. Miss Strudwick was a statuesque lady, with a formidable bosom, given to wearing black or dark-crimson clothes in a heavy fabric. She listed mountain-climbing as one of her hobbies in reference books. I used to find this puzzling, because I could not imagine her ascending a rockface. But she was unquestionably a person of authority. She measured the success of her rebukes by whether a girl was reduced to tears. Tears were evidence of the girl's shame and regret for her misbehaviour. I used to sit in her study, stubborn and defiant, refusing to cry. In consequence, our interviews lasted a long time.

I was undoubtedly badly behaved. I was also a slob, covering my gymslip with a large jersey and rarely brushing my hair. At one history lesson the brilliant but peppery teacher Miss Patrick presented me with a cheap hairbrush in front of the whole class.

I dreamed up ways of breaking school rules and shocking my teachers, not least to impress my schoolfellows. I was good at climbing, so I shinned up the lead pipes that clung to the side of the science block to the third storey. I recall staring into the window of the chemistry class, only to confront the appalled expression of the chemistry teacher. I must have seemed as much nightmare as reality. In many of these escapades, my companion was Gillian Ayers, later an outstanding abstract artist.

On one particularly offensive occasion, I climbed up the long curtains across the front of the big assembly hall, invisible from the platform but visible to the girls, contorting my face into grimaces. Those on the platform could not comprehend the gales of laughter from the hall. Miss Strudwick sent a letter to my parents, who spoke to me sternly. It made little difference. So this time I was threatened with expulsion, and only my mother's pleas to the school authorities gave me a second chance. I was in revolt against what it was to be young in 1940s England, though not against England itself.

The compensations, however, for me at least, were many. The school had teachers who loved their subjects and who made them come alive. History, English literature and – even though I hardly grasped the subject – physics stirred our imaginations. Teachers like Rosamund Jenkinson and Margaret Higginson, later headmistress of Bolton Girls' School, gave me a lifelong love of poetry. Even now, snatches of verse from John Donne to W. H. Auden come to mind, illuminating my own awareness. My schoolmates and I spent hours clustered around the tepid radiators in the damp winter cold, talking about religion and poetry, war and politics, until we reached a kind of nirvana where being vaguely hungry didn't seem to matter. The school was a haven, too, of music. Herbert Howells was musical director, working with Imogen Holst, daughter of the composer Gustav Holst, who had spent many years at St Paul's as what today would be called the resident composer. The *St Paul's Suite* he composed there was regularly performed by the girls. The words and music often come back to me: 'O, let us render thanks to God above,/What has one to fear who follows Him in all His ways?'

School lore decreed that we must never speak to strange boys in the street on our way to or from school, not even those from St Paul's Boys' just down the road. We found our friends, rivals and competitors from among people of our own gender. We did not grasp that we were members of the second, invisible sex.

One of my friends, Gill Groser, was the daughter of the Vicar of Stepney, a lovely man of immense compassion and kindness. Through them I got to know the East End, badly damaged by bombing. After air raids, Gill and I would cycle around the ruined churches and gashed houses, revealing their pathetic innards of baths and pipes and torn wallpaper. We met her father's parishioners too, stoical, sharp-witted and enduring.

At home, I had the task of carrying Amy's little girl Marian, who was four, down to the air-raid shelter in our garden – it was an Anderson shelter, a sandbagged half-circle of galvanised steel over a pit measuring about nine feet long, seven feet wide and five feet deep, into which we all crowded when the siren went off. There were usually five or six of us – my parents, my brother when not at boarding school, Amy and Marian, and me. The babies and toddlers were put at the back because the nearer you were to the entrance, the more likely you were to be injured by bits of flying debris. Children and old people came next; my father in his bowl-shaped steel ARP helmet guarded the door.

My other task, which I imposed on myself, was to climb all over the house picking up shrapnel. Nobody told me to do that, I just enjoyed doing it. It was a good reason to go up to the roof and see London burning. I used to cycle to major incident areas with friends in order to see if we could save somebody, but also because I suspect we found it very exciting to watch huge buildings in flames. One night in early 1944, it was Hammersmith rather than the East End that bore the brunt of the raids. Picking up my friends the Meyer twins, Margaret and Helen, on my way to school, I found their terraced house in Talgarth Road spewing smoke and flame from the incendiary bombs that had dropped inside. Well trained, we gingerly doused them with sand on the ends of long spades from buckets prepared for just such an emergency. School, when we got there, had been bombed, and substantially damaged. Most of the pupils and teachers were to be evacuated to Oriel College, Oxford, though I didn't go with them.

It was during one such raid that I met Herbert Morrison, the Home Secretary and former Leader of the London County Council. My parents and I had been guests at a party at 55 Park Lane hosted by a wealthy Scottish builder sympathetic to the Labour Party, Sir John McTaggart. I had pleaded with my parents to let me come with them, because I was as ever bewitched by politics, and longed to meet Labour MPs. The men and women I was to meet in my early years in the Labour Party would provide further evidence of the capricious nature of the education system. Ernest Bevin, then Minister of Labour, and Herbert Morrison, the Home Secretary, had both left school at fourteen. Clement Attlee was a product of Haileybury, a traditional public school with close ties to the military. Douglas Jay and Dick Crossman inhabited the most meritocratic and rarefied height of academia, both having been former pupils at Winchester College.

A particularly fierce air raid during the party in Park Lane drove us all to the basement shelter, where I found myself sitting next to Herbert Morrison. For the next two hours until the all-clear, I badgered him, argued with him and told him what he ought to do. Fortunately for me, he was amused. We kept in touch, starting with a lunch only a couple of weeks later at the House of Commons, where he showed me the document he would have to sign to commute a death sentence to life imprisonment.

'Sign it,' I said.

'But you don't know anything about the case.'

'It doesn't matter,' I replied. 'I don't believe in capital punishment.'

'Neither do I,' said Morrison, 'but it's for Parliament, not me, to make the laws.'

Herbert Morrison understood that his job as Home Secretary was not only to uphold law and order, but to defend individual freedom and civil liberties. He had to administer the wartime emergency law, Defence Regulation 18B, which allowed the government to intern people suspected of being Nazi sympathisers without due process of law, but he always leaned in the direction of liberty. He released Oswald Mosley, the leader of the British Union of Fascists, from internment on 20 November 1943, in the middle of the war, an action that caused immense controversy. Responding to an angry House of Commons, and indeed to criticisms from some of his own Cabinet colleagues, Morrison said: '. . . while considerations of national security must come first, I am not prepared, subject to this overriding consideration, to let anyone die in detention unnecessarily. This policy is based not on the inexpediency of making martyrs of persons who do not deserve the honour, but on the general principle that those extraordinary powers of detention without trial must not be used except in so far as they are essential for national security.' A conscientious objector in the First World War, he understood and sometimes even defended those with nonconforming opinions.

Young politicians benefit immensely from having a mentor, an established political figure who is willing to guide, advise and help them. Scores of able young men were assisted to become parliamentary candidates in the 1940s and 1950s by Hugh Dalton (Attlee's Chancellor of the Exchequer from 1945 to 1947) and Rab Butler, to mention only two. But few established politicians took young women seriously as potential parliamentary candidates, and all of them knew what gossips would make out of a mentor relationship. Morrison, a man of huge exuberance and high humour, enjoyed sparring and flirting with women. He was rumoured to have had affairs with several women in public life. But I mean something different – he actually *liked* women as individuals. He thought they were bright and sensible. He had met and appreciated some remarkable women on the London County Council, one of the great local governments of the interwar years. He had helped Ellen Wilkinson, Edith Summerskill and Barbara Castle launch themselves into political life. Funny, instinctively wise, never patronising, he became my political mentor during those wartime and early postwar years.

I, in turn, offered him cheeky and uncalled-for advice. He invited me to lunch in March 1951, when I was twenty, to tell me that Clement Attlee had offered him the post of Foreign Secretary, since Ernest Bevin was too ill to carry on. I didn't congratulate him.

'Let me ask you a question, Herbert,' I said. 'What is the MRP?'

'I have no idea,' he responded.

'Then you shouldn't be Foreign Secretary,' I declared triumphantly, and went on to inform him that the MRP (the Movement Républicain Populaire) was one of the important centre parties of France, and a partner in several of the short-lived coalition governments of the Fourth Republic. I was, of course, showing off. But my instincts about Morrison's unsuitability for the Foreign Office were right.

Herbert Morrison was a perfect example of the adage that there are horses for courses in government, as elsewhere. Brilliant at the Home Office and, before that, in local government, where he had an instinctive feel for public opinion, he never took to the Foreign Office. He got on badly with the officials there, who idolised Ernest Bevin. He knew little about foreign affairs and was not particularly interested in learning more. For Morrison's reputation, it was a disastrous appointment, and one that undermined the ebullient self-confidence and cheeriness that had been his hallmarks as Home Secretary.

I had met Morrison during what was called 'the little blitz', while fairly intense bombing was still going on. When my school had been damaged in the spring of 1944, it was too late to get into another school that academic year, so I was sent to tutors. One obvious place to find good tutors was Cambridge, so I spent three months living in the house of Rosemary Roughton, my shipmate on the *Serpa Pinto*. One of my tutors was the literary critic John Hayward. Like my St Paul's teachers, he bequeathed to me an enduring love of poetry.

Frequent disturbances, being uprooted from place to place, were familiar accompaniments of the war years in London. For some families it was an almost daily occurrence, moving from home to the safety of London's deep Underground tunnels; for others it was periodic, being evacuated for weeks or months, returning home, then being sent away again. So departing to live once again with strangers – for I did not know Rosemary's family – was neither unusual nor upsetting. At least I knew Rosemary, and I was not very far from home (though travel in wartime was slow and subject to long, inexplicable delays). I could call my parents by telephone at the weekends, though it was expensive. And there was the challenge once again of a new place and new people.

The Roughtons' home, 9 Adams Road, was a busy household. Alice Roughton, an overworked general practitioner, was immensely hospitable, opening her large, rather run-down home to anyone who needed a roof. The food on offer was mainly potatoes; there wasn't enough time to produce much variety. Her husband was a mathematician of reputed genius. He spent much of his time in the United States, and when at home, kept himself out of the way in his own room, accepting and returning meal trays left outside his door. We didn't often see him. The liveliest denizens of the house were members of one of Germany's great modern ballet companies, the Jooss Ballet, who had left Germany as a group sometime in the 1930s. Making the best of their circumstances, they practised in the bare sitting-room. Rosemary and I sometimes joined them, learning the five foot positions of classical ballet and playing bit parts in rehearsals of their most renowned modern ballet, the ironic and bitter *Green Table*, a satire on the world of international diplomacy. Occasionally members of the ballet would dance in the garden, sometimes wearing very little and scandalising the neighbours, members of Cambridge academia.

At the end of Adams Road, where the town yielded to the flat, fertile countryside, was a field of wheat, home to a galaxy of skylarks. I would lie on my back for hours, looking up at the huge East Anglian sky with its majestic slow-moving clouds, watching the larks soaring up towards the sun, emitting a waterfall of song. The sun, the sky and the song would embrace me, and I would feel one with nature, as I had in the dark lakes of Minnesota.

After this thoroughly agreeable interlude, I went back to formal school, not to St Paul's, still being repaired, but to Talbot Heath, a girls' school in Bournemouth. My mother wanted me to be close enough to her to be able to come home at weekends. Bournemouth was only twenty miles from Lyndhurst, where we had our family cottage. My mother was staying there more and more, so that she could write undisturbed. The cottage was not distant from the war; Southampton, only ten miles away, was pounded by air raids. But its remote situation, and the great beeches and oaks around the hamlet, gave one a sense, if not of safety, at least of peace.

As I have said, my mother was a worrier, a condition with which I failed to sympathise. Indeed, some streak of insensitivity led me, as a child and adolescent alike, to exacerbate her anxiety. I would go out walking in the forest and get lost. It wasn't difficult to do. The wide green avenues between the big trees, and the paths that wound among the heather and the bracken, could look much like one another. In those days there weren't any sign-posts, and outside the cycle paths and small car parks on the edges of the tarmac roads, there aren't many now. I was even more unhelpful when I returned from my three years in Minnesota in the autumn of 1943, rattling the bars of this least confining of cages.

For my parents allowed me far more freedom than most chil-dren of my age enjoyed. They let me go on a cycling holiday in Cornwall with my schoolfriends when I was fourteen, and to Switzerland for a week on my own when I was fifteen. Yet if my mother asked me tentatively where I was going when I mounted my bicycle, I would reply with the one word 'Out!' Then I would cycle off to see the effects of the latest air raid. In London, one of my favourite pursuits was to climb over the edge of the new Bailey bridge across the Thames, halfway between Chelsea Bridge and the elegant Albert Bridge, and to clamber down to the steel joists above the indifferent brown river.

For reasons a psychoanalyst would understand better than I ever have, I felt the need to prove myself by doing whatever frightened me. Getting lost in the New Forest or climbing under the bridge I found only mildly scary. The much greater test was to overcome the fear of strange men, a residuary consequence of the attempted gang rape Rosemary and I had escaped on the *Serpa Pinto*. I had been inculcated with the law of silence, *omertà*, first at Christ Church Elementary and then at Oldfeld School where bullying was a way of life among the pupils, but either unknown to or sedulously ignored by their well-meaning teachers. So telling my parents about my experiences and my fears was unthinkable. First, they were still strangers after my absence in the United States. Second, I was my own person. Seeking their help would have been, in my eyes, contemptibly feeble. I would have to find my own way to cope.

The way I chose was provocative. I wanted a companion for my long lonely walks, and I persuaded my parents to let me have a dog. My first, a little fox terrier puppy, highly bred and expensive, panicked whenever there was an air raid. Early in 1944, air raids were still quite frequent. In between the thump of bombs and the whoosh of anti-aircraft guns, I would hear my puppy screaming in panic. My mother, sensible in most things, was convinced he might have convulsions and bite little Marian. In vain I begged, pleaded, shouted at her. She would not change her mind. So the terrified puppy was 'put to sleep', and I notched up a resentment I had never felt about being sent to the United States.

The puppy's successor was a resilient mongrel collie called Treve. He became the companion of my next three years. He was allowed into the air-raid shelter, dozing by Marian and occasionally licking us both. Treve accompanied me on my late-night walks along the Embankment to Chelsea Bridge and back. Often on these walks I would pass lonely men, leaning on the river wall and smoking a cigarette. As I approached them, sometimes in the thick dark of a night blended with fog, I would identify a house close enough to run to, its lights glimmering at the edges of the black-out curtains on the ground floor. That never happened, although on several occasions I was followed, and once or twice quietly propositioned. When I began these walks, slipping out of the basement door late at night without my parents knowing, I felt sick with fear. But after a month or two I began to feel that I could handle whatever situation I might find myself in.

My mother loved the Allum Green cottage, and so did I. In my memory, it was always sunny there. New Forest ponies would wander by, and as the evening drew in, roe deer and the occasional stag would crop the grass on the greensward in front of the cottage. For my mother it was a place of healing. It soothed her anxieties and calmed her fears. She and I would go for long walks in the afternoon, walks embroidered by her knowledge of the wild flowers, birds and butterflies we moved among. She knew the names of the different butterflies, from chalkhill blue to red admiral. She could tell thrush from warbler, blackbird from field-fare, by listening to a few bars of their song. Few wild flowers, however small or humble, were anonymous. Ragged robin and violet, vetch and primrose, they pirouetted on banks and in meadows innocent of pesticides and weedkillers, an exquisite miniature creation. The barriers I had built against any intimacy crumbled. The forest brought everything into the perspective of eternity.

My mother had imbibed from her earliest years the love of nature with which Victorian England lived so harmoniously. That reverence reverberates in the poets she loved, Wordsworth, Coleridge and Southey, Thomas Hardy and Walter de la Mare. She could remember many lines of poetry, and her bookshelves were home to many handsome collections. As a little girl, she had revelled in Swinburne and Meredith, the Rossettis and Tennyson's *Idylls of the King*. Some of these poets are now little read, their romantic and elaborate style being too saccharine for modern taste.

Going for a walk with my mother was as rich an experience as visiting a great art gallery. As a little child I had regarded walks as a boring ritual, punctuated by occasional moments of excite-ment, a wall to balance on or a tree to climb, but since our routine daily walks were through Embankment Gardens, oppor-tunities for excitement were few. Walks in the New Forest were altogether different, as if I had walked through Alice in Wonder-land's looking-glass into a magical secret place. Indeed it seemed right that the girl who was the original inspiration for Alice, Alice Hargreaves,* had lived, after her marriage, only a few miles away.

To this day, the New Forest inhabits a part of me. It is a

---

* Alice Liddell married Reginald Hargreaves in 1880, and they lived at Cuffnells, on the outskirts of Lyndhurst.

poignant sweet recollection, like a poem or a song. An uprooted beech tree, a clump of bracken, a sun-streaked brown pool are signposts on my travels through the forest. It has many moods, from the intense ecstasy of young green leaves in the spring to the mournful soughing of bare trees in winter storms. If each of us has a sense of where we belong, this is mine, my earthly paradise. My year in the New Forest brought cohesion to my life. It was as if a shaken kaleidoscope of experience settled back into a new and pleasing pattern. My relationship with my mother had become an easy, loving friendship. Amy and I had an unspoken understanding of what made her happy. I had found a home in which I was able to be free.

By the summer of 1944, the tide of war was ebbing from the New Forest: leaving it resembled Macbeth's wood moving from Birnam to Dunsinane, from Hampshire to France. The tented camps and the trenches emptied as the troops poured out to fight the first battles of the Second Front. Tanks and trucks processed head to tail along the road from Bournemouth to Southampton. By July, the glades and heathlands were falling silent again. Birds and squirrels began to repossess their natural kingdoms.

I was soon back at school at Talbot Heath in Bournemouth. During the week, I stayed with one of my mother's pacifist friends, Ida Hillman. Her husband Bob, an ice-cream maker before the war, had become a sausage-maker, conjuring sausages out of all kinds of material better not investigated too closely. They were firm Labour Party supporters and lived in Boscombe, the shabby relation of prosperous Bournemouth. Ida was a woman of firm convictions and great resilience, a kind of Mother Courage, but she was also a nagger. I had not come across anything of this kind before. I believe now that nagging is the response of talented women utterly frustrated by the circumstances of their lives to those around them, in particular their husbands and children. Nothing I could do was right. Put a teacup in an unaccustomed place, answer the door when someone else should, wear the wrong clothes – everything was cause for bitter and continuing complaint. I enjoyed school, but dreaded the end of each school day. Escaping, I retreated to my little room with the excuse of having homework to do, or went off to local Labour Party meetings. On Friday afternoons, I mounted my bicycle the minute school was over and hurtled along the highway through the great oaks and beeches of the forest – which was not without its own hazards, among them lonely soldiers still camped there, who exposed themselves as I cycled by. I would increase my pace, and wonder how they could imagine this to be an enticing approach.

The Second World War was moving towards its end. The news was all about the ruthless advance of the Allies across France and into Germany, caught in a giant pincer grip between the Atlantic Ocean and the Soviet Union. My mind began to turn back to politics. My father had gone to San Francisco for the founding conference of the United Nations, and my mother decided to return to London in time for the general election of 1945, though she played no active part in it.

I got back to London for the election night, having been granted special leave by Talbot Heath School to do so. The mood was one of hope. The returning soldiers were determined that peace was not going to bring a repetition of the interwar years, the dole queues and the Great Depression. It would bring instead a democratic socialist revolution. The long-delayed election result in July 1945 was to be a prelude to that dream.

Despite the hardships and dislocations, the fuel crisis and the shortage of dollars, the new Labour government embarked on a major programme of reconstruction and reform. All the time I could spare from the demands of School Certificate examinations, and more than I should have spared, went into politics. Most of my efforts were devoted to the Chelsea Labour Party, a curious hybrid of refugee Marxists, young lawyers, pragmatic bus drivers and idealistic artists. The Party's chairman, Ben Hooberman, was a former intelligence officer who had recently been demobilised after service in India. He was to become famous as the lawyer for Les Cannon and Frank Chapple in the 1961 case – Byrne and Chapple v. Foulkes and Others on electoral fraud in the Communist-dominated ETU, the Electrical Trades Union.

The local Party secretary, Margaret Schufeldt, was a middle-aged Jewish refugee from Germany deeply steeped in Marxism, and widely read in that philosophy. She found the British Labour Party puzzling, primitive and certainly disappointing. I was the youth representative on the general management committee, not that there were many youths in Chelsea for me to represent. My official position meant that I had to attend general management committees every month. I became active in the Labour League of Youth, the Labour Party's national youth organisation, and was elected to its executive committee. At that time the League of Youth was busily engaged in building the new postwar society and therefore little trouble to its elders. It was being relaunched, like the Labour Party itself, after the wartime pact which precluded electoral battles between the main parties in the coalition government.

In May 1948 some unusually innovative official in the Control Commission which administered the British zone of occupied Germany, perhaps Frank Pakenham himself, invited the Labour League of Youth to send two representatives to the first postwar conference of the German Jungsozialisten, the youth wing of the SPD, Germany's Social Democratic Party. Frank Pakenham, later Lord Longford, was Chancellor of the Duchy of Lancaster, and in that capacity responsible for the British-occupied zone. He believed that reconciliation between the German and British people at every level was an essential precondition of a new Germany. Our visit was part of the programme to re-educate young Germans in the ways of democracy. Because I could speak a little halting German, learned at school, I was one of the two chosen.

Tom Deacon, my twenty-year-old colleague, and I, not yet eighteen, drove across a ruined and hungry Germany in a British Control Commission car, threading our way through cities of rubble and the blackened skeletons of houses. People emerged out of the cellars and holes where they were living. The only currency with any value was cigarettes. I was appalled by the desolation all around me, and by the hollow-eyed despairing people. Close to Hof in Bavaria, our destination in the American zone, we spent the night in an American army hostel, guiltily eating hamburgers for supper. On my way to bed, I saw girls my own age and younger being offered to soldiers in exchange for chocolate bars. The horrors of war, so insistently present to my mother, began to come home to me.

We reached Hof in time to hear Kurt Schumacher, leader of the SPD and the survivor of a concentration camp, open the conference. Emaciated, a man consumed and compelled by his own internal fires, Schumacher described for us young people his vision of a new socialist Germany. Nothing we could say after that seemed worth saying. Yet our very presence, the symbol of a new comradeship, meant that our halting introductory words to the conference, 'Genosse und Genossen, Brüdern und Schwestern . . .', were cheered to the echo. We ate our cabbage and potatoes and dreamed of a better world.

Until the next day. The next day our German comrades told us that at the railway station, not far from the Czech–German border, there was a train full of Czechs who had fled across the border after the Communist putsch of February that year. Many of them were fellow socialists, since the putsch had toppled the elected postwar social democratic government of Edvard Beneš and Jan Masaryk. They were being forcibly returned to Czechoslovakia. The German delegates begged us to intervene with the Occupation authorities to save them. So down to the station we went, to be confronted by scores of desperate people locked into livestock wagons, hammering on the wooden walls and trying to tear out the bars, shouting that they would be condemned to salt mines and stone quarries if they were sent back. We went to the American commander, for this was the American zone, and pleaded with him to let them go. But he was bound by the pitiless deal made at Yalta in 1945, the deal that sent hundreds of thousands of refugees from Stalin's tyranny, including many Russian prisoners of war, back to their deaths. Tom and I were able to rescue just one young man, by hiding him under a blanket and bribing the German driver with cigarettes to keep his mouth shut. We let him off when we got back to the British zone, not daring to take him further. We never saw him again.

What I saw in Germany did not destroy my ideals, but it did bring home to me that even our own governments and our own allies could behave brutally, whatever the charters and declarations of commitment to freedom and justice might say. No nation was immune from cruelty; the veneer of civilisation was indeed thin.

I had been dimly aware of the impact on my mother four years before of the publication of her pamphlet, called in the United States *Massacre by Bombing* and in Britain *Seed of Chaos*, condemning saturation bombing. She had been reviled in both countries by political leaders and by Church leaders as a kind of collaborator, someone soft on the Nazis. She had been ostracised, not least by some of her fellow authors, and found old friends wanted nothing to do with her. It had been a painful and disillusioning time. Now I saw for myself what she had been protesting about. I began to identify much more closely with her. I saw that saturation bombing, sometimes known as carpet bombing, the fate that befell Hamburg and Dresden, was a method of mass indiscriminate killing. Today we would call it a crime against humanity. Furthermore, it was a crime against humanity that was counterproductive even in military terms. There is considerable evidence that Germany mobilised a higher proportion of her civilians for war work, especially married women, than before the bombing began.

In December 1947 I had been offered an open History scholarship at Somerville College, Oxford, despite – or perhaps because of – a stormy interview. Something my mother had inadvertently said, about Somerville squeezing me in if they could as the daughter of an old Somervillian, persuaded me that her influence was the reason for the offer. I wanted in any case to go to the London School of Economics, and had only tried for Somerville as a dry run for LSE. So I didn't much care if the scholarship offer was withdrawn. I walked into the Principal's office, announced that I didn't want her bloody scholarship, and turned to march out, clothed in self-righteousness. But the Principal was Janet Vaughan, scientist, socialist and iconoclast. Intrigued by my rudeness, she rose from her chair and seated herself cross-legged on the floor, then patted the space beside her and said: 'Come and tell me why you are so bloody angry.' From that day, we became great friends.

I took the scholarship, partly because of Janet Vaughan, partly because having attained it meant, in those days, that I could bypass A levels. I was bored with school, saw no further worlds there to conquer, and was keen to get back into the real world.

With most of the year to fill in before starting at university in October, I decided to work on a farm. I had spent several of my holidays at a community farm in Frating, Essex, established during the war by conscientious objectors and supported by my mother, among others. I liked farm work, and I started there as second cowman to a herd of Ayrshire dairy cows, handsome red-and-white animals of uncertain temper. The farm manager was a former blast-furnace man from Consett, County Durham, a stocky man in his forties with black hair and a square, strong face. Joe Watson was a remarkable man, a committed Christian socialist, who came south in the 1930s when County Durham had become one long dole queue, and got to know the leaders of the community movement who steered him into farming.

I made friends too with Trevor Howard and his wife Enid. Trevor, a Cambridge history graduate with a First Class degree, was a pacifist who became a farm worker as an alternative to military service. Head of the poultry department, he taught me that even hens have a personality, albeit limited. He and Enid, a woman of vigour and resilience, became lifelong friends of mine. I was one of those who persuaded Trevor to follow his vocation and become an Anglican priest.

It was at Frating that I had my first encounter with discrimination against Catholics. Early one morning, I was sitting under a cow completing the milking the machine had not finished, amiably chatting to the head cowman, a pious Methodist. He asked me idly what denomination I belonged to. When I replied 'Catholic', I heard his stool and milk pail crash to the floor of the dairy. He stormed out of the barn into Joe Watson's office, and told him he was not prepared to work with me. Joe, an Anglican churchwarden, told him that in that case he would not be working at all. For days afterwards we milked in fraught silence. But in the end curiosity about the Catholic Church, the scarlet woman of Rome, got the better of him, and we began to talk again.

I suppose I was a bit in love with Joe. I had never met anyone like him. So after five months on the farm I decided to go to County Durham, to learn more about where he came from. I thought I could find a job on a sheep farm for the summer. But it was the wrong time of the year for shepherds' assistants, and I could not find a job. So, driven as much by injured pride at my failure to find employment as by desperation, I took the advice of other girls at the YWCA in Newcastle where I was lodging, and cycled to Whitley Bay to look for a job in a hotel. Through the front window of one of them, the Cliffe, I glimpsed the manager, and asked him if he had any work for me. I told him, lying, that I had several months of experience as a waitress. I don't think he believed me, but he saw a strong young farm worker, and he put me to work scrubbing pans and cleaning rooms for eighteen shillings a week, with occasional waitressing duties when things were busy.

The hours were long, seven in the morning until ten at night, with a couple of hours off in the afternoon, one day off a week and an occasional free weekend. The hotel staff, most of us girls in our teens, shared beds in three rooms in the hotel's attic. The water was almost always cold and there was only one bath between us. My room-mate believed in the old adage 'Ne'er cast a clout 'til May is out', and remained in the same vest and knickers for weeks at a time.

Our customers were a mixed bunch. Some were salesmen, some were spivs – that sharply dressed guerrilla army of wide-boys living off the black market and the credulity of the locals – and a few were deep-sea divers. Tips were rarely more than six-pence, and sometimes the sixpence was accompanied by a hefty pinch on the thigh or bottom. We perfected the technique of accidentally spilling hot soup into the laps of the most persistent offenders. The hazards of a young waitress's life are many, the rewards few. We were allowed to eat up food that was left over after all the guests had been served. If there wasn't any, the staples were chips and sweet tea. On Sundays, I cycled over to the little town of Blaydon, where the senior railwayman and his wife, friends of the Watsons, filled me up with homemade scones.

On the rare weekend when I had both Saturday and Sunday off, I cycled over to Windermere in the Lake District to stay with my Great-aunt Muriel and my Great-uncle Leigh. Aunt Muriel liked drama. On my Friday evening cycle ride from Whitley Bay to Windermere, I had taken a short cut over the fells near Holehird, their large house in the Patterdale valley, only to fall, with my bicycle, over a large rock. The bicycle was twisted, and I was scratched and bruised. I carried it down the hillside, arriving well after midnight on my great-aunt's doorstep. As soon as Muriel saw the dishevelled and bloodstained figure in the dim hall light, she burst into delighted applause. That was the way she liked young people to be.

Tyneside and County Durham were, from southern England, places apart, stoical, gritty, generous and direct. Their politics were Labour, Labour as a faith, an unquestioned way of life. The annual miners' gala was like a saint's day in Italy, a parade of thousands of miners carrying colliery banners, winding their way up the hill on which Durham Cathedral stands above the deep-brown river. It was a land of ravaged beauty, for between the pits with their gaunt winding wheels and heaps of staining black slag were woods and valleys, moors and streams, and views that swept from horizon to horizon.

At the end of the summer season I left Whitley Bay, my week's wages in my pocket, my new friends left behind. I hadn't discovered another New World, but I had discovered another England.

CHAPTER 4

Oxford Idyll

The University of Oxford in 1948 had burst the bounds of its own majestic, stifling traditions. The bells still rang from St Mary's, the university church, the river wound its weedy way through Christ Church Meadow, but the undergraduates were no longer neophyte adults. They had been aged by experience. Many had lived out the kind of history their tutors only taught.

The war had brought home to Winston Churchill's coalition government how deep were the wells of talent in the nation, and how poorly that had been recognised. Men and women who had left school at fourteen became outstanding military officers, or organisers on the Home Front. Recognising their potential, the wartime government had introduced the Further Education and Training Programme, offering ex-servicemen and women the opportunity and the means to go to university, paying for them to graduate after an intensive two-year 'emergency' course. Many of these students had never dreamed of a university degree before the war, and their working-class families would not have conceived of it either. The war, however, had propelled them into positions of responsibility, of having to make decisions not only for themselves but for others. In doing so, they had gained confidence. They filled the new vacancies in the professions, in management and in the new public services. Hundreds became teachers, probably the most impressive generation of teachers ever to enter the state schools. Collectively, their aspirations and their self-confidence eroded the walls of the old class system, bringing to the United Kingdom a level of social mobility not seen before or since, a social mobility enhanced by an ambitious programme of good-quality public housing and a move away from selective education.

I met many of this wartime generation of ex-service students at Oxford, and very impressive they were. One of my friends, Bill Pearson, was the son of a waiter and a chambermaid. Before the war he would not have seen the inside of a university. He was promoted to captain, lost his leg in battle, and at Oxford became both president of his college's Junior Common Room and an outstanding cricketer. He went on to become the West Midlands director of the CBI, a magistrate and a marriage guidance counsellor. A degree from a respected university provided the launching pad for him to achieve his aspirations. These men had no time for the artful pretentiousness of pre-war Oxford. Indeed, they had no time to waste. Many students who had chosen to take the two-year shortened wartime degree lived on ex-servicemen's grants which left little scope for luxuries or even necessities. They needed to earn money, and to do so quickly.

In spite of that, university activities flourished like flowers in a desert after rain. A wealth of ideas and aspirations had been stored up in the long, parched wartime years. Central to those ideas and aspirations was the determination to bring to an end the long civil wars of Europe, and in Britain, to create a fair and classless society which offered everyone jobs and opportunity. The demobilised servicemen and women knew that the pressures of finding a job and making a living would soon reassert themselves. So these precious university years had to encompass every ambition, achievement and satisfaction that could be crammed into them.

To be a girl just out of school in this intense and impatient company was daunting, but hugely exciting. My experiences had been colourful by the standards of most eighteen-year-olds, but seemed insipid beside those of men who had stormed the beaches of Italy or carved their way through the jungles of Burma. The undergraduates who had come straight to university from school seemed not only callow but, in an odd way, old-fashioned.

In material terms, Oxford was an austere place in 1948. The country was coping with a fuel crisis so serious that trains could not run for lack of coal, and households were strictly rationed. Food was plain and rooms were cold. Somerville, my college, served a diet heavily dependent on potato cakes. At night my friends and I would cluster round a single-bar electric fire, huddled in blankets and drinking cocoa made with the ubiquitous dried milk of postwar England.

One of the favourite meeting places of self-proclaimed socialists was the British Restaurant in the Plain beyond Magdalen Bridge, a relic of wartime, where students could buy sausages and mash or carrot pie for controlled prices. Another was Fuller's, the teashop in the Cornmarket, which offered iced Victoria sponges, walnut, coffee and lemon, expensive enough to ornament only tea parties for favoured friends. It was distinguished, too, by the frequent presence of a resplendent Ken Tynan, the legendary figure of that Oxford era, dressed in a gold satin shirt and dazzling freshmen with his eloquence about the theatre and the latest books.

The theatre was a magnet for young people starved during their years in the armed forces, or as evacuees in the countryside, of opera, drama and the arts. Their attraction to these activities coincided with a flowering of talent in the postwar Oxford years that was astonishing. Ken Tynan may have been the most admired and the most talked about, but many others less inclined to self-publicity found their place in the Oxford University Dramatic Society (OUDS) and in the Experimental Theatre Club. Jack May and Ronald Eyre launched their careers at

Oxford. So did Robert Robinson, the distinguished broadcaster, with whom I used to go punting late at night on the starlit Isis. Prominent among the undergraduate directors were John Schlesinger, devoted to his craft and hard to please, William Gaskell, radical and innovative, and Tony Richardson. Tony was like a caged hawk, restless, brilliant, yearning to be free of conventional barriers in the theatre and in life alike. He and I used to go for long walks, beside Oxford's misty canal or in the Cotswold hills. He belonged to the high windy moors of Yorkshire, not to the cultivated prettiness of Oxfordshire's parklands. He wasn't easy to talk to, though sometimes his conversation would take flight. I always felt that California was the wrong place for him, but by the time he moved to Hollywood we were no longer in touch, and I couldn't tell him so.

Refusing to acknowledge limitations of time or energy, I plunged into the world of university dramatics. I started modestly enough with the Experimental Theatre Club, mainly acting in new plays. Jean-Paul Sartre was much in fashion at the time, his troubled existentialist works leaving a wake of unanswered questions behind them. By my second year, however, I had moved on to the more traditional OUDS. I took part in their summer tour of the United States in 1950, playing in Ben Jonson's *The Alchemist*, in which Robert Robinson played the servant Face. I also played Cordelia in a production of *King Lear*, directed in Oxford by Tony Richardson and in the United States by Alan Cooke, in which Peter Parker, with whom I was to fall in love, took the role of Lear. We had our West End debut in the modest Fortune Theatre off Drury Lane; the few reviewers were kind to us.

The tour was something of a revelation, for we travelled around several Midwest universities as well as others on the East Coast, among them Purdue University in Indiana, Miami University at Oxford, Ohio, and Tufts University in Massachusetts. Our audiences reacted as Shakespeare's contemporaries might have done, identifying the actor with his or her character. So I was regarded as a sweet and upright girl, while my friends Jo Page, playing Goneril, and Josée Richards, later Robert Robinson's wife, playing Regan, were seen as dangerous hussies, to be avoided by local young men.

In his direction of the play Tony Richardson was, as in all things, absolutist. The dead Cordelia had to be presented by King Lear, her father, on outstretched arms as if on an altar. He then had to speak for several minutes that great soliloquy that begins: 'Howl, howl, howl, howl! O, you are men of stones!' Peter was a strong man and fit, but I was no featherweight. So a sling was arranged over his shoulders, which I held on to under his crimson cloak like a terrier grabbing its lead, during the interminable if moving address. The play, however, overcame such distractions with the sheer force of the plot. To this day, when I hear the commanding opening of Mussorgsky's 'Great Gate of Kiev' from *Pictures at an Exhibition*, which accompanied Lear's entrance, I am translated to the dark stage of the Fortune Theatre, just before the curtains opened, for our first and only week of public performances in England before the American tour.

Politically, too, Oxford buzzed with activity. Thousands of students joined the political clubs, and hundreds turned up to their meetings. The Oxford University Labour Club had some fifteen hundred members, and two of its most prominent former chairmen, Tony Wedgwood-Benn (as he was then known) and Dick Taverne, were still in residence. Tony Crosland, dashing in a white silk scarf and a paratrooper's beret, was the Club's senior treasurer. The Conservative Association, recently chaired by a serious-minded student of chemistry called Margaret Roberts, had fallen under the benign sway of William Rees-Mogg, whose deliberate and well-paced style of speech marked him out early as a sage.

It was immediately after arriving at Somerville in the autumn of 1948 that I encountered, for the first time since we met as children, Val Mitchison, daughter of Naomi Mitchison, herself a member of the brilliant Haldane family. Caustic, witty and beautiful, with black hair, blue eyes and a bone-china complexion, Val was to become one of my closest university woman friends. On hearing who my mother was, she commented, 'Oh, I see, the intellectual nouveau riche!'

Together we went hunting for the Labour Club. I managed to track down the secretary, Will Camp, at Oriel College. He invited me to tea. Tea, it should be explained, was the social highlight of the day, since few students could afford to take someone else out to dinner. Will was writing a novel, *Tell it Not in Gath*. I was impressed. He offered to read me excerpts. When he had finished, I remembered what my objective was. 'I want to join the Labour Club now,' I said. 'Who is the chairman?' Will frowned. 'It's Peter Parker,' he replied, 'and once you meet him you won't be interested in me.'

He was right. I saw Peter from a distance at the first big meeting of the Labour Club. The speaker was Emmanuel Shinwell, Minister for War, who had been under bitter attack from the Tories since the terrible fuel crisis of the previous winter. The meeting was tumultuous, with heckling and counter-heckling. I sensed that Peter, in the chair, was hugely enjoying himself.

That evening, at the dinner for the speaker held at the Mitre Hotel, Oxford's best, the tumult continued. Sitting opposite Shinwell, the senior treasurer could not contain himself: Tony Crosland waded straight in, disputing Shinwell's arguments and quarrelling with his policies. It was obvious that Shinwell had had enough, but how could the chairman remove the senior treasurer? After a whispered consultation, the strikingly handsome Florence Elliott, a fiery member of the Club's executive committee who liked a challenge, was persuaded to lure Tony away. She went up to him and suggested they could both have much more fun if they left the dinner than if they stayed. He followed her out of the room like a lamb, and Shinwell recovered his composure.

Peter Parker radiated energy and delight. He never walked. He danced, he strode, he bounced with a kind of powerful grace. His voice was an actor's, modulated and rich, controlled for the particular purpose it was serving. He played leading roles in everything he did – politics, the theatre, reading poetry on the BBC, rugby, in the college Junior Common Room – by stimulating and motivating others rather than by coercion and command. But there was an underlying toughness about him. Commissioned as a major at the age of twenty-three, he had had what was called 'a good war'. But it was a war that had taken the lives of his two elder brothers. The only surviving child of his family, he lived with an intensity that suggested he was living for all three young men, not only for himself.

His experience of the loss through war of those closest to him echoed the experiences of my mother, who spoke, at his invitation, to the Labour Club in my first term. When Peter telephoned me at home, my mother, who answered the call, was thunderstruck. 'It's Roland's voice,' she said. Reminded of the fiancé my mother had lost in the First World War, my father was, understandably, less taken with Peter after that.

From the moment I saw him presiding over the Shinwell meeting, I was bewitched; it was truly a *coup de foudre*, something I would earlier have denied was possible. I tried to think of ways to meet him, without becoming obsequious. We did meet again, when he was judging auditions for parts in Experimental Theatre Club plays and I was one of those participating.

I visited his room in Lincoln College at the end of my first term to wish him a happy Christmas and to tell him my mother and I would be spending a week in Bedford, where Peter's family lived, because she was researching a book on John Bunyan, the Puritan preacher and author of *Pilgrim's Progress* who had lived and preached in the town. Peter was sitting by the fire reading a poem by W. H. Auden. He read it out loud to me. 'The way is certainly both short and steep,/However gradual it looks from here,' it ran.

'Look if you like, but you will have to leap.' As a guide to our love affair, it was a good description.

Through politics and acting our lives criss-crossed, and by the spring of 1949 I was in love with him, and he, a little, with me. But I was too young for him, too much the tomboy, too immature. In the year and a half of our love affair, he taught me a great deal, not only about acting, politics and poetry, but also about dancing. I still remember the Commemoration Ball at Lincoln College in the summer of 1949, wearing a ball gown in a loud yellow-and-brown pattern and being introduced to the then Rector, Keith Murray, his impeccable evening dress complete with white gloves. Peter and I danced all night.

I had to concentrate my political energies on the Labour Club, because the Oxford Union Society, still the arena for the most prestigious debates, barred women members. Very rarely, there was an outside woman speaker, even more rarely, a female undergraduate. The Union boasted among its officers some conspicuous figures. Robin Day was later to make *Question Time* one of the most popular political programmes on television, and Uwe Kitzinger was to help construct the European Community. Few of the men, however, took the women's cause seriously. So with Ann Chesney, the warm and ebullient chairman of the University Liberal Club, and other aspiring women student politicians, I started an alternative debating society, open to both sexes. Occasionally we took militant action to protest against the Union Society's discrimination, in one incident chaining ourselves to the railings around its premises. For years after, amendments to the Union's rules that would have permitted women to join were put to the vote of the existing members, both senior and junior, and were – predictably – lost. It was to be my first, and not my last, encounter with what would today be called institutional sexism.

Fortunately, there were many undergraduates who were not attracted by the Union's pretentious and self-conscious style. One of them was Bill Rodgers, born in Liverpool where he attended the Quarry Bank High School, who became treasurer of the Labour Club when I was chairman. He took his politics seriously and organised the Labour Party group within the Club, young men and women who met every week to talk about policy. He was then, as later, a brilliant political organiser. It was an excellent preparation for his first major job in politics as General Secretary of the Fabian Society. It was also the beginning of our lifelong friendship.

I spent a lot of my evenings with friends, fellow undergraduates who remain friends of mine today. Among them was Phyllis Cook, daughter of a police officer in Birmingham, who with Val formed my Somerville triangle. Phyllis was very different from Val, a source of common sense, calm and loyalty. Another to become a close friend was Hilary Rubinstein, son of my mother's lawyer Harold, a gentle, loving man devoted to writers and writing. After working for his uncle Victor Gollancz, Hilary became a leading literary agent. In Oxford, he was regarded as an arbiter of culture. He was also a person of great warmth, capable of consoling those with broken hearts or family problems.

My favourite bolthole outside the restricted confines of the colleges was the tiny Wellington Square flat of my friends John and Eileen Spencer, whom the university permitted to live together because they were a married couple. John, a Quaker, had been a conscientious objector during the war, and was allowed to work on farms as his national service. He became first a farm labourer in Yorkshire, then a horseman in Lincolnshire, ploughing with powerful Percheron horses. A more tolerant government than that following the First World War gave COs who had done their national service the same opportunity to attend university as was enjoyed by veterans of the armed forces, so John came up to Oxford in 1947. He and Eileen were deeply involved in helping in the reconstruction of Germany. John helped to organise the first meeting between Oxford undergraduates and German students, when a group of thirty went to Bonn University for three weeks in the summer of 1947. To this day, Oxford and Bonn remain twinned cities. In 1948 Oxfam had just opened its first shop, sending parcels to a hungry and devastated Europe, an endeavour which also involved Christian Action, founded by John Collins, Dean of Oriel College, two years earlier.

The Spencers' flat was the venue for many late-night discussions. I had my own corner of the sitting-room floor, stocked with old newspapers and unread messages. One of their frequent visitors was Robert Runcie, who had been in Bonn with John in 1947. He was agonising about whether or not to enter Holy Orders. Tall, with a light, rather affected voice and a preoccupied manner, it did not at first seem credible that he had been an officer in the Scots Guards and a recipient of the Military Cross. It took a much longer acquaintance to take the measure of this brave and committed man. We had long conversations about theology and politics, he exploring the depth of his faith, I trying to resolve why I had chosen, as a young adult, to be baptised a Roman Catholic. Our hosts, both brought up in the Quaker tradition, reminded us of the uncompromising demands of conscience, no respecter of institutional rules.

In the summer vacation of 1949, Val and I decided to travel to Austria, where a Young Socialist camp was being held near Klagenfurt in Carinthia. The attraction was not so much the camp as the prospect of visiting Tito's Yugoslavia next door. We had two friends in the British Army Intelligence Corps, stationed in Austria under the Occupation, who were to be in the strictly geographic sense our fellow travellers: David Lane, later to become High Commissioner in Trinidad and Tobago and Ambassador to the Holy See, and Michael Summerskill, son of the redoubtable Edith, the Parliamentary Secretary in the Ministry of Food in the postwar Labour government. Val and I hitch-hiked part of the way, at one point in a car whose driver carefully removed part of the panelling in order to conceal smuggled packages before crossing the border.

We went through some of the ruined cities of Germany, strange spectral places in which gaunt men and women emerged from cellars and holes in the ground looking for bread and cigarettes.

The camp was a place of organised enthusiasm. Early every morning we were woken in our tents by the loudspeaker broadcasting the strains of 'We are of the Younger Generation'. The days were taken up with lectures, workshops and hikes. Food was black bread spread with lard, very occasionally garnished with a slice of German sausage. Among the participants were a brilliant young Scot, editor of the socialist journal *Forward*, George Thomson, and his wonderful, warm and unpretentious wife Grace. We were to become close companions in the years to come, fellow MPs, fellow Europhiles and eventually fellow founding members of the Social Democratic Party. To the heavy ideology-laden atmosphere of the Klagenfurt camp, the Thomsons brought something of the calm optimism of the Scottish Enlightenment.

Val and I went off after this brief ideological brainwashing to pursue our main purpose, the visit to Yugoslavia. Currency controls were fierce, intended to keep visitors out, and the penalty for smuggling in money was years in prison. Unperturbed, we folded the dinars we had obtained from Michael and David in the knots of our neckerchiefs, on the theory that if we were strip-searched we could always pull the scarves over our heads without unknotting them. On the train inspectors did come by, but limited their search to the usual scrutiny of passports and papers.

We arrived in the town of Bled and hired a room along with our friends Michael and David, who had joined us there. The lake nestling within its protective mountains was deep blue and inviting. There were few visitors, and we were readily identified because of speaking English. Among those few visitors was Tito's doctor. He wanted to talk to us about his distinguished patient, but to do so he felt obliged to swim far out into the lake and converse while treading water. He told us a bit about Tito's growing strains with the Soviet Union, his determination to maintain his country's independence, and the consequences of the rivalry between Communists and Chetniks during the war. Our trip to Yugoslavia was, however, dominated by hunger more than by politics. In spite of the smuggled dinars, we had very little money, and in any case food was strictly rationed. The only thing that seemed to be in abundant supply was plum jam. Each morning in our room we doled out provisions for the day: a couple of slices of bread, a piece of sausage or cheese, perhaps an apple, a couple of squares of chocolate. I remember the feeling of pure hatred I experienced when Michael spread plum jam on his chocolate – the triumph of hunger over good manners!

Back at Somerville for the autumn term, it was brought home to me that discussions with friends, politics and acting took up much of my time, indeed too much, according to the college authorities. I held an open scholarship, and was therefore expected to maintain a good academic standard, and to be an example to my fellow undergraduates. Somerville was an intensely competitive college, dedicated to demonstrating that women were intellectually as able as men. This was translated in terms of the proportion of First Class degrees won by the college, compared to its high-flying masculine rivals such as Balliol and Magdalen. My subjects of study were philosophy, politics and economics, pompously known as Modern Greats. I enjoyed politics, and in particular political philosophy, but with modern philosophy I could not come to terms. My father had told me about the philosophers he admired, T. E. Marshall, Jacques Maritain and Bertrand Russell, who pondered the nature of society and the concept of justice. Contemporary Oxford philosophy, by contrast, was dominated by logical positivism. I found it clever, arid and devoid of interest. When my thoughtful and patient tutor, Philippa Foot, looked intently at her sofa and asked me why it could not be both red and green all over, the question irritated me. It obviously couldn't be both. What more was there to say?

Economics was more attractive. I was fortunate in having a wonderful tutor, a woman for whom the word 'gaiety' might have been invented. Margaret Hall was elegant, brilliant, vibrant and occasionally frivolous. She wore scarlet suits and very high heels, and had a mind like a razor, precise, sharp and effective. She exemplified what I wanted to be – an outstanding professional, an attractive woman, and a wife and mother. She understood that for me economics was not an interest but a tool. When I was carpeted for failing to maintain the standards of work required of a scholar, it was she who interceded for me. It was she, too, who wrung from me a reluctant promise to spend more time on my weekly essays.

It was acting, my second love after politics, that had to be sacrificed to these demands. Despairing of ever making sense of logical positivism, I turned to two friends at Balliol who were famed for their command of the subject, Tom Sebestyen and Bernard Williams. Bernard was a favourite student of the renowned and mercurial Freddie Ayer, of whom I was in awe. He was also winning a reputation as one of the most brilliant undergraduate students of philosophy and classical studies in the university at that time. Tom Sebestyen, his inseparable friend, was the son of Jewish refugees from Hungary. A man of deep culture, Tom was torn between the excitement of philosophy and the desire to become a businessman, a drive that took him first to France and eventually, in 1989, back to a newly liberated Hungary.

If I mastered enough philosophy to obtain a good but undistinguished Second Class degree, it was due to them rather than to any efforts of my own. But these intensive seminars led to more than a degree. The three of us became close friends. Bernard and I were to get to know one another even better when we were both in North America in 1952, far away from the circle of friends we moved among at Oxford.

My last year at Oxford, October 1950 to June 1951, was overcast by the sorrow of losing Peter. He had won a Commonwealth

My parents, George Catlin and Vera Brittain, Glebe Place, 1935

With my mother and John, Sidmouth, 1932

Winifred Holtby, John, my
mother and Phyllis Bentley,
Glebe Place, 1932

With my mother, Glebe Place, 1936

With my mother and John, 1933

With my brother John,
St Paul, Minnesota,
1943

With John at the Allum Green cottage, 1939

My mother speaking at a peace rally, 1938

With my mother, Whitehall Court, November 1965

'*Isis* Idol', Oxford, 1949

With Bernard Williams after our wedding at St James's, Spanish Place,
2 July 1955

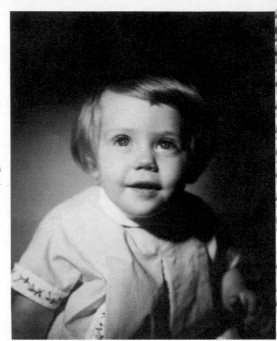

Rebecca aged eighteen
months, 1962

Prospective Labour
parliamentary candidate
for Hitchin, 1963

Scholarship to Cornell University in New York State, and was now engulfed in the excitement of America. But there were some compensations. The Labour Club in my term as chairman, the first woman to be elected to the post, attracted splendid speakers such as Dick Crossman and a high-flying junior minister called Jim Callaghan. I thought him very attractive and made toast for him and some of my friends on the tiny gas fire in my college room. Some of the Club's keenest members were invited to join a select group convened by the socialist thinker G. D. H. Cole. I was the only female member of the Cole group, and I was there on sufferance. Cole himself, a gaunt and rather chilly man, regarded women as inefficient organisms, once telling me they had too many protuberances.

The compensations were not only in the political field. In my last summer term I got to know Roger Bannister, then contending for the title of the fastest miler in the world. Sometimes I would run with him when he trained, puffing along in his wake. I was his partner at the Amateur Athletics Association dance, the evening after he won the mile race in 4 minutes 7.8 seconds, against such fine runners as John Parlett, Len Eyre and Alan Parker. That summer, on our way to Val Mitchison's family home in Carradale on the Kintyre peninsula, the two of us hiked through the Trossachs, getting lost all one night in drenching cold rain. But when we did arrive, Roger discovered the long white sand beach edging the bay. That evening, he ran like a deer, his fair hair turning gold in the setting sun. Val's mother Naomi, a connoisseur of men, was as transfixed as I was by the sheer beauty of his movement in that magical setting.

Oxford is a courtesan, bestowing on each of the university's students his or her own moments of enchantment – swimming in the muddy water of the Isis on a hot summer afternoon beside the buttercup meadows; borrowing a dozing punt late at night, the pole scattering the stars reflected in the water; balancing on the spikes that topped Somerville's walls after some late-night escapade before dropping into the shadows of the college garden, and falling in love, somersaulting and tumbling into love, the qualification for life that no amount of study could ensure.

My three years at Oxford were not to be the sum total of my student life. Maybe I wanted to prolong my studies. Perhaps I wanted to revisit my American childhood paradise. I don't remember now, but in any case in my last term I applied for a Fulbright Scholarship to study economics at Columbia University in New York, combined with field studies on the political action programmes of American trades unions. McCarthyism, that virulent populist form of anti-Communism, was then at its height. Having been on the winning side in the war, the politicians and people of the United States could not understand why they had been cheated of the peace and tranquillity they had anticipated. Now, only five years after VJ day, war – this time the Korean War – had demanded American troops and American treasure. The invasion of South Korea by North Korea was seen as yet another step in the Communist bloc's objective of world domination.

The United States had already seen Communist regimes established throughout Eastern Europe over the reluctant people of Poland, Hungary and most of the other countries in the region. The Soviet Union had blockaded West Berlin in 1948, compelling the Western Allies to mount an expensive air bridge to get supplies in as the only alternative to war. The Communist cause, declared Senator Joseph McCarthy, had been aided and abetted by home-grown fellow travellers and secret Party members, and it was these people the Senator pledged to identify and denounce. A brilliant self-publicist, McCarthy's method was to produce lists of named suspects, to the delight of the media and the horror of the administration. The careers of many innocent and patriotic public servants were ruined by rumour and innuendo. But in the lists there were some, most notoriously Alger Hiss, who actually had passed government files on to the Soviet Union.

Running scared, the State Department, McCarthy's favourite target, began to impose political conditions on the issue of visas. Among those trapped by this restriction was one very small fish – me.

There was no analogous movement to McCarthyism in the United Kingdom, despite the existence of powerful Communist parties in Italy and France. Britons felt grateful to the Russians for their part in the victory against Hitler, and had a greater appreciation than did the United States of the sheer scale of their human losses. Building on that gratitude, and on a profound yearning for a peaceful world, Communist parties and their associates were constantly engaged in promoting peace conferences and peace movements. They attracted many idealists and people of goodwill who in no way shared a commitment to Communist ideology.

In 1949 one such peace movement, the World Peace Council, brought together internationalists, social democrats and fellow travellers behind the idea of an international petition for peace, to be signed by political activists and student leaders, culminating in a huge peace conference in Stockholm. It called for an absolute ban on all nuclear weapons. As the newly elected chairman of the Oxford University Labour Club in 1950, I wanted to avoid a split within the Club on whether or not a delegation should be sent to the conference. The best way to do so, I decided, was to ensure that students from other Oxford political clubs, above all from the Conservatives, were invited too. So I went to see my friend William Rees-Mogg, now ensconced as their new Conservative Association chairman. Over a relaxed breakfast, he was perusing the *Financial Times*. I described my dilemma, and he agreed to take part in the preliminary conference in London as the Junior Common Room representative from his own college, Balliol. Halfway through the conference, he walked out, along with many of the Labour and Liberal delegates. But crucially for me, he had undoubtedly been there.

I was successful in obtaining the Fulbright Scholarship, but I found myself barred from entering the United States on the grounds that I had signed the Stockholm Appeal. So I persuaded William to write to the American Ambassador, pointing out that he himself had attended the preliminary conference, and could not conceivably be described as a fellow traveller of any kind. Was the United States proposing to forbid the entry of British students whatever their political beliefs? Recognising the absurdity of the position, the Ambassador presumably interceded. In any case, I was permitted to enter the United States.

William's generous gesture brought its own reward. In 1949 I had been features editor of *Isis*, one of the two main student periodicals, and I continued to contribute articles and profiles from time to time. The newly elected Conservative Association's chairman was a natural subject for the regular '*Isis* Idol' profile. In it, I recalled William's daily obeisance to the *Financial Times*. The profile was picked up from among the press cuttings by its editorial staff, and William was duly invited to the interview that launched his distinguished professional career, during which he became editor and later a columnist for *The Times*.

Before leaving for the United States in January 1952, I needed to earn some money to supplement my scholarship. I managed to get a temporary job at the Cherry Blossom factory by the Hogarth roundabout in Chiswick, making tins for boot polish. The women sorted out the metal pieces cut by the men, which were then joined together, filled and labelled, ready for dispatch. It was a cheerful job and as a team we worked well together, listening to the BBC radio comedies loudly broadcast over the crackle of metal-cutting. But then we were instructed by our shop stewards to work more slowly. Those who took no notice were compelled to do the same job over and over. We resented the orders, for most of us were piece workers, paid only for what we produced. So we came in for verbal abuse, including colourful descriptions of our looks, our shapes and our prospects. Some of the men stood around the platform we were working on, commenting on our legs. So we demanded trousers from the management, and got them. It was my first, but not my last, encounter with shop steward power.

The boat train for the *Mauritania* was filling up, the last passengers manhandling their trunks and tin cases out of the luggage vans. On the platform families were hugging one another, seeing off GI brides, new emigrants and excited students like me. But all the same, I was cast down. My parents were there, and so were Amy and Charlie Burnett, my surrogate parents. But there was no Roger to be seen. The train began to ease out of the station and gather speed. Then, at the end of the long platform, he appeared, weaving through the crowd, running faster and faster. He was just able to catch up with the carriage where I was standing with my head out of the window, time enough to thrust a bunch of flowers into my hand and to kiss me a literally moving goodbye. This farewell epitomised for me the end of the Oxford chapter of my life and the beginning of a new adventure.

CHAPTER 5

America Coast to Coast

Columbia University sprawls across Morningside Heights in the northwest of Manhattan. Beyond it lies Harlem, then as now a neighbourhood of run-down and often charred brownstone buildings decorated with rusty fire escapes, high-rise public-project apartments and littered empty lots. Columbia is a private university with a good academic record, but far removed geographically and aesthetically from the manicured green lawns and neoclassical buildings of its Ivy League fellows. We students divided our time between classes and seminars on the campus, and the vibrant, noisy life of New York. I lived in International House, a large and gracious student hostel on Riverside Drive overlooking the broad Hudson River and the New Jersey palisades on the other side. Two-thirds of the hostel's residents were from overseas, a third from the United States. There were lots of cultural and social activities to bring us together. One of my fellow students was Leontyne Price, later to become a world-famous opera singer. She would trill in the shower next to my room. Through her I became familiar with *Porgy and Bess*, that epic of the American South, and with the other works of George Gershwin. Another of my friends was Guido Declercq, a serious-minded scholar from Flanders, dedicated to the revival of his war-scarred province.

I found the United States in September 1951 very different from the confident, trusting country I remembered from my wartime years as an evacuee. Columbia was wracked by suspicion and mistrust. In one of my first seminars, my insensitive if unwitting behaviour nearly wrecked a fellow student's career. Marvin Lee had been a marine serving in Korea. He was a clever, sardonic man of strong left-wing sympathies. Trying to express his opinions while protecting himself from the witch-hunters, he had devised a contorted sociological language which was very hard to understand. Detecting in the jumble of jargon a familiar theme, I asked him, 'Why don't you just explain Marxism without all that gobbledegook?' The class froze. Here in their midst was one of those 'traitors' Senator McCarthy had warned them about. Everyone stared at Marvin. The silence was shattered by the professor, Aaron Warner, who bawled me out for not knowing what I was talking about. He and I both knew I was right, but now I understood what I had done. I came greatly to respect him. After the class, Warner confronted me outside. 'What the hell do you think you are doing? Do you want to destroy his whole future?' After that, I guarded my tongue in class, but spent hours arguing with Marvin in the twilit coffee bars near the campus.

The other university I got to know, mainly through weekend visits, was Cornell, where my father before the war had been a professor of political science. Cornell had a renowned School of Labor Relations, a useful source of material for my episodic study of the American trades unions. The university stands at the hub of several dramatic gorges, opening out into the Finger Lakes, a region of turbulent rivers, tumbled rocks and trees clinging to the steep edges. Swimming at night in the clear cold rockpools and in and out of the high waterfalls was to bond with elemental nature.

My most fateful weekend visit was to Connecticut, ablaze with the gold and crimson leaves of the early fall, maple, beech and oak. I had been invited to her home by Mo Walton, the mother of the sculptor Marion Putnam who had been my hostess during my wartime summer holidays. Mo was a tiny, twig-like woman in her eighties, with blazing blue eyes. A generous and discriminating patron of music, she had supported Béla Bartók in his early penurious years as a refugee in the United States. She suggested I might like to bring a friend, so I asked Bernard Williams, the fellow undergraduate who had taught me enough philosophy to get me through my Oxford finals, and who was now training in Canada to fly jet fighters in preparation for active service in Korea.

My hostess was greatly taken with the slim, dark young man in his RAF officer's uniform. He was quite tall, had glossy dark-brown hair and the good looks of a filmstar. She and I met him at a railway station close to her home in Connecticut. Mo drove her large American sedan with reckless panache. She could only just see over the top of the driver's panel. Bernard loved driving fast, and enjoyed the way Mo just missed parked cars and the edges of the wooden bridge we crossed. She responded happily to his enthusiasm. Bernard and I spent the weekend walking in the stupendous woodlands, listening to the music for which they provided a fitting stage, and writing poems to one another, not love poems but exercises in exploration. Mo was intrigued by this unusual form of communication. She played the part of an elderly Cupid. Bernard and I marked the end of his leave with a visit to *Guys and Dolls* in New York, the musical that best catches the spirit of that restless, vibrant city.

This, my third, American visit culminated in a journey from coast to coast, the objective of all the foreign scholars who could assemble the necessary time and money. Three of us shared the trip: Rodney Donald, a wry, reserved Scot I'd known at Oxford, treasurer of the Oxford Union and now a student at Harvard Business School, Guido Declercq, my serious music-loving Flemish colleague at International House, and me. Between us we managed to buy a small, elderly Mercury car. We hoped to sell it on the West Coast for more than we had paid for it. The Mercury boiled over in the Appalachians, a couple of days' drive from our starting point in Boston. We were nowhere near a town, or even a garage. So we walked to the nearest farm to ask for water to pour into the radiator. The farmer's wife, clearly curious about us, invited us to share the family's meal. As we ate, she inspected us closely. She had never heard of Belgium, and had only a dim idea of Britain. As she and I were washing up, she inquired, 'Where you come from, do y'all eat with knives and forks?'

While we were awaiting repairs in West Virginia, I heard about a miners' strike in the mountains. Labour relations in the Appalachians were savage and confrontational. The work was grim, the pay low, the owners interested only in maximising their profits. In John Lewis, leader of the miners' union, a Welsh immigrant of beetling black eyebrows and snowy thatch of hair, they had met their match. It came as a shock, nonetheless, to see that the pickets carried shotguns they fully intended to use if anyone tried to cross the line. That evening there was a party in one of the local village's battered shacks, to celebrate the day's successful picket. As I was about to drink the transparent liquid offered me, one of the miners knocked it out of my hand. 'That's pure hooch,' he said. 'If you drink it, you'll go blind.' So I added the illegal corn-whiskey of West Virginia to my litany of American experiences.

We proceeded hesitantly through Kentucky, Tennessee, Alabama and into Mississippi. We had not anticipated the segregation of the races, nor the depth of poverty we found there. Unknowing, we blundered into black diners and black motels, leaving a stunned silence in our wake. The cabins of the Mississippi delta were the slave cabins of a century before, decrepit and weather-beaten, without bathrooms or lavatories. In the fields, black people toiled. Among the featureless small towns of used car lots, drugstores and mom-and-pop grocers, we encountered suspicious red-faced white men. In one little East Texas town we were ordered to leave by the local sheriff, beer belly dented by the belt of a gun holster. We couldn't understand why, until he pointed to the Massachusetts licence plate on our old car. 'We don't like Yankees here,' he announced. The wounds of the Civil War festered still.

We did not find in the Deep South the elegance and courtesy its historic reputation promised. Instead, we encountered resentment and coarseness. Stopping one night in a one-motel town we were informed that there was just one double bedroom available. 'No good,' we said, 'there are three of us and one is a woman.'

The proprietor leaned over the stained counter and winked. 'Easy, honey,' he said to me. 'You just turn over in the middle of the night.'

My friend Guido was so appalled by this lack of delicacy that he contrived a curtain of shirts and underwear knotted together, to screen off my part of the bed.

As we drove across West Texas and then into New Mexico, Nevada and California, the sense of space liberated my being, as it had when I first travelled by train from Montreal to St Paul. That space was not just empty land, mile after mile of tundra or forest, as it might have been in Newfoundland or Siberia. It was purposeful space – mountains, canyons, grasslands and deserts – but on a huge scale. We spent days crossing the wheatfields of Kansas and Iowa, often at night when the heat was less intense. Later, Rodney remembered driving for miles while Guido and I argued about whether animals have souls, drawing on the arguments of St Thomas Aquinas that both of us had been brought up on. As we reached the Rocky Mountains, the scenery became dramatic. We parked in the middle of the night near the rim of the Grand Canyon, to await the dawn. The sun rose, starkly lighting, tier after tier, the towers and minarets of that magic chasm, first pink then yellow, catching the breath in our throats. Driving on through the Sierra Nevada, we reached eventually, at the end of the continent, the radiant coast of California. The highway from the mission church of San Luis Obispo through Big Sur to Carmel must be one of the loveliest in the world. We stayed with a friend of Rodney's at his ranch in Santa Rosa and then went on to San Francisco, like ancient Rome crowning its seven hills above its dazzling bays. There Guido left us, after a memorable farewell dinner. Rodney and I went on to Oregon, where I had planned to visit Madge Lorwin, the wife of a dedicated Foreign Service officer McCarthy had falsely accused of being a member of the Communist Party. Rodney and I parted to pursue our own separate ways back east.

The case of Val Lorwin, whom I had met shortly after arriving at Columbia, was a classic example of the way the Senator operated. Val had been accused by a former lodger, Harold Metz, of having held meetings in 1935 with 'strange-looking people'. According to Metz, Lorwin had waved his red membership card at these meetings to underline his arguments. But the Communist Party card in 1935 was a sixteen-page black booklet. It was the Socialist Party membership card that was red. Then in January 1951 Val was suspended from the State Department as a security risk, but in March 1952 was reinstated, following strong protests from those who knew him and had worked with him. Nevertheless, in December 1953 he was indicted on three criminal counts of falsely denying his Communist connections. The case came to trial in May 1954, and ninety-one witnesses, including many federal officials, testified on Val's behalf. Not a single witness was found to support Metz, and the case was thrown out in the next month. Val Lorwin described the outcome as 'a tribute to American sanity and justice', but the long ordeal had undermined his health and his self-confidence. He died in 1982.

My return east was to be devoted to my research project, the political action programmes of the trades unions. The person I most wanted to interview was Dave Beck, the legendary and formidable leader of the Teamsters' Union, the most powerful single union in North America, and a law unto itself. Dave Beck was more than a union leader – he was at that time effectively the political boss of Seattle. It was rumoured that he had invited the town's leading figures to discuss the financing of the new cathedral, and had then locked the door and let no one out without a substantial donation being pledged or made. Stalinist in the control of his union and ruthless in the exploitation of his power, Dave Beck was cordially loathed by the union federations, and particularly by the CIO, the Congress of Industrial Organizations, whose modern-minded leaders, especially the social democrats Walter and Victor Reuther of the Autoworkers' Union, regarded him as a predatory dinosaur. In 1959 he was convicted in a federal court of income tax evasion. He went to prison in 1962, was paroled in 1964 and pardoned by President Gerald Ford in 1975.

Arrived in Seattle, I asked for an interview with Beck. The voice at the other end of the telephone sounded dumbfounded. A *student* asking to interview the great Dave Beck? There was a long silence. The voice said it would ring back. That evening it did, briefly and to the point. 'Get out of town,' it commanded. I went off to see the local secretary of the CIO to ask his advice. He didn't ponder it for long. 'I guess you'd better,' he said. And so I did.

Travelling east by Greyhound bus and hitch-hiking (once with a man who kept a loaded revolver in his car's glove compartment), I made my way via St Paul and Madison to St Louis, Missouri. The city was home to one of the most lively CIO regional organisations in the country. The account the officers gave me of organising new factories, recruiting members and running political campaigns on behalf of the Democratic Party was very impressive. We got on so well that we talked into the evening, and my companions asked me if I would like to accompany them to a nightclub where there were drinks, gambling and a floor show to be enjoyed. Maybe the invitation was intended as a test of my English sangfroid, for on arrival we passed through a long passageway supervised by several large men with suspiciously bulging jackets, then into a dark room lined by fruit machines where the floor show was about to begin. Nothing so far in my life had prepared me for what I saw, a show of such raw obscenity, leaving so little to the imagination, that I was numbed rather than shocked, every sensibility I possessed bulldozed. This had one advantage: my companions clearly admired my old-world sophistication. It confirmed their image of Europe as a society of roués.

From St Louis I made my way to Chicago, host to the 1952 Democratic National Convention, the high point of my trip east. In those long-ago days, presidential nominees were still selected at the Convention by delegates from the forty-eight states, themselves chosen in local conventions of party activists, or occasionally in primary elections. Some delegates were mandated to vote for a particular candidate, quite often a state's 'favourite son'. Others were not, or were released when their candidate no longer had any hope of being chosen. The voting took place only after an intricate process of lobbying, barnstorming and trading delegates' votes in smoke-filled rooms – and these rooms did indeed reek of alcohol and tobacco.

Governor Adlai Stevenson, the leading contender, I had met earlier in the year when I was a member of a pompously entitled 'Young Atlantic Leaders' tour. One of my fellow members was John Baker, who was to become a judge and chairman of the historic National Liberal Club in central London. We had gone to Stevenson's comfortable, crumpled home in Libertyville, Illinois, at his invitation. He sat cross-legged on the floor in gym shoes and slacks, surrounded by me and my fellow students, answering with wit and grace every question we could throw at him. I was briefly transfixed by a hole in the sole of one of his gym shoes, which endeared him yet more to me. The impression he made was formidable, despite the understated, almost apologetic manner. Phrases he quoted stay with me still: 'A lie runs round the world while the truth is pulling on its boots'; and his moving response, drawn from the Old Testament, to his eventual nomination: 'I seek only to do justly, to live rightly, and to walk humbly with my God.' Charming, civilised and urbane, Adlai Stevenson entered my Pantheon of political heroes, those I most wanted to resemble should I ever become a politician myself.

Stevenson refused to campaign for the nomination at the Convention. Indeed, there is some question whether he wanted it, in a year when the Democrats, owing to the extreme unpopularity of President Truman and 'his' war in Korea, were unlikely to do well. Stevenson's rivals were not so inhibited. Senator Estes Kefauver, the gawky and cantankerous senator from Tennessee, and Robert Kerr, the oil millionaire senator from Oklahoma, both fancied their chances. Indeed Senator Kefauver was to be the front runner on the first two ballots. Each hoped for trades union support, for this was the decade in which the unions were powerful political players, especially in the Democratic Party. The CIO had its own office at the Convention. Its assistant director, Telford Dudley, was an acquaintance of mine, first encountered when I had interviewed him in New York for my Fulbright thesis. He was conducting discussions with the leading candidates about their commitment to labour's interest, the quid pro quo being financial and other help in the Convention ballots, and in the subsequent presidential campaign.

My acquaintance was enthusiastic about helping me in my research. I had no sophisticated bugging devices, not even a Dictaphone. Both he and I were intrigued by how I could learn what actually went on between the unions and the would-be Democrat presidential candidates. My presence as a foreign visitor might be inhibiting. So we agreed I should hide under one of the beds in the hotel room. Invisible to all, I lay in the dust in the bedroom where the discussions were being held, listening avidly to every word. My education in American politics could not have been more direct or more immediate.

Soon after returning east from the Convention, I received a telegram summoning me back to England for a selection conference for the Harwich constituency, which I had come to know years before when I worked as a cowman in Frating, Essex, after leaving school. The Party chairman was Joe Watson, who still managed the farm there. Joe liked the idea of a young woman contesting this solidly Tory constituency, and he rightly judged that being a parliamentary candidate would set me on the road to a political career. The challenge was irresistible. Abandoning my thesis and the last few months of my Fulbright Fellowship, I returned to England in November 1952. But before I could think about fighting elections, I needed to find a job.

CHAPTER 6

Mirror and Marriage

I had rushed back from the United States that November after only eight months of my year-long Fulbright Fellowship, lured by the chance of fighting a parliamentary constituency, albeit a pretty hopeless one for a Labour candidate. But I needed a job, not only to earn my own living but to help meet the costs of campaigning. Luckily for me, at least one employer was as keen to offer me a job as I was to acquire one.

A journalist from the *Daily Mirror* was waiting for me on the dock at Southampton, and he offered me a job on the spot for the sensational salary of £14 a week. The *Mirror*'s proprietor, Cecil King, had read an '*Isis* Idol' feature about my friend Val Mitchison and me, and had told his staff to track us down and hire us both. I didn't immediately accept. It wasn't the kind of job I had in mind, so for a couple of months I applied fruitlessly for other jobs. Eventually in late January necessity drove me to join the *Mirror*.

The *Daily Mirror* of the 1950s was a successful tabloid which managed to combine brilliant popular journalism with a crusading purpose. It was supportive of the Labour Party without being uncritical, committed to making the welfare state work effectively, and open-minded in its approach to such causes as equal rights for women and the abolition of capital punishment. There was substance in its populism. Its editor, Sylvester Bolam, was greatly admired in Fleet Street for his professionalism, and journalists were proud to say they worked for the newspaper. It was also tough, persistent and inquisitive, pursuing stories until the human interest or the scandal was husked out of them.

Val became the paper's junior royal family reporter, covering all their movements, and did it well. I, however, was a disaster. I started well enough, settling into the atmosphere of thick cigarette smoke, half-empty tea mugs and frantic phone calls. The other journalists in the newsroom were friendly enough, though they had no time to give me much advice on covering a story. In the evenings after work, they repaired to the local pubs, swapping news and gossip, and putting away large amounts of beer and whisky. My evenings were taken up by political meetings or Fabian study groups, so I didn't offer to go with them. The Fabian Society, which I had joined, offered welcome opportunities to discuss politics in depth.

The one subject of intense interest to my fellow reporters was my expenses claim. My extremely conscientious mother had brought me up to be self-righteously honest on financial matters. Indeed, she had been known to write to the tax authorities to inquire if she had been under-taxed, and to return to out-of-the-way shops if she had been undercharged in case the shop assistant had to pay for her mistake out of her own small wages. So I diligently filled in the exact sum I had paid for a taxi or a train fare. But my expenses came out at a quarter or less than those of most of the other reporters. My colleagues told me I had to pad them, or they would all be in trouble. They took my expenses form and filled it in with ghostly taxi journeys and mythical tips to useful contacts. I realised my life would become impossible if I, an unbearable Goody Two Shoes, went on arguing, so I simply destroyed the form they had devised and replaced it secretly with one of my own.

I got a big break on my first assignment as a news reporter, a routine stint trailing the Duke of Edinburgh who was playing polo that Sunday at a sunny Cowdray Park. I was just dozing off after an uneventful afternoon, lulled by the distant thud of hooves on newly mown grass, when the *Mirror*'s veteran photographer shook me awake. 'Get down to the ground fast,' he hissed, 'the Duke is holding forth.' I got there just in time to hear the Duke, in between swilling champagne from his silver winner's cup, declare, 'And I don't give a damn what the Church of England may say', for the benefit of those opposed to sport on the Sabbath. Wild excitement broke out at the *Mirror*'s end of the telephone line when we reported back to the news desk. 'Get back here pronto,' we were ordered. The photographer and I hurtled down the road to London, breaking every speed limit. The next day, there on the front page was his photograph and my story, much hacked about by the tyrants in the subeditors' room but bearing, incredibly, my first byline.

And nearly my last. With the exception of one other story, I never again made the front page. I was reduced to investigating house fires yielding sad tales about pets lost in the flames, strictly page seven stuff. I attended weddings where it had been rumoured that someone would declare there was an impediment to the marriage, so that I could write up the story of the weeping bride or deceived bridegroom. I had some awful assignments, like the time a photographer and I went to the home of a woman whose little daughter had been burned to death after her nightdress caught fire. The mother had cried herself into a state of desolation where tears no longer came. Determined to get a heart-rending picture, the photographer picked up a handful of ashes and asked her if that was all that was left of her child.

There were some wonderfully absurd moments, too. The *Mirror*'s great rival was the *Daily Sketch*. The photograph of a young woman on her way to becoming a society celebrity had appeared in the *Sketch*. The *Mirror* had been told that 'she' was actually a man who had successfully fooled its rival newspaper. Great excitement again. The *Mirror's* top reporter, Mary Malone, and I were dispatched to follow the car that took the society beauty from London to an unknown destination, which turned out to be somewhere on the English–Welsh border. The car, closely shadowed by us, managed to shake us off in the narrow hilly roads, but we finally tracked it down to a fine country house standing in handsome parkland. We camped just outside the grounds, so that we could resume the chase if the quarry tried to escape. But that, of course, was getting us nowhere, and the prize of showing up the *Sketch* was ebbing away.

Then our news desk dreamed up a wheeze. Mary was to impersonate a long-lost relative from Latin America, and I was to be her English friend. This, it was hoped, would give us access to the mansion and from that vantage point we might be able to learn the true identity of the society beauty. So Mary and I duly dressed up, and swept up to the front door in a prestigious car hired for the purpose. The butler, clearly confused by the manner of our arrival, left us waiting in the elegantly furnished front hall. Not long after, a person stormed in. 'Get out,' he shouted, 'you are no relations of mine!' Get out we did, rather quickly. Back at our camp on the park edge, we contacted the news desk from a public telephone to explain our failure. The editor had already been called by an outraged notable, obviously a person of considerable influence, who had told him in no uncertain terms to call his hounds off. We were pretty sure we were pursuing a man in drag, but there was no way we could prove it to our editor's satisfaction.

Most of the time I hated my job. There were long periods of boredom, reading other newspapers, half-heartedly trying to identify possible stories and then piecing them together. One of the subeditors had read somewhere an old wives' tale to the effect that men who carried purses were always mean; I was given the odious job of telephoning scores of celebrated men to find out if they carried purses. One of them was the ballet dancer Robert Helpmann.

As soon as I had put my question, he snapped at me, 'I suppose you are trying to prove I'm mean?', and put the phone down. Days spent like that filled me with gloom. I used to think of ways to get an answer. Maybe pretending to be the plumber? Or casting myself on the mercy of the respondent? No, I was a pariah and I knew it. Two years after Cecil King's brainwave had been acted upon, I was pressingly invited to resign. So I did. I felt humiliated, but far from disappointed. I was comforted in my humiliation by being singled out to appear in a new medium that was just beginning to become widely recognised – television.

In the autumn of 1952, I had been selected as prospective Labour candidate for the safe National Liberal and Conservative constituency of Harwich.* Far from a triumph, my selection was something of a fiddle. No one else wanted to stand. These were dog days for Labour, defeated at the general election of 1951 and doing badly even in the mid-term of the first postwar Conservative government, whose Prime Minister was the manifestly ageing Winston Churchill. Labour, still led by Clement Attlee, was racked by differences between left and right. Those differences were intensified by the conviction on the left that the 1951 election had been irredeemably lost by the determination of Hugh Gaitskell, Chancellor of the Exchequer, to cut public expenditure in order to finance the British contribution to the United Nations-led defence of South Korea. In this bleak political climate, few aspiring Labour politicians were interested in fighting a safe Conservative seat. The selection committee was offered the choice of Joe Watson, the constituency chairman, who made it clear he had no desire to be the candidate, or me.

For the media, however, the selection of a twenty-two-year-old

* The National Liberal Party was a relic of the 1933 national government, a group of Liberals opposed to their own Party's decision to remain in Opposition. In practice, by 1952 National Liberals were indistinguishable from Conservatives.

woman to fight a parliamentary constituency was at least something new. I was chosen to be one of six representatives of the
Queen's generation to participate in a turgid and very Reithian
BBC series ponderously entitled *Our Concern Is the Future*, which
it undoubtedly was. Television at that time was little more than
radio with pictures. Each of us had to talk for fifteen minutes
direct to the camera about our personal vision of the second
Elizabethan age. It is hard to imagine that anyone other than our
doting parents watched us.

The series elicited a heavy-handed rebuke to Lieutenant-
General Sir Ian Jacob, the BBC's Director-General, from the
Prime Minister himself. On 30 May 1953, Churchill protested to
Jacob about having two Labour candidates on the programme
among the six representatives, the other being my erstwhile love,
Peter Parker:

> In the current television series *Our Concern Is the Future*, two
> prospective Labour candidates are being used, Mr Peter Parker,
> candidate for Bedford, and Miss Shirley Catlin, candidate for
> Harwich. No Conservative politician is taking part in the
> series . . . I consider it most important that the BBC should not
> only be impartial, but should be seen to be impartial in its polit-
> ical attitude, and I would be glad if you would give me your
> comment on these facts.

Ian Jacob's reply was spirited and unapologetic:

> We do maintain a meticulous tally of the appearances of MPs.
> We have not done so for prospective candidates, nor did the
> Board of Governors when they considered the matter believe
> that we should do so, even if we could. When people other
> than MPs are appearing in programmes of general interest they
> are judged on their competence and not on their political
> views. We are often unaware of these. The choice of Mr Peter

Parker and Miss Shirley Catlin in the series *Our Concern Is the Future* was made on their outstanding qualities as representatives of the younger generation ... I do not think the occasional appearance of a candidate, who may or may not make a good impression when he does appear, is a matter which can justify attacks on our impartiality.

In January 1954 my prospective candidature turned into a real one. Sir Stanley Holmes, the longtime MP for Harwich, a man distinguished by his total silence in the House of Commons, was elevated to the peerage, presumably for his unqualified loyalty. The National Liberal and Conservative candidate groomed for the succession was Julian Ridsdale, a glass manufacturer, an amiable, florid man. While the by-election was in too safe a seat to be exciting, the newspapers were delighted to have a diversion in a dull political season, and printed lots of pictures of 'the schoolgirl candidate' in long socks and woolly scarves. The weather that January was fiendishly cold.

Harwich was a disparate constituency. The town after which it was named was an ancient, decaying port, with some handsome old harbourside buildings and a small fishing fleet. Further down the Essex coast was Clacton-on-Sea, a popular day trippers' destination before the war. It was by this time a town of families in semis and bungalows, struggling hard to be respectably middle-class, some running bed-and-breakfast accommodation catering to the holiday trade, still then content with windswept pebble beaches, pier-end shows and chips. In between the two towns was Jaywick, an exposed cluster of beach huts and bungalows that had been inundated in the east coast floods of 1953. I had visited Jaywick at that time. Bits of buildings and furniture were floating helplessly in the muddy grey water, beyond which was the capricious and menacing North Sea. People who had seen their flimsy homes destroyed were wandering about in Wellington boots or steering little skiffs among the debris, trying to save whatever they could. The only other town of any size, also on the coast, was Frinton-on-Sea. Frinton fancied itself as far removed from the hoi polloi, an early example of a gated community. Indeed, it was so exclusive that visitors had to get permission to pass through the barriers into the town. Labour candidates were not particularly welcome.

I concentrated during the run-up to the by-election on Harwich itself and the scores of small villages in Tendring parish, my best prospect for attracting Labour votes. I spoke at over a hundred meetings, three or four a night, ploughing through snow, mud and the darkness of the countryside, for this was long before the invasion of sodium street lights. One such meeting was with the dreaded National Farmers' Union. Despite much cosseting by the postwar Labour government and the popularity of Tom Williams, the former Minister of Agriculture, the farmers of Tendring parish remained true blue to the last man. As I arrived at the school hall, a drumbeat of sticks and staffs greeted me. It only stopped when I asked if they preferred to ask no questions and to have none answered. I won at least a little respect by being able to distinguish a Jersey from a Friesian, an Aberdeen Angus from a Hereford. Having been a cowman had, it turned out, its political uses.

Elections in the 1950s and 1960s were dominated by class. I could walk up the garden path and guess nine times out of ten how the people in the house would vote. Most of those in council houses would be Labour voters. But if the little garden was carefully laid out with miniature flowerbeds and little box hedges, the inhabitants would be Conservatives. The presence of garden gnomes was almost always definitive proof of Tory voters. Bungalows and semidetached interwar 'builders' specs' usually housed Conservatives. Victorian terraces were harder to judge, and might be Labour if there was a pram in the front hall.

In the rural villages, almost no one would admit to voting Labour. I met many farm workers in tied cottages who did not dare to vote because they did not believe the ballot was secret, and they feared to lose their homes. I spent hours in back gardens among the washing lines and bean poles trying to persuade them otherwise. Day after day I inhaled the smell of poverty, rotting linoleum, coal dust from the kitchen range, wet woollen jerseys and inside walls puffy with damp.

The press were amused by the pretensions of the 'schoolgirl candidate', for these were the years before women's lib. My mother and father had instilled in me the confidence that girls were intellectually and socially the equal of boys, and a strong sense of social justice that made discrimination repellent. But at door after door as I canvassed the constituency, the woman who answered my knocking would call into the dark house behind her, 'Jim [or Joe or Harry], how do we vote?' Years later, I was to be reminded of that when I met tribesmen in the Rajasthani villages undisturbed by India's 1994 constitutional amendment requiring that one-third of village councillors would henceforth have to be women. They were convinced the women would do exactly as they were instructed by their menfolk.

I lost the by-election, with a decrease of 0.2 per cent in the Labour share of the vote, to 40.9 per cent. To hammer home the point, I lost Harwich again at the general election in May 1955, eighteen months later. But I won priceless assets. The first was the experience of campaigning. The second was, however modestly, national recognition, for now my name and photograph were in all the national newspaper files, and I would be rung up to comment on young people's views or young women's opinions of various political events and policies.

Within the Labour Party I became a popular choice as an additional speaker, or mover of a vote of thanks. On one auspicious occasion, I was invited to move the vote of thanks at the annual conference of the Labour Party's Eastern Region to Clement Attlee, still leader of the Party but by this time clearly reaching the end of his time in that position. Attlee presented a long speech – more properly described as a lecture – on the role of China in the world. The audience was restless and disappointed at this rather tedious discourse. 'For Heaven's sake, do something!' the chairman of the meeting hissed in my ear. My job was to thank the former Prime Minister. By sheer luck, I had been given a few months before a scrap of paper from Attlee's office in the Commons by my friend Val, whose father Dick Mitchison was MP for Kettering and a member of the Shadow Cabinet. I had kept it. It was, I believe, written by Clement Attlee in his years as a social worker in Limehouse before the First World War. I read it out to the Labour audience, saying that this was what the former Prime Minister had written in 1912:

> In Limehouse, in Limehouse, before the break of day
> I hear the feet of many men that go upon their way,
> That wander through the city, the grey and cruel city,
> Through streets that have no pity, through streets where
>   men decay.

This was the Clement Attlee the Labour Party loved – abrupt, controlled, modest, but also burning steadily with the slow flame of his socialist convictions. They rose to their feet and clapped for minutes on end. The verse's author, however, remained unimpressed. When I was introduced to him after the meeting, he snapped, '1911, actually.' That ended the conversation.

I learned in Harwich a lot about shoestring campaigning, for we had very little money and a big constituency to cover. I learned how to make a few hundred pounds go a long way in producing leaflets and stickers, especially if there was a sympathetic local printer. I discovered how to beguile the local press, always hungry for stories, by writing up humorous accounts of meetings, and delivering them the day before the paper went to press. I learned how to rally volunteers by taking out canvassing teams with a couple of experienced people who promised to arrive promptly on the doorstep if any voter asked difficult questions or became hostile. We taught canvassers not to be over-optimistic, and to recognise that most people are polite and therefore reluctant to say they are going to vote against you. We learned how to interpret body language and circumlocutions which really meant 'No'.

I grew to understand a little about the people of Britain at that time – stoical, sceptical individuals with a rooted commitment to fairness, a tough-minded sense of humour, and an insistence on keeping their feet on the ground.

Ernest Bevin, Labour's great postwar Foreign Secretary and former General Secretary of the Transport and General Workers' Union, had once said that the saddest thing about the British people was the poverty of their aspirations. That was true too, the obverse of their virtues. Few of the hundreds of working men and women I met in the Harwich constituency in the 1950s, and during many other elections at that time, aspired to greater heights or horizons than those of their parents. Britain, in that respect, was very different from the United States. Full employment, secondary education for all, and the attrition of the class system were to change that, but its accomplishment would take more than a single generation.

True to their populist mission, the tabloids had plucked a suitably romantic conclusion out of my two unsuccessful attempts to enter Parliament. I might not be an MP, but I would be a bride. Bernard Williams, the Oxford friend I had invited to Mo Walton's house in Connecticut in that magical fall of 1952, was now a Fellow in Philosophy at New College, Oxford. We had seen a lot of each other since we had returned from North America. He had thrown himself enthusiastically into the 1955 general election campaign in Harwich, making speeches and canvassing. It was not something philosophers generally did, but Bernard always believed that philosophy should explore how people live and the relevance of moral philosophy to practical living. He once said that truths about human life were known to virtually all human beings except moral philosophers. So although our career patterns followed very different paths, we found it easy to communicate about politics. The same cannot be said about philosophy. I found Bernard's expositions of the Greek classics very exciting and relevant to much in contemporary political behaviour. But the school of analytic philosophy of the time lay beyond my interest and my understanding.

Bernard's interest in politics ran deep. Far from removing himself from the pain and crudeness of making political choices, he threw himself into examining the arguments and the consequences. He welcomed the chance to discuss such matters with the wide range of people with vastly different experiences that one encounters in the world of active politics. He did not see himself as superior because of his education or his learning. He was always open to learning more. Throughout his life, he contributed to the public arena, participating in or chairing commissions on public schools, gambling, obscenity and censorship, and the misuse of drugs. He once said he had done all the vices. His last involvement was with the Labour Party Commission on Social Justice, established by the then leader, John Smith, in 1992 and chaired by Gordon Borrie. It was a subject close to Bernard's heart.

Before Bernard and I married, I shared for two and a half years a rickety flat with two wonderful friends, Helge Kitzinger, who had been at Somerville with me, and Madeleine Zimmermann, a contemporary of mine at St Paul's Girls' School. The flat was on the top floor of a Victorian terrace called Colville Mansions, just off the Portobello Road. We had found it after a discouraging search through west London, in which we were offered flats without baths, flats with cockroaches in possession, and even flats with mirrors in the ceiling, a reminder that Bayswater had long been a favourite venue of the oldest profession. Colville Mansions was at least reasonably light and airy, but the trouble was the roof. It leaked so badly we had to sleep with buckets around our beds, and eventually with a tarpaulin draped over the worst holes. This, however, was but a foretaste of what was to come. One evening, with a mild roar, the entire front cornice of the building collapsed into the street below. Decades later, in the House of Lords, I met Lord Colville of Culross. I wondered if I should ask him if he owned the Mansions.

The young Bernard was in perpetual intellectual motion, like a dragonfly hovering above a sea of ideas. Everyone he encountered, every event that occurred were material for his insight and his wit. His conversation was a work of art, though never consciously so, revealing the depth of his reading and the richness of his knowl-edge. He was a joy to be with, and I cannot recall any occasion when we had nothing to say to one another.

He could be cruel too, sometimes filleting a personality with the sharp daggers of well-chosen words. I invariably rose to the defence of his victims, whether it was an inept colleague or a bumbling driver holding up his car. We occasionally had short, sharp clashes in which he complained that I did not take his side. With the benefit of hindsight, I see now that I underestimated how difficult it was for an ambitious and brilliant young man to have a wife equally strongly committed to a career, still rare in the 1950s. Some men could not forbear trying to humiliate him; more than once, at some gathering, an older man stretched out his hand and said to Bernard, 'This must be Mr Shirley Williams, I presume?' As ever, the publicity attracted by politicians was absurdly disproportionate to that extended to most other walks of life.

Bernard was the most consistently fascinating person I have ever met, but he was not easy-going. Nor was he faithful. Hugely attractive to women, he basked in their admiration. He used to tell me that clever women were much more bewitching than stupid ones; beauty and intelligence went together. That was something I liked in him, for the women he knew as friends and lovers were never just sex objects. He appreciated them fully as

people, and it was as individuals that he tried to understand
them.

As for getting married, Bernard was keener than I was. I cherished my freedom, and asked myself whether I wanted to take on
the obligations of matrimony. To me marriage was a sacrament. It
involved vows that had to be kept. It was an 'honourable estate',
profoundly different from a love affair between unmarried people.
Infidelity destroyed trust, and trust was indispensable to any long-
term relationship. Bernard took marriage seriously, but did not
rule out the possibility of divorce. On my part, there was a personal element as well. A bit of me still yearned after Peter, though
by now he was firmly married to my erstwhile Oxford rival, Jill
Rowe-Dutton. There is a timetable built into life, and by the mid-
1950s many of my contemporaries and friends were getting
married. Helge and Madeleine were being courted too. Helge's
suitor was my friend from my Oxford days, Hilary Rubinstein. I
was 'best man' at their wedding, a month after mine. Helge and
Madeleine both admired Bernard, a frequent visitor to Colville
Mansions, and were enthusiastic about our marrying. So I said yes
to his proposal.

Our wedding on 2 July 1955 was a fashionable affair. We were
married at St James's, Spanish Place, the Roman Catholic church
off Marylebone High Street where my parents had married almost
exactly thirty years earlier in June 1925. The ceremony was followed by a lavish reception at Hutchinson House in Curzon
Street. My bridesmaids were Helge and Madeleine, my flower girl
Marian, Amy's daughter, and my page Peter, her son. The best
man was George Engle, a wise and understanding friend of
Bernard's and a fellow student who went on to become chief parliamentary draftsman, the person who oversees the drafting of
laws.

Both my parents approved of the marriage. Bernard's were
much more dubious about it. His father Owen, a Welsh civil

servant whose great passion was the theatre, was a Freemason. I remember once at their home in Reigate climbing into the attic to retrieve something for Hilda, my mother-in-law, only to discover to my amazement the ornate regalia of a leading Freemason. Hilda had a sternly nonconformist background. Both she and Owen lived for their brilliant son, and were worried that he had fallen into the clutches of a Catholic. His mother warned him that priests would be coming up the footpath to our door all the time. These warnings had no effect on Bernard. He had become great friends with a young Italian Jesuit priest, Giancarlo Colombo, a man with the dark, elongated features of an El Greco painting, who combined a passionate faith with an exceptional mind. Giancarlo was no acidulous celibate. He once told Bernard that had he not been called to the priesthood he would have made a world of women. But he never broke his vows. Not long after Bernard and I married, Giancarlo told us of his desire to visit Bruges, the medieval Flemish town, on his way back to his monastery in Bormio in the Italian Alps. The three of us went there together, and spent a couple of days exploring the Béguinage, the haven for religious lay women, and the churches. We then drove across Switzerland, where Giancarlo as a Jesuit was not permitted to travel and had to take off anything that showed he was a priest. Yet early in the mornings in little Swiss villages, people mysteriously appeared at the church where Giancarlo was saying his daily Mass.

When we said goodbye, Giancarlo thanked us for our friendship, and hinted that we might never meet again. We protested – after all, Italy was not far. But he seemed to know something we did not know. A year later, he slipped while carrying a heavy cross up to Mass in the mountains, and fell with it into a deep ravine.

Bernard and I spent our honeymoon on Lesbos in Greece, at the invitation of his student Demetrius Nianias, whose family lived on the island. Demetrius was later to become its representative in the Greek Parliament. His uncle had a house in a lemon grove, overlooking the bright-blue sea. In the evening, going to parties and dancing outdoors in the velvet air, we noticed many young women holding hands with one another. The spirit of the great poet Sappho was still alive on the island.

In 1954, the year before I got married, after my enforced resignation from the *Daily Mirror* in October 1953, I had decided to look for a new job on a broadsheet rather than a tabloid. I thought a future MP, which is what I fully intended to be, should know something about finance, and in particular about the City of London. In the mid-fifties the *Financial Times* had become akin to a postgraduate college for aspiring young Conservative politicians, many of them recent graduates. Several of my university contemporaries, among them William Rees-Mogg and Nigel Lawson, were already installed there. But it was not to prove so easy for a woman, and a Labour one to boot. The editor, Gordon Newton, whose name was legendary among the newspaper's staffers, was no feminist. He liked to tell the story of his wartime experience when suitable young men were hard to find and he had to employ, reluctantly, several women. One had come to him with a tedious article that began 'Brazil is in the Western hemisphere'. Newton told her to leave the sentence out. 'Oh, God!' she had responded. 'Isn't it?'

The newspaper's proprietor, Lord Drogheda, a man of great charm and grace, looked askance at employing the woman who, William Rees-Mogg had told him, was known at Oxford as the Red Queen. His opinion was mollified, however, on learning that I was a Roman Catholic. He eventually agreed to confirm my appointment, concluding the interview by saying, 'You may not be any good, but at least you're cheap', which indeed I was in those days of very unequal pay. I earned only half what my male Oxford contemporaries earned, and as a journalist in the International Department I had no place at the all-male editorial lunch table. I didn't allow myself to get too resentful at this differential treatment, and I enjoyed myself thoroughly at the

Financial Times, learning a good deal about the working of markets, about commodity exchanges and even about monetary policy. Peter Galliner, the head of the International Department, which handled syndicated articles for respected foreign publications, was not only immensely knowledgeable, he also had such excellent contacts throughout Europe, the Soviet bloc and beyond that at times I assumed he must be some kind of intelligence agent.

There were only a few of us in his department, and we had to work hard to meet the rising demand for *Financial Times* material. One of my colleagues was the London correspondent of the *Nihon Keizai Shimbun*, a Japanese man who was obviously horrified to share his office with a woman journalist. He and I argued all the time, sometimes asking Peter to settle matters of fact. Years later, Kakuei Tanaka became the Secretary-General of the Liberal Democratic Party of Japan, an immensely influential position in that rarely challenged party of government. On a ministerial mission to Japan in the 1970s, I called on him in my official capacity. As I was leaving, he indicated that he had a gift for me; the exchange of gifts accompanies almost all formal meetings in Japan.

Into his office came two men bearing a huge model of a pagoda, four or five feet long, which he presented to me. Tanaka, I thought to myself, you've got your own back now. The pagoda was unportable. It found a resting place in the attic of the British Minister to Tokyo, and for all I know may be there still.

After Bernard and I were married, we moved into sounder but less exciting accommodation than my rickety shared flat, a ground-floor flat in Clarendon Road, near Notting Hill Gate, in those days far from being the fashionable neighbourhood it later became. The community's dustbins lined the outside of our bedroom wall. Twice a week, we were woken up by the clang of bins being emptied. The flat was in an ugly modern block, but lacked most of today's modern conveniences. Instead of a refrigerator, there was a primitive metal box misleadingly called the Osokool, which embodied the principle of evaporation as a way of keeping food cold. It yielded a regular harvest of soured milk and perspiring butter. Jerry-built, the flat's walls were thin enough to make our neighbours' conversations part of our own. But just having a flat to oneself was a huge luxury in the 1950s. Thousands of couples were compelled to share with their parents for lack of anywhere to live.

Given the difficulties of finding affordable accommodation, the Rubinsteins and Bernard and I decided to be more adventurous. West London had many large houses, three or four storeys high, built for big families with resident servants. They were much less expensive in relation to liveable space than the smaller houses for one family of three or four people. So we decided to share, and bought a big nineteenth-century detached house with a small garden at the back in Phillimore Place, Kensington, for £6800. It had four storeys plus a basement, and seven bedrooms. The move was exciting for all of us, an experiment in living with two, and later three, families in one house. It turned out to be just one excitement in a sensational year.

The 1955 general election had produced yet another Conservative government, but at least the leadership had changed from that of the ailing and confused Winston Churchill. Anthony Eden I had been taught by my parents to admire. He was seen by them as the man of principle who had resigned in February 1938 at the time of the Munich Agreement, much influenced by the League of Nations' failure to oppose Mussolini's invasion of Abyssinia in October 1935. He was at last Prime Minister. Now there would be someone at the top who understood a world that was changing fast, in which many countries were becoming independent nations for the first time as the great empires crumbled away. But we were wrong. Eden's reputation had been established by his early understanding of the menace presented to the world by the European dictators, Mussolini and Hitler. Now he saw a new Hitler in a man who was at worst a reckless nationalist, Gamal Abdel Nasser. To Eden, Colonel Nasser's nationalisation of the Suez Canal was tantamount to Hitler's annexation of the Rhineland, an intolerable breach of the international status quo that had to be stopped. His attempt to do so, which led him to lie to the Cabinet, Parliament and the country about his reasons for intervening in Egypt, became known as the Suez crisis. It set British politics on fire.

At first the Labour Opposition was hesitant to criticise. Hugh Gaitskell, leader of the Labour Party following Attlee's retirement in 1955, had a Jewish wife, and had seen Nazism at close quarters. He was keen to protect Israel. But he became more and more angry as he discovered that the planned Suez intervention was based on deceit by a very ill Eden and those immediately around him. The Cabinet itself was deeply split, and several ministers resigned, among them Sir Edward Boyle. I remember him telling me many years later that the Prime Minister had been so ill he would slip off his chair in Cabinet and show clear signs of distress.

Within a matter of days, Britain was at war with itself. There were huge demonstrations pro and anti the government. With my friends I organised a protest lobby of young men all wearing bowlers and carrying black umbrellas, based on the theory that this would have much more effect on Conservative MPs than a demonstration of the usual left-wing types. Indeed, it did. Some Conservative MPs were quite shaken by it. A number of young officers refused to serve in Egypt, and there was a fierce reaction that went far beyond the traditional left.

Little by little it emerged that the leaders of Britain and France had conspired with Israel to seize the Suez Canal, on the flimsy excuse that they were intervening between the combatants, Egypt and Israel. Fleet Street rumour dated the planning of that intervention to several weeks before it took place. Emotions ran high, on the one side a national pride inflamed by the retreat from

Empire; on the other, outrage at the government's clumsy decep-
tion. Hugh Gaitskell denounced the government as the facts
became clear, and was in turn attacked as a traitor to his country.
So high did feelings run that Gaitskell himself was caught up in a
scuffle in the Commons with an enraged Conservative MP
behind the Speaker's chair. At public meetings far from London
convened to condemn the illegal invasion of Egypt, groups of
young Tories would turn up to barrack the speakers. On one occasion at Bury St Edmunds, where I was one of the speakers, an
organised band surrounded the audience chanting 'Kill Nasser!'
and 'Hang the Gyppos!' There was the strong scent of a lynch
mob in the air.

Almost coincidental with the Suez crisis was the uprising in
Hungary on 23 October 1956 against the Soviet Union. It was
brutally put down by Russian soldiers and Russian tanks. How far
this happened because the Western powers were divided and
diverted by the Suez business, I do not know. Certainly, no serious
attempt was made to support Hungary's desperate leaders. I
remember listening to the radio day after day and hearing the
voice of the Hungarian Prime Minister, Imre Nagy, calling for
help. 'Save our souls!' he pleaded, and it was like a drumbeat
against the gathering thunder of the Soviet artillery. Imre Nagy
and his closest colleagues were hanged for their defiance by the
Soviet authorities.

To Anthony Eden, the Suez crisis must have seemed like
another opportunity for a heroic stand against a dangerous enemy.
For many of the rest of us, it was an anachronistic and absurd
reversion to the great days of the British Empire. Looking back, I
recall the French saying, 'Plus ça change, plus c'est la même
chose.' It is hard now not to be struck by the many analogies with
the Iraq War fifty years later.

The Suez crisis was the moment when Britain came painfully to
confront the loss of her empire and the diminution of her power.
This diminution was rubbed into our wounds by President

Eisenhower's warning that the United States would cease to support sterling unless the intervention was immediately brought to an end. *Et tu, Brute!* Poor Eden, once the world's conscience against a dictator, was now betrayed by his closest ally in his efforts to stop what he believed to be another such. Yet Eisenhower was undoubtedly right.

The other harsh lesson was from Hungary. The West would make no attempt to overturn the Yalta agreement or breach the Iron Curtain that was erected to make it real. The democracies might condemn, but they would not intervene. I understood that, but could we not have opened our borders to those fleeing tyranny in the Soviet empire long before the fall of the Berlin Wall in 1989? It did not happen. Like the Czech socialists I had met in Germany in 1948, the Hungarian rebels were quietly swallowed up by the prisons and labour camps. Only a few managed to escape. As a small compromise with conscience, Bernard and I took one of them, a young man called Laszlo, and put him up on our sofa for eighteen months until he finally emigrated to Canada. Laszlo was a volatile, ambitious young man who found the constraints of being a refugee in a strange country hard to take. Before he left for Canada, we asked him what he would like as a farewell celebration. 'I would like to spend an evening at the Pigalle,' he replied, the Pigalle being a blowsy nightclub in Piccadilly. As the chorus line of half-clad girls passed by him, their big breasts wobbling and bouncing above their tinsel miniskirts, Laszlo could contain himself no longer. Leaning forward, he seized a barely contained bosom. We were all three asked, urgently, to leave.

Long after the Suez crisis, a chance meeting in 1985 enabled me to add a personal footnote to what I knew about this tumultuous moment in Britain's postwar history. William Clark, Anthony Eden's Press Secretary, dying of liver cancer, asked me to visit him at his Oxfordshire mill house. He had found out the truth about the Suez adventure, he told me, from Earl

Mountbatten, who had taken it for granted that Clark was one of the small inner circle in the know.

Mountbatten's remarks led Clark to piece together what had actually happened, that France and Britain had conspired with Israel to occupy the Suez Canal, while pretending that they were intending to stop a conflict between Israel and Egypt. The one room that had not been carefully closed off to separate the few who knew from the many, including Cabinet ministers, who did not, was the gentlemen's lavatory, and it was there that the crucial conversation took place. Once Clark's suspicions had been confirmed, he went straight to the Cabinet Secretary, Sir Norman Brook, and submitted his resignation. He agreed to postpone a public announcement until all British troops were out of danger. Crossing Whitehall shortly after he had resigned, Clark was accosted by David Maxwell Fyfe, the Lord Chancellor. 'You are a very able young man,' said Maxwell Fyfe. 'You had no responsibility for the decision. You should not feel constrained to resign.' Clark looked at him. 'Is that what you said at Nuremberg?' he asked. Maxwell Fyfe, Britain's prosecutor at the Nuremberg war crime trials, never spoke to him again.

CHAPTER 7

African Liberation

In January 1958, Bernard was invited to spend a term teaching philosophy at the new University College at Legon, near Accra, in Ghana. Ghana was the first British colony in Africa to become independent, in 1957, and its first Prime Minister, the powerful, brooding and impetuous Kwame Nkrumah, was a hero figure among African nationalists. The opportunity to be present at the creation of the new Africa was hugely attractive. Bernard was given leave by his college, and in September that year I resigned from my job at the *Financial Times*, which I had greatly enjoyed. I was hugely excited by the prospect of going to Africa and in any case it was time to move on.

Bernard and I reached the country by way of Morocco, where we spent a few days exploring Rabat, and Senegal, where we visited Dakar, then very much a French colonial town, its elegant avenues bordered by trees. Ghana was an ebullient and enchanting country. Market women sported undulating portraits of Dr Nkrumah printed on the colourful kente cloth that strained over their rounded buttocks and hips. Dusty little boys mimicked the strut of their departing colonial rulers, and then collapsed in mirthful heaps, delighted at their own performance. The colonial

rulers, in their creased khaki shorts and, for the most traditional, pith helmets, were not amused. One expatriate white
driver stopped his car next to me as I was exploring the vivid and
messy market. 'Get in,' he ordered. 'We don't want them to see us
walking.'

Above the teeming shacks and huts of Accra, a great arch had
been erected in the colours of the new Ghanaian flag, bearing the
inscription 'Freedom and Justice'. From the transistor radios just
beginning their invasion of Africa trilled the words of the national
anthem, 'Ghana! Land of Free-Dom!' Heavy road-making equipment from the Soviet Union, including snowploughs, blocked the
red laterite roadsides, heralds of a modern infrastructure that
always seemed just about to happen. Ghana was independent and
relatively rich because of years of good cocoa prices and careful
administration by the Cocoa Marketing Board. The problems
could be dealt with tomorrow.

The first time the University College's Land Rover dropped me
in Mampong, a village on the scarp that divided the humid green
coastlands from the dry hills of Ashanti, I was scared. As the car
departed I was left in total blackness. There was no electric light,
only the shrieks of alarmed birds and the shrill grumbling of mon-
keys in the velvet darkness of the bush. Then the dark was dotted
with little lights, each one a hurricane lamp carried by a student
of the People's Educational Association to lead me to the unlit
mud-brick schoolroom where I was to teach. The PEA had been
started by Thomas Hodgkin, then at the Oxford University extra-
mural department. The students themselves, cocoa farmers,
market traders, fishermen and carpenters, were impeccably dressed
in white shirts and shorts or in richly woven kente cloths. Before
each evening class, the sullen brown river foamed with Persil,
used to wash people and clothes alike. My lectures, on development, the Commonwealth and South Africa, were manna in this
education-hungry land, as, a century before, were WEA lectures
for the coalminers in the valleys of South Wales.

Ghana was visibly torn between the old world and the new. Many traditional Ghanaians lived close to a world of spirits whose invisible rules had to be respected. On one starlit night, Bernard and I had gone for a walk beside the wild sea, innocently trespassing on a site sacred to the ancestors of the Ga tribe. Out of the shadows of the bush, figures emerged, and began a mysterious dance that increased in intensity, weaving in and out of the palm trees and the huge waves crashing on the shore. I remember too the blasphemy I unwittingly committed by sitting on an over-stuffed Victorian chair in the house of a senior chief. Inevitably it turned out to be his throne. Only the pouring of many libations of local brandy overcame the enormity of my behaviour.

But the spirits could be helpful as well as embarrassing. I gained enormous prestige among my economics students for my uncanny ability to detect plagiarism in their essays. Given the paucity of books on economics in the university library, this was not difficult. A laboured student paper on classical economics would suddenly sprout the elegant analysis of a Marshall, or the powerful argument of a John Maynard Keynes. The hapless writer of the essay would be aghast at my discovery.

Our most surprising encounters with traditional West Africa occurred in the Christmas vacation. We drove to the remote Northern Territories over corrugated unpaved tracks, through dry, lion-coloured country, to visit the parents of one of our favourite students. At the kraal of neat round huts where his family lived, we found a scene reminiscent of medieval paintings of Adam's Fall – dogs, goats, hens, flowers, and human beings of all ages dressed in leaves. The student's parents, despite their lack of clothes, were people of great dignity. We sat down and ate goat stew served on yam leaves. The conversation, translated by our student from the local language, turned on the transition to the modern world. Fast young girls, the parents told us, insisted on wearing clothes. We were given two fine wooden carvings, which I have still, that exemplified the tradition: a king and queen, each seated on a stool and wearing ceremonial headdress but nothing else.

I was beginning to learn a little about comparative cultures. I had already encountered different values, demonstrated more often in practice than in theory. I upbraided my students, many of whom were Christians, for tolerating polygamy. It was one manifestation of the inequality of the sexes in Ghana, which had been brought home to me when an entire work group of women breaking stones in a quarry, most of them with the newest baby strapped on their backs, cheered when Bernard offered me his hand to pull me up a steep slope.

The students considered my criticism philosophically; was it true, they asked, that some families in England put their elderly parents in nursing homes and only visited them once a week, or even more rarely? Was this not disrespect for the old? No decent Ghanaian family, they pointed out, would dream of doing such a thing.

Kwame Nkrumah himself embodied his country's transition to the modern world. Charismatic and ambitious, he was also superstitious, consulting witch-doctors and astrologers before making important decisions. He was a brilliant speaker with the capacity to inspire his audience. I heard him on several occasions, a handsome, compelling personality in his traditional West African tunic, entrancing his listeners with the vision of a Black African renaissance of which he was to be the leader. Thinking of him years later, I was reminded of Adlai Stevenson's poignant comparison of himself with Jack Kennedy in 1960. 'Like Cicero,' he had said, 'when I speak they listen. But he is like Demosthenes. When he speaks, they march.' And so it was with Kwame Nkrumah.

Pursuant to his purpose, Nkrumah convened the first All-African People's Conference in Accra in December 1958. He invited the eight African independent states, some of long standing like Ethiopia and Liberia, others such as Guinée newly minted from colonial status, as was Ghana itself. He wanted to discuss the emergence of 'an African personality in international affairs'. Africa, Nkrumah declared, had for too long spoken only through the voices of others. Alas, it continued to do so, for in the euphoria of launching the great conference, no one had taken account of the fact that Africa possessed no common language. Delegates from Tunisia and Morocco, observers from Guinée and Senegal, spoke in perfect French to a largely uncomprehending audience. Disaster was averted only by the conscription of every member of the University College who had even a smattering of French to come and translate the proceedings. Most of the translators were, inevitably, expatriate Britons. I found myself translating, as best I could, into rudimentary French the words of the Ghanaian Finance Minister, Mr Komla Agbeli Gbedemah. He would stop after a few words and gesticulate angrily at me, not realising that I had to hear a complete phrase before I could translate it into passable French.

I was impressed by the impact of French culture on the Francophone Africans I met at the conference. I was later to learn, on a short trip to Togoland, how sharp was the distinction between the small educated elite, the *assimilés*, and the bulk of the population, the *indigènes*, in the French-African empire; nevertheless, the acceptance of that elite as French citizens bore favourable comparison with Britain. Léopold Senghor, the great poet and political leader of Senegal, was continuously elected to the French National Assembly between 1946 and 1958, and in 1983 he was elected to the Académie française. Gaston Monnerville, Deputy from French Guiana and grandson of a slave, served briefly as Under-Secretary of State in charge of the French colonies before the Second World War – the first black man to hold a position in the French government – and in 1959 became President of the French Senate. Such an appointment would have been unthinkable in the Britain of the 1950s.

The French Republic had invested heavily in the education of that African elite in the history and culture of France. Suitably qualified young Frenchmen conscripted for national service could opt to teach in France's colonies, overseas departments and territories, rather than train for the military. The products of that investment were manifest at the All-African People's Conference. I remember overhearing a conversation between two of the Francophone Africans at the end of the first day. 'Voilà justement l'esprit cartésien,' said one to the other. It was not a remark frequently heard in even the better British common rooms.

After our visit to the Northern Territories we drove our battered car to Lagos, Nigeria – or, to be more precise, we tried to. Somewhere in the deep bush of the Togo–Nigeria border, the car breathed its last. Dazzling butterflies as big as the palm of a hand fluttered by, and brightly coloured birds chattered and squawked in the high canopy of the rainforest. We seemed to be alone with only animals for company. Then, as the evening drew on, we became aware of being inspected closely. Amid the thick green leaves of the plants and trees all around us it was possible to discern several faces and inquiring bright eyes. A car also on its way to Lagos stopped. 'Are you in trouble?' the driver asked. We explained what had happened. 'Well,' he said, 'you won't be able to get anyone to tow it to Lagos for hours, and by that time everything movable will have vanished – tyres, lights, upholstery. It's what the people in this jungle live on.' I was reminded of Cornish fishermen scouring the wrecks of ships cast up on their rocky coast before the days of coastguards and lighthouse keepers. So we abandoned the car in the bush. The only consequence was that we were charged duty by the assiduous Nigerian customs officer on scrap metal imported into Nigeria, when we told him what had happened. At least he didn't try to argue that we were importing a car.

Arrived in Lagos, we stayed at the home of Oladipo Onipede, a friend of mine from New York's International House, where I had lodged while a student at Columbia. Oladipo was a Yoruba who ran a commercial college for aspiring business people, secretaries and managers. Lagos was a noisy town, much more volatile and quarrelsome than Accra. Indeed, Ghanaian friends had questioned our decision to go to Nigeria for Christmas. 'The Nigerians,' one told us, 'are the Romans of Africa. We are the Athenians.'

In Oladipo's courtyard, Bernard and I had a big room open on one side. We shared the courtyard with a rather amiable sheep which was known as 'the goat', and was to be sacrificed for Christmas dinner. We became rather fond of her, and it was a grim moment when she had her throat cut just outside our room. Life went on all around us all the time; there was no secure retreat into privacy. The day before we returned to Accra, Bernard's status as an Oxford University teacher now being well known in the neighbourhood, we awoke to find at least twenty men sitting cross-legged and silent in the courtyard, politely waiting for us to wake up so that they might press the claims of brothers and sons who fancied going to Oxford.

I loved West Africa, but it was not without its traumas. Some were mild, like the necessity to wash every lettuce leaf and tomato in antiseptic, given that the main form of fertiliser was human manure. For years afterwards green salads always tasted to me of Milton, the powerful antiseptic we used. Others were more disturbing: the warnings about scorpions and snakes had to be observed. Particularly menacing was the green mamba, hard to see in the grass, which we were told actively pursued human beings and could slither as fast as a man could run. Stories abounded of green mambas being found in larders and beds. A colleague of ours, a rather sensitive young academic, failed to notice one climbing up his trouser leg. He had to remain still for a couple of hours until the snake woke up, and returned by the route it had taken.

For me the worst trauma was the first of a series of miscarriages that I experienced in various parts of the world, which taught me quite a lot about the differences in the treatment of women among obstetricians. I had been warned that there was a high risk of miscarriage in tropical countries, but I had very little idea of either the symptoms or the after-effects. When I saw an array of knives and scissors on the table in the little cottage hospital that served University College, just before I was operated on after the miscarriage, I didn't know what the doctor was going to do – maybe even perform a hysterectomy? In proper British tradition, I wasn't told; there was nothing for it but to grin and bear it.

From Ghana I returned to England in January 1959, leaving Bernard to finish the term. We met in Rome for an Easter holiday, and then went back to Oxford. In the summer of 1959 Bernard was appointed lecturer in philosophy at University College, London, whose provost was his friend Noel Annan.

A general election was expected soon, and I was looking for a constituency to fight where the result was not preordained, as at Harwich. There was a vacancy for a candidate in Southampton Test, which adjoined the safe Labour seat of Southampton Itchen, represented by Horace King, who was to become the Speaker of the House of Commons in 1965. I had local connections because of my parents' cottage in the New Forest some ten miles away, where I had spent most of my school holidays. The by-election at Harwich in 1954 had conferred on me a reputation as a determined campaigner, and so I was selected to become the prospective Labour candidate for Southampton Test. The Conservatives had been in office for eight years. They had the Suez debacle to their discredit. Those living on state pensions and benefits felt strongly that their incomes had not kept up with the general improvement in the standard of living. But during the campaign this hardly counted against the persuasiveness of the first wave of postwar prosperity, summed up in the Tories' brilliant slogan: 'Life's better with the Conservatives. Don't let Labour ruin it.'

Inexplicably Hugh Gaitskell, the Labour Party leader, a man of scrupulous integrity who had masterminded an impressive campaign, let himself get sucked into a foolish and unconvincing series of promises about better pensions and public services, combined with a pledge that income tax would not be raised. Even more damagingly, he claimed that purchase tax, the main sales tax at the time, would actually be reduced. An able Chancellor of the Exchequer, Gaitskell had worked out that continuing economic growth would enable public spending to increase without higher taxes. But concepts like 'the buoyancy of the revenue', no doubt understood by academic economists, sounded like a gimmick, and a meretricious one, in the course of an election. 'We've got him,' Harold Macmillan exulted to his speech writer George Crist, on reading in the newspapers of Gaitskell's latest pledge. Stopping the car he was in at the time, he held an impromptu press conference on Wandsworth Common. 'If this is an auction,' he told the rapidly assembled journalists, 'I'm not in it.'* Macmillan himself saw in that phrase the epitaph to Gaitskell's campaign. And so it proved. Once again the Labour Party – and its candidate in Southampton Test – were defeated. The Conservatives romped home, on a turnout of 78.7 per cent, to a majority of a hundred seats.

The 1959 election defeat spurred Gaitskell's determination to modernise the Labour Party. He recognised that the traditional working class on which Labour had depended for support was eroding, as prosperity enabled more people to aspire to middle-class lifestyles. He also understood that Labour's socialist ideology, in particular nationalisation, did not appeal to them. Polls indicated that most nationalised industries were far from popular. The heart of the matter, to Gaitskell, was not public ownership – though he envisaged a moderate extension of it – but equality of opportunity, the centrepiece of Tony Crosland's 1956 book *The*

---

* Alistair Horne, *Macmillan: The Official Biography*, vol. 2, *1957–1986*, Macmillan, 1989.

Future of Socialism. And that depended more on tax policy, economic growth and public services, in particular health and
education, than on nationalisation.

The Labour Party Conference in November 1959, shortened to
only two days, turned itself into an autopsy of the general election. As the debate unfolded, speakers became more savage and
more bitter, not least because Gaitskell went straight for the jugu-
lar. He had a perverse, if courageous, instinct for choosing the
worst times and places for his crucial battles. He proposed now to
rewrite Clause Four of the Party's Constitution, the sacred text of
British socialism, above all the common ownership of the means
of production, distribution and exchange. He consulted neither
the Shadow Cabinet nor the National Executive Committee.
That may have been why he underestimated the visceral opposition to his proposal.

On the second day, however, the mood of the conference
changed. Ian Mikardo, the darling of the left, lost his seat on the
National Executive Committee. Stunned by this result, even the
left wing of the Party was prepared to listen to speeches by Denis
Healey and me deploring the bickering within the Party. It would,
I said, be a gift to the Conservatives. We should concentrate
instead on the objectives we shared, in particular the modernisation of the public services. 'Does it really make sense,' I argued,
'that when someone has an accident in a 1959 car, he should have
to be admitted to an 1850s hospital?' The speech, from a member
of the new generation of Labour activists, attracted considerable
press attention.

Hugh Gaitskell was that rare creature, a passionate intellectual.
Rationality was his creed. His limited patience was strained
almost beyond endurance by the stolid prejudices of the trades
union leaders he depended upon, and the colourful sophistries of
his left-wing critics. Born in India of Civil Service parents, he was
as much a liberal as a socialist. He cherished liberty, detested
racism, and believed in the redistribution of income and wealth to

achieve social justice. He was never attracted to the European Community, for as a political entity it threatened to eclipse the Commonwealth. The Commonwealth embodied Gaitskell's deepest convictions, including internationalism and interracialism, and it had developed out of Britain's imperial history with which his family had had close connections.

Gaitskell had an extraordinary capacity to command the loyalty of those closest to him. He was a man who attracted disciples. His strength lay in part in the depth of his commitment to changing the Labour Party, not only to win elections but to transform Britain itself; in part in the sensitivity and vulnerability of the diffident, charming man glimpsed through the public carapace. No one was less aptly described as a desiccated calculating machine, Aneurin Bevan's absurd epithet for him. Gaitskell was capable of unrestrained enjoyment, flinging himself into dancing, which he adored. At Labour Party Conferences he would set ideological differences to one side, twirling across the floor with Barbara Castle, herself a splendid dancer. Towards the end of his short life, he fell wildly in love with a wealthy Conservative hostess, Anne Fleming, wife of James Bond's creator, Ian Fleming, disregarding his friends' counsels of discretion. He was as besotted as a boy in love.

Those of us within Gaitskell's circle – and I was only at the outer edge – were ready to take on any political battle for him. We thrilled to his call at the 1960 Party Conference, during the struggle over unilateral nuclear disarmament, to 'fight, fight and fight again to save the party we love'. We were determined to break the shackles of Clause Four. And we were shattered, to the point of tears, when he declared at the 1962 Conference that a thousand years of history should not be abandoned to seek membership of the European Common Market, a mission on which Harold Macmillan had just embarked.

Our house in Phillimore Place had become by now something of a magnet for our friends, who found the combination of philosophers, politicians and writers they often found there stimulating. Hilary Rubinstein was working for his uncle, the left-wing publisher Victor Gollancz, not easy to work for but a man constantly engaged in the great issues of the day and interested in new and unconventional writers. Bernard loved the open, worldly atmosphere at University College, London after the more cloistered atmosphere of Oxford. As for me, 1 had been appointed General Secretary of the Fabian Society in 1960, following my friend Bill Rodgers. Fabian publications were being more widely noticed as the prospect of a change of government dawned. The wartime generation of political leaders was passing away, and the ground was being laid for a new era of politics. We friends in Phillimore Place were caught up in the ferment of discussion, plans and aspirations that were to characterise the 1960s. The *Sunday Times* in 1966 described Bernard and me as 'the New Left at its most able, most generous and sometimes most eccentric', though I never found out the nature of the eccentricities they had in mind.

After the 1960 Party Conference, Bill became engaged in mobilising Gaitskell's supporters under the banner of the CDS, the Campaign for Democratic Socialism. I kept my distance from the CDS, convinced that, to be of use to the Party, the Fabian Society had to remain above the battle. Since the members of its executive committee ranged from Dick Crossman to Tony Crosland, my prudence may have been justified. But it also suited me personally to hang a little loose in the deeply divided Party. Even then, I was something of an outsider. I was never invited to join XYZ, for instance, a private club which brought together Labour's intellectuals for dinner and conversation. I resented this, for many of its members played a much less prominent role in the Labour Party than I did; but then it was an all-male institution, and I was beginning to learn what my place was – if not a tea-lady, then at best a secretary.

Less than three thousand members strong, the Fabian Society

wielded a remarkable degree of influence. Many of the Labour
Party's leading figures served on its committees. Distinguished academics were pleased to write policy pamphlets for the Society,
receiving not a penny for their work. Fabian headquarters were in
a damp, narrow Georgian building in Dartmouth Street,
Westminster, with a main room on the ground floor where meetings were held, three tiny offices on the first floor, and a dark
basement full of mouldering Fabian pamphlets, some by earlier
Fabian authors such as George Bernard Shaw and H. G. Wells.
Only a very few people were aware of the eminent backlist of
Fabian authors. I learned about one of them when he made a substantial offer for sole control of it. I had met him at a meeting to
which he, a newly selected parliamentary candidate, had invited
me as a speaker. He offered me a lift back to London from
Buckingham where the meeting took place. I expected an Austin-
Morris or a Ford Escort, and was surprised when a Rolls-Royce
drew up. It seemed a propitious backdrop for a publishing deal,
though I felt obliged to refuse. The candidate's name was Robert
Maxwell.

The subjects that dominated political thought in the Fabian
Society during my four years as General Secretary were the construction of the welfare state – in particular, pensions, the
management of publicly owned industries, and the structure of
government. Richard Titmuss, the London School of Economics
professor with the gaunt face and burning eyes of an El Greco
saint, presided over the series of pamphlets on the welfare state, to
which his younger colleagues, Brian Abel-Smith and Peter
Townsend, made distinguished contributions. Michael Shanks,
my former colleague on the *Financial Times*, edited the major
Fabian work on the management of publicly owned industries.

There was also a covert group on the structure of government,
covert because some senior civil servants privately offered us
advice. It produced a pamphlet called *The Administrators*, whose

most radical proposal was to create a new Department of Economic Affairs. The key Fabian recommendation was to give the new department control of public investment, hopefully introducing a long-term perspective on Britain's economic development into Whitehall's thinking. The recommendation was effectively blocked by the Treasury. The proposal was later put into practice with the creation of the Department of Economic Affairs by the 1964 Wilson government, but still without control of public investment. Shorn of effective power, the new department lacked the clout to survive amid the savage and secret rivalries of Whitehall.

Alongside the work on domestic policy, the Fabian Colonial Bureau, later the Fabian Commonwealth Bureau, had a considerable influence on the government. The Fabians possessed a rich network of contacts in Asia and Africa, the heritage of their long battle against imperialism. Leaders from Pandit Nehru to Julius Nyerere were nurtured on Fabian doctrine, and many made the Colonial Bureau their first port of call in England. Dr Rita Hinden, later editor of the journal *Socialist Commentary*, ran the Bureau with strong support from Arthur Creech Jones, Attlee's Colonial Secretary, and later from George Thomson, Harold Wilson's Commonwealth Secretary. It became an indispensable source of information for Labour spokesmen on colonial and Commonwealth affairs.

One of the most important issues during this time was the Macmillan government's proposal for a Central African Federation, bringing together Northern and Southern Rhodesia and Nyasaland. The Central African leaders Kenneth Kaunda, Joshua Nkomo and Hastings Banda were strongly opposed, believing the Federation would reinforce the hegemony of the white community and delay yet further the independence of their countries.

I knew Kenneth Kaunda, a determined but gentle politician, from the day he had walked into one of my People's Education

Association classes in Accra in 1958. I had introduced him to my class as one of Africa's emerging leaders. He had demurred, saying, 'I am only a student come to learn, like the rest of you.' I wrote the submission to the Monckton Commission on the Central African economy for these leaders. I tried to explain it to Dr Hastings Banda, an authoritarian with all the confidence of the old-fashioned general practitioner he had long been. As far as he was concerned the submission might have been in some utterly strange language, but since it was written by a young woman it probably didn't matter anyhow. He was right; the Central African Federation was an idea that was stillborn, not least because of the hostility of the Prime Minister of Southern Rhodesia, Ian Smith.

By this time Helge and Hilary had a son, Jonathan, born in 1956, and a daughter, Felicity, born two years later. I had miscarried a second baby in 1959, but not long after becoming the Society's General Secretary I became pregnant again, a condition which greatly alarmed my Chairman, Tony Crosland. Looking with distaste at my burgeoning figure, he urged me to go home. 'This is obscene,' he told me. He was, I thought, horrified that I might go into labour there in the office.

My daughter Rebecca was born at University College Hospital on 20 May 1961. The only one of my four potential children to survive to full term, she was to me a miracle, a tiny human being with every finger and toe perfect. I was given her to hold, still pink, blue and silver from the amazement of being born, her black hair in wet tendrils over her round head. I passed her to Bernard, who held her like a piece of fine china, his sharp and sensitive face softened by his emotions. I was back at work within a couple of weeks, taking Rebecca with me. As the Society's General Secretary I was able to decree my own rules. The baby slept in a carrycot under my desk, comforted if she cried by my small devoted staff, in particular the wonderfully humane administrator,

Gladys Cremer. It was all somehow very unFabian, but then the Fabian Society itself was adapting to a new world.

As Rebecca grew up, learning to crawl and then to walk, she spent more of her time at Phillimore Place. She learned to walk in Greece, when Bernard and I were on holiday with his friend and student Demetrius Nianias, his wife Nan and their son Georgy. Rebecca spent hours under a big umbrella on the balcony in Athens watching Georgy walk. By the time we had got to Mykonos, a fortnight later, she was able to walk confidently along the side of the harbour where the boats were bobbing at anchor, closely followed by Bernard, a devoted father.

Back home at Phillimore Place the child population had multiplied. The Rubinsteins' third, Mark, was born a few weeks before Rebecca, and our tenants Frank Windsor, the TV actor of such noted series as Z Cars, and his wife Mary had produced a daughter, Amanda. Looking after them all was much easier than it would have been for a nuclear family living on its own. All the adults worked outside the home, but at different times of the day. I was usually away in the afternoons and evenings, since the main vote in Parliament was at 10 p.m. following several hours of debate, so I was often around in the mornings, at least until I became a minister. Bernard would be at home during the university vacations, and Helge, who was a marriage guidance counsellor, conducted many of her consultations at home too. There was always a familiar adult around, for the small but significant crises that erupt in family life, the scratched knee or the dead goldfish. So the stress and guilt that afflict so many families were minimised.

My mother, as she grew older, derived much pleasure from her grandchildren. John, my brother, and his wife Jennifer had by this time two sons – Daniel, born in August 1954, and Timothy John, in June 1961. They rented a flat in a mock-Victorian castle in Kingsgate on the Kentish coast. The flat had views across the Channel, and a small sandy beach where the children could play.

My mother's relationship with her grandchildren was rather formal. She did not change their nappies or play football with them. She never had done much of that, and she may have forgotten how. But she deployed her own particular skills to their delight, telling them stories and giving them story-books for birthdays and Christmas that she had written herself. She was heartbroken when John abandoned his wife for his secretary, Elaine. Both my parents took Jennifer's side, and relations with John, already strained by his repeated demands for money to be invested in his small property company, came close to breaking point.

In 1963, when Rebecca was two years old, I was selected as prospective Labour parliamentary candidate for Hitchin, Hertfordshire, a county constituency much altered by a big inflow of new voters. The field of contenders for the candidature was rather weak, because Hitchin, with its four thousand-plus Tory majority, was not regarded as a likely win for Labour in the forthcoming general election. But ambitious young politicians had overlooked the rapid growth within the constituency of the new town of Stevenage, with its concentration of workers in the aerospace and other high-tech industries. It was a town tailor-made for Harold Wilson's message about the white heat of technology – indeed, so much so that Wilson, now Leader of the Labour Party following Hugh Gaitskell's untimely death in 1963, appeared early in the campaign on the balcony of a house in Stevenage to deliver the message himself.

Hitchin also happened to be a constituency with an agent, Jack Ward, who was an organisational genius. He had worked out that the combination of the new electors in Stevenage with the high-minded, progressive electorate of Letchworth, the first Garden City, should swing the vote our way. He urged me to make contact with as many voters as I could, stressing the need for a new Britain that would put the old barriers of class and gender behind it, a new Britain that I as a young woman could easily identify with. It was the challenge I had been waiting for. And Jack was right. The swing in Hitchin was the highest of any constituency in the county, and nearly twice that of the southeast as a whole.

I may have been helped by my brief appearance on the third of Labour's television election broadcasts, holding a basket of groceries and comparing prices with a similar basket of five years earlier. It was not a very inspired piece of television, but it was a gesture towards women voters, who were still very much seen as housewives. There were many working wives in Stevenage and I encountered virtually no prejudice against women candidates among the voters. Bernard and I campaigned together, and on the election leaflets was a photo of our little family.

I was lucky to have tough, devoted and resilient supporters in the constituency party. Several of the survivors remain friends to this day. Philip Ireton was a railwayman whose genius lay in an extraordinary understanding of local government finance, a subject I must admit to finding yawn-making. He was self-taught, but no one could out-argue him on this esoteric subject. In any dispute on the matter, it was crucial to have him on your side. Occasionally, as we met at local or county functions, he would draw me to one side and whisper to me what must have seemed to others juicy gossip. The whispers were almost invariably nuggets of information about public accounts.

Hilda Lawrence and her husband Bill were pioneers of the new town. Born and brought up in east London, they were among the first families to move to Stevenage when it exploded into thousands of homes. They devoted themselves to building a balanced society, in which sport, drama and music developed alongside the schools, churches, pubs and hospitals that make up the tapestry of the town. They were brave, too, confronting the critics of anything new, fighting to keep the central Fairlands Valley out of the hands of developers and, later on, backing me against the militant element on the general management committee of the local party.

If you are an MP, such men and women are beyond calculation: they tell you what you are doing wrong, yet do so against a background of affection and loyalty. There were others like Hilda and Bill: Michael and Ann Cotter; my constituency agent Jim Caldwell – successor to Jack Ward – and his wife Terry; and, in Letchworth Garden City, Stanley Grant, an accountant with the Commonwealth Finance Corporation who at every election used to canvass half the town in which he lived, some three or four thousand homes. I often stayed with him and his wife Helen during election times.

My victory at Hitchin sometime after midnight on 16 October 1964 tipped the balance of seats in favour of Labour, though Labour's hair's-breadth victory was not confirmed until Brecon and Radnor reported the next day. Exhausted and elated, I drove to the top of the hill just south of Stevenage on the A1 highway. I looked down at the lights of Stevenage and the surrounding villages, and at the thousands of people I now represented. These were my people, the people I was elected to serve. I was at last a Member of Parliament.

CHAPTER 8

Women in the House

Newly elected as the MP for Hitchin, aged thirty-four, I was now in a Labour government with a majority of just four. Like almost every other new MP, I caught my breath as I climbed up the stone stairs that lead to St Stephen's chapel, flanked by statues of past statesmen who once debated there, and on into the central lobby, the place where constituents come to meet their MP. I was walking into eight hundred years of history, marked by conflicts, scandals, struggles and epic events, as well as individual acts of courage, commitment and defiance. It was at once awesome and inspiring.

The House of Commons is, however, indifferent to new MPs. There are no welcoming ceremonies and very little preparation. No one then told you much about the rules that govern its operations, nor about the complicated geography of the old buildings. Only since the early 1990s have MPs been able to have an office of their own. I spent the first three months of my new life without an office or even a desk, looking for somewhere I could dictate replies to my voluminous constituency correspondence, two hundred or more letters a week. I hunted for telephones that were not already commandeered. Mornings were taken up with meetings of

Commons committees, or listening to individuals or groups of constituents anxious to influence legislation. I could not work from home because, given the government's fragile majority of only four, to be absent from a vital vote was an unforgivable offence. So I would dash home to give my little daughter supper and a bedtime story before returning for the 10 p.m. vote and perhaps an hour or two's work after that.

The persistent demands on an MP can overwhelm the aspirations that brought him or her into Parliament. Yet there are moments when one becomes acutely conscious of Parliament's place in history. In the summer of 1967, Bernard and I had gone to Romania for a holiday at an inexpensive resort on the Black Sea with our friends Peter and Barbara Metcalfe, both of whom were active members of my constituency Labour Party, Peter being a leading councillor, and their daughters Caroline and Victoria, of a similar age to Rebecca. We took turns to look after our three little girls busily building sandcastles and peering at a nearby nudist colony populated by fat middle-aged men. When our turn for three days off came, Bernard and I went to the Carpathian mountains, jagged as tigers' teeth, where we found a small hotel. I handed over my passport, with its description of my new occupation as a Member of Parliament. The elderly hotel clerk looked carefully at it, and then murmured under his breath, 'Mater Liberorum!' Exiled to this remote location for the nostalgia he felt for the freedoms of the defunct Hapsburg Empire, he had a Ph.D. from the University of Vienna. I often recalled his words, not least on the rare occasions when the Commons defied the government of the day to defend individual liberties or the rights of minorities.

But I was not just an MP – I was that rare bird, a woman MP. My first action on entering the House of Commons in October 1964 was to go everywhere that had previously been barred to me as a non-Member. Pushing open the door marked 'Members Only', I received a sharp reminder of my secondary status. For behind the door was a row of gleaming urinals. Women MPs, a small minority of only twenty-nine when I was first elected, had been allocated two cosy little rooms marked 'Lady Members', with an ironing board, an iron and a chintz-covered settee to rest on.

The arrival of women in the Commons was not, of course, entirely new. The first signs of these exotic new arrivals had appeared some forty-five years before I got there. The pioneers were formidable personalities, some with a background in local government, others from the social and financial elite. I had met a few of them when I was still a child. My father, ever keen to advance my future career, had once introduced me, a scruffy teenager, to the first ever woman MP to take her seat, the wealthy and acerbic Nancy Astor. 'She wants to be an MP,' my father said. The great lady looked at me with distaste. 'Not with that hair!' she declared. She had already perceived what was to be a big negative factor in my political career.

Among my mother's friends was Dr Edith Summerskill, tall and handsome, her Roman profile emphasised by the forceful hats of the 1940s New Look. She had been a junior Minister for Food in the Attlee government, useful as a doctor in advocating nutritious but unfamiliar and sometimes disagreeable products. Her medical qualifications gave her unchallengeable status, which she used to good effect. Married to another doctor and mother of a son, Michael, and a daughter Shirley (who was herself to become an MP), she became a role model for me, at once a public figure and a successful wife and mother with strong feminist views.

One of Labour's iconic female figures after the war was Bessie Braddock, earth mother of Liverpool and a powerful voice in the movement. Two younger women were already becoming stars: Jennie Lee, wife of Aneurin Bevan, and Barbara Castle, the fiery red-headed 'Lancashire lass' who was to become one of the most influential and certainly the most attractive figure on the left. So I didn't feel isolated or alone. There was a certain camaraderie among the women MPs, which even extended beyond party. We wanted to see one another do well. We knew what we were up against, the unstated but pervasive view that women weren't up to the hard choices of politics, that they at best might contribute to 'soft' subjects like health, pensions and education. Indeed for four decades no woman was appointed as a minister to departments other than these.

Ten years later when I became a member of the Cabinet, in October 1974, as Secretary of State for Prices and Consumer Protection, I had to face an hour of parliamentary questions, most of them hostile and designed to prove that Labour, just elected, was responsible for the high rate of inflation. I felt like St Sebastian, the target of arrows from every direction. Out of the corner of my eye I could just see a figure behind the Speaker's Chair intently watching my performance. It was Margaret Thatcher, Shadow Environment Secretary. When my ordeal was finished, I retreated to the Lady Members' Room, where she was ironing a dress. 'You did well,' she said. 'After all, we can't let them get the better of us.'

When I was first elected I made friends with several male

contemporaries who got into Parliament at much the same time. We'd met early on in the Labour Party, at Oxford or, later, in the Fabian Society. Among them were Bill Rodgers, Roy Hattersley, Peter Archer and Frank Judd. We were destined to serve as MPs and later as ministers in four Labour governments, as well as being Shadow ministers in Opposition. So I was one of a close and mutually supportive cohort, and that went a long way to compensate for the loneliness of being a woman in a world of men. We remain friends today.

Yet as a woman I was inevitably an outsider. MPs, especially the older ones, enjoyed the deeply masculine, clubby societies they had made for themselves. There were two kinds of clubby society. The Conservative version was lived largely outside the Commons, in the elegant clubs of St James's and Pall Mall, with occasional incursions from Liberal and even Labour politicians, notably Roy Jenkins. Inside the Commons, it took the form of dinner parties or intimate drinks in the Smoking Room or on the terrace. I once went into the Smoking Room with a Labour colleague, to be greeted by a veteran of the place who leaned over my well-covered shoulder and hissed at my escort, 'This is obscene!' The Labour version was more like a traditional working men's club. It was lived almost entirely inside the Commons, in one of the many bars, with heavy beer-drinking and gossip until late at night, often including journalists from the Commons lobby. Many Labour MPs represented constituencies far from London – in Scotland, Wales and the North of England – much too far away to commute. Salaries in the 1950s and 1960s were meagre, so many of these MPs lived in dreary rooms or flats without their wives and families. 'Going home' to these places was unattractive. Furthermore, apart from the first Attlee government of 1945–50 and the second Wilson government of 1966–70, Labour administrations did not enjoy sound majorities. That meant most Labour MPs had to stay around for fear of a vote being called unexpectedly.

Women were excluded from nearly all the clubs that male MPs

belonged to. Mrs Thatcher was never invited to join the Carlton Club before she became leader of the Conservative Party in 1975, when she was offered honorary membership. I was never invited to join the Reform Club, segregated until 1981, nor the more exclusive Party clubs for self-selected 'coming young men', like The Group in the case of Labour. I can still remember, as a junior Minister for Education and Science in 1967–9, having to walk through the basement of the Reform Club and then to ascend by goods lift to the room where a group of scientists and ministers were meeting to discuss the importance of genetic factors in health. It was as if a woman walking across the large ground-floor hall would pollute the hallowed surroundings of the club.

Did clubs matter? Yes, they did. They were where networks were established, networks that were important for selection, promotion, exchange of opinion and information. Women politicians were excluded, outside Parliament, by the segregation practised by clubs. On the inside, they often excluded themselves, not wanting to be part of a heavy-drinking culture, or to be the butt of stories and jokes. I used to spend my evenings answering the pile of letters from my constituents, a pile that never seemed to diminish. I wasn't very sociable. I found it easier just to be a minister, with red boxes of official correspondence to add to the constituency letters, because they provided an acceptable excuse for my absence from the bars.

As I noted earlier, finding a mentor is important to an aspiring young politician. A mentor knows the ropes and can make connections with established people in the Party and in Parliament. Again, there was a big difference in this respect between the situation of young men and that of young women. There were few established women politicians in any case during these postwar decades, other than those I have mentioned, and their own positions were not secure. For young men, on the other hand, mentors were not hard to find. On the Labour side, men such as Hugh Dalton, and on the Conservative side Rab Butler, commended

their protégés to winnable constituencies, and later to their colleagues as junior ministers or parliamentary private secretaries, the
lowest rung on the greasy pole of political power. I was again
lucky, the serendipity no one can plan for, having met Herbert
Morrison, the wartime Home Secretary, during that air raid in
London back in 1943. He was unique – the only significant male
politician at that time to help bright, committed youngsters
regardless of gender. Whispers, of course, went around; as far as I
was concerned, there was not the slightest basis for them.

I was surprised by the prejudice I encountered among some of
the older MPs. The Conservative 'knights of the shires' were gallant and patronising. On one occasion I got back to the House
from a meeting to hear the division bells ringing. It was a day for
private members' bills and I didn't know what this one was about.
I asked my 'pair', the Opposition MP who would agree to abstain
from a minor vote if one of us was committed to a meeting or lecture outside the House, a kindly and genial Conservative. He
refused to tell me. I pleaded with him, as the time to vote trickled
away. He patted me on the head. 'Don't you trouble your pretty
little head about it,' he said. It turned out to be the bill to legalise
homosexual acts between consenting adults. Older Labour MPs
representing the trades unions, too, were often uncomfortable
with women MPs, unlike those from a local government background who had much more experience of women as colleagues.

The solidarity among women MPs never amounted to organising an official women's caucus, as happened in the United States'
House of Representatives, but there were occasions when we
made common cause. During the passage of one particularly hard-
fought bill, we had numerous divisions with MPs crowded into
the lobbies like passengers in a rush-hour Underground train.
After each division, one or two women MPs revealed that they
had been sharply pinched by an unknown assailant. The following day, many of us got together and decided to retaliate. When
there was next a series of divisions, we agreed we would wear

stiletto heels, fashionable at the time, and stamp as hard as we could on the foot of the pincher. The day after, an elderly MP hobbled into the tea room. We were full of concern. What had happened? Had he been run over? No, he replied angrily. He had gout. But no one ever pinched us again.

I came to realise how often the achievements of women politicians grew out of their father's belief in them. Look at the list of women leaders and look at their fathers. Time and again, the daughter has realised the father's ambitions not only for herself but for him too. Indira Gandhi, Benazir Bhutto and Sirimavo Bandaranaike in Sri Lanka became the leaders of what one might call dynastic democracies. There was either no son to take up the baton, or the son was unfitted to the task. Margaret Thatcher, Barbara Castle, Jennie Lee and I were all examples at a less exalted level of daughters living out their fathers' aspirations. The relationship between fathers and daughters has not been greatly studied, but it is, in my view, a key to understanding how some women become leaders. There is a variant on the theme – the woman who seeks to carry out her husband's frustrated ambitions. Begum Khaleda Zia of Bangladesh and Cory Aquino of the Philippines came to the leadership of their countries after their husbands were assassinated. These women were determined to pursue their husbands' legacies. Hillary Rodham Clinton may have wanted to fulfil the ambitions of a gifted husband who frittered away some of the time granted him as President of the United States. In all these instances, the role and example of the male relative are crucial.

Most women MPs in my early years in politics were unmarried or childless. Several of those who did have children were personally wealthy, or had married wealthy men and were able to rely upon trained and authoritative nannies for the care of their children. One of these well-off MPs, Lady Tweedsmuir, a junior minister at the time, handed over her newest baby in its carrycot to a suitably responsible-looking policeman to care for while she attended a meeting, as to the manner born. Another woman, an impressive young MP who was not rich, my colleague Helene Hayman, later the first Lord Speaker, had to smuggle her son into the House. There were no rooms she could use to care for him, so from time to time we shared my ministerial room.

Politics is a hell of a profession to combine with motherhood. When I was first elected, and indeed for a decade after that, the House of Commons routinely sat until 10 p.m. or even later during weekdays, from Monday to Thursday. My efforts to get home from 5 p.m. to 7 p.m. for Rebecca's bedtime were all too often thwarted, and replaced by a telephone call to my husband or my house part-ners Helge and Hilary, to say that I couldn't make it. Three things made my life just about possible: a helpful husband, sharing a home with devoted and tolerant friends and being able to rely on my daily household help, Margaret Curry, who was willing to be pressed into service on urgent occasions as a baby-sitter and nanny.

Hours have been substantially shortened by the 'modernisation' of the House of Commons, but at a high price in terms of the effectiveness of that House. Reform will need to go a great deal further, with a view to empowering Select Committees, extending parliamentary oversight to quangos and treaties, and scrutinising legislation effectively, including holding hearings and citizen con-sultations, if the Commons is to matter and if women are to play a serious part in it. The parliamentary vote, so often controlled by the Whips, has its ultimate place, but it is neither a subtle nor a successful way to establish the accountability of the executive to the legislature or to the people.

At least as important for women is reform of the voting system, as Robin Cook, the reformer who led the House of Commons after being sacked as Foreign Secretary by Tony Blair, well understood. Countries in Western Europe that have a proportional-represen-tation voting system all have a substantially larger share of women in their legislatures than does the United Kingdom.

Shorter hours in the Chamber have not meant shorter hours at work, but instead more time for the constituency. It is not only that voters are better informed and much more demanding. Emails have added a whole new dimension of interaction – a good thing, but yet more work. So the contest for an MP's time becomes more acute, especially in the case of a parent. Many children see very little of their MP parent; in those sectors of our society where nannies don't exist, grandparents and neighbours are vital. Even with their help, life becomes a series of small tugs on the heart-strings; another disappointment, another unintentionally broken promise. Of course this is now the common experience of children with two parents working away from home, but don't let us kid ourselves. So-called 'quality time' on Sundays or during holidays cannot fully compensate. 'It takes a village to raise a child,' Hillary Clinton told the Democratic National Convention in Chicago in 1996, quoting an African proverb. A shared home is the nearest thing to a village in today's urban world. In my case, the 'village' was made possible because of the generosity of my friends and the willingness of my then husband Bernard to take an equal part in bringing up our child. In fact, I owe my career to Hilary and Helge Rubinstein, with whom Bernard and I shared our home for fourteen years, and I am conscious that I exploited them. Rebecca was brought up with their family of four, in particular with their second son Mark, born only a few weeks before her.

I am puzzled that so few couples with young children choose to share a home. First of all, a big house shared is much cheaper for each family to buy than two or three separate houses. Second, as any parent knows, it is far easier to manage two or three children of a similar age than children who are several years apart. Mark and Rebecca were an inseparable pair. They would share an easel in the back garden, busily drawing and painting for hours at a time. Mark was an ebullient, happy boy whose joy in life was infectious; she was a serious, thoughtful and conscientious little girl. They complemented one another. Of the Rubinsteins' two older children,

Jonathan was an imaginative, gentle boy with the sweetest of natures, and Felicity, a bright and bold little girl full of ideas; Ben, the youngest, was an angelic-looking child with a charming and quirky disposition. Between the four parents, Hilary and Helge, Bernard and me, we could usually ensure baby-sitting and occasional expeditions for the children. We could also share the entertainment of visitors – authors, politicians and academics among them – enriching our own networks of friends and acquaintances.

Neither we nor the Rubinsteins ever attempted to split the house up by separate entrances to the upper floors, and we never needed to. During the years we shared the house we never had a serious row, though we often had vigorous discussions about what we were doing and the people we met. Fundamental to the whole arrangement were mutual trust and mutual values on most things. We also approved of one another's marriages. All four of us were friends in the deepest sense. We could not have imagined swapping spouses, fashionable in the 1960s, nor were any of us ever tempted to do so.

In 1964 Bernard was promoted to the Chair of Philosophy at Bedford College, London – at the time, one of the youngest people ever to have become a full professor. His formal achievements were remarkable. Three years later, in 1967 at the age of forty, he was offered a prestigious appointment as Knightbridge Professor of Philosophy at Cambridge University. He combined this with appointments to significant public inquiries and commissions in every decade of his career. Even more impressive than his formal achievements was his recasting of contemporary philosophy from the minute analysis of language enjoined by logical positivism to deliberations on the richer challenges of moral philosophy. For him, an ivory tower was an uncomfortable place to be. He had this in common with my second husband, Dick Neustadt, who resisted academic pressure to move from practice to theory in his study of politics.

Bernard's great love outside his professional subject was music, and in particular, opera. In the seventeen years he and I were married, it was Mozart whose operas appealed most to him. He chose *The Marriage of Figaro* as the entry music for our wedding. Towards the end of our marriage, it was Richard Wagner who captivated him, especially the Ring cycle. I went to see it with him when I was expecting our daughter Rebecca. Somehow the heaviness and vague discomfort of pregnancy have been associated in my mind with this opera cycle ever since. Still the politician, I found Wagner's evocation of pagan gods and heroes off-putting, and I was conscious of the association some found with Aryan myths.

I should have thought more deeply about the changes in Bernard over these years. Like many other reasonably happy spouses, I took my husband for granted. Yet both aesthetically and in lifestyle, our ways were diverging. He developed new friendships, some with people I didn't like. He began to dress differently, abandoning the pullovers and corduroy jackets of his years at UCL and Bedford College for the safari suits and smart denim jackets that were becoming fashionable. And he decided to accept the Cambridge Chair, although it would mean abandoning his happy life in London. These were all signs of a new restlessness, but I failed to take them seriously.

Because Cambridge was only twenty miles from the northern edge of my Hertfordshire constituency, Bernard and I thought we could combine our careers by buying a house in a place close to the constituency while I continued to live in Phillimore Place during the week. One sunny afternoon in the summer of 1967, driving around looking for a suitable property, we came across an old house in a pretty Hertfordshire village called Furneux Pelham. We asked the man mowing the lawn if he knew of any house for sale in the village. 'Well,' he said, 'I was thinking of selling this if I met people I liked who wanted to buy it.' Within minutes we were inside the house. He explained that he and his wife, both bobsleigh enthusiasts, only used the house at weekends and were thinking of moving back to London. They warmed to us, and we to them. An hour later, we had settled on buying the house, a half-timbered listed building, part of which dated back to the fifteenth century, plus half an acre of rough meadow, for £15,000. We lived there together for three years, mainly during weekends and holidays.

I had a sense of foreboding about the move. Spending half the week apart meant that Bernard, wonderful company and very attractive, would build more new friendships of which I was not part, since most of my weekends were taken up with constituency commitments. Sundays were the only days we spent together, and then often with mutual friends. It was foolhardy of me to think our marriage could survive, but it was tempting to believe it could. Gradually we grew apart, Bernard spending more and more of his time with his new friends. Our marriage began to crumble. Although I didn't yet know it, he was falling in love with Patricia Skinner, the wife of one of his colleagues.

During a holiday in the summer of 1970 on a ranch in Wyoming, chosen by Bernard because of Rebecca's love of horse-riding, an enthusiasm she and I shared, I began to realise that something was badly wrong. Bernard seemed detached, far away. I told him that he seemed like a stranger. By the time we got back to England, I knew why.

For more than a year Quentin, Patricia's husband, and I strove to save our marriages against the *coup de foudre*, the compelling passion that had engulfed Patricia and Bernard. We failed, perhaps inevitably, and by the end of 1970 they had left to set up home together in Grantchester, just outside Cambridge. Rebecca, now nine, adored Bernard, and had spent much more time with him than would most children of her age with their fathers. Losing him, as well as the comforting presence of her other family, the Rubinsteins, were bitter hardships to endure.

When Bernard left me for Patricia it was not only my marriage, but the household we friends had created, that broke up. I moved to Furneux Pelham in 1971 to live near my constituency, and sent Rebecca to the local school, fifty yards from the house. In 1972, Hilary and Helge sold Phillimore Place and moved to Notting Hill.

Things got much tougher after I moved to Hertfordshire. I depended on my former household help Margaret Curry; she agreed to live there temporarily with her husband Michael, who had just retired from a job with London Transport. I also depended a great deal on close friends within the constituency, particularly Peter and Barbara Metcalfe. Rebecca spent a lot of time at the Metcalfes' house in Stevenage with their daughters Caroline and Victoria. It was as good a solution as one could hope for, but there was still the pain of missing key moments in my child's life: school plays and athletics matches, prizes and teachers' evenings, being there to provide comfort after a fall, or at the loss of a much loved kitten or goldfish.

Every working mother knows this pain; being an MP, like being a nurse, a solicitor or a waitress, is accompanied in our hard competitive world with rising commitments at work. I suppose it is the price we pay for demanding equality between men and women, and all the good things that go with that. But there will be no satisfactory solution until men share domestic burdens much more equally, especially the upbringing of children and the care of elderly relatives. That in turn requires new patterns of work. Such changes are, thankfully, at last beginning to occur.

Trying to live two lives, that of a working woman and that of a traditional wife and mother, has proved very difficult for most women, and has undoubtedly been a factor in the existence of the 'glass ceiling', the de facto limit to their professional or business careers. But the emergence of women as leaders is not a modern phenomenon. The difference is that those historic women leaders were able to pass their domestic responsibilities over to housekeepers, nannies and servants. In the long histories of monarchies and empires, women from time to time succeeded to leadership: in my own country – to mention only the most memorable – Queen

Elizabeth I, Queen Anne, Queen Victoria and Queen Elizabeth II. In other countries, women leaders have been seen as mothers of the nation: Golda Meir, Indira Gandhi, Isabelita Perón, Corazón Aquino and Ellen Johnson-Sirleaf, sometimes binding up historic wounds. Little boys, learning a national history in which there are female as well as male heroes, will more readily accept an elected female leader; so will young men, swearing oaths of loyalty as police or army officers to a woman head of state. Here is one reason why, paradoxically, it has been harder for Americans to accept a woman president than for Asians and Europeans, despite the powerful position of American women in many other spheres of society.

I'm inclined to agree with the American sociologist Carol Gilligan, who wrote a book in 1982 entitled *In a Different Voice*. Her thesis, based on a great deal of research, was that girls learned from babyhood the language of association. Their conversations revolve around relationships rather than around individuals. They are socialised into the family, learning to help with ordinary chores rather than encouraged towards individual enterprise. Out of this early nurturing one would expect to see a politics of consensus emerge rather than an adversarial politics of competition and conflict. So it has proved, in some countries and cultures – for instance, Scandinavia. But surely not in Britain, whose first woman Prime Minister, Margaret Thatcher, was among the most distinctly adversarial politicians in recent experience.

She was one of those women others describe as 'the only man in the Cabinet', or 'the only member of the Government with balls', implicitly underlining a male concept of what leadership is all about. Mrs Thatcher established over two terms of office her control of the Cabinet, getting rid, one by one, of those she called the 'wets'. With the sole exception of Janet Young, Leader of the House of Lords and therefore distant from the daily battles in the Commons (at that time the Conservative Party had a large inbuilt majority in the Upper House), every Cabinet member was a man. I once asked Lynda Chalker, an outstanding Minister for Overseas

Development (from 1989 to 1997), why she had never been made a Cabinet minister. 'I don't think Margaret much cares for girls around her,' she replied, laughing.

Margaret Thatcher's remarkable power over her colleagues went unchallenged until near the end of her third term of office, although some of her policies were deeply disliked by many of them. One factor, of course, was the admiration in which she was held by many Conservative activists, an admiration close to hero-worship, especially after the Falklands War. Another lay in the traditional upbringing of many Conservative men. For them, women were figures of unquestioned authority – not only their mothers, but their authoritative and disciplined nannies and the matrons at their boarding schools. Women were to be obeyed. I have always believed that many Conservative politicians were in awe of the Prime Minister and simply didn't know how to challenge her.

As she grew older, Mrs Thatcher adopted an increasingly monarchical style. Her Cabinet began to look like a court. There was her vizier, or wise counsellor, Willie Whitelaw. 'Every Prime Minister needs a Willie,' she once said with unconscious irony. There were her squires, the handsome Cecil Parkinson and the bold Michael Forsyth. And there were lots and lots of young Rosenkavaliers too, boy warriors in twill trousers and striped shirts who would gladly have given their lives for her.

She was not the only woman leader who conformed to a historic, even a mythical, female role. In 1969, having been a junior Education Minister, I visited a primary school in Bombay, now Mumbai, to look at the methods of teaching. Bangladesh was struggling to become independent of Pakistan, and the children were invited to illustrate this aspiration. Many of them depicted the Prime Minister, Mrs Gandhi, seated on a cloud and touching the fingers of the infant Bangladesh, a rough evocation of Michelangelo's fresco of God Almighty touching Adam into life on the ceiling of the Sistine Chapel. In the children's minds may have been such Hindu goddesses as Kali or Durga, female divinities of awesome power.

Such women leaders are not role models for most modern British women, who dislike the adversarial style of our politics, back-benchers cheering or shouting at their teams like fans on the football terraces. The wider public doesn't like the style much, either. A different style is emerging and becoming respected, seen in the quiet work of building consensus, finding an agreed way forward, bridging party as well as ethnic, gender and religious divisions. In Europe, Angela Merkel, first woman Chancellor of Germany, exemplifies the new style. So do Ellen Johnson-Sirleaf, the first female President of Liberia, and Gloria Arroyo, President of the Philippines.

The media have not adapted to the new style, which they find dull. They still live in a world of stereotypes, where women politicians fall into four categories: the dragon, the sexpot, the carer or the chum. They concentrate on appearance – hair, clothes, shape – and on private life. That marvellously sparky ex-MP Edwina Currie was once driven to say to a persistent photographer, 'I've got two degrees as well as two legs, you know!' The media's stereotypes can be devastating. The photograph of Tony Blair in 1997 surrounded by scores of new women MPs, some elected through a selection process restricted to women, captioned 'Blair's Babes', was the tersest dismissal conceivable of all that effort and dedication.

The tide, however, rolls steadily in. There are few areas of national or, indeed, of international life in which women do not play an increasing part, reaching the highest positions in once wholly masculine areas like banking, policing, judging, even in the military. But that is not the most important evidence of this quiet revolution. More important is the emergence of men as carers, involved fathers and grandfathers taking pleasure in parenthood. We are learning that the most satisfactory societies are those that welcome the contributions of men and women alike, both to work life and to family life, recognising that they are complementary, and that neither needs to dominate the other.

CHAPTER 9

Junior Minister

My ministerial career in Harold Wilson's 1964 administration began happily. A day or two after the general election of 16 October 1964 I had a call from Kenneth Robinson, the new Minister of Health. He was a slim, elegant man with a small moustache and the disciplined bearing of the naval officer he had been during the war. I did not know him well, though I had met him at a number of Fabian functions. I did know he was someone who believed women had a lot to contribute to politics. His wife, Elizabeth, was a fine artist. I have one of her graceful paintings on my bedroom wall to this day.

As a boy, Kenneth had longed to become a doctor, as his father was before him. But his father died young, and his mother could not afford to maintain him through the many years of training required. He had to leave school at sixteen, and find work as an insurance broker. It took the war to unlock his potential. During his service in the Royal Navy, Kenneth rose to the position of a lieutenant commander in the Royal Naval Volunteer Reserve. In 1949, he won a by-election in St Pancras North, a constituency he represented until 1970. His boyhood dream was realised in an unexpected way when Harold Wilson appointed him Minister of

Health in October 1964, although the position was at that time outside the Cabinet. No other position in the government would have meant so much to him. For Kenneth was not really a party man. His consuming cause was a health service free and accessible to everyone. His other main interests were the arts, in particular the visual arts and opera. Shortly after my election in Hitchin, he invited me to become his Parliamentary Private Secretary.

To be the PPS in the case of many ministers is to be a bag-carrier and errand boy. In the case of Kenneth Robinson, the job offered an immense opportunity to learn how government worked. He took me to departmental meetings and encouraged me to express my opinions, to the surprise of his civil servants. He discussed policy choices with me, and talked about the decisions he had to make, including priorities for expenditure. At that time, much of the money was going into new hospitals to serve new and expanding towns, following the programme initiated by one of his predecessors as Minister of Health in the Conservative government, Enoch Powell. Kenneth loved the NHS, and fought for it with a quiet obstinacy that inspired the devotion of his own department – a sentiment that was not so evident towards his bullying and contentious successor, Dick Crossman. I shared that devotion. I remember when Kenneth showed me the list of hospitals to be constructed. Among them was the Lister in Stevenage, the new town in my constituency. In November 1972 it was formally opened by the Queen Mother. Yet he had never responded openly when I had pleaded with him for the hospital to be built.

On 20 April 1968 Enoch Powell delivered his notorious 'rivers of blood' speech about the perils of allowing Commonwealth immigrants into the United Kingdom. Kenneth was furious. Powell, Kenneth observed to me, had been assiduous in recruiting men and women from the West Indies to staff the National Health Service. It could not have worked without them.

Kenneth was not a politician in the sense of being good at building up support within the Party for himself. Our main office was at the Elephant and Castle, some distance from the House of Commons, which suited Kenneth, who cared much more for his department than for the shenanigans of Parliament. Given that the NHS was Labour's flagship achievement, it was strange that Wilson did not appoint him to the Cabinet in 1964. He may have thought Kenneth was too likely to fight the NHS corner whatever the circumstances, and that judgement may have been correct. Or it may have been that Dick Crossman, an ambitious minister, was already planning a new superministry for himself to head. In one of his restless reshuffles, not only of men and women but often of whole departments, Wilson did create such a ministry, combining Health and Social Security. Dick Crossman was duly appointed to be its Secretary of State. It was an intolerable situation for Kenneth, but allowed Wilson to placate his domineering colleague, among those closest of all in the Cabinet to the Prime Minister.

Relieved of his post in October 1968, Kenneth was sidelined as Minister for Planning and Land, a typical Wilson fudge. It was a Potemkin department, façade without substance, as became clear when the post was abolished a year later. For Kenneth Robinson, a man to whom status meant little and substance everything, the job was an insult. But Harold Wilson, a kindly man, found it very hard to sack people. Fortunately Kenneth proved a great success in life beyond politics, becoming in 1972 Chairman of the English National Opera, and later the author of a well-received biography of Wilkie Collins.

In April 1966 I moved into my first formal ministerial post, Parliamentary Secretary, the lowest rung on the political ladder. The Ministry of Labour, to which I was to go, had been described by its minister Ray Gunter as 'a bed of nails'. He was a canny right-winger, born just a few years earlier in the same South Wales mining town as Roy Jenkins. A strong trades unionist, he had been General Secretary of the TSSA, the railway salaried staffs' union, before entering Parliament. Ray was proud of his working-class origins, imbued with instinctive common sense, and unflappable. He had learned how to fight his corner, not least against the hard left in the trades unions. He and his wife had a flat in Artillery Row which they had transformed into a railway-man's cottage, a coal fire in the grate and a green baize cloth over the kitchen table. At the end of a hard parliamentary day, Ray and I would drink mugs of tea there, he in his vest and braces, his wife in her pinafore.

The Ministry of Labour lived in an atmosphere of perpetual crisis, for it was the peacemaker in the many strikes that wrenched the British economy in the 1960s and 1970s, strikes that were to erode support both for the trades unions and for the wider Labour movement. Its timeframe for action was usually twenty-four hours or less. It had a remarkable team of conciliators and arbitrators, led by the peerless Conrad Heron. Shirt-sleeved and exhausted, these civil servants would wrangle for hours over the phone or in the ministry's gloomy meeting rooms, trying to find a basis on which a strike might be averted or settled. The men they dealt with, senior trades union officials, were themselves running scared of their shop stewards.

Ray Gunter had some sympathy with their position, but he knew how easily inflated claims for more pay could wreck the embattled Labour government, for all that it had just been re-elected in March 1966 with a substantially increased majority of ninety-seven. Productivity was poor, and the country was running into a balance-of-payments crisis. It was becoming difficult to sustain Britain's global role. The union leaders understood that too. Conflicting loyalties surfaced at all our meetings, except in those with the hard left. For them a moderate Labour government was a diversion from the path to revolution. They saw no conflict at all.

The National Union of Seamen was one of the unions run by the hard left, and one in a crucial bargaining position. The union called an official strike on 16 May 1966, just six weeks after the re-election of the government. Exports piled up at the ports, and stocks of imported goods, including food and fuel, began to run low. In June, as the strike dragged on, Ray Gunter became ill in the House of Commons and was compelled to take sick leave. I was the only other minister in the Department, so decisions had to come to me. I also had to attend the Cabinet, reporting occasionally to my dauntingly senior colleagues on the day-to-day developments of the strike and our efforts to end it. On the most critical matters the Prime Minister was consulted. From beginning to end, he took a close interest in what was going on, interpreting the strike as a conspiracy by 'a tightly knit group of politically motivated men', a description that stirred controversy among his Cabinet colleagues.

The new government's key members had decided not to devalue sterling. In this, they were influenced by still burning memories of Ramsay MacDonald's Labour government, re-elected in 1929. That government had resigned over a financial crisis in 1931, which was followed by MacDonald's becoming head of a national government, mainly of Conservatives but including some Liberals, at the behest of the King. The Liberal Party split on the issue; those who joined the government were to be called 'National Liberals'. Ever afterwards he had been reviled as a traitor to the Party by many Labour MPs. In addition, many Commonwealth countries, including India and Australia, held a large part of their reserves in sterling, and would feel utterly betrayed by a devaluation. Ministers believed that, to maintain international confidence in the currency, the seamen's demands must be resisted.

By constitutional convention, a Parliamentary Secretary and a Permanent Secretary are of equal status. So, if they disagree, a third and more senior person must resolve the difference between them. Given Ray Gunter's absence, there was no such senior minister in the Department, and it was the Prime Minister who had to resolve our disagreements. The Ministry of Labour's Permanent Secretary in 1966 was Sir James Dunnett. A gruff and short-fused civil servant of the old school, he had firmly opposed the appointment of a woman minister to his Department, betting – wrongly – that Ray would share his prejudices. He now reinforced that earlier opposition by refusing to speak to me. He would offer his advice only to the Prime Minister. For several fraught weeks, as the strike wore on, the subtle and charming Deputy Secretary, Denis Barnes (whose wife Patricia was a well-established novelist), had to shuttle up and down the corridors conveying my thoughts to Sir James, and his to me.

The seamen's strike was settled early in July for a wage increase well above inflation that deeply damaged the government's anti-inflationary policies. Inevitably, sterling weakened, and the cost of Britain's role east of Suez became increasingly hard to sustain. As voluntary restraint on wages crumbled, the government fell back on its second line of defence, a statutory prices and incomes policy. Such a policy attracted the furious opposition of both the left, including the trades unions, and the right, including the employers' organisations. Frank Cousins, the Minister of Technology and former General Secretary of the Transport and General Workers' Union, resigned in a huff. He had not been an effective minister, for he could never get used to the constitutional restraints of ministerial accountability. Nevertheless, his going dealt a further blow to the government's relations with the unions.

Hammering the prices and incomes policy into place against such massive resistance was the kind of job George Brown, Deputy Prime Minister and First Secretary for Economic Affairs, positively relished. George was a force of nature, brilliant, unpredictable and capricious. Caution had been left out of his personality. He was the Italian tenor of politics, unable to keep his feelings to himself, unable to hold a drink, even a modest sherry, and unable to suppress his anger at his fellow ministers' lack of loyalty towards him.

His innovative, burgeoning mind had never been disciplined by the conventions and constraints of a higher education. Consequently, he was more original than the rest of us, but also hugely impatient and highly sensitive. Like Jim Callaghan, he was very conscious of his educational limitations compared to most of his colleagues. Labour politicians of an earlier era had accepted that the Labour Party was a marriage between intellectuals and trades unionists, each bringing to the table his or her experiences and interests. But as higher education expanded to take in a growing proportion of the population, those who had never had access to it began to feel its absence more keenly.

Bill Rodgers, my friend from university days, now Parliamentary Under-Secretary at the Department of Economic Affairs, and I were the junior ministers responsible, under George, for getting the contentious Prices and Incomes Bill through Parliament. George's intermittent presence at the committee scrutinising the bill was not much help to us. His rhetorical, impassioned support fanned the flames of opposition. Hour after hour we argued in committee, once for thirty-six hours on end.

Only the euphoria of exhaustion kept us going. The committee's chairman, Harold Lever, a man of high intelligence and even temper, used wit and sympathy, qualities he possessed in abundance, to steer the bill through the House. On the morning after the long committee hearing, he invited me back to his luxurious flat in Eaton Square to have a bath before the final meeting started again in a couple of hours' time. Resting in the marble bath with its gold taps, and then eating breakfast served on a tray by a butler, with a crisp white tablecloth, coffee and croissants, restored my good humour. Harold and his wife Diane had understood exactly what was needed to keep me going. On that last day, as the committee stage finally came to an end, George Brown seized me in an impromptu dance. 'Squeeze and be loved!' he bellowed. 'Squeeze and be loved!'

*

After nine months at the Ministry of Labour, I was promoted in January 1967 to be a Minister of State at the Department of Education and Science, in charge of schools. The Department was housed in an ugly, heavily reinforced building in Curzon Street, formerly the wartime headquarters of MI5. It had a flotilla of ministers, three Ministers of State and a Parliamentary Secretary, as well as a formidable Secretary of State. 'You are going from a ministry where the time scale is twenty-four hours to one where it is eternity,' Denis Barnes told me. It took me twenty years to realise that he was right.

My new Secretary of State was Anthony Crosland, described by Dick Crossman as the Labour Party's only other thinker. Tony was a man who relished intellectual argument. More than any other minister I have ever known, he surrounded himself with clever, iconoclastic friends and acquaintances, people who challenged his ideas and criticised his policies. He conducted a perpetual think-tank in his own home, inviting anyone interested in education to come and discuss their ideas with him. Some of the regular participants would clash sharply with Tony, though others kept silent, wary of his savage tongue. But he never rubbished anyone who put forward a serious, well-thought-out case, however much it might be at odds with his own thinking. He was an impatient man; he could be merciless to the time-wasters, the pompous and the vague. For Tony was a man with a purpose, indeed a vision, the vision of a classless society where every child would have the opportunity to fulfil his or her potential. He had set out that vision in his book *The Future of Socialism*, published in 1956. Now he had the opportunity to make that vision a reality.

I was included in his 'brains trust' as a regular member, not least because Tony respected my husband Bernard's intellect and debating skill and invited him as well. On Saturday nights, the regular time for the brains trust, we would be firmly told that there would be a break in proceedings, when Tony, as regular in his Saturday habits as I was in attending Mass on Sundays, would watch *Match of the Day*, a glass of whisky in his hand, slippers on his feet, sometimes wearing his old Para beret and jacket to help him feel utterly relaxed. Before and after this sacrosanct time, we would discuss comprehensive schools, tertiary and sixth-form colleges, how to integrate the state system and the public schools, how to encourage the flock of recently created polytechnics to pioneer new forms of higher education rather than mimic the traditional universities. Abolition of the eleven-plus examination, under which less than a quarter of the nation's children were selected for a grammar school education, was our guiding star.

Tony had inherited from Michael Stewart, his quiet but equally committed predecessor, Circular 10/65, which required every local education authority to submit a plan for going comprehensive. In October 1966, fortified by the increase in Labour's majority, Tony had reinforced the message by linking school building to an LEA's willingness to go comprehensive. Money would not be forthcoming for new selective schools. The only lever he possessed to get LEAs to comply was the power to approve or reject school building proposals, and even that power was heavily qualified since most new school building was needed for 'roofs over heads' as the tide of children born in the baby boom, between 1958 and 1962, surged into the primary schools.

Education at that time was almost wholly devolved to the county and borough councils. So much depended on the goodwill of the education administrators in the counties and the cities, for we knew it would be difficult to get the legislation we wanted through Parliament. There was, fortunately, a lot of goodwill. Education committees on the whole disliked selection, and parents were increasingly resentful when their children failed the eleven-plus because they could see how that failure would constrain their future job opportunities. The economy was demanding more school leavers with good literacy and numeracy, as well as other skills. As I started working on the plans submitted by the local education authorities from all over the country in response to Circular 10/65, the strength of support for comprehensive schools became obvious. But there were some authorities that were strongly opposed. Some, like Kent and Tameside, openly fought us. Others, like Norfolk, simply failed to respond. This last was the cleverer way to deal with our imprecations, but only worked for authorities with slow-growing child populations that had little need for new schools. It took a long time for the overloaded Department to catch up with these practitioners of peaceful resistance.

Local education authorities were encouraged towards a new, comprehensive, system by a generation of parents who no longer accepted the stagnant class divisions of the pre-war years, and wanted much greater opportunities for their children. Education was already benefiting from the inflow of emergency-trained teachers, and from the recruitment of outstanding men and women as education administrators and inspectors. The establishment was changing out of all recognition. As early as the mid-1950s, the first experimental comprehensive schools were launched, in Anglesey and soon afterwards in Leicestershire. From the point of view of local authorities in rural areas, or those comprising a mixture of towns and villages, comprehensive schools were a cost-effective way to meet parents' ambitions for their children. Because they were initiated by local authorities and not by the central government, they took many forms.

That comprehensives had parental support was clear from the pace of change. In 1965, before Michael Stewart's first circular, on encouraging comprehensive schools, 8.5 per cent of children in the eleven-to-fifteen age group attended comprehensive schools. Six years later, the figure was 35 per cent, and ten years after that, 85 per cent. This extraordinary transformation was not mainly due to central government policy. Indeed, the Department's weapons were limited to the school building programme and to persuasion. The movement continued remorselessly under Labour and Conservative governments alike, not only because most local authorities favoured comprehensive schools, but so did most parents and most teachers. It was a reform that had, like the 1944 Education Act, broad public support. Local education authorities that were adamantly opposed, like Kent, have kept their selective systems right up to the present day. Their results are not great advertisements for the old way, being little better than average overall.*

Some strongly Conservative authorities, like those in the West Country, Devon and Somerset, were enthusiasts for the comprehensive system, though many of their county councillors were products of private schools. Some Labour authorities, like Durham, were far from keen, since many of their councillors were products of grammar schools. Much depended on the personal opinions of local leaders, or of their education officials. It was only later, in the 1970s, that comprehensive schools became political footballs, following the organised attacks on state education by the so-called Black Paper writers. The Black Papers were written by teachers and educational journalists who were passionate opponents of the comprehensive experiment. The best known was the MP and former grammar school headmaster Dr Rhodes Boyson. But the comprehensive schools as such provided little ammunition for these critics. Outside London and a handful of other inner-city spots, they settled down into a widely accepted neighbourhood system. Most children went to their local primary school and then to a common secondary school. These began to offer a wide range of courses, including those for pupils taking public examinations all the way up to A level, the gateway to higher education.

Not only were the schools rooted in their neighbourhoods; in

---

* Kent LEA ranked fiftieth out of the 148 LEAs in England in 2007. Ten of the 118 worst-performing schools (where less than 15 per cent of pupils achieve five GCSEs at A–C) are in Kent or the neighbouring (also selective) Medway Towns LEA.

the 1960s and 1970s, before the selling-off of council houses, many of those neighbourhoods were themselves socially comprehensive. In the new towns, for example, like mine in Stevenage, up to four-fifths of the housing was owned by the Development Corporation, the appointed body that ran each new town until it had reached its target population. In older towns the proportion owned by the council might be a third or more. Council tenants comprised people with very different jobs and a wide range of incomes; there were a lot of sour jokes about the new Rover standing outside the council house. But the links between school and community were treasured for their own sake, as fibres of civic society. School governors were drawn from that local community and after the Taylor report of 1978, boards of governors included teachers and parents from the schools as well.

What did play into the hands of the critics, not surprisingly, were the antics of a small number of militant left-wing teachers, mainly in London, protagonists of what was called progressive education, eschewing competition and distrustful of discipline. They called themselves the Rank and File. Attending and speaking at the annual conferences of the teachers' unions, held over the Easter period, was one of the crosses junior ministers – and sometimes senior ones, too – had to bear. They were often raucous and hostile, fuelled by the anger of these elements. Many hardworking teachers were disinclined to give up their Easter holiday to attend them.

The newspapers routinely reported the conferences, but what attracted their attention even more were the occasional outbursts of militancy in individual schools. The most notorious of these took place in Islington, where for eighteen months between 1974 and 1975, a radical majority of teachers at William Tyndale School, led by headmaster Terry Ellis, flatly refused to teach basic subjects or to impose any kind of discipline on their pupils. These tedious requirements, in the view of the Tyndale teachers, were all part of class brainwashing. Parents complained bitterly, and then began to withdraw their children from the school. The events at William Tyndale fed into the picture of trendy, irresponsible left-wing teachers who got away with anarchy while the local authority looked the other way. Certainly the Inner London Education Authority, to which the school was answerable, was slow to intervene. But William Tyndale was a primary school, not a comprehensive. Its problems were the unaddressed problems of the inner city, not those of the comprehensive school.

Politically, London was sharply divided between the Conservative-dominated suburbs and the Labour-dominated inner area. It was also more socially divided than much of the rest of England, apart from a few major cities like Manchester and Birmingham. It was in these socially divided urban areas that battles over comprehensive schools were most acute. The ILEA worked hard to establish a comprehensive system within a context of old school buildings, separated sites, and differing parental expectations. It had gifted and highly radical leadership from Frances Morrell, from 1983 to 1987. It stirred up enough controversy to be abolished by the Thatcher government in 1990.

On the whole, the partnership between the local authorities and the Department of Education and Science worked well. Secretaries of State in those days were rather like American presidents – they operated by persuasion. To get anywhere they had to carry with them powerful partners, in the shape of the local authorities and the teachers' unions. Once the specific grant for education was abolished in favour of a general rate support grant, the education authorities had to fight their corner against all the other demands upon the local authorities. The LEAs at first banded together in an organisation called the Association of Education Committees, led by a redoubtable and canny negotiator, Sir William Alexander, who knew every trick in the complex game of rate support grant. To strengthen them, the AEC was superseded by a new Council of Local Education Authorities, for which Sir William had only scorn. The weakness of the LEAs lay in their dependence on central government for almost all their expenditure on education. But that weakness was not exploited in the 1970s.

The Crosland vision, which I shared, was one of an inclusive, cohesive society of which the schools would be the building blocks. It was not that of a narrowing ladder, with pupils falling off at every rung. Tony was not sentimental about children. Indeed, I don't think he particularly liked their company. But he cared passionately about equality, and was driven by a controlled anger against the privileges, patronage and preferment that so clutter up British society. Because he knew exactly what he wanted to achieve, few of the counter-arguments deflected him, but they did serve to make his policies consistent and robust. He conducted his Department collegially, so that everyone, however junior, was encouraged to express his or her own views. Reticence or syco-phancy had no place in those exchanges. Fortunately, Tony had many remarkable civil servants in his Department; some already enthused about the ending of selection. The most formidable of these was Toby Weaver, a man with his own agenda. He sold Tony on the idea of a binary higher education system – traditional uni-versities on the one hand, and on the other, polytechnics based on the earlier concept of technical colleges promoted by David Eccles, another of Tony's Conservative predecessors. Tony's famous Woolwich speech on 27 April 1965, drafted by Weaver, set out the concept in some detail.

Tony wanted to attract some of the new wave of students who would emerge from the comprehensive schools towards more applied, practical higher education. He was very much aware that Britain lacked both entrepreneurship and advanced technical skills. He also knew that most higher education institutions yearned to be universities, and that, once they achieved that status, they would tend to copy the traditions of the long-established ones. Tony's Permanent Secretary, Sir Herbert Andrew, was a tradition-alist, but one who understood the limitations of selection for secondary education. He was a man of detail rather than strategy, so that he and Tony worked amicably together. But he was no six-ties radical. When I arrived, the second woman minister in his Department, he was troubled. 'I have no young woman at present that I can release to be your private secretary,' he told me. Coming from the rough-and-tumble of the Ministry of Labour, I found this odd. 'Well, give me a man,' I said. Sir Herbert looked shocked. 'But Minister,' he replied, 'you might be travelling. You might need . . . uh . . . a safety pin!'

Like other public-school-educated socialists, Tony was a bit of a romantic about the traditional industrial working class, a char-acteristic he shared with Tony Benn, whom he called Jimmy and loved dearly. He liked to think of himself as Grimsby man, iden-tifying with the likes and dislikes of the Lincolnshire east-coast constituency that elected him in 1959. Grimsby was a big fishing port in Tony's day; work was tough and often conducted in the bitter cold, rain and sleet from the North Sea. Watching football and drinking beer were among the few diversions in this hard life, and Tony fiercely identified with both. As well as snobbery, Tony hated Puritanism, perhaps because he had been brought up within that sternest of sects, the Plymouth Brethren. As a young eco-nomics don at Oxford, he had sometimes seemed to be trying to shock the ghosts of his ancestors. By the time I came to know him well, he had discovered the delights of a marvellously happy rela-tionship with Susan Barnes, whom he later married, herself a fine journalist of high intelligence and acute sensibility.

Given that I was the second female Minister of State in his Department – later to be joined by a third, Alice Bacon – Tony was depressed at my arrival. We, this monstrous regiment of women, Jennie Lee, Alice Bacon and myself, were a varied bunch. Tony was scared of the forceful Jennie. He used to ask his private secretary, that most intimate of Civil Service functionaries, to arrange his diary so that he never had more than fifteen minutes with Jennie. She was Minister of State for the Arts, specially appointed to that post by Harold Wilson, and saw herself as an autonomous minister charged with getting as much money as possible for them. Tony found her approach of nagging and pleading combined hard to deal with. It made little difference in any case, he told me, because Jennie felt in no way constrained by her formally junior role as Minister of State: if Tony didn't concede what she demanded, she would go straight to Harold and get the money anyway. Her instincts were sharp. She realised that Harold carried a burden of guilt about her late husband Nye Bevan, the man he had once resigned with on the issue of health charges, for having distanced himself from his former left-wing associates. She could rely on that sense of guilt to get her what she wanted.

Comprehensive schools in the 1950s, when a few experiments were initiated, and even in the 1960s, were not a matter of particular contention between the parties. Edward Boyle, Minister of Education in Macmillan's government, had been cautiously in favour (though his local party was less enthusiastic). When he retired from politics in 1970, to become Vice-Chancellor of the University of Leeds, I asked him why. By way of reply, he told me that his agent had been to see him in 1965 about the bill to abolish capital punishment, on which there was to be a free vote. Edward told him he would be voting for abolition. 'Sir Edward, Sir Edward!' cried the agent. 'We've given you race relations. We've given you comprehensive schools! For God's sake, give us capital punishment!'

The issue of comprehensive schools did not so much divide the parties, then, as divide traditionalists from modernisers within the parties. If County Durham's all-Labour Education Committee disliked them as much as did Conservative Kent, Conservative Devon was as willing to experiment as Cheshire. 'My son wouldn't have got through the eleven-plus,' a leading Conservative county councillor told me, 'so we had to send him to a private school, but I think it's a first-rate idea, and I'd have sent him to a comprehensive if there'd been one.'

Working with Tony Crosland was immensely stimulating. Everything either he or I wanted to do was tested by the critical intelligences of Michael and Sasha Young, John Vaizey and Tyrrell Burgess, Christopher Price and many others. Unlike most leading politicians, Tony did not restrict his circle to disciples and sycophants. He enjoyed argument, and wanted to pit his own ideas against the best brains he could muster.

I was keen to persuade Tony that we could accept smaller comprehensives than the very large ones with which the experiment began. Parents understandably disliked vast schools where the head teacher did not know the names of the pupils, and where children coming up from the small and friendly primary schools felt engulfed in a sea of others. But since comprehensives had to offer all their pupils the opportunity to take Ordinary and Advanced level examinations, they had to have sixth forms, and these had to be of a viable size. This, in turn, determined the size of the school. In areas where only a quarter or a third of the children stayed on after the age of sixteen, a viable sixth form offering a choice of subjects at A level might require as many as ten or twelve entering forms. Where half or more of the children stayed on, the school could have as few as five. After much discussion, Tony allowed some LEAs to go ahead with small comprehensives. One of them was Hertfordshire, my own county.

While I was Minister of State for Education I devoted some of my energies to starting nursery classes and nursery schools. Growing numbers of married women were going out to work, and were looking for safe carers for their children. Then, as now, there were not enough nursery places, and many women had to resort to untrained childminders. Some were good, but others took on as many infants as they could, lining them up in cots with a view to keeping them quiet. I envisaged maintained nursery schools to be central hubs for the care of young children: they would run book and toy libraries, and training courses for childminders, as well as keeping an eye on the minders in their immediate area. As happens so often, however, I was not in the Department long enough to see my ideas bear fruit.

I enjoyed Tony's leadership for only eight months, between January and August 1967. Indeed, he was the Secretary of State for only two and a half years. But in that short time he had changed the character of his Department into one suffused with the comprehensive ideal; he had given the Labour Party a goal to work for; and he had put into practice the tenets of social democracy, equal opportunity and social justice. He was never again, after his stint at Education and Science, in a position to further these objectives. But he had begun a process that had a lasting effect on British society.

Yet in one respect Tony was bounded by his times. He had little feeling for diversity, and neither gender nor race equality imbued him with the passion that class discrimination engendered. He hardly noticed the discrimination against girls and women that undoubtedly thrived in educational circles, not least the strongly held belief that girls were no good at science and mathematics, the so-called hard subjects. Determined to tackle poverty, he was not notably aware of the poverty among ethnic or national minorities, some of them of long standing, like the black Britons of Cardiff's Tiger Bay and the Irish and black communities of Liverpool. I suspect Tony would have said that he approached poverty as a problem to be remedied whoever the poor might be.

And this he did. His determination to counter the educational consequences of poverty was demonstrated by the successful creation of Educational Priority Areas, which attracted extra funding for teachers and for schoolbooks and equipment in the poorest areas. Ministers have wrestled with the problem ever since, but none have come up with a more successful formula. They rarely look behind them at the achievements of their predecessors, always believing they have a better answer.

In August 1967 Tony was moved to the Board of Trade, to be

replaced by Patrick Gordon Walker, elected in March 1966 for Leyton in northeast London, the constituency that had rejected him little more than a year before. I found him cautious and conservative. In my absence on a family holiday, Alice Bacon, the Minister of State newly appointed to the Department, firmly ordered the files on schools to be moved into her office, and used her seniority to persuade the compliant Gordon Walker to switch me from schools to higher education and science.

The science portfolio I found fascinating. I visited Jodrell Bank to hear Bernard Lovell explain how his radio telescope could probe back into space and time to tell contemporary human beings about the origins of the universe. I went to CERN in Geneva, and watched atoms being smashed in a proton accelerator, the fragments leaving traces in a bubble chamber that revealed the complexities of subatomic structures, the world in a grain of sand. I saw, at the Rutherford Laboratory, an early experiment in fusion forcing together the atoms of a cat's eye – not the real thing but the tiny sparklers used to mark roads. I felt privileged to be the sole student of these glittering tutorials from the best scientists in the country. Many were also among the best scientists in the world, for the freedom and autonomy then granted to research scientists in this country attracted brilliant men and women from all over.

My new ministerial role, however, was not to be the calm contemplation of the mysteries of science. The student revolution of the late 1960s was waiting in the wings.

I got my first inkling of the coming unrest on a visit to France in 1968 to attend an Organization for Economic Co-operation and Development (OECD) meeting on comparative educational opportunities. I was proud of the British record, nearly a third of students in universities coming from families of skilled and unskilled workers, far above the proportion in most other European countries. But the representatives from the Soviet bloc easily trumped my figures.

I had been duly impressed until a reporter from the French Communist journal *L'Humanité* suggested I ask them how they defined 'working class', and in particular how Communist officials defined themselves. My theoretical knowledge was getting patchy now that I was nearly twenty years distant from my university years, and I had forgotten about the dictatorship of the proletariat. Those officials were part of that proletarian dictatorship, and therefore entitled to describe themselves as working class. If they were part of a social revolution, it was a remarkably self-interested one. As I pondered this interpretation of equality early one morning I watched students outside my hotel window in Paris ripping up the cobblestones, potential ammunition against France's dreaded riot police. Escaping my accompanying civil servants, I went down to the Panthéon. It was occupied by students, and on its hallowed walls was spray-painted the bold slogan 'L'imagination au pouvoir!', an impeccably French call to action.

It was not easy to unravel the motives behind the student revolution of 1968. The Vietnam War had engendered huge opposition among students, sharpened in the United States by the dreaded prospect of being drafted. Indeed, the revolution there began to melt away once the government abandoned selective service, a form of conscription with exceptions for certain categories of young men, in particular those following higher-educational courses. Many a son of an elite family escaped service in Vietnam by pursuing one postgraduate course after another. In some European countries, conditions for the vastly increased cohort of university students were truly grim, herded as they were into huge lecture halls with little or no personal contact with their professors. This was certainly not true of Britain, where students studied in small classes, usually fewer than ten to each lecturer, on fairly generous grants. Moreover, unemployment was low, so graduates could expect to get decent jobs.

The ethos of the time, however, expressed in the lyrics and the beat of popular music, was one of rejection; rejection of the stuffy,

respectable materialism of their parents, rejection of compromis-
ing governments, rejection of the paternalism of the traditional
universities. Sexual freedom, apparently made safe by the invention of the pill, undermined conventional morality, especially
morality based on the fear of pregnancy. The new generation felt
itself to be emancipated.

All over Britain, universities erupted. As Minister for Higher
Education, I had to find out why, and to deal with it if I could. In
Birmingham, the Vice-Chancellor and I were barricaded in his
room, and only managed to escape through the central-heating
ducts. In Edinburgh I stood beside the Principal, Michael Swann,
as he shouted through a megaphone demanding a hearing for us
both. At Essex University, as I went into a students' meeting, a
young woman said to me, 'I wouldn't go in to that lot if I were
you.' The meeting boiled and surged like an angry sea. In
Southampton, seeing hundreds of students gathered around the
steps of the main building to demonstrate against me, I asked the
driver of my car to drive slowly enough for me to leap out and run
into the mob, calculating correctly that the students would fight
among themselves for the privilege of getting at me. My formidable, wry and unflappable Parliamentary Private Secretary, Bob
Mitchell, the MP for Southampton Test, warded off the banners
crashing down on my head.

The student revolution petered out quite suddenly, maybe just
because it lacked in Britain any convincing cause. Ted Short, my
new Secretary of State, appointed in April 1968 as successor to
Patrick Gordon Walker, and I drew up a bill which gave students
representation on university courts and academic boards. Unlike
some of our European neighbours, we refused to yield on assessment or examinations in which students had no voice. Soon, the
exquisite tedium of academic committees blanketed even the
fiercest student revolutionary. They had got what they wanted,
and they found it a hollow prize.

I learned from this experience three things: first, that the political leadership in a democracy must be a blend of toughness and compromise; neither, on its own, leads to a satisfactory outcome. Second, that with a few honourable exceptions, I did not want to share my trench with academics. Few would stay around when the attack came. Third, I discovered that, for the media, the story was everything. I remember descending in the lift from my office in the Department of Education's old building in Curzon Street, still skirted by its protective concrete walls, into a lobby filled with students. They were punishing Ted Short, a dedicated former teacher with impeccable socialist credentials. At the call 'Action!' from the television producer who had got inside with them, they started punching their fists in the air and shouting 'Short OUT!', a cry that punctuated my dreams.

In that hot and revolutionary summer, I managed, through a little selective string-pulling among my American friends, to get myself appointed as page, the person who arranged meetings and interviews, to the Connecticut delegation that was attending the 1968 Democratic Party Convention in Chicago. The city was dominated by Mayor Daley, one of the Midwest's most notorious political bosses. The Convention was in turmoil. The President, Lyndon Johnson, his vision of the Great Society drowned in the mud and blood of Vietnam, had announced that he would not stand again. There was no single evident successor, and the Party was torn between moderate hawks and extreme doves who demanded immediate withdrawal. Foremost among these was the enigmatic poet-statesman Eugene McCarthy, worshipped by the idealists of the peace movement. The Connecticut delegation, a large one, had not been mandated to vote for any particular person by its state caucus, and therefore offered a tempting field for candidates keen to pick up votes. Victories in a state primary could commit that state's delegation. But the final decision on who would be the 1968 Democratic candidate for President would be made by the Convention.

The delegation was minded to vote for Senator McCarthy,

but felt that they should hear from him first. I was sent off to invite him. The senator kept me waiting quite a long time while he finished an interview with the editor of a high-school magazine. He showed little interest in meeting with the delegates from Connecticut. I too admired him, but I was driven to the unwelcome conclusion that he was not serious, although so much was at stake. He was indulging himself in being the centre of attention.

Down in the park that bordered Lake Michigan, politics had indeed become serious. The Yippies, a radical sixties mutant of the Hippies, had set up camp and were proselytising for peace in Vietnam. They were not the kind of group that appealed to Mayor Daley, and he had decided on the very day I visited with two or three other Labour MPs to drive them out. Interested observers, we suddenly found ourselves in the midst of a fierce battle, as the Chicago police, swinging batons and weighed down with revolvers, piled into the astonished Yippies. The police were using Mace, newly deployed to deal with civic disorder, a vicious and stinging powder which could do severe damage if directed at the face. I was fit and fairly young, so it was not hard for me to outdistance the corpulent Chicago officers. But at least one of my parliamentary colleagues, Anne Kerr, was seriously injured. The experience was in sharp contrast to the way in which I saw the then Home Secretary, Jim Callaghan, deal with a more threatening demonstration in Grosvenor Square in the heart of London.

In the autumn of 1968, a march had been planned to assemble at Speakers' Corner in Hyde Park, to protest about the Vietnam War. The route would take the marchers perilously close to the American Embassy in Grosvenor Square, which had been attacked in an earlier demonstration in March of that year. On that occasion, ten thousand people had besieged the Embassy. The demonstration had turned into a violent confrontation with the police. Now, seven months later, the atmosphere in London was

Mark Rubinstein and Rebecca, 12 Phillimore Place, 1964

A party at Tony Crosland's house, 1965, among them Tony and Susan Crosland,
Bernard and Rebecca Williams, and me

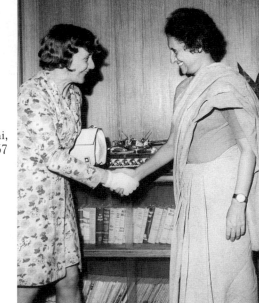

Meeting Indira Gandhi,
Delhi, 1967

Shadow Home Secretary, Brook Green, 1974

My stepmother, Delinda Catlin, with Morag, 1978

A rainy demonstration in support of *Solidarność*, with MPs David Ennals and John Roper, 1980

The SDP gets down to work, March 1981. *Back row:* Bill Rodgers, me, Roy Jenkins, David Owen. *Front row:* Christopher Clark, Eileen Spencer

Launching 'A Fresh Start for Britain' with David Steel, 16 June 1981

SDP candidate meets a horse, Crosby, November 1981

After the count at Crosby, 26 November 1981

Campaigning in Cambridge with Bill Rodgers, 1987

With Dick Neustadt at our engagement party, John F. Kennedy School of Government, Harvard, 1987

Our wedding at Old Hall Green, 21 December 1987. Roy Jenkins and his wife Jennifer beside Dick and me

In New Hampshire
with Dick and
Rebecca, 1987

With my niece
Larissa, 1985

Dick and my
nephew Alexander,
1988

again tense. Thousands of demonstrators were known to be coming, and both the media and the police expected a lot of trouble. London was so empty that Sunday morning, it seemed like a deserted city. Some shop fronts were boarded up. Nervous young policemen waited in blue vans to be summoned.

I had asked Jim Callaghan if I might join him at the Home Office, since many in the crowd would be students, and I felt a sense of responsibility for them. I was also convinced by now that I wasn't bad at dealing with demonstrations. Jim was in a room in the Home Office equipped with closed-circuit television sets linked to cameras monitoring the route. With him were the Metropolitan Police Commissioner, Sir John Waldron, and the senior officer with direct responsibility for the handling of the march, Commander John Lawlor. It was a sunny day, but there was a feeling of apprehension in the room. Jim stood up, relaxed as a cat stretching, and said he felt like a walk. And walk he did, through an empty Whitehall and down to the Embankment where the demonstrators were forming up. 'Nice day for a march,' he said. 'Shouldn't think there'd be any trouble.' The marchers were stunned. Here was the establishment itself, in person, the class enemy, the oppressor, ambling among them wishing them an enjoyable day.

Jim went back to the command room and watched the march take shape. It got angrier by the minute. In Trafalgar Square, hundreds of people were shouting, trying to break through the police cordons to get to Grosvenor Square, away from the agreed route. Scores of police linked arms, shoving them back into place. At one moment, the police line broke, as demonstrators made a concerted effort to reach the American Embassy. Jim looked at the Commissioner. 'Horses, maybe?' Some mounted police began to push the breakaway group back. Everywhere the cameras in our room showed a teeming, heaving pile of marchers and policemen grappling with one another. Jim said calmly, 'I don't think we need anything more. The next demonstration will start where this one stops.' No water hoses, no jeeps, no tear gas, no guns – certainly, all being used against demonstrators elsewhere in the world. Indeed, the demonstration ended with some of the marchers and police officers linking arms and singing, ironically, 'Auld Lang Syne'. As for me, I learned another lesson – never use more violence against your citizens than the absolute minimum needed to maintain order.

CHAPTER 10

A Stint at the Home Office

My final post in the 1966 Wilson government was, as it turned out, at the Home Office. Jim was still there. I had always liked him because he remained human, untouched by the awful arrogance that divorces so many top politicians from the real everyday world. I didn't, however, always see eye to eye with him, especially on the thorny subject of immigration. We confronted one another in particular on whether the government would abide by the promise its predecessors had made, to allow East African Asians whose lives or property were threatened by post-colonial governments to settle in the United Kingdom.

Harold Wilson, always looking for a clever ploy that might resolve problems at a stroke, decided that Jim and I would make a good team to deal with Northern Ireland – the seasoned Protestant Home Secretary and the enthusiastic Catholic Minister of State. Northern Ireland at the time was administered by its own devolved Parliament, but came under the broad umbrella of the Home Office. Civil rights marchers, most of them from the minority Roman Catholic community, were coming into confrontation with a wholly Protestant provincial government. Harold's ploy did not appeal to the Unionists, who had governed the province from Stormont ever since Ulster had refused to join the Irish Free State in 1922.

In my new capacity as a junior Home Office minister with responsibility for Northern Ireland, I was sent on a goodwill tour of Boston in 1969, the purpose of which was to discourage Irish-Americans from collecting money for arms for the Provisional IRA. A favoured venue for this mission was outside Catholic churches after Mass. My companion on the tour was the Irish Consul-General, who had some difficulty persuading Irish-Americans that the Republic of Ireland wanted nothing to do with the IRA.

Like other Home Office ministers, I was a potential target for the Provisional IRA. I had been visited at home in Hertfordshire by my local constabulary, who offered me an alarm, only to admit that it would take at least ten minutes for them to get to me from the nearest police station in the event of it going off. With evident relief, we agreed that an alarm was pointless, but I did promise to look under my car before starting it. However, the British Embassy requested protection for me while I was in the United States. The protection was forthcoming, but only in the most grudging way imaginable. Boston's police had not shed their resentment at Britain's role in the history of Ireland, as they perceived it. On my first night in Massachusetts, I slept uneasily in a hotel room with a large policeman snoring on the other side of the door. The next day I was due to move from Boston to Cambridge just across the bridge, the home of Harvard University, where I was to attend a reception in my honour. The reception had been organised at the British Consul-General's request by Richard Neustadt and his wife Bert. Dick, a professor of government at Harvard and an adviser to presidents, had spent a sabbatical year in 1961–2 teaching at Nuffield College, Oxford, and had returned that autumn to undertake his short intensive study for President Kennedy of the crisis following the unilateral cancellation of Skybolt, the weapon the UK planned to rely on for its nuclear deterrent. This mission had brought him into contact with senior civil servants in the Foreign

Office and the Ministry of Defence. The British establishment thereafter regarded him as a trustworthy friend and valuable contact.

The Boston police duly drove me in a small convoy of police cars to the middle of Eliot Bridge, the nearest crossing of the Charles River to where Dick and Bert lived. The convoy stopped, and I was informed that this was the point at which the Boston police district ended. I was turfed out to walk the rest of the way to the Neustadt house, dragging my suitcase. The incident did at least give me a good introductory story for the guests at the reception, and indeed for my hosts.

My responsibilities at the Home Office extended beyond assisting Jim on Northern Ireland to the three 'Ps' – prisons, probation and pornography. Pornography meant that I had to skim a pile of pornographic magazines each weekend to ascertain whether they had stepped over the line as obscene publications, and should be banned. The Civil Service wrapped the pornographic material in brown paper, and then sealed the package with sticky tape, which enabled them to check whether it had been opened or not. After the first day or two of amazed discovery, I found the endless pages of huge breasts and naked women straddling chairs numbingly boring. Heavily made-up, used-looking women, most of them wearing wisps of underwear in pink or black, displayed themselves to the reader. Some photographs suggested sadomasochism – chains and whips in the background, or bonds and manacles ornamenting the bored models. I began to feel a bit sorry for the men who were turned on by pornographic pictures. They seemed such pathetic counterfeits.

The climate on the banning of obscene publications had been transformed by the case of *Lady Chatterley's Lover*, D. H. Lawrence's famous novel, in 1960. It had been the centrepiece of a great battle between distinguished witnesses, including writers, bishops and academics. My father had been among them. The judge found against banning the novel. The successful campaigners went on to press for legislation against allegedly obscene publications, and plays too, to be repealed. That did not happen until after I had left the Home Office, so I was the last of the guardians of public morality. I developed a quick inspector's eye for sadism as I made my way through the pile, and then tried to decide whether pictures of women being whipped while dressed as schoolgirls were demeaning, or might even elicit copycat behaviour among the nation's paedophiles. These I mainly banned. The inescapable conclusion I reached was the extraordinary intensity of the hatred some men feel for women – and the inexplicable willingness of some women to play up to that hatred.

As prisons minister, I decided my first step should be to go to one, not as a visitor but as an inmate. I had seen a little of prisons as an MP, and the one thing I knew for sure was that they were not the holiday camps the tabloids alleged them to be. The prison service in England and Wales still conforms to the Victorian tradition, embracing the twin missions of punishment and rehabilitation. Few things are more evocative than smell, and my nose still recalls the peculiar odour of disinfectant, urine and decay that pervaded the old prisons with their long grey wings around a central hub. 'Slopping out' was the daily routine in most prisons when I was the minister, hence the acrid smell of urine.

Pigeons would get caught in the wire-netted windows, or between the bars and the window panes, and would flap there until they died, rotting grey and white feathers their sole memorial. The small cells had hard narrow cots, and little other furniture; in the most crowded prisons, inmates might spend eighteen hours a day in there. Those serving long sentences were usually able to attend trade classes or work in a workroom at a routine job, but little provision was made for the thousands who were mentally disturbed or illiterate. They were not trained for a job outside crime, and without that, rehabilitation was something of a chimera. Sadly, little has changed since that day.

Becoming an inmate proved to be bureaucratically extremely

difficult, but in the end I managed to get the authorities at Holloway prison to agree that I might spend twenty-four hours there under the guise of being an offender, and they would not inform any of their staff that I was actually a minister. Whether they kept to the promise I do not know, but I did go through the business of being accepted into the prison, stripped and searched, given prison clothes, endlessly laundered and totally lifeless, and put in a stained and grubby cell. I had to explain to my cell-mates, and later during association (the period when prisoners are allowed to spend time together), what I was in for. I decided the hardest to check up on was prostitution, so I told them I was 'on the game'. The 'game' extended to a wide spectrum of women, from the elegant mistresses of Mayfair to the cheap £5-a-go end of the business around mainline stations such as King's Cross and Victoria. So it wasn't difficult to 'associate'. I found the conversation highly enlightening.

One of the worst aspects of prisons at that time was the dearth of washing and toilet facilities. Slopping out meant that at night prisoners had to use a pot or a bucket as a lavatory, and then had to throw the contents out every morning. Showers and baths were few and far between, as were flush toilets, sometimes shared by thirty or forty people. Getting decent toilets into the prisons became one of my minor causes. I battled against obtuse opposition among some of the officials, just to convert a couple of cells in each wing into toilets and washrooms. Even today, many prisons' facilities are grim.

To my surprise, I came to have a high regard for prison officers. With a few exceptions, they were not the bullies or turnkeys I had expected. Many that I met were committed to rehabilitating the men and women in their charge. At that time, the late 1960s, most of the older prison officers were capable people whose prospects had been blighted by an education limited to elementary school. The ceiling was not so much glass as stone. Attracted by a caring job that was also tough, they tried hard to get through to their charges. Theirs was a kind of rough warmth I hadn't anticipated. But the same wasn't invariably extended to me. Some prison officers thought that the appointment of a woman minister to this forbidding job was absurd. In one or two of the prisons I visited, it was made clear that no toilet facilities could be found for me. In others, it was a test of nerves rather than an issue of restraint; prison governors had considerable autonomy, and the radical governor of one top-security prison introduced me to a roomful of convicted murderers, then left me there with my Civil Service secretary for three-quarters of an hour.

My brief sojourn in Holloway prison deepened my respect for the probation service, my third Home Office responsibility. Probation offered those near the end of a prison sentence, or sometimes as an alternative to it, a path back to citizenship and self-respect. Probation officers befriended prisoners but did not pander to them. An inspired idea at the time, probation seems to have been relegated to a minor role in the spectrum of means to deal with crime. I don't know why – maybe because it predates New Labour and New Conservatives and thus seems old-fashioned.

Jim and I worked together harmoniously on Northern Ireland, for we both knew that discrimination had to end, and that power had to be shared. He had an acute political instinct. He could feel in his very being how the public would react to a given decision or action, and indeed how the Labour movement would. Like Herbert Morrison, he possessed as Home Secretary an enviable sense of the balance to be struck between freedom and order. He never overstepped the self-imposed limits on his own power.

But on one issue, already mentioned, we fell out badly: the plight of the East African Asians. In 1968, the Asian residents of Kenya were threatened with expulsion, or worse. These were the men and women who had chosen British citizenship, rather than Kenyan, at the time of the colony becoming independent. They had been promised by the then Conservative government's

Commonwealth Secretary, Duncan Sandys, and its Colonial
Secretary Iain Macleod the right of abode in the United Kingdom
should they be expelled or threatened with the loss of their property or even their lives.

In the 1960s, there had been some nasty racial incidents.
Patrick Gordon Walker, the Foreign Secretary in waiting, had
been defeated first in his Smethwick constituency at the 1964
general election in a bitterly racist campaign, and again at a by-
election in Leyton in 1965, thought to be a safe Labour seat.
Rumblings had come from the Tory right, soon to be articulated
in the oracular and doom-laden prophecies of Enoch Powell, and
the Wilson government was running scared of populist racial prejudice. Jim, observing the impact of Powell, a brilliant orator in
some ways reminiscent of Oswald Mosley, feared an uncontrol-
lable backlash against any substantial immigration of non-whites.
I saw only that the legal rights of these British citizens were being
overridden, despite the pledges of an earlier government.

The received opinion of the time, which I never found convincing, was that harsh controls over immigration were the quid
pro quo for tolerance at home. Of course, there was some truth in
it. Britain, a densely populated country, could not absorb an
unlimited number of immigrants. But to thus argue that we could
take almost none, however strong their claims, conflicted with
our past experience. Immigrants, and in particular those fleeing
persecution, had made a huge contribution to Britain, not least
because of their gratitude to the country that offered them a
haven. They had also borne more than their fair share of deaths
and injuries defending us: think of the Gurkhas and the Fijians.

But the Cabinet would have none of it. The quota for East
African Asians was set at fifteen hundred heads of households plus
their families, whatever promises had been made, and that was
that. Furious at what I saw as a breach of faith, I argued with the
Home Secretary, lobbied my colleagues, and finally organised a
little group of junior ministers, among them Eirene White, Joan

Lestor and Reg Freeson, who were prepared to resign if no concession was made. The concession we got was a tiny one. In his winding-up speech, Jim Callaghan, in a throwaway line, murmured: 'Of course, if they are in danger we'll have to take them.'

I asked Jim if I could seek a meeting with the then Foreign Minister of India, Swaran Singh, to find out whether his country would agree to take the East African Asians temporarily, in the event that threatened members of that community could not get entry immediately to the United Kingdom. Mr Singh gave me a gracious welcome in Delhi, and said that his own country was so big it would hardly notice a few tens of thousands of refugees from East Africa. But on one point he was rightly adamant. The United Kingdom could not renounce its obligation to its own citizens. Those who could not get immediate entry could 'queue' in India, but must retain the right to a legal abode in the United Kingdom. India's Foreign Minister then added cheerily, 'Some will die here, and a lot of others will just decide to stay.'

The anticipated expulsion of Asian Kenyans did not take place in 1968. The possibility did, however, elicit a powerful open letter from Iain Macleod, MP, former Colonial Secretary (1959–61) and one-time editor of the *Spectator*. Writing in the magazine on 23 February that year, Macleod rebuked his former colleague Duncan Sandys, Commonwealth Secretary at the time of Kenya's independence, for trying to abandon the pledge that had been made to Kenyans who opted for British citizenship at the time. 'If I understand your position correctly,' Macleod wrote, 'it is as you told the *Sunday Telegraph*, that it was certainly never intended to provide a privileged backdoor entry into the UK. Leaving aside the emotive words, that is exactly what was proposed: special entry in certain circumstances, which have now arisen. We did it. We meant to do it. And in any event we had no other choice.' He added, even more mordantly, 'Your Kenyan constitution is devastatingly clear. So is Hansard. So are all the statutes. And so therefore is my opposition. I gave my word. I meant to give it. I wish to keep it.'

In 1972 Idi Amin, President of Uganda, did what Jomo Kenyatta had threatened to do in Kenya. He expelled Uganda's Asians, some fifty thousand people, and confiscated their property. Edward Heath's Home Secretary, Robert Carr, made it clear in January 1973 that the government would honour the pledges given at the time of Kenyan independence. He faced with grace and courage the opprobrium of an angry Conservative Party Conference that October. Over the next few months, 28,000 East African Asians came to Britain and thousands more went to India. Now on the Opposition front bench as Shadow Home Secretary, I whispered under my breath 'Amen'.

The publicity associated with being a woman minister, and the fact that I had already spent several years in the United States both at junior high school and as a Fulbright scholar, enabled me to build up my own personal special relationships. I began to be invited to give lectures and seminars. It was a good time for think tanks, and I got involved in two of them, the Aspen Institute and the Chicago Council on Foreign Relations.

The Aspen Institute, in Colorado, was the inspiration of Mortimer Adler, a German immigrant to the United States who was determined to create a new Athens in his adopted country, a place immersed in the great classics which would adapt their teachings for the modern age. Aspen, when I got to know it in the 1970s, was directed by a brilliant and generous internationalist called Joe Slater. He used the money lavishly made available by the Institute's patron, Robert Anderson, chairman of the oil company Atlantic Richfield, to create networks linking liberal-minded intellectuals, and statesmen and women in Europe, Latin America and Africa with influential Americans. Members of these networks met at seminars in Aspen and, later, at European venues such as the Institute's centre in Berlin to debate and discuss the great issues of the day. The Institute's headquarters, seven thousand feet up in the Rocky Mountains, were exciting modern buildings in a carefully cultivated bright green landscape park surrounded by mountains and crystal in the high dry air. To this remote intellectual Valhalla the great and the good found their way. As if all this wasn't enough, Aspen had its own excellent summer orchestra and a cluster of small, smart and expensive boutiques downtown.

Joe Slater had a rare capacity for identifying exceptional people. It was at Aspen that I met some of the most remarkable men and women I have ever encountered. Outstanding even by the Institute's elevated standards was Bohdan Hawrylyshyn who, as a boy, had fled from a displaced persons camp in occupied Germany shortly before he was due to be repatriated to his native Ukraine. He became a lumberjack in the forests of northern Ontario, took an engineering degree at the University of Toronto and by 1968 had become director of the Centre d'Études Industrielles in Geneva, an institution supported by Alcan that trained a new generation of business and industrial managers. Hawrylyshyn became one of the world's foremost thinkers on management. Recognising how rapidly traditional management practices were becoming obsolete, he was among the first to offer short courses for directors and chief executives. He was among those who saw the new Great Crash coming, driven as business and finance were by short-termism and an obsession with the bottom line.

In 1981, Hawrylyshyn started an international management institute in Geneva, at which I used to lecture regularly. In 1989 he returned to his beloved Ukraine to found a similar institute there. I was a member of the board for ten years, and also served on an international advisory body to Ukraine's Parliament with Geoffrey Howe, now Lord Howe of Aberavon, and George Soros. On my frequent visits to Ukraine I followed the country's troubled path to independence.

In 1975 the Shah of Iran, Reza Pahlavi, who had visited Aspen with his wife, issued an invitation to Joe Slater to put together a group of Aspenites to take part in a special conference to be held in Persepolis in honour of his wife, the Shahbanou. The Shah's legitimacy as Emperor of Iran was questionable. His father had occupied the throne in a bloodless military coup and Pahlavi was anxious to do everything he could to establish his right to it. To this end, he had invited many distinguished guests to Teheran to celebrate the twentieth anniversary of his accession, and had himself represented Iran as head of state on high-profile visits abroad. The Aspen conference, with its roll-call of illustrious American participants, was intended to demonstrate yet again the links between the Shah and Persia's glorious history, not least the 2500-year span of the Peacock Throne. I still remember the hoarse voice alleged to be that of the Emperor Darius rumbling from a stone sarcophagus at the opening ceremony. It reminded me forcefully of the Commendatore in Verdi's *Don Juan*.

Joe included me in an otherwise largely American delegation, along with the Australian Foreign Minister Andrew Peacock and his stunningly glamorous wife Susan. Among the American members of the group were Richard Holbrooke, later to become the US ambassador to the UN, and Robert Mann, leader and first violinist of the famous Juilliard Quartet, and his wife Lucy, who were to become great friends.

Persepolis, the centre of the celebrations, was a revelation. I had had no idea that Persian civilisation, the splendour of its art and the beauty of its buildings, rivalled that of Athens, with the difference that Persepolis had suffered much less disturbance from history. We climbed up stairs edged by friezes of chariots, soldiers and dancers in black marble on terracotta walls. We walked on carpets thickly scattered with bright images of birds and flowers.

The moment came for tributes to the Shah. I felt very uncomfortable. I was his guest and I assumed he was a popular leader, but I also knew that he had a brutal secret police force in the Savak, which would tolerate no critics. So, when my turn came, I tried to square my conscience by asking the Shah to deal with these outrages on the grounds that he wanted to be a modern leader admired beyond his own country, and would therefore need to meet these conditions. My speech did not go down well with my American colleagues, many of whom felt I had been discourteous.

The Persepolis party reeked of hubris. It was a hugely expensive celebration in a poor country. It emphasised a claim to the succession that was in fact shaky. In the pitiless words of the *Cambridge History of Iran*, the Persepolis party 'appears to have marked the beginning of an obsession with personal aggrandisement and with military might which substantially contributed to the Shah's overthrow'.*

We went on to Isfahan, a fabulous city of blue and gold mosques, arches and gateways of filigree stone and pilgrims in spotless white robes and turbans, and then to Shiraz. Shiraz was then a city of roses and Moghul gardens, oblong silent pools reflecting the stars and the lanterns in a visual fugue. Ever since that visit, I have been aware of the delicacy and fragility of ancient civilisations. Iran is among the very few that remain.

Dick Holbrooke and I shared an urgent need to find out how strong was the support for the Shah among ordinary Iranians. Neither of us were convinced by the propaganda. So we rustled up a couple of English-speaking Farsi students, hired a car and set off with the Peacocks on the day set aside for a special visit to admire the Shah's famous agricultural revolution. We suspected the farms and villages we would be shown would in fact be showcases for the regime.

A few miles outside Shiraz we found a village with stockaded farms, rather like one of those traditional French domains with walls around them. As we approached in the car, which the villagers probably thought indicated the presence of an official, shutters were pulled down and gates closed. By the time we reached the village, it looked like a place besieged. It took some

* Peter Avery, G. R. G. Hambly and C. Melville (eds), *The Cambridge History of Iran*, vol. 7, *From Nadir Shah to Islamic Republic*, Cambridge University Press, 1991.

time for our student guides to persuade the villagers that we were not from Teheran, or even from a regional office, but visitors from abroad.

Eventually one or two of the braver men agreed to talk to us. The tale they told us was a sad one. Many of their small farms had been commandeered by government officials to form large tracts of land that could be used for industrialised agriculture. The compensation had been small and the opportunities for work on these new estates were non-existent for middle-aged and older farmers. It was a matter of indifference to the government that their means of livelihood had been taken away. They had been promised clean water, but much of this had been diverted to the needs of the agricultural revolution. They were not allowed to keep the Koran or any other religious symbols in their houses nor to carry out Muslim rituals. They seemed to both of us people ripe for revolution should an inspired leader come along, which of course he did four years later – the Grand Ayatollah Khomeini.

Richard and I were sufficiently concerned by our visit to ask to see our respective ambassadors in Teheran. Mine was obviously rather bored by this sudden arrival of an irrelevant Opposition MP. Like his American equivalent, he assured me that nothing I told him was new, the Shah was indeed solidly entrenched on the Peacock Throne and the United Kingdom had the best of all possible relations with the regime.

As a junior minister in Harold Wilson's second administration and a Cabinet minister in his third, I was largely unaware of the personal torments of guilt and fear he endured. He came across to me as businesslike, clever and unpompous. His ministerial appointments, like his policies, took into account the opinions of the Party, both in Parliament and in the country. He could not be fairly accused of cronyism, except in his bizarre choice of Labour peers. His personal and political secretary Marcia Williams has, on occasion, been accused of influencing his selection but she has always denied this. His management of the Cabinet was low-key. He gave everyone a chance to speak. But he made sure there was a core of loyalists who could be counted on, and he arranged the Cabinet agenda with his Cabinet Secretary, Sir John Hunt, in a way that minimised trouble – sometimes by just leaving out items his more irritating ministers were pressing for. In this respect, Tony Benn and I were both affected, for both of us pushed items for Cabinet discussion that were outside our specific Department responsibilities. Wilson's summing up of Cabinet discussions was masterly. I once challenged his conclusion, busily counting heads myself. The Prime Minister abruptly reminded me that summing up was his prerogative.

His strength was a remarkable ability to manage a party that was already deeply divided on ideological lines. He drew on his reputation as a left-winger, established early in his ministerial career and apparently confirmed by his resignation from the Labour government in 1951 over the Chancellor Hugh Gaitskell's rearmament budget. Past left-wing views, however, did not determine his assessment of his colleagues. He was aware that many of his most talented ministers were people of the centre or the right.

Harold Wilson was surprisingly ungrand. Like his predecessor Clement Attlee he was not attracted by money or bright lights. He would have eschewed the modern horror of being a celebrity politician. The Isles of Scilly, his family refuge, were where he spent his holidays, walking the dog and paddling in long, old-fashioned shorts on the edge of the beach. He was approachable, accessible to Labour MPs and to Conference delegates, but he was not naturally sociable. The outer ring of his personality was permeable, but the inner ring was impenetrable. Its guardian was Marcia Williams, flanked by a small kitchen cabinet of confidants and old associates. Marcia's brother and sister both worked for the Wilsons at various times.

I related to Marcia in terms of her office. I accepted that she controlled access to Harold, though I recall no occasion when I wanted to see him that she refused. I treated her with respect, but never sought to be close. I had no idea of her extraordinary influence, and only faint intimations of her acute political mind.

I was puzzled by some characteristics of the Prime Minister, not least his obsession with leaks and the media's treatment of him. Some of the people in his inner ring had business associations with Eastern Europe. In the 1960s and 1970s the Cold War had to be taken seriously. After all, the brutal suppression of Czechoslovakia's Prague Spring had occurred as recently as 1968. There were officials high up in the Intelligence Service who distrusted Harold because of his friends. He was acutely aware of that suspicion, and indeed reciprocated. When he appointed me to the Cabinet, he took me into the Cabinet Room and pointed to a small object in the corner of the ceiling. It was, he told me, for bugging Cabinet discussions. I remember thinking that my boss was getting a bit paranoid. Years later, when I read *Spycatcher* by Peter Wright, former Assistant Director of MI5, I realised that Harold had reason for his suspicion. Margaret Thatcher should have set up a tribunal of inquiry into Wright's attempt to subvert constitutional government. Instead she used the Official Secrets Act and Robert Armstrong, Cabinet Secretary, to try to prevent its publication.

Marcia's influence over Harold was pervasive. Not only did he consult her over political decisions and over management of the Party, he allowed her to determine whom he saw. She made huge demands on his time and energy. He responded to her entreaties even when he was exhausted or burdened by affairs of state.

Explanations of her extraordinary influence over him are many. The tabloids were, as ever, convinced it was sex, and some of them ferreted away – unsuccessfully – to find evidence, including attributing Marcia's children to the Prime Minister. (Their father was in fact Walter Terry, political editor of the *Daily Mail*.) My own opinion is that Marcia's influence over Harold flowed from his concern for her, and guilt. The concern arose from her intense and sometimes volatile personality. The guilt came from distancing himself, and later becoming alienated from, his old left-wing associates. Marcia usually identified herself with them, and their differences became acute over the issue of Britain's membership of the European Community in Wilson's third administration. He had been persuaded that membership was important on economic grounds. She remained implacably opposed. Tensions over Europe both in the Cabinet and in his kitchen cabinet exhausted Harold. His energy drained away and his resignation in March 1976 did not come as a complete surprise. He was haunted by the knowledge that one of his close relatives had developed Alzheimer's at an early age. He was determined to leave office before any such disintegration of his remarkable mind became apparent.

Harold's record as Prime Minister and leader of the Labour Party has been underestimated. As Prime Minister, during a period of unremitting economic difficulty, he maintained full employment but was unable to restrain inflation. Unwilling to break trades union power by allowing mass unemployment, as Mrs Thatcher was later to do, he tried the alternative policy of income and prices restraint – first voluntary, then statutory, then through a so-called social contract, which conceded substantial power over government policies and priorities to the trades union leadership. It failed, but it was a failure rooted in a commitment to social justice.

In his relationship with the United States, then as now the predominant military power, Harold played his cards cleverly, if at the cost of considerable humiliation to himself. Strong pressure was brought to bear on him by Lyndon Johnson, a formidable President and a bully, to commit British troops to the war in Vietnam. Johnson's need for allies was as great as George W. Bush's need for allies in Iraq, for in both cases the war lacked international approval or the imprimatur of the United Nations.

Harold was in a weaker position vis-à-vis the President than was Tony Blair in 2002. Britain's economic position in the 1960s was shaky; indeed, it culminated in the decision to devalue sterling in 1967. American cooperation in lending Britain large sums of money to prop up sterling was vital. Yet Harold managed to maintain reasonable relations with both President Johnson and with his own Parliamentary Party, where passions raged against the war in Vietnam, fuelled by television coverage of the devastating American air attacks. On at least one occasion, the President's resentment of his guest's obstinacy in keeping the United Kingdom out of the war led to the Prime Minister being left in his room without dinner. Harold understood the need to keep his cool. Whatever the humiliation, he swallowed it. What mattered was staying out of the Vietnam War without wrecking the special relationship.

In another way, too, Harold's achievement as Prime Minister has been underestimated. He was without prejudice. He did not judge people on their colour, race, gender or class. Members of his government were drawn from many backgrounds: there were former miners and former academics, trades union officials and landowners. He was the first Prime Minister to appoint women as ministers outside the 'family' departments to which they had traditionally been consigned – with the sole exception of Margaret Bondfield, appointed Minister of Labour by Ramsay MacDonald in the second minority Labour government, in 1929. Now they were appointed to departments that had never had a woman minister before: the Foreign Office, Transport, the Home Office, Economic Affairs, Overseas Development, and as Paymaster-General. Barbara Castle, the pioneer in several of these ministries, once said to me that she was personally responsible for the installation of ladies' lavatories in more ministerial suites than anyone else. I don't believe Harold had a conscious policy of positive discrimination. He simply appointed whoever he thought would be best for the job. His triumph undoubtedly was his success in keeping his truculent and bickering party together. Party unity was always his first and greatest commandment; to achieve it required both imagination and innovation.

His proposal in 1975 to renegotiate the terms under which Edward Heath had taken the country into the European Community bought him precious time. When it became clear that the new (if not very different) terms negotiated by Jim Callaghan as Foreign Secretary could not bridge the divisions between the pro- and anti-Europeans within the Party, he seized upon the device of the referendum, so temptingly proffered by Tony Benn. He then for the first time in history allowed his ministers to argue publicly with one another, suspending collective Cabinet responsibility for this issue alone. He kept himself out of the national debate until very near the end, when the victory of the Yes campaign seemed probable. The outcome enabled him to reunite the Party after the campaign, and by the time its new-found unity had fractured again, he had left office.

CHAPTER 11

Private Grief, Public Unrest

I had moved to Furneux Pelham in an effort to save my marriage but once Bernard had gone it proved a difficult move to sustain. During the week I saw little of Rebecca, who was now at a local primary school. Margaret Curry and her husband Michael had stepped in to hold things together, but they wanted to retire to Ireland so it could not be a permanent solution. I decided to move back to London. The Labour government had been defeated by Edward Heath's Conservatives in 1970, so my career as a minister had come to an end for the time being. As a Shadow minister, I could get home in the early evenings, even if I often had to return to the House later for a 10 p.m. vote. Furthermore, in Opposition it was no longer my responsibility to be present for every important vote, whenever it was called, to ensure there was a majority for the government.

My former sister-in-law Jennifer, with whom I had remained on close terms since her divorce from my brother John, had been living with her three sons, Daniel, Timothy and William, in Brook Green, Hammersmith. She had been seeing quite a lot of John's friend and mine, Robert Balfour, who ran his family's estate in Scotland near Clackmannan, on his infrequent visits to

London. Robert, who was single, eventually asked Jennifer to marry him, and she agreed to move to Scotland with her two younger sons. My purchase of her Brook Green house in an attractive Victorian terrace surrounding a small common suited us both.

Hammersmith was at this time still a selective borough, so Rebecca had to sit the eleven-plus examination in order to get into a grammar school. She became a pupil at a direct-grant school, Godolphin and Latymer, a good traditional girls' school only a short distance from our new house. She was eleven now. I offered a pleasant third-floor flat in my house to the grown-up son Tristan, and later to the daughter, Amanda, of my friends Kenneth and Betty Allsop, in exchange for their company for Rebecca. The arrangement worked well, but only because Rebecca was a conscientious and hard-working pupil determined to do well in her O levels, and, fortunately for me, she was blessed with similar friends.

The catastrophe that had overtaken my private life had coincided with a crisis for the government of which I was a member. Many people are familiar with the experience of crises coming in droves, so that there seems to be no escape from them. It seemed like that to me in 1970. Everyone had expected the Labour government to be re-elected. Indeed, the odds on a Labour victory were so long that the bookies stopped taking bets. On 12 June, six days before polling day, NOP gave Labour a lead of 12.4 per cent.

Yet confidence in the government was fragile. The pound had been devalued on 18 November 1967, despite heroic efforts by the Prime Minister to avoid any such disaster. In the first three years of Wilson's two 1960s governments, between 1964 and 1967, devaluation had been the word no one could speak. Behind the scenes, senior ministers clashed bitterly on what was the best strategy. Tony Crosland held that the government should have devalued immediately on its re-election in 1966. Roy Jenkins, at that time Home Secretary but after November 1967 Chancellor of the Exchequer, shared that view. I agreed with Crosland, but as a junior minister I was outside the decision-making loop and not even supposed to know what was going on. We junior ministers had in fact quite a good idea of what was happening. Most of us believed devaluation was preferable to the alternative, a savage deflation. But when it was announced, belief in Labour's ability to manage the economy was badly damaged. Furthermore, devaluation was slow to rectify the balance of trade. The troubling run of monthly trade deficits in 1967 that had preceded devaluation continued into 1969. By the autumn of that year, however, the economy had dramatically turned the corner. In September there was a huge rise in exports. Figures for the first three-quarters of the year showed the government well on track for its target of a £300 million surplus on the balance of payments – indeed, even for a surplus on visible trade, an almost unthinkable achievement. Edward Heath, the Conservative leader, predicted that this recovery would not last – and that was the issue on which the election turned.

There was another source of apprehension about the government's ability to govern – its stormy and sometimes servile relationship with the trades unions. It is hard now to credit how much time and effort Harold Wilson and his ministers devoted to sorting out strikes and other industrial disputes. Trades union leaders now expected to find themselves summoned to the Ministry of Labour, or even to No. 10 Downing Street, for beer, sandwiches and hours of talk. Their ability to compel senior ministers and even the Prime Minister to disrupt their schedules for long periods fed their sense of their own importance. But it did little to smooth the path of industrial relations. For the paradox was that these very same leaders were losing control over their members. The power of shop stewards, working day to day in the same workplace as ordinary members and sharing their grievances, was growing; that of union officials, often elected on a small turnout of members' votes, was diminishing.

The re-election of the Labour government in March 1966 had been swiftly followed, in May, by the national seamen's strike; it lasted for six weeks. The Liverpool dock strike in October 1967 had held up £100 million worth of exports and fed the loss of confidence in the pound that preceded the devaluation of sterling. So the government was harried by industrial troubles, and the powerful influence of the trades unions within the broader Labour movement meant that legislation to limit industrial action was out of the question.

Now, in the run-up to the 1970 general election, Harold Wilson again had to devote time and attention to an industrial dispute, diverting him from the campaign. The printers' unions had threatened to strike on 9 June. But so deep were the internal differences between SOGAT, which represented the less skilled printing trades, and the National Graphical Association, that they would not even agree to sit around the same negotiating table. Although the strike was settled a few days before the election, voters were reminded of their government's impotence in the face of union power.

The single most important factor reversing the public's favourable view of the government was not the printers' strike, however, but the publication three days before election day of trade figures that seemed to bear out Heath's charge that the government was not out of the woods as far as the economy was concerned. Heath had talked during the election of 'a bogus story of sham sunshine', an unattractive phrase that nonetheless caught the mood of a questioning public. The May figures seemed to bear him out – a trade deficit of £31 million. It was little use the government pointing out that the figures included over £18 million for two jumbo jets. Nor did the government know, at that point, that the Treasury had seriously underestimated the value of exports. It was too late.

One month's trade figures would not have so radically altered the course of the election had there not been a deep-seated

unease about the administration's economic and industrial management. It would have taken more than the two-year record of
an outstanding Chancellor of the Exchequer, Roy Jenkins, to
eradicate that unease. Persuaded that the Labour government
had still not mastered the balance-of-payments problem, the
public voted in the Conservatives. Fortunately for me, they did
not vote in a Conservative MP in the Hitchin constituency.
Many of my Stevenage constituents were employed in fairly well-
paid industries, aerospace and engineering, and the new town
had grown rapidly over the previous four years. On their daily
lives the government's economic agonies had not made any deep
impact.

The Conservative government that came into office with a majority of thirty had one overriding objective: to take the United
Kingdom into the Common Market. That objective had at last
been made possible by the retirement from the presidency of
France, in 1969, of General Charles de Gaulle, whose suspicion of
Britain as a Trojan horse for the United States had on two occasions led him to veto its application for membership. It seemed
just that Edward Heath, who had spent three hard years as Lord
Privy Seal from 1960 to 1963 trying to negotiate terms for British
entry, only to be derailed by de Gaulle's veto, should now have
another opportunity. For Heath believed unswervingly that
Britain's destiny lay with the European Community. As his autobiography *The Course of My Life* made plain, his commitment to
constructing a new Europe that included Britain went back to the
beginning of the Second World War.

  For the next three decades, British politics was to be racked by
dispute over Britain's relations with the European Community. As
had been the case with the Corn Laws in the nineteenth century,
divisions within political parties outweighed the divisions
between them. And, as with the Corn Laws, the arguments were
not about making a single important decision. They were about

Britain's future in the world. Harold Wilson had made a new application for membership of the EEC in May 1967, with the support of a clear majority of the Cabinet and of the Parliamentary Labour Party. That application too had been vetoed by de Gaulle, to the relief of some members of the Cabinet. But Wilson had said, after the French veto, that he would not take no for an answer. That enabled Heath to present a common position.

In Opposition, however, Labour moved rapidly towards rejection of the EEC. The Party's shift from government to Opposition had freed all the critics and sceptics to mobilise against it. Some believed the Commonwealth offered an alternative grouping, though the struggle with white settlers in Rhodesia and black nationalists in East Africa somewhat lessened its attractions. Many critics were convinced that the EEC was a capitalist conspiracy that would block Labour's policy of nationalising key industries. They compared European social democracy not with the patchy reality of socialist government in Britain, but with the socialist Utopia of their dreams. For by any objective standard, the social model adopted in northern European countries was far ahead of that in Britain, in respect of the quality of public services, the level of social benefits and the size of the gap between rich and poor.

The politics that swirled around the European question had little to do with objective standards, though, and everything to do with stereotypes and ancient prejudices. At the Labour Party Conference of October 1970, a resolution opposing British entry to the EEC was almost passed. By the spring of 1971, several Shadow ministers were signalling their opposition to membership. Such is the adversarial nature of British politics that it is difficult to maintain a bipartisan policy on any important issue. In the process of fighting Mr Heath's government, the Labour Opposition convinced itself that, since he was wrong on everything else, he must be wrong on Europe too.

Scenting an opportunity, the Labour Party's National Executive

Committee, where the antis now held a bare majority following Tony Benn's conversion to their cause, demanded a special conference. It became clear that the special conference, to be held in July 1971, would vote against British entry to the European Economic Community, though not necessarily by the two-thirds majority required to confirm a Party policy. Harold Wilson, the Houdini of politics, was now faced with the classic dilemma: how to hold his riven party together. He could not afford to lose the left, who were still his strongest supporters. He did not favour ruling out membership completely. He was, however, anxious not to offend the pro-Europeans, either, among whom were his most influential and able ministers. He came up with a fudge so ingenious that only a master chef could have produced it.

Harold told the July special conference that, had he been Prime Minister, he would not have accepted the terms Edward Heath had negotiated. Labour should unite against membership on the terms offered. As Ben Pimlott pointed out in his biography of Wilson, nobody believed him.* But he had found the one way to hold his party together, and for Harold that was the bottom line.

At the Labour Party's annual conference in Brighton in October 1971, a resolution opposing British membership of the European Economic Community on the terms negotiated by Edward Heath was carried overwhelmingly. This decision persuaded Harold and his Chief Whip, Robert Mellish, to impose a three-line whip – the toughest discipline there is – on Labour MPs voting at the end of the forthcoming six-day debate on Europe. A Shadow Cabinet called on 19 October, just before the debate began, endorsed the decision. Imposing the three-line whip broke promises made to Roy Jenkins and the other pro-Europeans by both Wilson and Mellish that there would be a free vote, a breach made even more painful by Heath's tactically wise decision to

* Ben Pimlott, *Harold Wilson*, HarperCollins, 1992.

declare a free vote for the Conservatives. I was among the sixty-nine Labour Party MPs who voted with the government to endorse entry.

1970 was a year I might have celebrated. It was the year when I was first elected both to the Shadow Cabinet and to the National Executive of the Labour Party. Press stories described me as a coming politician, one to watch. The media demanded comments and sought interviews. But I did not give a damn. I could hardly bring myself to read them, and they gave me no pleasure when I did. My beloved mother was dying. My brilliant, mercurial husband had fallen in love with someone else. Those things were terrible enough. The probable break-up of my family was even worse. Close friends offered to take Rebecca into their own family, but I knew I could not bear such a separation. She was the most precious person still left to me.

Three years earlier, in the autumn of 1966, my mother had fallen over a pile of builders' rubble on her way to give a talk one dark evening at the Church of St Martin-in-the-Fields in Trafalgar Square. Her broken arm mended, but the fall precipitated a gradual deterioration of her nervous system. She lost the use of her legs, and then, for a writer the cruellest blow, the use of her hands. She was fearful of losing her reason, but that never happened. Instead, she lost the power to speak.

My mother's lifelong housekeeper, Amy Burnett, by now a deeply cherished friend, looked after her for the first two years of this strange debilitating illness. My father was the soul of devotion, while maintaining his lively interest in everything that was going on. In the last year, when my mother needed round-the-clock nursing, she moved to an expensive nursing home in Pimlico, near to their flat in Westminster, where there was little human warmth or sympathy. My father and I found instead a small home in Wimbledon where the lady in charge genuinely cared for her patients. My father and I went to see my mother almost every day. In the last few months of her life, I talked to her eyes, which alone were capable of a response. I loved her with a fierce protective love, and felt angry that someone who had given so much to the world should face such a prolonged and cruel death. It was agonising to see the slow ebbing of her faculties. She died on Easter Sunday, 1970. It seemed an appropriate day. On her memorial are carved only the words 'Blessed are the peace-makers', from Matthew V.

Bernard and I, together with Paul Berry, my mother's dear friend and biographer, scattered her ashes as she had requested on her brother Edward's grave in the lovely war cemetery above Asiago in the Italian Alps. It was a golden autumn day. Italian families were eating their picnics around the little cemetery. I was marking two deaths, that of my mother and that of my marriage.

While the demands of public life at times seem unendurable, they also compel one to endure. The eyes and the ears of the media are everywhere; there are few hiding places. So one learns composure, to keep hand and eye steady, to never let go except with the most trusted friends. That discipline helps, acts as a life-line when the foundations themselves crumble away. The show must go on.

By 1971, my father was beginning to recover from the loss of my mother. He had already been grieving through the three long years in which she had lost her faculties, her ability to walk, to write and ultimately to speak. He had been assiduous in his care of her, and when she could no longer be looked after at home, in his long daily visits. So after her death he had no reason to feel guilty. She herself had long wanted to die. He was still in good health, and kept in touch with friends and acquaintances. He had not lost his pleasure in life. So when an old friend living in Australia, Delinda Gassmann, herself recently widowed, wrote to tell him she was planning to spend a holiday in England and would enjoy his company, he responded with alacrity.

Delinda, part-Italian, part-English, was no shrinking violet. She had lived an adventurous life, managing hotels in England, Australia and New Guinea, and had been widowed three times. She explained to inquirers that she had loved all her husbands, and used to boast, 'Never divorced, dear, never divorced.' She was happy to take the initiative in marriage, and the gaps between her marriages were short. There could be no comparison between her and my mother, for they were as unlike as two people could be. Delinda was dogmatic, vivacious, sociable, and did not enjoy intellectual matters. She loved to cook, to design and make clothes, especially elaborate hats, to dance and to argue. She was also direct and honest. As my father aged, she kept her side of the implicit bargain, looking after him briskly but affectionately until he died, in January 1979.

Time does slowly heal, though it leaves scars behind. As I emerged from my own cocoon of wretchedness, I began to enjoy Opposition. I had never experienced it before. In October 1971 I was appointed Shadow Home Secretary. In Parliament I was blessed with an opposite number of integrity, moderation and deep seriousness, Robert Carr, one of the fine but later endangered species of politicians known as one-nation Conservatives. I didn't agree with him on everything, but I sometimes found disagreeing a bit artificial. The elaborate minuet of British parliamentary politics can conceal passionate mutual hostility. It can also disguise genuine mutual respect.

I would not have been Shadow Home Secretary had it not been for one of those vagaries of chance that sometimes derail political fortunes. A group of rebel Conservatives had put down an amendment to the European Communities Bill calling for a referendum before Britain could sign the Treaty. My fellow pro-Europeans and I had miserably voted against the bill as it proceeded through the House of Commons after our rebellion on the second reading. This amendment, however, raised fundamental constitutional issues. Roy Jenkins, George Thomson and Harold Lever all opposed the idea of a referendum on principle. They regarded referenda as the anathema of representative government, instruments that could be easily manipulated by irresponsible populist politicians. I did not agree. I believed that a referendum on a constitutional matter of such importance, concentrating on fundamental issues, would provide the opportunity for a massive national debate consulting and informing the people. So when Roy Jenkins, George Thomson and Harold Lever resigned from the Shadow Cabinet over the decision on 29 March 1972 to vote for the amendment, I did not do so. When elections for the Shadow Cabinet took place the following autumn, I stood and was elected at the top of the list. In a typical gesture intended to heal the gaping divisions in the Parliamentary Party, Harold then re-appointed me Shadow Home Secretary.

It was not to last for long. In October 1973, under great pressure from his supporters in Parliament, Roy stood for the Shadow Cabinet and was elected. Without the backing of some pro-European and anti-referendum MPs, I dropped from joint first to eighth place. The obvious spokesman role for Roy was that of Home Secretary, now that Wilson had appointed Denis Healey as Shadow Chancellor and Jim Callaghan as Shadow Foreign Secretary. There was no other major Shadow position. Harold Wilson put the decision off for several weeks, but I deferred to Roy as the more senior and prestigious figure. I was moved to Social Security, clearly a demotion, and from my point of view, far less exciting.

However, in the autumn of 1973 Carol Bracken came to work for me, and life changed markedly for the better. Carol was, like me, a single mother, with an only son, John, only a little younger than Rebecca. She had uncompromisingly high standards in professional and personal matters alike. The demands she made on herself were unrelenting, embracing a commitment to help all my constituents. No one, however obsessive or self-absorbed their demand for assistance, was left out. Carol became their advisor and friend. When she left my employ after my election defeat in 1979, both she and I felt bereft. We kept in touch, however. Fourteen years later, in 1993, when both of us were happily married – me to Dick, she to her brilliant husband from the Treasury, David Savage – Carol came back to work for me until she and David moved to King's Lynn to devote more time to their shared love of the arts and architecture. She was, and is, a remarkable woman, whose insights into the human condition are lucid and sensitive.

In 1974, after a stormy battle with the miners and the introduction of a three-day week to save electricity, Edward Heath lost the general election to Harold Wilson. The country believed that Labour could settle the strike, and in that it was proved right. But Edward Heath's question 'Who governs Britain?' was not to be so easily disposed of. The question haunted the next two Labour terms of office. Ultimately, it was a question the Party was unable to resolve.

I had been summoned to lunch shortly before the 1974 election by William Armstrong, Cabinet Secretary and head of the Home Civil Service. This was the man Edward Heath relied on, and often took down to Chequers with him at the weekend, to brainstorm about the country's problems. Armstrong was deeply troubled. He envisaged a possible collapse of constitutional government. I did not dismiss his fears. I had in 1970, the last year of Harold Wilson's government, heard the rumours of planned coups and stories about private armies training in remote parts of the country. Harold himself believed these stories and, as Peter Wright's disturbing book *Spycatcher*, which would be published in 1987, showed, he was not wrong.

The new Labour administration began with an evasive answer: Britain would be governed on the basis of an agreement between the unions, the employers and the government. The central dilemma of how to attain low inflation without rising unemployment – the dilemma that haunts all social democratic governments – would be resolved by a voluntary 'social contract'. Wages would be limited to an agreed ceiling, and employers would be penalised if the ceiling was exceeded.

I entered the Cabinet in February 1974 as Secretary of State for Prices and Consumer Protection. It was a daunting job. There had been massive increases in oil prices in 1973, the outcome of a decision by the cartel of oil producers to punish nations that had supported Israel during the Yom Kippur War. The threshold agreement reached between Mr Heath and the unions triggered wage increases automatically when there was a rise in the cost of living, adding to the impact. Prices were going through the roof. In the month I took on my new job, the annual inflation rate exceeded 13.5 per cent. The job of Conservative backbenchers in the new Parliament was to demonstrate as quickly as possible that I was personally responsible for inflation.

As Prices Minister, I was the junior member of the triumvirate charged with implementing the social contract. Day after day, as inflation soared, Denis Healey, the Chancellor of the Exchequer, Michael Foot, the Employment Minister, and I discussed with one another and then with the trades unions what might work. The trades union leaders, the so-called Neddy Six – for all of them were members of the NEDC, the National Economic Development Council – were not of one mind. Those like Hugh Scanlon of the AUEW, the engineers' union, whose members were skilled workers, resisted the narrowing of wage differentials. Those like Jack Jones of the TGWU, the Transport and General Workers' Union, many of whose members were low-paid, wanted a flat-rate, across-the-board increase. On one thing both were agreed: there was to be constant pressure for restrictions on prices. In July 1975, on the eve of the government imposing a statutory incomes policy, Jack Jones managed to persuade his fellow trades union leaders to accept a £6 a week flat-rate increase, which greatly benefited lower-paid workers. It was successful, halving inflation without any substantial increase in unemployment. A second year was agreed with considerable difficulty, this time for either £2.50 or 5 per cent on existing wages, not to exceed a maximum of £4.

My part in the social contract was to deliver stable or at least only moderately rising prices for necessities. At every meeting, the trades unions would press for tighter controls over prices and profit margins, while back in the Department, I came under pressure from representatives of the Retail Consortium, the CBI, the food manufacturers and other interests to relax the stringent price code originally imposed under the Heath government. I had three things on my side: the fact that the price code was inherited from the Conservatives, which undermined partisan criticism; the fact that the Price Commissioner, Sir Arthur Cockfield, was a well-known Conservative and former Cabinet minister; and third, the disunity of the manufacturers and retailers, who rarely agreed on a single approach.

Two early decisions rescued me from the fate implicit in my impossible job. Mine was a new ministry, in part carved out of the Ministry of Trade and Industry. New ministries, especially those created for political reasons by Harold Wilson, enjoyed a very short lifespan. When I learned that other departments were planning to unload their deadbeat civil servants on my new ministry, I decided I had to make a stand. I called the Prime Minister and told him I could not accept the position he had offered me unless I could choose my own Permanent Secretary. Rumours had reached me that I was about to get someone all of Whitehall had been trying to dispose of.

Harold was not inclined to agree with me. He pointed out that ministers were not free to choose their own civil servants, and that objections like mine were rare and not to be encouraged. So I told him I would have to make public my reasons for not accepting the job. He asked me who I had in mind. I couldn't think of a name, so I asked if I could call back. I then rang my good friend from my Ministry of Labour days, Denis Barnes. 'Who's good?' I asked him. He thought for a while, and then told me the names of two civil servants he considered to be outstanding. I rang the Prime Minister back with the names. He was impressed. 'How did you choose so well?' he asked. And that was how I came to get one of the best Permanent Secretaries, Ken Clucas, and one of the best Deputy Secretaries, John Burgh, in all Whitehall.

My other early decision was to keep Sir Arthur Cockfield on as Price Commissioner. I had toyed with the idea of appointing a Labour supporter. On the evening of my Cabinet appointment, I was invited to a farewell party for Sir Arthur, who assumed he would now be dismissed, at his flat. His wife met me at the door. 'You are about to meet the most intelligent man you have ever encountered,' she whispered to me. This unexpected introduction duly impressed me. Sir Arthur, I realised, was a man of stubborn and unimpeachable integrity. His commitment to public service would in no way be influenced by his political preferences. In that case, a Price Commissioner who was widely known to be a Conservative would be far more effective in dealing with the employers than a Labour appointee. And so it proved. Sir Arthur was relentless and unbending, formidably knowledgeable in his administration of a price code so complex it would not have disgraced the scholastics of thirteenth-century canon law.

I was able, by bargaining price code concessions against voluntary price restrictions, to obtain agreement on a limited list of essential foodstuffs and other goods whose prices would be kept down by government subsidy and by the retailers' own cross-subsidies. This 'price-check' system, along with requirements that goods had to be labelled with their prices and weights, helped us to get voluntary limits on wages. What would have surprised Adam Smith, who believed in free trade and competition, was the employers' strong resistance to publicising prices. It was the harshest battle I encountered. Ignorance was the Achilles heel of consumers – they did not know where to go for the lowest prices, and nobody told them. So I insisted that goods were labelled with prices, and that Citizens' Advice Bureaux and local authorities informed shoppers where particular goods were cheapest.

In the fraught bargaining sessions over prices and profits, the techniques of the interests involved were very different. The union leaders went in for declamations and threats of non-cooperation. The employers, more subtle, tried to charm me. On more than one occasion, the chief executive of a major company tried to embrace me in the lift; others invited me out to dinner. These were tactics reserved for women ministers, but they told me something about the vanity of the men involved.

The social contract did not come without a cost. The trades unions gained an influence over legislation that I felt, uneasily, was incompatible with proper democratic accountability. They called for legislation to be brought forward, for instance, on dock-workers' and trades unions' rights, while indicating resistance to other proposals. Their support for the government's inflation policy was indispensable, since the alternative was high interest rates and consequent unemployment. As one interest among many, however, they were becoming too dominant for the good of the country.

The trades union leaders were also paying heavily themselves for the social contract, in terms of grassroots support from their own members. As wage restraint was demanded, year after year, shop stewards began to organise powerful internal opposition. Why should they and their fellow workers voluntarily hold back while prices rose? What were they getting out of it? Many shop stewards were men of the left, and they regarded the government as playing the employers' game. Thus the currents of discontent flowed ever more strongly, menacing the government's efforts to hold the dykes.

CHAPTER 12

Jim Callaghan: Old Labour's Last Hurrah

Jim Callaghan became Prime Minister on 4 April 1976, less than three weeks after the resignation of Harold Wilson. When Cledwyn Hughes, Chairman of the Parliamentary Labour Party, told him he had won against five formidable opponents, Jim muttered, 'And I haven't even got a degree!' His response encapsulated two themes that had run through his life: a deep regret that he had never been to university, and a deep gratitude to the Labour movement for allowing him to overcome that handicap.

As the historian Peter Hennessy has memorably said, Jim Callaghan was the embodiment of the spirit of 1945, the year when a triumphant Labour government led by his mentor, Clement Attlee, for the first time ever came to power with a majority in the House of Commons. Jim Callaghan's political life ran in tandem with the rise and the decline of democratic socialism. The British version of that ideology was wedded to the parliamentary system, and therefore the Labour movement looked to Parliament to redress its grievances. It supported candidates first Liberal, then Labour, to represent its interests in the Commons. It was distrustful of theory, pragmatic in its approach; and, at that time, moderate in its demands.

The trades unions wanted to be seen as a respected part of a wider society. Their members might be politically reformist, but they were also often conservative in their behaviour and in their moral values. In this too Jim Callaghan was cut from their cloth. He had deep reservations about the so-called permissive revolution with which Roy Jenkins and his friends were associated. The nonconformist teachings of the chapel were still part of his character. He revered, and sometimes envied, the education so many of his colleagues had enjoyed and now took for granted. Education was a treasure to be cherished and respected. It was not meant to be the playground of teachers with extreme ideologies, some of whom rejected the discipline implicit in learning itself.

Jim brought to the premiership some useful baggage from his earlier political roles in the most senior offices of state: Chancellor of the Exchequer, Foreign Secretary and Home Secretary. As Chancellor, albeit an unconfident and uncertain one, he had learned a good deal about the weakness of the British economy, so exposed to the international winds through sterling debt and a fragile currency. As Foreign Secretary, he had seen aspirations to world power crumble, but he had also managed, as Harold Wilson's lieutenant, to produce a compromise on the Treaty of Rome that enabled that government to hold together. As Home Secretary, conventional though he was on criminal justice matters, he had shown courage and boldness in his dealings with Northern Ireland. He had wound up the B Specials, detested by the Catholic minority, and had refused to bend in the face of bigotry on either side. Jim had seen as much of human folly as any politician in the land. Yet he never lost his humanity. He was, and felt himself to be, like the rest of us.

I had remained at the Department of Prices and Consumer Protection after Wilson left office. We were still engaged in negotiations to get a further eighteen months of incomes policy in place. I had managed, as already mentioned, to negotiate a package of measures to keep the prices of essential goods down, including a range of nutritious if unexciting food subsidised in part by the Treasury, in part through cross-subsidisation by firms. The price-check system was supported by a lot of information about prices, including comparisons, between different stores, of the same goods. This price transparency was more resented by the retailers than anything else I did. Those little sticky labels on everything people buy were part of my legacy, if such a pompous word can be appropriately used here.

What we needed to do, above all, was to keep inflation down without using the powerful but cruel weapon of mass unemployment. For the men and women of Jim Callaghan's generation, whose childhood memories went back to the Great Depression, the shabby dole queues and the misery of trying to make frayed ends meet, inciting or even tolerating mass unemployment was unthinkable. That was true for Edward Heath as well. So both leaders trod the stony, and eventually impassable, road of prices and incomes policy. That policy put a heavy burden on civic society, requiring restraint by strong interests that often failed to see the point.

The foundation of the government's domestic economic framework was its prices and incomes policy and that in turn required the acquiescence, if not the enthusiasm, of the trades unions and the employers. It was to be the testing ground not only of us, but of the Labour movement itself.

Denis Healey, Michael Foot and I, as Prices Minister, worked well together. Denis is a colourful, ebullient personality, combative and life-loving, with an unusually rich hinterland outside politics. He is an exceptionally gifted photographer, who published a remarkable collection of his work in a book called *Healey's Eye*, and is immensely knowledgeable about music, which he adores. I once made the mistake of appearing on a BBC music quiz with him. I lamely remembered a few favourite pieces, from operas by Verdi, which I had immensely enjoyed. He got every single excerpt right – the composer, the movement, the number and description of the work and the date. On top of that, he has written one of the best political autobiographies ever published, appropriately entitled *The Time of My Life*. To all of this can be added a brilliant military career and a wonderfully fulfilling marriage to a sparkling, sympathetic and insightful wife, herself a writer, Edna Healey.

Yet he was never a serious candidate for the leadership. He was unpredictable, behaving rather like a strongly served tennis ball hitting a soft spot and then bouncing sideways. You could never be sure what he might do. He was a loner, enjoying his family and a few close friends, mainly not politicians, so predictions about his behaviour from colleagues were not particularly helpful. He had been brusque with many of them, or scorched them with his brilliant, brutal humour. He was not a popular figure in the Commons tea room. I liked him very much.

Michael Foot was, and is, adored in the Labour movement, a movement he himself idealised. Neither the trades unions nor the many left-wing groups that found shelter within that big tent were as high-minded as Michael thought. They saw in Michael's kindly image of them what they would have liked to be, and they loved him for it. His own commitment to democratic socialism took the form of a passionate belief in social justice coupled with an equal passion for Parliament. Like the great nineteenth-century reformers, he linked the two, holding that the former could only be achieved through the latter. Michael was a radical, a reformer, an inspirer, but lacked the element of brutality political leadership requires. His judgements on national issues were too much affected by partisan proclivities. But he and I shared similar ideals. We trusted one another as people, even if we didn't trust one another's judgements. We were both optimists.

The difference, however, was that I believed power tended to corrupt, even in the hands of the left, and therefore had to be checked and constrained. His political morality was much more black and white. Unlike Michael, I began to be concerned about the concessions made by the government of Harold Wilson to the trades unions. We had worked together with mutual appreciation, and in my case huge admiration for his love and understanding of literature, but we fought bitterly over the Trades Union and Labour Relations Bill introduced after the October 1974 general election. Along with Roy Jenkins, the Home Secretary, I fought hard in Cabinet against imposing the closed shop, especially in the newspaper industry, and against extending it to editors as well as journalists. Like Michael, I had been a member of the National Union of Journalists, but I felt freelance writers should continue to be able to express themselves without having to belong to the union.

By the spring of 1976 I had had quite a long stint in Canute's chair, trying to order back the tide of inflation, and I was ready to move somewhere else. But in appointing his Cabinet the new Prime Minister left me where I was. I was, though, completely unprepared for the event that precipitated my move.

Roy Jenkins was the man many of us expected to be offered the job of Foreign Secretary. It was the only position, short of Prime Minister, that would have kept him in the new Labour government. But Callaghan saw him as so committed to the European Community that everything he did as Foreign Secretary would be questioned and attacked by both the left and the Eurosceptics, groups that only partly overlapped. Jim had had his fill of Party contention, and he was not about to multiply the reasons for it. Tony Crosland, Roy's friend and rival, who had abstained on the famous 1971 yes vote on the EEC, was a more detached figure and a person who never saw Europe as being of the first importance. So Jim offered him the post. Roy, deeply disappointed, went instead to the other position for which he had been proposed, that of President of the European Commission. His departure from the Cabinet in September 1976 precipitated a reshuffle.

I was in New York when the telephone rang in my hotel room. It was the Prime Minister. He mentioned Education and Science. I was reluctant. Rebecca was at a voluntary-aided school in a part of London which at that time was still selective. The Inner London Education Authority, pursuing the policy of introducing comprehensive schools, had decided that voluntary-aided schools would have to choose between going independent and becoming comprehensive, a choice much resented by the parents at her school. At one or two school meetings I had attended to support the choice of going comprehensive, I had encountered their anger. A few parents had sworn and spat at me. This was not something entirely new in my experience, but I was worried for my daughter. I told Jim it would be very difficult. He was getting understandably irritated. 'You're very hard to please,' he said. I knew I couldn't expect him to leaf his way through every possible vacant Cabinet post, like someone trying to sell a suit, so I agreed to do it.

In those distant days, a good Prime Minister would keep in touch with his Cabinet members, but would not try to tell them what to do. Jim used to invite ministers to come and talk with him face to face about what they intended to do, and how much support they were getting from their Department; he might even telephone occasionally on a particularly contentious issue. But we were left to run our own Departments. You knew your track record would be an important factor in your promotion or demotion, but there was no detailed interference. Later Prime Ministers, Tony Blair even more than Margaret Thatcher, sought to micro-manage Departments they believed to be politically sensitive, or were personally interested in. I would not have wanted to be a Cabinet minister in a situation where key decisions were taken over my head (and sometimes without consultation) by someone in the No. 10 Policy Unit directly accountable not to me but to the Prime Minister.

Soon after I was moved by Jim Callaghan from the Prices and

Consumer Protection Department to Education and Science, I stood against Michael Foot for the deputy leadership of the Parliamentary Party. I had been elected to the Shadow Cabinet by my fellow Labour Members of Parliament every year but one while we were in Opposition, and had been a Cabinet member since the election of the Labour government in February 1974. Over the whole of that period I had also been an elected member of the National Executive Committee. My colleagues in the moderate Manifesto group, anxious about the accelerating lurch to the left in the Party, were desperate to challenge Michael as the iconic figure of the soft left, and thought I had the best chance to win.

So I stood against him, shortly after Jim became Prime Minister, but without his support. He probably felt my time would come, but certainly not yet. Many in the Parliamentary Party wanted a leadership that combined the right and the left, and this the Callaghan–Foot team promised. Michael won by 38 votes, 166 to 128, a smaller margin than his supporters had predicted.

When I first became a junior minister, in March 1966, advisers were rare creatures existing at the most elevated levels of government, where they deliberated with Prime Ministers and senior Cabinet members. Relations with the media were conducted by government press officers, many of whom were scrupulous in their efforts to be objective. When I rose to Cabinet level myself, I was allowed to have two advisers, Stella Greenall and John Lyttle. Stella had been adviser to Fred Mulley, my predecessor as Secretary of State for Education and Science. I asked her to stay, which she agreed to do. She had spent twenty-four years as an official of the National Union of Students and had become something of a legend. No one understood the intricacies of student financing better than she. Stella was the originator of the mandatory grants system, adopted by the Macmillan government in 1962, which conferred free higher education on a whole generation of university students. The universities did not charge tuition fees; there were also maintenance grants for those who could not otherwise afford to go, in a university system that was largely residential. Stella left the Labour Party a year after Tony Blair's election as Prime Minister, outraged by the introduction of tuition fees. 'We have created a monster,' she declared.

Stella liked working behind the scenes. She let her ministers take the credit for her dedicated work. She had a quiet persistence that brought results and won the respect of the Department's civil servants. I could rely completely on her careful research. Her husband Philip was devoted to an unusual hobby, numismatics, and built up a remarkable collection of historic coins which Stella left to the British Museum.

My other adviser, John Lyttle, who came to work for me in 1974 when I became Secretary of State for Prices and Consumer Protection, would have made an outstanding investigative reporter. He understood the intricacies of the Labour Party and guided me around the shoals of the Parliamentary Party and the National Executive Committee. John also got to know the civil servants in my newly created department and won their respect. He acted as a progress-chaser, reporting on which of my policies were being energetically pursued, which were being obstructed and which were being left to wither on the vine. A minister cannot sack a civil servant, but can steer responsibility for delivering new policies towards those most likely to advance them. John understood both my departments better than I did, and would know exactly where each initiative stood. Education was a controversial area, and comprehensive schools were a flagship Labour policy. Within the department there were passionate supporters and strong sceptics. These differences were reflected in the rate at which such policies progressed.

John never made the perilous assumption that taking a decision was enough; he knew it was the beginning of a process, and not its end. Nor was he inclined to tell one what one wanted to hear; the truth, however unwelcome, had to be told.

John was a complex, sensitive, driven man. Gaunt and drawn, he lived on whisky and cigarettes. He had close friends, but was not a party-goer. His commitment to his job, like his loyalty, was extraordinary. He was no sycophant; his analyses of his various employers were candid, even piercing, but he conveyed his views only to the persons concerned and to a few trusted friends

The friendship between John and me, which had survived the strains of breaking with the Labour Party and launching the Social Democratic Party, crumbled when he applied to become the new party's chief media officer. That John Lyttle was a brilliant press officer no one could deny. The publicity he engendered for the launch and the crucial period of by-election successes that followed it played an essential part in the party's survival. Not unreasonably, John felt he deserved the post. There was within him, however, an insistence on truth-telling that eschewed compromise, a kind of whimsical obstinacy. Asked during his job interview what his strategy would be for television, John made his contempt for the medium clear. Television, unlike the print press, did not interest him. It was a response that killed his chances of getting the job.

John never forgave me. Loyalty works both ways, and in his view I should have used my considerable influence to get him the post. I thought that was wrong, even though I knew better than anyone else just how good he was. So John joined Roy Jenkins's team, directing his talents to promoting his new employer, and to my disadvantage.

When Roy stood down as the SDP's leader in 1983, John found a new position as special assistant on public affairs to Robert Runcie, the Archbishop of Canterbury. Runcie's term as Archbishop was not unclouded. He clashed painfully with Margaret Thatcher over his uncompromising commitment to social justice, powerfully expressed through the Church of England's Faith in the City project. Runcie was also caught up in a hostage crisis, when Terry Waite's well-publicised mission to

free Iran's hostages led to his own capture in January 1987, just a
day before Lyttle took up his post. Well over half John's time was
taken up with looking for Terry Waite. John would vanish for
weeks at a time, only to reappear fitfully from the shadowy alleyways of Middle Eastern politics. He held secret meetings with
leading figures in Iran, the Lebanon and elsewhere in the Middle
East, becoming a kind of unofficial ambassador whose work was
much valued by the Foreign Office. I saw John only occasionally
in these years, and never managed to heal the breach between us.
John, who had suffered for a long time from a heart condition,
died in 1991.

It was not long after the death of Mao Zedong that my Department received an invitation from the Chinese government to
send an official delegation to discuss cooperation on scientific
research and higher education. I had visited Hong Kong in 1965
with a parliamentary group examining the colony's majestically
slow progress towards democracy. We advocated that a majority of
the Legislative Council should be elected. It took many years for
that to happen. But while I was less than impressed by the rate of
political progress, I was astonished by the remarkable efforts made
to house those who had fled the mainland. There were masses of
gaunt high-rise flats, but they were lightened by little gardens
clinging to rooftops and balconies. Every space was utilised. I had
never travelled to mainland China but the taste provided by
Hong Kong made the prospect exciting.

   Four of us went to Beijing on 20 July 1977: apart from me,
my Permanent Secretary Sir James Hamilton, my Senior Chief
Inspector of Schools Sheila Browne, and my private secretary Mr
R. C. Jones. As soon as we arrived, we were taken to the sarcophagus of Chairman Mao, a large transparent edifice on the side of
Tiananmen Square in which rested the embalmed body of the great
leader, mildly orange in colour. We all stood with our heads bowed
for several minutes. I reflected on the tradition of embalming the

bodies of leaders, a tradition shared by the Communist Party and the Catholic Church, and not one I find beguiling.

Negotiations started soon after this requirement had been satisfied, in the traditional setting, a square room with hard upholstered chairs ranged side by side along the walls. This did not make discussion easy. I sat next to the minister and our rather stilted conversation was respectfully listened to by the assembled officials. What did become clear was that the newly liberated Chinese officials were seizing the opportunity presented by the accession to power of Deng Xiaoping to rebuild their disrupted education system, and were gratifyingly turning to the United Kingdom to help them do it. We had already set aside some money for scholarships for Chinese exchange students in science.

By the end of the first day, before the inevitable banquet, we had the outline of an agreement. It was just as well. The next day, 23 July, I received a curt summons to return home immediately. A vote had been called, and, as so often happened during the Callaghan administration, the Whips were scurrying around for votes and weren't sure they had enough to assure the government's survival. So two days after landing in Beijing for this historic meeting, I was being rushed back to England. Obliged to change planes there, I tore through the crowded streets of Hong Kong in a police convoy, with traffic being held up at every crossroads. I left behind bemused Chinese officials, convinced that there must have been an attempted coup against the British government. The pedestrian truth, of course, was that this was just one more instance of the idiosyncrasies of the British parliamentary system.

My officials successfully completed their mission, and several hundred Chinese scholars arrived in British universities over the next few years. Many returned to senior academic positions. Seven years later, the Chinese government invited me back to see how successful the exchange had been. I invited the Rubinsteins to accompany me. Our Chinese hosts insisted that we travel in a convoy of three black cars, a big one for me and the senior local officials accompanying me, a middle-sized one for the Rubinsteins, who were assumed to be servants rather than friends, and a third small car for the luggage. In vain we suggested that we could all share the one big car.

In all other respects, it was a marvellous trip. In Xian, China's ancient capital, I complimented the local Communist leader on the survival of so many of the ancient temples, given the widespread destruction of historic China during the Great Cultural Revolution. 'We are far from Beijing,' she replied. I learned later that the People's Liberation Army had been ordered by the local leaders to protect the monuments against the ravages of Mao's young vandals.

We were among the very first Westerners to see the terracotta army of Ying Zheng, the first Emperor of China, exhumed. We were taken to the huge burial ground, of which only a small part had been uncovered from the sand in which it had been preserved for many centuries. To look down on the arm of a half-buried warrior still futilely brandishing his sword, or on the head of a whinnying horse, the sound long since silenced, was to feel part of a long-forgotten civilisation, and to share in the irreversible march of history.

In Guangzhou, already waking up to its commercial potential, the story was very different. The manager of the best hotel, where we stayed, had discovered that Hilary was the editor of *The Good Hotel Guide*. Desperate to get a mention, he showed us the elegant 'Presidential Suite', reserved for the most important VIPs. It had a well-controlled small river running through banks of polished stones, as well as a modern bar. The Rubinsteins were promised that they could stay there on their next visit.

Ideology, in 1984 Guangzhou, despite the prospect of riches, was far from dead. I ordered a taxi to take me to its old Catholic cathedral. As soon as my Chinese minders grasped my intentions, they appeared beside the taxi insisting that I should not go. I told the driver to take me there. An undignified scuffle broke out, with

The Senior Advisory Council of the Institute of Politics, John F. Kennedy School of Government, Harvard, 1988. *In back row among others:* Senator Edward Kennedy (Chairman), Richard Thornburgh, Senator Culver, Ron Brown. *Front row:* Katharine Graham, John F. Kennedy Jr. and me

The broken umbrella: on a march in 1988 to commemorate the seventieth anniversary of the granting of the vote to women over thirty

At Ring Lake ranch, near Dubois, Wyoming, 1989

My favourite photo of Dick, 1988

With my South African friends:

The writer Nadine Gordimer and her husband Reinhold Cassirer, Johannesburg

With the South African stateswoman Helen Suzman and Paddy Ashdown in London

Colin Legum with me, Fish Hoek, Cape Province, 1990

Party of friends in Cape Cod, 1990

A farewell party at the Institute of Politics, 1990

Opening an agricultural college for Seva Mandir in Rajasthan, 1997

With Dick and Helena Kennedy on a British Council visit to Brazil

With Paddy Ashdown and British UNPROFOR peacekeepers, Skopje, Macedonia, 1999

Dick and me with William Keegan in Moscow

The Liberal Democrat delegation visits India, 2002. Among others, Navnit Dholakia, Ann Dholakia, Greg Simpson, Norman Lamb, MP, Manmohan Singh and me

Women at the Crossroads conference in Cape Town, 1999

With the writer Naomi Mitchison on her 100th birthday, Carradale, Argyll

At the British Library with its architects Mary Jane Long, Colin St John Wilson, and my nephew, Timothy Brittain-Catlin

Near Petra, Jordan. Time out from a meeting of the Steering Committee of the UN World Women's Conference, 1995

me jumping into the car and the minders trying to pull me out. Eventually the taxi and I broke free, and I found myself in the crowded backstreets where everything that could possibly be eaten was being cooked, where bicycles and rickshaws were fighting for space, where some wooden stalls were being used to display vegetables and spices and others used as beds.

The cathedral, when I got there, was a pathetic sight. Its roof was wrecked, the rain kept out by a tarpaulin. The sole human inhabitants were a very old European priest and an equally old Chinese woman. It was clear that no one dared come to the cathedral. I left them some money, and made my way back to the hotel. There was no other foreigner to be seen.

In a lecture Jim Callaghan gave at Ruskin College, Oxford, on 18 October 1976 he made plain that he cared a great deal about education. He had heard from his friends and from his children a good deal about 'child-centred' education, lax discipline, and teachers who failed to teach. He was aware of the unease of parents, especially aspiring working-class parents, who were bemused by some of the methods their children encountered. Jim's ear was always closely attuned to the concerns of voters, not just politically as a guide to how they might vote, but because he felt responsibility towards them. In particular, he thought that boys and girls from poorer homes might miss out on their one opportunity to realise their potential. He was also troubled by criticism from employers that school-leavers were neither fully literate nor fully numerate, and were not properly trained for jobs in industry. Serious shortages of maths and science teachers made it unlikely that these problems could be rectified quickly.

Jim had a strong conviction that traditional teaching methods were best. He distrusted what was called 'progressive education'. It was a distrust shared by large numbers of parents, whose worries found voice in the Ruskin speech. Many young teachers, however, rejected traditional methods. The teachers' unions had a highly radical left-wing fringe which had no time for testing and examinations that established academic pecking orders among the children. Though most teachers were moderates, the moderates rarely asserted themselves at teachers' conferences against the clamorous voices of the radicals.

Furthermore, Jim appreciated that any large-scale change in education methods, coming on the heels of the reorganisation of schools to become comprehensive, would need the support of the public. To that end he suggested that there should be a great debate on the subject, conducted in every region of the country, to which representatives of industry, trades unions, parents and local authorities should be invited. It was an early example of something that became fashionable much later on – consultation with the users of public services. The press was predictably sceptical, the educational experts disdainful. But the regional conferences were useful. They showed strong support for comprehensive schooling, coupled with concern about the wide differences between the curricula followed in different schools. These differences created serious problems for children moving from school to school, a much more common occurrence than in the less mobile communities of pre-war England and Wales. There was also a strong undercurrent of worry about the mastery of basic literacy and numeracy, shared not only by parents but also by employers. Those concerns prompted the first tentative steps into what was called 'the secret garden' of the curriculum.

Following the regional conferences, I drafted a Green Paper, *Education in Schools, A Consultative Document*, for the first time proposing that there should be a core curriculum of fundamental subjects, and that core curriculum should take up around half the time children spent in school. I asked the local education authorities to review current curricular arrangements with their teachers. But there was not enough time to implement this proposal before the 1979 election brought in a Conservative government. Eight years later Margaret Thatcher's third administration enacted a much more draconian national curriculum which laid down in detail what should be taught in almost the whole of the school year.

The teachers' unions were profoundly suspicious of my intentions. Given that I had virtually no powers except those of persuasion, and the government lacked a majority to bring in legislation, I needed the teachers' goodwill to achieve any reforms at all. But I wanted more than their goodwill. I wanted to give them confidence in themselves and in their professional standing. I was very much aware that good teachers were vital to the country's future prospects, yet teachers had a much lower status in their own eyes, and in the eyes of the wider public, than professions such as medicine and the law. I concluded that a professional body which would be consulted about entry levels into the profession, about standards of professional behaviour including agreed grounds for dismissal, and about requirements for in-service training would do an immense amount for their self-confidence. As my own contribution, I made O level passes in English and mathematics a minimum requirement for entry into the teaching profession.

The teachers were organised in rival unions that competed with one another for members. Relations between the two largest, the National Union of Teachers and the National Association of Schoolmasters/Union of Women Teachers were strained. Terry Casey, the General Secretary of the NASUWT, was a combative man with a knobbly face and an emphatic, even demagogic, style of speaking. He was aggressively masculine. He had once introduced me as the ministerial speaker to his annual conference by explaining that there were 'manbrains' and 'womanbrains', and that as 'womanbrains' went (which was not far) I had quite a good one. I swallowed down my irritation, and made only a humorous reference to it in my own speech. The General Secretary of the NUT, an old friend of mine from university days when he had been President of the National Union of Students, was Fred

Jarvis. Fred cared deeply about education and about opportunities for all children, but he had a very contentious union to lead. The NUT had as powerful a left wing as the Labour Party; it was led by London teachers and was waxing increasingly militant, particularly about pay.

I put my proposition about a general teaching council to these two unions and their smaller, more moderate companions, the Assistant Masters' and Mistresses' Association (AMMA) and PAT, the Professional Association of Teachers. The latter two were enthusiastic, but the quarrel between the two larger unions had become so sour that they would not even meet in the same room to see me. Since no teaching council could work if they were not prepared to cooperate with each other, as well as with me, I had to tell them I would not be able to go ahead. My threat failed, and the idea at that time of a general teaching council was stillborn.

To sustain comprehensive schools against their critics, now rallying under the banner of the so-called Black Papers writers, I needed the support of parents. The first step was to accept the recommendations of the Taylor Committee on School Governors and Managers. In its 1977 report, A New Partnership for our Schools, the Committee had proposed that school governing bodies should have two parent governors elected by the parents and two by the teachers, while others would represent the local community and the non-teaching staff. The Taylor recommendations broadened the social base of governing bodies, and rooted local schools even more closely into the communities they served.

My other proposal to win parental support ran into considerable opposition, not least from my own Party colleagues. Schools, I recognised, were very different from each other in their internal arrangements, in their approach to school discipline and in their teaching methods. Some favoured progressive approaches, others much more traditional ones. Among secondary schools there were also coeducational schools and single-sex ones. Choices between schools on these grounds seemed to me in no way incompatible with the ending of selection, any more than need be the choice of a faith school rather than a secular school. I wanted to see diversity among schools, as distinct from a selection-based pecking order. I believed, and still do, that this kind of choice would strengthen support for comprehensive schools. But the Labour left and the union left did not see it that way. Led by Tony and Caroline Benn and quietly supported by one of my junior ministers, Margaret Jackson, they opposed my proposals in the Party and in the Parliamentary Party. Furthermore, whereas I believed a consensus going well beyond party loyalties would safeguard the comprehensive schools, they believed with equal fervour that such a consensus would compromise the principle itself.

My championing of comprehensive schools had by this time made me a highly controversial politician and a target for the Tory media. I was foolish to put myself right in their line of fire. In August 1976 a group of Asian women, employees of the Grunwick Film Processing company in north London, had been on strike for months against what they claimed were poor pay and conditions. As a longstanding member of their staunchly moderate trades union, APEX, which had sponsored me as an MP, I decided to visit their picket line in May 1977 along with my fellow union members and ministerial colleagues Fred Mulley and Denis Howell. We wanted to draw attention to the objectives of the strike, which had attracted little media coverage. I was motivated by a feeling that the Asian workers should not feel isolated and unsupported in what I believed to be their just grievances.

Huge press attention followed, as we had hoped. But what also followed, three weeks after our visit, was a mob of militants who clashed repeatedly and violently with the police. Ignoring the three-week gap, the tabloids gleefully fingered my colleagues and me as the instigators of the violence. In the context of growing industrial strife, I was marked by the Grunwick affair as if by a tattoo. Failure to anticipate what the Tory press might make of my intervention was one of the biggest mistakes of my career.

Margaret Jackson and my other junior minister Gordon Oakes were embroiled by now in the miserable business of closing teacher-training colleges. The dramatic decline in the birth rate since 1961 meant that there were insufficient posts for the number of teachers being trained by the colleges, teachers who would be looking for jobs in the early 1980s. It was one of the most painful decisions I have ever had to make. Dedicated principals and senior staff begged me to relent. I knew that smaller classes improved educational standards more than anything else, and I longed to have the money to enable local education authorities to employ all those would-be teachers. The government, however, was caught up in its worst budget crisis since the period of devaluation ten years before. The International Monetary Fund was pressing for large cuts in public expenditure as a condition of lending money to sustain sterling. There was no way out for me, or for the colleges.

I was equally conscious of the consequences of the ebb tide in births for the universities. I went to see the Committee of Vice-Chancellors. I had found the vice-chancellors I had met to be civilised and pleasant company, but very reluctant to make any decisions, especially those that might be unpopular with their own university constituencies. I had discovered way back in the days of the student revolution of the 1960s that few academics were good companions in a trench. It seemed to me that the only way for them to avoid a painful shrinkage in student numbers until the birth rate rose again was to open their doors to part-time and mature students, and to people on short professional and executive courses. I believed that the universities would benefit from a more socially and demographically diverse student body. In this I was influenced by my American experience. Given the government's budgetary problems, I could also see that the very generous provision made for the universities – high ratios of staff to students, student grants including living expenses, residential rather than local universities for most students – was unsustainable. Nor was it only a budgetary issue: the universities in the 1970s enjoyed great autonomy and an academic freedom unparalleled elsewhere which attracted brilliant men and women to them despite modest pay, and I did not want to see that put at risk.

The ancient universities lived comfortably in their ivory towers, blissfully disregarding the world outside. Desperate to wake them up, I wrote my own speech without consulting my civil servants, laying out what came to be called 'the thirteen points', proposals for change that might enable the universities to protect their core values against the gathering storm. The speech, and I, were dismissed with contempt. The university leaders could see that the Labour government was on its way out. They saw no pressing need to change their ways. One distinguished Cambridge head of college, Sir John Butterworth, told me pityingly at his college high table one evening that I should stop worrying. At least three alumni of the college were likely to be ministers in a new Conservative government. Oxbridge, he said, would get exactly what it wanted.

A decade later, Roy Jenkins was fighting to get the House of Lords to accept an amendment to Kenneth Baker's Education Reform Bill of 1988 to protect academic freedom. The University Grants Committee had been abolished, and government, not the universities, was determining which departments were to be closed.

The Prime Minister was soon unable to devote any more of his time to education or indeed to anything much other than the country's economic plight. Inflation was continuing, driven by the huge increases in oil prices introduced by OPEC in 1973. The government had committed itself to social investment as part of its deal with the trades unions to restrain wage demands, and was perceived in the international markets as a 'tax-and-spend' administration. Sterling was once again under pressure. The US Treasury took a sour view of the United Kingdom's prospects, and its Secretary of the Treasury, William Simon, was disinclined to help. Neither he nor Germany, whose Chancellor Helmut Schmidt was also approached, was willing to make large loans available, though Schmidt did indicate that *in extremis* he could be counted upon.

There was irony in the situation Callaghan found himself in. Large reserves of oil and natural gas had been discovered in the North Sea within British territorial waters. Big investments had to be made in drilling and pumping equipment, including the monster oil platforms that had to withstand the rigorous weather conditions of the northern ocean. Royalties from the oil would not be received until the end of the 1970s, still three years away, but would then flow into the Treasury at the rate of an estimated £2 billion a year. Callaghan's government was paving the way for the bonanza that buoyed up Mrs Thatcher's regime for the whole eleven and a half years she was in power.

In an effort to establish confidence in the international financial markets, Jim Callaghan and his Chancellor Denis Healey put together a package of cuts in public expenditure amounting to £1 billion, introduced a surcharge on employers' National Insurance payments, and promised cash limits on expenditure in future; but to no avail. All the package did was to infuriate the Labour left and elicit charges from them of betraying Labour's ideals. The country was being driven towards borrowing from the International Monetary Fund; both Prime Minister and Chancellor knew that the conditions attached to any loan would be stringent indeed. They also knew that accepting such conditions might well break the government, as Ramsay MacDonald's had been broken in 1931 – and there was no fate more dreaded by a social democratic administration.

Jim faced the prospect of his government disintegrating over the issue. He could not suspend collective responsibility, as Harold Wilson had done over membership of the European Community, for the decision that had to be made was one for the Cabinet, not one for a referendum of the people. So the Prime Minister embarked upon the most intensive and exhaustive debate of any in modern times. It took up most of October and November 1976, with nine full Cabinet meetings and many more meetings of Cabinet Committees. He was determined to give every Cabinet member his or her say, so that no one could claim afterwards to have been bounced, silenced or misinformed. He conducted the whole operation with exemplary patience, listening to every point of view, letting the Chancellor reiterate that the markets demanded substantial cuts in public expenditure and would have to be satisfied. Although it turned out later that the estimates by the Treasury of the public sector borrowing requirement, the PSBR, were seriously exaggerated, that was not the crucial point. The Labour government was believed by the financial markets to lack financial discipline, to be unwilling to grasp economic realities, and to be profligate with public spending. Whatever the statistical reality, these impressions drove their actions, including the selling of sterling.

It was remarkable, in hindsight, that Jim was able to take two months to reach the decision the IMF was demanding. The media in the 1970s were not subject to today's information revolution that requires instantaneous responses, nor were the world's financial markets fully globalised. Controls over capital movements were still in place, being finally dismantled only in the 1980s. The IMF debate was a classic example of how Cabinet government is supposed to work. It may no longer be possible in the post-Internet world.

The Cabinet discussions clustered around three positions, that of the Chancellor Denis Healey, that of Tony Benn and his supporters, and that of Tony Crosland and his associates. Healey's position was that most but not all the IMF's demands had to be met, requiring cuts of £1.5 billion in expenditure in 1977–8, and a similar amount in the estimates for the following year. This came on top of the cuts already made in July 1976, and the commitment then to cash limits for public expenditure (which would see its real value fall by the level of inflation). Tony Crosland took the view that the July cuts should suffice, that the PSBR estimate was probably wrong (he was correct in this) and that the government should stand up to the IMF. Tony Benn saw in the crisis the opportunity for the socialist economy he wanted. Cabinet members had been asked to submit memoranda for discussion. Tony Benn called for import controls (which would have breached European Community rules) and a siege economy.

At the end of the exercise, all of us understood better the economic forces with which the government had to contend. The compromise that was finally reached fell short of the IMF's original demands, amounting to cuts of £1.5 billion in 1977–8 and £1.5 billion in 1978–9. The sale of £500 million of government shares in the oil company BP was substituted for an equivalent cut in public expenditure.

After a tense stand-off, the IMF eventually accepted this outcome. The final confrontation between Denis Healey and Johannes Witteveen, Managing Director of the International Monetary Fund, was so fierce that it ended in the Chancellor telling the distinguished Dutchman to take a running jump. If the IMF insisted on the full pound of flesh, he threatened, the British government would call a general election, invoking the issue of the rights of a democratic government. I could not help wondering what would have happened if ours had been the government of a developing country in Asia or Africa instead. But once the agreement was reached, the markets turned about and the pound strengthened.

For nearly two years after the IMF crisis, the Callaghan government navigated through calmer waters. Deals were made with the Liberal Party, led by David Steel, under which the Liberals were consulted about forthcoming bills (but not about the government's programme), so they could indicate whether they would offer support. The government agreed to direct elections to the European Parliament, a Liberal objective, but conceded nothing on proportional representation at home. Jim Callaghan, very much a Party man, came to respect David Steel. Steel might have looked like a schoolboy, but he had the judgement and sagacity of a statesman. Confidence in the government increased. Furthermore, royalties from North Sea oil began to flow into the Exchequer. Britain was moving rapidly towards self-sufficiency in oil and its economic prospects were brightening.

The BBC took great pride in its television documentaries, especially those intended to address the great issues of the time. In the summer of 1977, the Harvard economist Kenneth Galbraith was invited to compère a weighty series called *The Age of Uncertainty*. The final programme was to be a discussion among some twenty or so well-known people about the age we were living in, conducted over a weekend at the farm of Galbraith himself in Newfane, Vermont.

Newfane is five hours' drive from Boston's Logan, the nearest international airport. The BBC sent a large limousine to pick up the four participants who were arriving together from London: Edward Heath; Kay Graham, proprietor of the *Washington Post*, the newspaper that had revealed the Watergate conspiracy; Jack Jones, the General Secretary of Britain's largest trades union, the Transport and General Workers'; and me.

Without hesitating, Jack climbed into the seat next to the driver. The rest of us settled down in the luxurious back compartment. There was a discreet glass screen between front and back. Ted Heath, whom I had always thought of as an aloof, shy man, began to talk about the hazards of being at once a single man and a Prime Minister. Scores of ambitious Conservative mothers had sent him photographs, sometimes accompanied by appealing descriptions, of their daughters. They had accosted him with invitations to lunch or tea. One striking redhead regularly appeared at public meetings he was addressing, loudly applauding his more eloquent passages, and laughing excessively at his rather laboured jokes. 'I began to look out for her,' he told us, 'and then I noticed that everyone else did too.' The crowning moment of her intrusion into his life came in a ceremony at a yacht club on the Isle of Wight, where Ted was to be awarded a cup. 'As I came into the room,' he told us, 'I suddenly saw her.' Her back was turned to him. He crept up behind the group she was with, who seemed to be laughing a lot. 'I heard her say, ". . . and of course he always forgets his toothbrush." At that moment I caught the eye of the Duke of Edinburgh. He gave me a meaningful wink.'

We travellers from London arrived late at Newfane, and were slipping gratefully off to bed. Just as I was about to do the same, a young man came in with a message. 'Henry Kissinger is flying in from California, which is four hours behind us here He doesn't want to spend the evening on his own. Are any of you happy to stay up for him?' Henry Kissinger! The Secretary of State to Richard Nixon! I volunteered immediately. To my surprise, no one else did. So at one in the morning, London time, Henry Kissinger and I, along with a large number of cans of beer, found ourselves chatting in one of the Galbraiths' sitting rooms. Kissinger was in a mood to talk. Never a buttoned-up man, he told me about Nixon's paranoia, his prayers for forgiveness, with which he wanted to associate this distinguished colleague, and Nixon's dark suspicions of conspiracies by the media against him.

The next morning, only three hours later, Kitty Galbraith, Kenneth's delicately beautiful wife, asked me if I would like to go swimming with her. 'I like to go skinny-dipping in the beaver pond,' she said to me. Being conventionally English, I am not keen on skinny-dipping with people I hardly know, but I felt it was the custom of the country and it seemed starchy to refuse. So Kitty and

I, stark naked, dropped into the dark waters of the beaver pond. To my amazement, as I surfaced, I saw what appeared to be a scene from *Macbeth*, Birnam wood moving to Dunsinane. What appeared to be a small leafy copse was approaching. As it came nearer, Kitty and I sank into the pond, only our eyes and nostrils clear of the water. Past the pond marched a dozen or so secret servicemen, each carrying a branch. In the middle of them appeared the figure of Dr Kissinger, going for his morning walk.

The BBC weekend was both intense and absurd. At one point, Kay Graham angrily confronted the producer. 'Yes, I said you could record what I said,' she declared, 'but I didn't imagine you would have a microphone in the toilet!'

Besides being Secretary of State for Education and Science, I was Paymaster-General. This ancient title could not be feminised without becoming the butt of obvious jokes, so neither my predecessor Judith Hart nor I tried to alter it. The formal duties of this position were very light, involving oversight of public service pensions. In practice, the job of the Paymaster-General was to chair whatever Cabinet Committees the Prime Minister nominated. Mine included two highly contentious ones, industrial democracy and Scottish devolution.

There were three strands of opinion about industrial democracy: those who wanted none of it, which included most employers; those who wanted the trades unions officially represented on the boards of major companies, the view adopted by Jack Jones, and those who wanted a German style of industrial democracy, with representatives elected by the workers themselves to serve on the supervisory boards of companies. A committee of inquiry chaired by Alan Bullock, Master of St Catherine's College, Oxford, and biographer of Adolf Hitler, had reported in favour of the second alternative. In the light of what I knew about industrial democracy in Germany, and my reservations about trades union control, I favoured the third. It proved impossible to reach any kind of agreement in the Cabinet Committee, or indeed outside government, among the contending views. In the end, the idea of an official policy on industrial democracy was quietly buried.

Scottish devolution, though, could not be shelved in that way. Separate bills for Scottish and Welsh devolution had already gone through Parliament by July 1978, but there was no united enthusiasm for devolution in either country. In Wales, there was nothing approaching majority support.* As for Scotland, the bar to approval had been raised by an amendment moved by George Cunningham, Labour MP for Islington South and Finsbury, a clever, obstinately independent-minded backbencher, requiring that at least 40 per cent of the Scottish electorate (not simply of those who voted) must favour devolution in a referendum for it to go ahead. Looming over the whole procedure was the question asked by Tam Dalyell, the irrepressibly honest (and therefore inconvenient) MP for West Lothian, which still remains unanswered: if English MPs have no vote on devolved domestic Scottish legislation, should Scots MPs continue to have one on domestic English legislation?

A central issue in the case of Scotland was whether a devolved Scottish Parliament should have the power to raise taxes. This was the question referred to my Cabinet Committee. I believed that a limited right of taxation was critical to establishing a genuinely devolved Scottish Parliament. This meant that it would have to accept responsibility for its decisions. But there was strong opposition on the committee to any such recommendation. Indeed the government itself was divided on devolution, reflecting the deep disagreement in the two countries themselves.

The promised referenda were held in March 1979. In Wales the proposal was decisively lost. In Scotland, a tiny majority of those who voted supported devolution. But the turnout was low, and

* Kenneth Morgan, *Callaghan: A Life*, Oxford University Press, 1997.

George Cunningham's condition, approved by Parliament, of approval from at least 40 per cent of the Scottish electorate, was nowhere near being met. Barely a third registered their agreement. Devolution to Scotland would have to wait for another eighteen years.

Jim brought calm to No. 10. 'Steady as she goes', the old navy saying, seemed to sum it up. He was never rattled, as Harold Wilson had been, by rumours of conspiracies against him, nor was he obsessed by what the newspapers said. He did not shift ministers around, nor overnight create new posts, Harold's way of confusing his rivals and rewarding his friends. He had beaten off – in my view, mistakenly – Barbara Castle's proposals for trades union reform, so the unions had reason to be grateful to him. For the first two years of his government, the union leaders in response had delivered incomes restraint, though against increasing odds.

Jim Callaghan was a much better Prime Minister than Chancellor of the Exchequer or Home Secretary. The job suited him. He was a man for the broad canvas, interested in all aspects of society, instinctive in his feel for the values, not just the opinions, of his people. He was deeply rooted in his family and also in the land, distrustful of what we now call 'spin' and of political fashion. I remember him asking me whether I thought he could appoint Peter Jay, his son-in-law, to the plum post of Ambassador to Washington. Peter was a brilliant man, he said, but wouldn't people think it was nepotism? He was at pains to point out that it was not his idea, but that after David Owen had suggested it, he began to see the arguments for it. It was in my view, as I told him, an inspired appointment. For two years Peter and his wife Margaret, Jim's impressive daughter, dominated the Washington scene and projected the image of a vibrant young Britain. Jay's appointment, and indeed that of David Owen, the youngest Foreign Secretary since Anthony Eden, brought excitement and drama to the government.

By the autumn of 1978, however, the pent-up anger and frustration of the shop stewards, after three years of wage restraint and two years in which standards of living declined, began to boil over. The third year of the policy had been complicated, based on productivity agreements that were hard to understand. The shop stewards, close to their members in the factories and workshops, were becoming alienated from their official leaders, the trades union barons who were close to the Prime Minister and his deputy, Michael Foot. Jim Callaghan's reliance on old friendships and old loyalties was to prove insufficient. The world had moved on. The sense of solidarity that had sustained the Labour movement for so long was being replaced by a new, impatient individualism. Appeals to community sentiment were to prove ineffective when people saw their incomes and their status threatened.

Jim did not seem to me to be aware of this change in mood. Treasury computers in 1978 showed that a 5 per cent limit on pay settlements would bring inflation down dramatically fast. Within a year or so, the combination of pay restraint and the rising flow of North Sea oil would transform the country's prospects. There would be real improvements in standards of living. But prices in 1978 were still rising at about 7 per cent a year. A 5 per cent limit in income increases meant another year of belt-tightening. Jim could not count on winning an election decisively. The thought of a further Labour government whose majority depended on concessions to one minority or another, staggering on from one vote in Parliament to the next, must have appalled him. He needed to conserve his energies for governing the country in difficult times, not for bargaining in Parliament and endless in-fighting with his caustic critics in the Labour Party.

I have always believed that Jim's decision to delay the general election until the spring of 1979 emerged from a tragic overestimate of his own influence with the union leaders, and of their influence over their members. What I may have underestimated was his weariness with the endless bargaining he was involved in. Had the election been fought in the autumn of 1978, his own popularity, far ahead of that of his Party, might have carried his government on to victory. He had been a good and trusted Prime Minister, and the people knew it. On 7 September 1978 Jim told the Cabinet that there was to be no autumn election. I remember that Peter Shore, then Secretary of State for the Environment, and I both protested, pleading for a pay ceiling of 8 per cent, just above inflation, and an election that autumn. We were abruptly interrupted by the Prime Minister, who told the Cabinet that the timing of a general election was his prerogative and nobody else's. He would not accept any further discussion on the issue.

In October, opinion polls showed Labour slightly ahead of the Conservatives. It was to be the last such occasion. In the winter, all hell broke loose. Lorry drivers, school caretakers, local government workers and many others joined in a massive protest against incomes policy. Newspapers carried pictures of mountains of rubbish in the streets. Worse still were the reports that the dead lay unburied in hospital morgues up and down the country. The strikes turned into a kind of frenzy, in which otherwise decent men and women outdid one another in their callousness towards the public they were meant to serve. Returning from a summit meeting of world leaders in Guadeloupe, an island that in press photographs was made to look more than usually like a tropical paradise, the Prime Minister responded to media inquiries by playing down the crisis at home. Unable to see television programmes about Britain on his Caribbean island, he had misjudged the extent to which industrial strife was now beyond control.

By January, as strikes spiralled across the country, backing wild claims of 30 per cent and even 40 per cent pay increases, all pretensions to an incomes policy were abandoned. The Prime Minister himself, his reputation for negotiation and close ties with the unions in tatters, seemed to lose the will to fight. The government began to drift from one setback to another. In my own area, while the teachers did not strike, they refused to do anything beyond teaching itself. Since the school caretakers were on strike, that meant that no one took responsibility for the safety of children once the school day ended. Then, just before the election, the teachers' unions put in a surreal claim for a 36.5 per cent pay increase. I offered them 9 per cent and proposed to refer the rest of their claim to the Standing Commission on Pay Comparability, postponing whatever recommendation it made until after the election, just four days away. For this, I was denounced by Fred Jarvis, the NUT's leader, as a liar, which made headlines everywhere. I was accused of blocking the pay negotiation and uniting the whole teaching profession against me. My immediate reaction was one of disbelief and then of indignation. I had known Fred for thirty years. We had campaigned together for comprehensive schools. Nothing was to be gained for the teachers by such denunciations, nor for the children they taught. I was already angry that children had been prevented from going to school by caretakers' obstructiveness and the willingness of the teachers to hide behind them. But then I reflected on the situation we faced. Moderate and sensible leaders like Fred were being harried by their extremists. They were becoming desperate. Like drowning men, they grappled with their government and took it down with them.

The Cabinet did consider bringing in a state of emergency and using troops for essential public services, but flinched from such a course. It was doubtful how much impact troops could have made. It was also recognised that such an action would split the government and the Labour Party beyond repair. On 28 March 1979 the government narrowly lost the vote of confidence, and that precipitated a general election. In spite of an impressive campaign, Jim Callaghan lost the May election to Margaret Thatcher's Conservative Party, and the country embarked on a radically different political experiment.

CHAPTER 13

Labour Falls Apart

L abour's defeat in the 1979 general election was a source of great bitterness and rancour; the wrath of the left-wing activists was directed at Jim Callaghan. He had once been seen as a unifying figure in Labour's civil war, largely because of his opposition to Barbara Castle's 1969 White Paper, *In Place of Strife*. He had the reputation of being the champion of the trades unions. He had also been at best agnostic on the subject of Europe, and played little part in the 1975 referendum. He was, in addition, respected by Tony Benn, the trail-blazer of the left, for his forthrightness. On this score, Benn compared him favourably with Harold Wilson. But Jim had two strikes against him. First, his government had been defeated. Second, he was closely identified with incomes policy, the bugbear of the left.

On the first, it was vital for the left to demonstrate that they were in no way responsible for Labour's defeat. Yet the evidence to the contrary was clear. From a position in February 1979 of being eleven points behind the Conservative leader Margaret Thatcher, Jim had recovered to the extent of being thirteen points ahead of her by the end of the election campaign, three months later. He ran far ahead of his Party, which had started the campaign at

10.5 per cent behind, and ended 2 per cent behind.* If anyone could have won the election for Labour, it was the trusted and well-liked Prime Minister. With his instinctive sense for public opinion, Jim Callaghan was accessible and friendly. When he was at the Home Office, he and I quite often walked through St James's Park on our way to the House of Commons, accompanied only by a single police officer. Members of the public would come up and offer Jim their opinions on some current government policy, and he would almost always pause to hear them out. When he travelled to his Cardiff constituency on a Friday, the doors of his carriage were not locked; here, too, people would walk up the corridors to speak to him. His visit to the Embankment in London where the demonstrators were gathering just before the anti-Vietnam demonstration of October 1968 was wholly in character. He liked people. He was not one of those politicians whose contact with the public is limited to carefully controlled occasions.

But could Labour have won the election? Here Jim's judgement, in my opinion, on both the date for going to the polls and the proposed figure for pay increases under the incomes policy, was flawed. At Cabinet in October 1978, not long before trades union anger exploded, Jim announced that the new ceiling for pay increases would be 5 per cent, and that the election would be not in the autumn of 1978, but the following year.

Those of us who saw a lot of our constituents realised how deep the resentment over the incomes policy was. Many of mine were in skilled jobs – in aerospace, pharmaceuticals and other high-tech areas. They saw their margins being squeezed year after year, for one of the effects of incomes policy was to narrow wage differentials. They were highly organised, in strong and aggressive unions, and in labour markets where highly skilled people were in short supply. The national interest in reducing inflation and the

* Anthony King (ed.), British Public Opinion, 1937–2000: The Gallup Polls, Politico's Publishing, 2001.

market incentives for widening differentials were at odds with one another. Loyalty to the Labour government was not strong enough to bridge the gap for long. Jim had been much influenced by the optimistic 1978 Treasury computer forecast showing that a pay norm of 5 per cent would bring inflation down very quickly, leading to an improvement in incomes in real terms. But to the public, coping with inflation now running at 8.3 per cent, this pay norm meant a substantial reduction in their standard of living. Vainly, several of us argued for a norm of 8 per cent, which would have had a slower impact on inflation but would at least have allowed wages and prices to rise at a similar rate. Jim would have none of it. Nor did he respond to arguments for an immediate general election, which the government might have won, before the explosion that came to be called 'the winter of discontent'.*

These misjudgements were the Prime Minister's own contributions to the defeat. The winter of discontent destroyed the government and, with it, many of the hopes and aspirations that electors had associated with Labour. Yet a large part of the electorate remained loyal: on a high turnout of 76 per cent, the Conservatives got 43.9 per cent, Labour 36.9 per cent and the Liberal Party 13.8 per cent.

I lost my parliamentary seat, the only Cabinet minister to do so. My Conservative opponent, Bowen Wells, took Hertford and Stevenage by a majority of 1295. I was not surprised. I had worked hard over the fifteen years I had been the MP, and I knew many of my constituents personally, but there were certain factors working against me. Before the 1974 general election there had been substantial boundary changes because my Hitchin constituency had grown too big. I had lost Royston, Baldock and Letchworth, and gained Hertford and its surrounding villages. Letchworth, the Garden City, had long been a centre of support for me. It had

* From mid-October to mid-November 1978, Labour was polling 5 per cent higher in voting intentions than the Conservatives.

attracted many progressive families and sustained scores of voluntary organisations, from morris-dancing to human rights. Parts of my new constituency, on the other hand, were no longer the familiar territory I had spent a decade caring for. Hertford was a Conservative county seat, displeased at finding itself in a Labour constituency. Most of the pleasant villages I now acquired were also traditionally Conservative, and resentful of the new town of Stevenage thrusting its tentacles into the surrounding countryside. Perhaps the most important factor was the Conservative manifesto promise to allow tenants to buy their council houses. That promise split my vote, and that of many other Labour MPs representing new towns.

Stevenage, the first of the postwar new towns, had houses of high quality, built to Parker Morris standards, the kitemark of good public building. Most of the houses belonged to the New Town Development Corporation, were well maintained, and graced by young trees and pleasant flowerbeds. The town had good schools, a large park and a new hospital. Even the older neighbourhoods, built fifteen or so years before, had kept their value. The sale of these houses at a discount of a third for tenants who had lived in them for more than three years, ranging up to 50 per cent for those who had lived there for twenty years or more, was irresistible to those who could afford to buy. I remember one constituent I had helped coming up to me during the election campaign. 'You are a good MP, Mrs Williams,' he said, 'but you aren't worth £5000 to me.' The prospect of another Labour government taking away this golden opportunity swayed many votes.

Did I expect to be defeated? No, but I did think there was a good chance I might lose. I remember feeling intensely relieved that both my mother and my father, who had set such great store by my political career, were dead, for I knew their disappointment, indeed chagrin, would have been far greater than mine. As I went around the constituency in the tough slog of the election campaign, I realised how angry and disturbed my voters felt about the winter of discontent, especially the women. I felt, too, that an era in politics was ending. Mrs Thatcher represented a radical change in mood, away from the longstanding consensual politics of one-nation Conservatism towards a polarised society of conviction politics.

I was more concerned about how to handle the humiliation of the defeat than about the defeat itself. In my time in the House of Commons I had made many friends. But I had never fallen in love with the place; it was too clubby and exclusive for me. As for cov-erage of the defeat, I found the media were sympathetic, even sentimental about it. My main interview took place the day after the election, on the sunny morning of 4 May. I remember I was wearing a pink suit, since nothing even remotely funereal seemed to me appropriate. I was interviewed by Robin Day, an old friend from our Oxford University years, with whom I had appeared on the BBC's *Question Time*. Norman St John-Stevas, who had been Minister for the Arts under Ted Heath and was to become Minister for the Arts a second time as well as Leader of the House of Commons in the Thatcher government, treated me with gentle piety, as befits one mourning a deceased public figure. My family and many of my friends had called to commiserate, most of them assuming I would be downcast. There was a widespread assump-tion that my political career, at the age of forty-nine, was at an end.

In fact I was numbed rather than hurt by the result. All around me, Labour MPs were losing their seats. I was one among many victims, if the only one who had been in the Cabinet. The numb-ing helped me to be graceful in defeat, and to go round thanking my constituents for their support during my decade and a half as their MP. By Saturday morning, a good night's sleep and the prospect of freedom from the constraints of being a minister began to cheer me up. My old friends John and Eileen Spencer, who were staying at my house, remembered hearing me singing in the bath that morning. For there was not only freedom but also opportunity. I had woken up to a heady sense of freedom, as if I had got my life back after all the years of responsibility and discipline. I didn't know what I would do, but I did know I needed time to think. My daughter Rebecca had just been offered a place at Wadham College, Oxford, to study law, after getting good A-levels at her school, Camden High School for Girls. She had moved there after her first secondary school, Godolphin and Latymer, had chosen to go independent rather than comprehensive, a choice put to the school by the ILEA in 1976. So we no longer had to live in London. With the characteristic rapid response of Americans, I received within a few days a letter from the John F. Kennedy Institute of Politics at Harvard University inviting me to go there for a semester as a Fellow. Here was an opportunity to think about where I was going and, more important, where the Labour Party was going. I responded with alacrity.

Each semester the Institute invited six people associated with politics to conduct a course on a subject of their choice for those Harvard undergraduates who were interested. Almost all the Fellows were American, former Congressmen or campaign managers, occasionally well-known state or local politicians. Inviting a foreigner was unusual, but my gender proved to be an advantage: very few of the Fellows were women. The fellowship carried with it accommodation, in lodgings or a small apartment, a bursary sufficient to meet most of one's needs, a well-equipped office and the company of colleagues and students, all of whom attended a weekly Institute supper where everyone talked about current political issues, usually introduced by some famous visitor.

It is hard to imagine anything that could have been more congenial to me. At last I had the time to think about my years in government, to reflect upon the battles within the Labour Party and to ask myself what had gone wrong and why. I also found myself in the midst of a fascinating period in American politics. When Lyndon Johnson signed the Civil Rights Act in 1964, he is said to have commented as he put down his pen, 'We have lost

the South for a generation.' Richard Nixon proceeded to construct a Southern strategy on the basis of that remark, one that
implied the betrayal of Southern whites by the Democrats, the
party that had always been associated with the South. Nixon had
been disgraced by Watergate, but his Southern strategy succeeded
nonetheless. The once 'solid South' fragmented. Democrats could
no longer count on its instinctive loyalty. By the mid-1980s, the
Republicans dominated Congress and the hugely popular Ronald
Reagan was installed in the White House, proclaiming that it was
morning again in America. The Republicans had triumphed over
a bad legacy. Maybe Labour could too?

This new opportunity gave me time to think about my own life.
After Bernard left, I had seen a lot of the political writer Anthony
King, Professor of Politics at Essex University. Tony was a frequent
and admired broadcaster on political programmes, for which I had
occasionally been interviewed. I was attracted by his directness
and his North American energy. Tony had lost his wife Vera,
whom I also knew, from cancer in 1970. Our bereavements drew
us together and we fell in love. One of his closest friends in the
United States was Dick Neustadt, whom he had befriended
during the sabbatical year Dick and his wife Bert, together with
their children Rick and Elizabeth (Beth), spent in Oxford in
1961–2. Dick and Bert invited Tony, Rebecca and me to spend
several summer holidays with them at Wellfleet on Cape Cod. So
we got to know that magical place of endless sand dunes fringing
a huge ocean, scores of little lakes dotted among the stunted oak
and pine trees, and sunsets of blazing primary colours. Dick loved
the Cape, his favourite place on earth. As soon as the summer
semester ended, he and Bert would head down there and stay for
two or three months at a time.

I spent a lot of time with Bert during these holidays. She had
been a traditional wife, catering for her husband's every need. In the
lovely phrase from the Old Testament, her price was far above
rubies. She would try to build a wall around his work time. She

shielded Dick from life's endless interruptions so that he could remain undisturbed in his study of the American presidency. Throughout their married life Dick had been supported and sustained by her. She had an almost reverential concern for his work and did all she could to protect his writing time. Their one-storey cottage in Wellfleet on the edge of Gull Pond, a lake three-quarters of a mile across, was a magnet for Dick's colleagues and even more for his former students and their families, who would trek across the continent or the ocean to see him. My stepdaughter Beth recalls in her biography of her father that Bert put a chain across the path to their door, bearing a notice. 'Man at Work,' it read. 'No Visitors Before 5 pm.' It wasn't entirely successful in deflecting the tides of visitors that swept in every afternoon and congregated on the sunny deck overlooking Gull Pond.

Dick was a slow writer, engrossed in ensuring that every word carried its full weight of meaning. His writing, as his daughter Beth lovingly describes it in her essay about her father in the same work,* had a density and depth that attracted students to read his books over and over again, each time discovering fresh nuances and subtleties. Some reviewers described Dick as a second Machiavelli. Whether Machiavelli refined with such exuberant intensity the advice he gave, I cannot say.

Bert had recently encountered the women's liberation movement, and had found it unsettling. Here was a completely different vision of the role of women from that according to which she had been brought up. She had been well educated at one of America's most renowned women's colleges, Vassar. She had held, after graduation, responsible and demanding jobs in Washington. Marriage, however, implied for her a different role – as helpmeet and supporter of a husband whose ambitions and aspirations would henceforth determine the pattern of their lives. Bert and I discussed

* Matthew J. Dickinson and Elizabeth A. Neustadt (eds), *Guardian of the Presidency: The Legacy of Richard E. Neustadt*, The Brookings Institution, 2007.

at length the different paths our lives had followed and whether women's liberation would enrich or simply complicate their lives. She took me with her to a Cambridge women's group, mainly discontented wives of academics, highly educated and clearly frustrated by the obstacles they had encountered to pursuing a career. She told me about an occasion that had clearly shaken her.

As the wife of a senior professor, Bert had readily accepted the traditional obligation to entertain the wives of new faculty members, almost all of them men, and to offer them useful advice. She strongly identified with her husband's university, Harvard. On one such occasion, she was explaining the ways in which wives could help their husbands in their careers. From the gathering of carefully dressed young women, some wearing hats and gloves to the tea party, there burst out a furious dissenter. Shaking with anger, she pointed at Bert: 'It's people like you who have betrayed us,' she shouted. Bert was not the sort of person just to get indignant at this breach of good manners. She took the memory away with her, and thought deeply about it. She began to question some of her own assumptions, and in doing so understood better her own daughter Beth, who at this time was in a phase of rebellion against her orderly and dedicated mother.

Dick, too, encountered the early ripples of the movement. The language of his early books – for instance, the first edition of his classic *Presidential Power* – was entirely masculine. It assumed that senior politicians and their advisers would all be men, even though already in 1960, when the book was first published, women in the United Kingdom and elsewhere in Europe were beginning to make a mark on their governments. Dick became a strong advocate of his own women students, famously battling for one of the most outstanding, Doris Kearns. He made her his teaching assistant, but could not persuade his colleagues to promote her to a tenured academic post. Instead she became a brilliant historian of presidents, writing about Franklin Roosevelt, Lyndon Johnson and Abraham Lincoln.

Dick was fascinated by politics, of which he had been a committed and ambitious practitioner, as well as an observer and student. Chosen by President Truman to be his speechwriter and assistant while still in his twenties, he had devoted himself to trying to understand the institution of the presidency, how it worked and how the very different personalities of successive presidents adapted to the role. After Truman left office in 1952, Dick had found a teaching job at Columbia University in New York, where he concentrated on writing a book on the subject. In the apartment below that of the Neustadts lived their friends David and Ellie Truman. David, a distinguished political scientist, was then Professor of Government at Columbia. Ellie became Dick's assistant on *Presidential Power*, the book that was to make him famous. Dick's manuscripts, invariably scrawled in ink on yellow legal pads, would be lowered at the end of a string from his flat above for Ellie to type. The book was of such densely concentrated observation, such incisive comment, that it made Dick's reputation in Washington and academia alike. Its sales were immensely lifted by a press photograph of President Kennedy just after his election carrying the book under his arm into the White House.

I was drawn to the Neustadts and to their lifestyle. Talking, swimming, sailing, canoeing and entertaining friends in their wonderful world of pine trees, sand and water, friendship and conversation. I didn't know it at the time, of course, but I had met my second husband.

At the end of 1979, after my semester at the Institute of Politics, I returned to Britain, to the National Executive Committee of the Labour Party and to the via dolorosa that was then the experience of everyone connected with the Wilson and Callaghan governments. My time away had enabled me to see more objectively what was happening. Those who live within dysfunctional families rarely regard themselves as dysfunctional, and so it was for us.

It was clear that the Labour Party was doomed to be unelectable – and if nothing changed, social democracy itself would be discredited. I was prepared to devote time and energy to making sure that did not happen.

I had lost my constituency, but I was still on the NEC. From that ringside seat I watched the Campaign for Labour Party Democracy* relentlessly pursue its objective of making the Parliamentary Party accountable to an NEC it could control. Mandatory reselection was the first goal: every Labour MP would be obliged, in the course of a parliamentary term, to present him- or herself for reselection by his or her general management committee on the basis of his or her record. On the face of it, this might look like an exemplary democratic measure, putting pressure on MPs to work hard for their constituents (there are always some MPs who fail in that duty). But in practice an MP's chance of reselection would depend upon the political complexion of the local general management committee. If it was a right-wing committee, it might assess the MPs' support for the parliamentary leadership. If it was left-wing, what would matter would be how that MP had voted on policy matters, especially those where the NEC had differed from the parliamentary leadership. In other words, whoever controlled the NEC would control the selection of the MPs too. Reselection would have more to do with the MP's political orientation than with his or her service to their constituents.

I was more pessimistic about the Labour Party's future than many of my parliamentary colleagues. Only a handful of them served on the NEC. Of the parliamentarians I was closest to, only Tom Bradley, elected from the trades union section, who had been Roy Jenkins's Parliamentary Private Secretary, and John Cartwright, elected by the Co-operative Society in the affiliated organisations

---

* A pressure group within the Labour Party advocating making MPs more accountable to local party general management committees.

section, were NEC members. John Golding, the outspoken and brave trades unionist and MP for Newcastle-under-Lyme, was a staunchly moderate NEC member, but I did not know him well. The media rarely covered the private meetings of the NEC in detail, though they gave quite extensive coverage to Party conferences, held at seaside resorts in the early autumn. Many MPs, already shaken by the election result, failed to see what was happening to their Party until they met together at the 1979 conference.

There was another reason for my pessimism. I was closely associated with the Campaign for Labour Victory, a group of moderates organised by Bill Rodgers arguing that Labour would be unlikely ever again to win an election if it pursued extremist policies. As a former member of the Labour Cabinet and a prominent opponent of the far left, I was invited to speak at scores of local Party meetings in the run-up to the 1979 Party Conference. At these meetings I would encounter hecklers, but also many good Labour Party members who were scared about what was happening to their local party. They would speak to me privately about moderate members being abused or intimidated. At this stage, although we observed the steady onward march of the hard left, none of us considered leaving the Labour Party. The Conservative Party was coming under increasing pressure from the right, from organisations like the National Association for Freedom (NAFF) and individuals like the authors of the education Black Papers.* It was still broadly a Heathite party, but we could see that its new leader, Margaret Thatcher, would be likely to take it in more dogmatic directions, and for us to join it was simply unthinkable. Our hope was that, sooner or later, the Parliamentary Labour Party would stand up to the NEC. That hope was to prove hollow.

---

* The education Black Papers, which strongly attacked progressive teaching methods (see p. 172), were written by Brian Cox, Anthony Dyson and Rhodes Boyson, MP.

Serving on the NEC was a grim experience. My heart sank at the thought of yet another meeting, yet another acrid and futile argument. The only compensation was the solidarity of our small group, the unexpressed loyalty we felt towards one another. Throughout the 1970s, my little band of allies and I put down resolution after resolution at meeting after meeting, and lost them all. Things got worse after Harold Wilson retired – Wilson had managed to avoid confrontations, repeatedly arguing that the Labour government might be put at risk. He retired in 1976, and Roy Jenkins resigned as Home Secretary in the same year. Roy had been a powerful ally, mobilising withering arguments against the hard left; but to no avail. Arguments carried no weight against those who had decided their positions long before the arguments were ever heard.

On one issue our small group of NEC members felt we might prevail: we demanded publication of the November 1975 report by the Party's National Agent himself, Reg Underhill, on the subject of entryism – there was no doubt that the Revolutionary Socialist Party and the Militant Tendency, two extreme-left groups, were trying to make inroads into the Labour Party rather than being independent. This technique became known as entryism. Reg Underhill was a quiet, utterly devoted Labour Party official, who wore his love and concern for the Party on his sleeve. I do not know whether he was an admirer of the traditional Bevanite left or of the Gaitskellite right; I suspect he had reservations about both. He was, however, a deeply parliamentary democrat. The refusal of the NEC to publish or even discuss his painstaking, carefully prepared report on what he saw as a serious threat to the Party was a staging-post in the journey towards political paranoia. The hard left had no wish to examine the cancer that was killing the Labour Party, and in this they had the support of the soft left, who indulged their emotions at the expense of their judgement. One of their number was the Party's General Secretary Ron Hayward, a Vicar of Bray who could switch allegiances instantaneously if it was expedient to do so.

I was outraged by this cavalier dismissal of Reg Underhill's report. Here was a man of impeccable loyalty and integrity, as everyone on the NEC knew, and who had given his life to the Labour Party. That his report was not even considered by the NEC, the body responsible for the health of the Party, and that we could not rally a majority of its members to insist on doing so, appalled me. The key issue, as this instance demonstrated, was not Europe, nor public ownership, but representative democracy. The hard left and in particular the Trotskyites regarded representative democracy as a sham, a way of disguising the interests of the property-owning classes. They shared with the Communists the belief that it was the Party, not the public, to whom elected politicians should be accountable.

I had witnessed Communism in practice many years earlier. In 1949, as described earlier in this book, I had visited Tito's Yugoslavia. My acquaintance with the country led me to read, a decade later, a seminal book by one of Tito's lieutenants, Milovan Djilas, entitled *The New Class*. Djilas's theme was that one-party states, even Communist ones, evolved a new ruling class which gave itself privileges as well as power. Unaccountable to an electorate that was offered no choice between different parties, this ruling class became more and more divorced from the people it claimed to serve. On my later visits to the Soviet Union I was to see this phenomenon for myself. In 1969 as a junior minister, I visited Moscow. The then Prime Minister Harold Wilson, whose own lifestyle was austere, had decided that ministers outside the Cabinet should share cars and travel standard class in trains and aeroplanes. So I was in the back of the plane to Moscow. We arrived at the airport, and no one left the aircraft. From my window I could see a guard of honour lined up at the bottom of the first-class steps. Time passed. Eventually an airline official came to my seat and asked if by any chance I was the minister. I was. I descended the first-class steps and briefly reviewed the guard of honour. It was clear that none of the Russian officials could imagine a member of another government, let alone one of their own, travelling standard class.

A small thing, maybe – except that after that I learned that the best schools, the best medical treatment, the best railway carriages and the best hotels were available only to the *nomenklatura*, Djilas's new class. The lives of the *nomenklatura* were risky. Their official lives, and, under such Soviet leaders as Stalin, even their biological lives, could be ended at whim. But while they survived, they enjoyed the privileges of the upper classes everywhere.

I blamed the hard left for its failure to see the rise of the new ruling class in the Soviet Union, but I could be blamed myself for failing to realise that the soft left was not irremediably committed to the hard left. It looked like that to me, encountering the solidarity of the broad left on issue after issue that came before the National Executive. The soft left was disappointed by the record of Labour governments. They were looking for ways to compel the parliamentary leadership to be responsive to the Party. But they were not, as I recognise now, enemies of parliamentary democracy itself.

The trades union movement had been from the beginning the rock on which the Labour Party was built. It saw itself as a substantial part of British society, and its leaders as partners with the parliamentary leadership. By the 1970s, the rock was splitting. There had always been some left-leaning unions, in particular in well-paid industries like printing, but they were more than balanced by the big general unions representing semi-skilled and unskilled working people. Now, under pressure from frustrated shop stewards and ordinary members too, the unions were becoming more militant. For eleven years they had worked within the constraints of an incomes policy, sometimes voluntary, sometimes statutory. The authority of the elected trades union leaders had been eroded by their commitment to the policy, which left many trades union members feeling they had been unfairly dealt with. As noted earlier, while the general unions benefited from the narrowing of wage differentials, those that represented professional and skilled workers greatly resented it. Paradoxically, it was these unions that moved to the left.

The unions had not supported an incomes policy without exacting a price in terms of legislation favourable to them. Laws like the Employment Protection Act, the Health and Safety at Work Act and the Industry Act, all passed in 1975, and the Trade Union and Labour Relations Act of 1976 had substantially strengthened their hand. Within the movement itself, shop stewards had gained power relative to the national leaders. A growing proportion of wage bargaining was conducted at local level. By 1977, only a quarter of the settlements were made at the national or regional level.

Why did Labour governments allow themselves to become martyrs of their incomes policy? Because they could not stomach the alternative. The economy in the 1970s was still primarily dependent for jobs on manufacturing. Twenty-four per cent of the labour force was so employed, with a further 13 per cent in the public services and 3 per cent in agriculture. Most of this labour force was organised in trades unions whose role was to bargain with their employers for the best possible wages and working conditions for their members. In a free market, the main constraint on their bargaining power was the threat of unemployment. The trebling of unemployment in the first three years of the Thatcher government, driven by harsh financial policies of high interest rates and cuts in public expenditure, was the alternative. It was complemented by laws abolishing the privileges and immunities conferred on the unions by Labour governments. Together these measures broke the power of the unions.

Looking back now, I would have to say that the Labour government of which I was part conceded too much to the unions. The Trade Union and Labour Relations Committee, half representatives of the government, half those of the unions, met regularly to examine proposed legislation. Full notice was taken of what the unions didn't like, or wanted changed. Governments are right to consult widely and to hear the opinions of their citizens, but in my view no special interest has the right to veto or amend legislation to suit its own purposes. Governments must govern for everyone. Nor should special interests be exempted from the normal processes of democracy. That is why Barbara Castle had been absolutely right to insist on secret ballots before strikes and to disallow secondary strikes. Labour had bent too far in its efforts to conciliate the unions. But as so often happens in politics, its Conservative successor went too far in the opposite direction. In the three years of financial austerity between 1979 and 1982, hundreds of sound businesses were destroyed, leaving areas of desolation in the old industrial areas and casting hundreds of thousands into unemployment. Many never worked again.

My perception of Labour's plight, and my pessimism about it, were much influenced by my position on the NEC. Colleagues still in Parliament, surrounded by a moderate majority of Labour MPs, were only dimly aware of it, as one registers the distant sound of thunder. At the Labour Party Conference in the autumn of 1979, MPs were shocked to find themselves the scapegoats of Labour's election defeat. Penned into a corner of the conference floor in the block of seats allocated to them, they were jeered and pointed at by angry delegates. Even among the MPs themselves, assumptions about what was happening depended a great deal on what part of the country one's constituency was in. In London and Liverpool, the battle was fierce. Moderate MPs had to spend much of their time and energy mobilising loyal party workers in their constituencies to show up at meetings and vote on resolutions. The tactics of the hard left, dragging the meetings out, moving resolutions when most people had gone home, upbraiding and sometimes intimidating their opponents, wearied local members with regular jobs and family responsibilities. Little by little, these men and women drifted away.

*

I was so preoccupied with the fight within the Party and by the need to make a living, now that I had neither a ministry nor a constituency, that I failed to take on board the significance of the Dimbleby Lecture of 22 November. Roy Jenkins, now President of the European Commission, had been invited to deliver this pres-tigious BBC oration, which he called 'Home Thoughts from Abroad'. Roy looked at politics through the perspective of history; he took a long view and a large view, which was why his personal ambition was always tempered by a certain detachment. Observing British politics, quarrelsome, partisan and petty, Roy described in his lecture the dominance of the two-party system and the erosion of popular support for it. He saw this system as one of the main reasons for Britain's comparatively poor per-formance as a nation. It was the system itself that needed to change.

Roy by now had moved away from the Labour Party; he no longer even mourned it. While he retained his association with many who were still in the Party, politically he was now closer to leading Liberals such as Jo Grimond, the Bonham-Carters and David Steel, the leader of the party since 1976. Roy's call in his lecture for a new centre party was music to Steel's ears. For David Steel, one of the shrewdest minds in politics, did not want Roy to join the Liberal Party. His mind was set on much bigger things: he wanted the Liberal Party to be the catalyst of a political upheaval, bringing two-party politics in Britain to an end.

Contrary to much media speculation at the time, I had had only intermittent contact with Roy in Brussels between 1976 and 1980. I admired him for his strong stance against racism and for his imaginative approach to criminal justice. My time as a Minister of State at the Home Office had convinced me that pris-ons were not an effective way to deal with non-violent offenders. Furthermore, in the 1974–6 Wilson Cabinet, Roy and I had found ourselves in a committed minority of liberal-minded ministers. On freedom of information, a Speaker's Conference to review the electoral system and the incorporation of the European Convention on Human Rights into British law, we stood together, attracting only one or two others; on freedom of information, though not on the other proposals, one of those few was Tony Benn.

The grandeur of Roy's thinking about politics attracted to him a circle of brilliant young men whose loyalty was total, men like John Harris, Anthony Lester, David Marquand and Matthew Oakeshott. Several of them had worked for Roy in one or other of his official posts. They were known to the media as FORJ, friends of Roy Jenkins. I sometimes thought of them as acolytes, but that was unfair. Part of Roy's attraction for them was his willingness to discuss, to be open to question, to carefully reconsider his own position in the light of what they said. He combined strongly held values with complete lack of dogma. His Dimbleby Lecture gave direction to their aspirations, and to many beyond them. I was not of their number, nor was I at this time a close friend of Roy's. Our lifestyles were dissimilar, and our friendships different. I was much more embedded in the Labour Party culture than he was, and I did not share his fondness for clubs. Nor could I, for at this time, as noted earlier, clubs were still a male preserve. What he most enjoyed, good conversation and good food, were to be found there. The subtle and nuanced quality of Roy's conversations with his friends sometimes made me feel pedestrian and clumping.

Yet the picture that many Labour people, and indeed the media, had of Roy was distorted. He was incredibly hard-working, yet wore his industriousness lightly. He was up before dawn, to read the newspapers and go for his regular morning walk, and got most of his writing done by lunchtime. He and his wife Jennifer had a charming house in East Hendred, twenty minutes from Oxford, but it was not one of those showcase houses full of expensive ornaments. It was a functional house, with wellington boots in the hall, papers in piles, and stone corridors. At weekends children clustered around their grandfather and clambered over him.

Roy had the capacity to change pace according to the day and the season. Jennifer was the lodestar, a person who never compromised her principles and whose integrity was absolute. Nor was she ever intimidated by Roy's reputation, though she carefully guarded it. I remember on one occasion her leaning over the lunch table to say: 'Roy, you are being insufferably pompous!' He took it like a lamb.

I saw the 1979 Dimbleby Lecture as an interesting set of observations, but not as sowing the seed of a new party – and that demonstrated the gulf that still separated my expectations from those of David Steel. I was not alone in this. David Owen, Foreign Secretary in Callaghan's Cabinet, had repudiated Roy's tentative steps towards a new party shortly afterwards, with the contemptuous dismissal, 'We will not be tempted by siren voices from outside.'* Leading Liberals like Cyril Smith and Timothy Beaumont, suspicious of Steel's motives, were equally unenthusiastic, seeing the whole thing as a Jenkinsite takeover. At a meeting of the moderate Manifesto group of Labour MPs in May 1980, I firmly told them, 'I am not interested in a third party. I do not believe it has any future.' But something was to happen that went a long way towards changing my mind.

The Labour Party's special conference of 31 May 1980 at Wembley, organised at the behest of the National Executive Committee, was supposed to agree on a new policy statement called 'Peace, Jobs and Freedom'. But its real purpose was to continue the attack on the last Labour government. The delegates came, like Mark Antony for Caesar, to bury Callaghan, not to praise him.

The conference indulged in an orgy of condemnation, with the former Prime Minister and the former Chancellor of the Exchequer, Denis Healey, being heckled and booed throughout their speeches. Hardly a single defender of the Labour government reached the

* Quoted in David Owen, *Time to Declare*, Joseph, 1991.

rostrum. Then suddenly, David Owen could stand no more of it. He strode up to deliver a short, furious speech, typically on the most contentious issue of all – the siting of US cruise missiles on British territory. He was jeered all the way through. It was at this moment that he completely reversed his earlier position. No longer the moderates' most brutal opponent of a proposed new party, he became its most impatient advocate. The intolerance and savagery of the conference delegates drove me, too, a further long step towards breaking away. The media coined the phrase 'the Gang of Three' to describe the three Labour politicians identified as the most likely to walk out – David Owen, Bill Rodgers and me.

David had learned from a journalist friend a few days after the conference that John Silkin, Shadow Minister for Industry, proposed to demand that Britain leave the European Community. John Silkin was one of those men who see themselves as future leaders, even if few agree with their self-assessment. He rarely missed an opportunity to advance himself. Intending to run for the leadership as soon as Jim Callaghan resigned, he saw his anti-Europe record as an asset of which Labour MPs should be reminded. Silkin's intervention enraged the three of us. We had been through all this only four years before. In 1972 I had broken with my closest Shadow Cabinet colleagues, Roy Jenkins, George Thomson and Harold Lever, to support a referendum whose result I believed would hold for at least a generation, only to see the authors of that referendum already repudiating it. David Owen as Foreign Secretary had based himself on Britain's commitment to the Community, firmly entrenched in the referendum result of 1975. But none of this seemed to matter now: the conference passed a resolution calling for Labour to reconsider Britain's membership. So much for the voice of the people.

Bill Rodgers and I had planned to meet after the Wembley conference to consider our position in the light of its decisions. Bumping into David, Bill suggested he come too. The three of us met in my flat near Victoria station a few days later, our anger and resolution stiffened by the news about John Silkin. There we worked out the first of our common statements. It denounced Silkin's call for Labour to support withdrawal from the European Community. On this we were of one mind. The Labour left inhabited a fantasy world in which the European Community was seen as a capitalist conspiracy. Never mind that the welfare state was much more generous in Germany, France and the Netherlands than in the United Kingdom. Never mind that France and Italy had a larger proportion of their economies in public ownership. According to these people, the European Community stood in the way of the left's unachievable dream of a command state planning its way to Utopia. Within a decade, the Labour left was to have more in common with Margaret Thatcher in its distrust of Europe than either had with the moderates in their own party.

Rebecca, now a university student, had followed these critical events closely. Home for the weekend, she peered into the sitting-room to find out what was going on. 'I wanted to see history in the making,' she told us. But none of us three yet saw it that way. What we had made up our minds to do was to plunge our banner into the earth and call upon Labour supporters to rally to it. We were to suffer further huge setbacks before we could make up our minds to leave.

The media had not shown much interest in the endless dreary battles within the NEC. They had not commented on the fact that few of the fifty new Labour MPs in the 1974–9 Parliament, thirteen of them victors in by-elections, had joined the Parliamentary Party's Manifesto group, which meant in effect declaring oneself against the incursions of the left. It seemed to me an early indication of what mandatory reselection would do to the party.* But our

---

* Eight moderate MPs were deselected during the 1979–83 Parliament; all but one of them voted for Tony Benn in the deputy leadership contest (David Butler and Dennis Kavanagh, *The British General Election of 1983*, Palgrave Macmillan, 1984).

public statement caught the media's interest. Fastening on the phrase 'There are some of us who will not accept a choice between socialism and Europe. We will choose them both', the Sunday newspapers were rife with speculation about a possible split. That speculation was given further momentum by a speech to the parliamentary press gallery by Roy Jenkins in the same week. Roy spoke there of the possibility of an 'experimental plane', soaring into the sky – his metaphor for launching a new party of the centre. I knew nothing of his intention to make the speech, nor did he consult me about it.

Just over a week after our statement, on 14 June 1980, the commission of inquiry into Labour's constitution that had been established the previous autumn met for a long session at Bishop's Stortford in Hertfordshire to pull its conclusions together. Those conclusions for many of us added up to the abdication of Jim's leadership and the weakening of the autonomy of the Parliamentary Party. We were not surprised, given the long retreat of the moderates on the NEC, but we were deeply disappointed. The parliamentary leadership had conceded mandatory reselection. It had also agreed to a new way of electing the Party's leader. He or she would no longer be chosen by the elected Labour MPs, but by an electoral college which would also decide on the terms of the election manifesto. Half that electoral college would consist of representatives elected by the Parliamentary Party, a quarter by the trades unions, a fifth by constituency parties and the balancing 5 per cent by the socialist societies and cooperatives. Given the inroads being made into the constituency parties and the trades unions, it would not be difficult for the left to establish a commanding position. The commission's conclusions were, of course, subject to the approval of the Party Conference to be held in September 1980.

The Gang of Three – Bill Rodgers, David Owen and I – like many of the MPs in the Manifesto group, believed that Jim Callaghan and Denis Healey should have flatly refused to have anything to do with the electoral college. I thought they should have said that the Parliamentary Party would not accept that the right of electing the leader should pass from MPs to an electoral college; Labour MPs, most of them moderates or soft left, would have rallied behind such a tough stand. Intimidated and abused, they longed for their leaders to provide them with both a shield and a sword. But Jim was exhausted. His natural ebullience had been drained by the years of in-fighting. Like many other political leaders, he misjudged the moment when he should have gone. His last few months in office were months of growing despair.

CHAPTER 14

A New Party is Born

On 1 August 1980, David, Bill and I took a significant further step, publishing in the *Guardian* and the *Daily Mirror*, the two newspapers most read by Labour supporters, a much longer statement of our principles than had appeared in June. 'The Labour Party is facing the gravest crisis in its history,' we began. And then, for the first time we speculated on a new party. 'If the Labour Party abandons its democratic and internationalist principles . . . the argument may grow for a new democratic socialist party.'

Hundreds of letters poured in from all over the country, many from Labour supporters. Overwhelmingly, they shared our consternation about what was happening to their Party. A few others were scathing – our departure would be good riddance. So we prepared for the battle we knew would come at the annual Labour Party Conference, to be convened at the end of September 1980 in Blackpool.

We could not have concocted such a surreal Labour Party Conference if we had tried. If the previous year's gathering had been unpleasant, wrote Ivor Crewe and Tony King in their book *The Birth, Life and Death of the Social Democratic Party*, the 1980 conference 'seemed to most right-wingers to be not only unpleasant but positively insane'. Proceedings opened with an amazing speech by Tony Benn, a rave about what the left would do with power when it got it. His list included the extension of public ownership to all the country's major companies – what Bevan had called 'the commanding heights of the economy' – the control of capital movements, withdrawal from the European Common Market, and the abolition of the House of Lords, which might try to block such radical reform. To achieve abolition might, Benn said, necessitate the creation of a thousand new peers pledged to abolish themselves. Many of those listening, including some on the left, recognised that this programme would need not victory in an election, but a revolution.

The Campaign for Labour Victory had presciently organised a meeting for that very evening, to be held in the Spanish Hall at Blackpool's conference centre. I was to be one of the speakers. The atmosphere was not just electric, it was incendiary. I had to fight my way through crowds of delegates, some intoxicated by Tony Benn's vision, to get to the hall. Some shouted at me, one or two even spat, while others, keeping their voices down, whispered encouragement. I hadn't written down what I was going to say, but I was buoyed up by a ferocious indignation. 'I wonder why Tony was so unambitious?' I asked. 'After all, it took God only six days to make the world.' The conference was bitterly split. In the end, control of the manifesto by the electoral college was defeated, but reselection was confirmed. The battle over who elected the leader was put off for yet another special conference which would decide on the composition of the proposed electoral college.

Tony Benn was at his apogee, the hero of the left with an appeal that went far beyond their relatively small numbers. He was to me an enigma. Personally he was the sweetest of men, concerned about his friends and colleagues, ready to help, funny and self-effacing. His socialist values ran deep, owing more to the

Levellers of the English Civil War than to Marx or Trotsky. The iconic leader for him was Colonel Rainborough of Cromwell's New Model Army, the man who declared during the famous Putney Debates: 'The poorest he that is in England hath a life to live as the greatest he.' Benn's charisma overwhelmed his reason, and his eloquence washed away his logic when he was responding to an adoring audience. One of my journalist friends observed that, during his speech to the conference, Tony held forth through the applause, not pausing for it to die down. He seemed to be in a self-induced trance. Indeed, some of his own supporters began to get worried. Comments were made on his staring eyes, even his sanity. The bonds between the soft left and the hard left began to fray. They were to snap only a few months later.

I was still balancing on the brink of leaving the Party. Then on 15 October 1980, Jim Callaghan resigned as leader, and everyone's thoughts turned to the election of his successor. After the disappearance of a few long-odds candidates, like John Silkin and Peter Shore, the choice boiled down to Michael Foot or Denis Healey. As I mentioned earlier, Michael was widely loved in the Party. A brilliant writer and polemicist, he could not be accused of belonging to the authoritarian left. He believed passionately in Parliament, and had made clear his opposition to those 'reforms' that were intended to weaken the Parliamentary Party. Like Harold Wilson, the first commandment by which he lived was to hold the Party together.

Opposition to him came from two sources: those who did not see him as a potential leader, and those who believed the time for cobbling together the contesting wings of the party was now over. I belonged to both points of view. I had come to respect Michael when we worked together on prices and incomes policy, but I did not see him as having the kind of mind that could grapple with an economic crisis. I thought him to have a romantic view of the left, shaped by his experience of the interwar period. But the left had evolved from a cat into a tiger.

Denis Healey met both requirements. As Chancellor, he had proved himself as tough as one would expect from a former tank officer who had helped to organise the wartime landing at Anzio. His pugilistic manner was balanced by a savage sense of humour. It wasn't easy to place him, for he was no man's disciple, and no one was his. He was a loner in politics, but a loner blessed by a marriage so happy it was always alive. Many of us on the right of the party saw him as our best hope, indeed by now our only hope. We waited expectantly for Denis to come over the brow of the hill, flags flying, trumpeting a challenge all of us could respond to.

It didn't happen. I still don't know why. No one could accuse him of being faint-hearted or cowardly. Maybe he decided a low profile would be a better road to victory. If so, he underestimated the concerns of a demoralised Parliamentary Party. They wanted a champion ready to fight for them. Responding to questions from a delegation of the moderate Manifesto group, still the largest in the Parliamentary Party, Denis produced a series of evasive and unsatisfactory answers. Asked at the end why they should vote for him, he snapped back with his old brutality, 'Because you have nowhere else to go.' But they had; from that meeting, many went off to build somewhere.

Michael won the election for the leadership by ten votes, 139 to 129. A few MPs on the right voted for him in order to bring the crisis in the Labour Party to a head. One of these was the late Neville Sandelson. One or two others thought he might be able to hold the party together; they doubted that Denis Healey could. Among these was the brilliant television producer and later European Parliament member Phillip Whitehead.

Foot's election horrified the Labour right. Many of them were now prepared to consider joining a new party. They were waiting for a lead, but it would be many weeks before that lead came. For me, leaving the Labour Party was like pulling out my own teeth, one by one. There was my former constituency party, many of whose members were friends, bonded by long chilly nights of canvassing, dealing with difficult cases at constituency surgeries, celebrating victories, mourning defeats. The general management committee had approached me to ask if I would like to stand again as their candidate, and I was torn apart by having to choose between betraying my principles and betraying my friends. I had to tell them that I was not prepared to do so.

I had little hope that we could win back the Party, but also little hope that we could frame a new party capable of surviving in the rough world of two-party politics. I was tempted by the prospect of a career at the John F. Kennedy School of Government at Harvard University, having already been a visiting Fellow at the Institute of Politics there. Denis Healey and Michael Foot had pleaded with me not to leave the Party, and Harold Wilson had told me that if I stayed, he would envisage me as 'one of a very short list' of possible future leaders. But what got to me most of all was the thought of having to stand on scores of platforms at the next election, expounding my support for policies I thought disastrous for the country. No senior position in politics could possibly compensate for that.

My old Oxford friend Bill Rodgers found the dilemma even more painful. Bill had been brought up in a strongly Labour working-class household in Liverpool. As I noted earlier, his natural genius for organisation had led him to found a small group of serious Labour supporters from within the amorphous ranks of the University Labour Club, of which I became chairman in the autumn of 1950. Bill's group met to discuss policy, not to listen to speeches by ministers and ex-ministers. It was after his time as General Secretary of the Fabian Society that he organised the Campaign for Labour Victory, to support Hugh Gaitskell in his efforts to excise Clause Four from the Labour Party constitution. Bill was highly valued by Gaitskell, and rapidly became indispensable to the Labour right. After Gaitskell's unexpected early death, Bill regarded Roy Jenkins as his natural successor. His relations with Harold Wilson were distant, but Harold had a good don's detached eye for talent. He knew that his government needed able people, so he appointed Bill to a series of difficult but influential positions.

Leaving the Labour Party was viscerally painful for Bill. He lived in Camden Town, a lively Labour borough. His children went to school there, many of his friends lived round about. So agonising was the pain of parting that he developed back trouble so bad he had to spend days lying on the floor. He was the most realistic of the Gang of Three. He never fooled himself about what the real world was like. But he was also, and this was less widely known, a man of strong passions. He offered loyalty and expected loyalty back.

David Owen had been much less involved in the Labour Party than the two of us. To begin with, he did not come from a Labour family. His mother, an Independent county councillor in safely Conservative Devon, had had little to do with Labour people. The main Opposition party in Devon was Liberal, and for them Mrs Owen had little respect. David had trained to be a neurologist, at a time when medical students lived a separate existence from other university students and when the hours expected of young housemen in hospitals were such as to preclude any other activities. By the time he entered parliamentary politics, as MP for Plymouth Sutton in 1966, the area he had always lived in, he had still seen very little of the Labour Party at national level. His commitment to the NHS made him a popular junior Health Minister. Barbara Castle described him to me as the best junior minister she had ever had. Indeed, his rigorous training as a neurologist, a profession that depends upon the capacity to make fateful decisions instantly and which requires its practitioners to obey or be obeyed without question, was an excellent basis for being junior to an able if volatile minister. It was also a good basis for autocratic leadership. David had many of the qualities of boldness, charm and quick intelligence needed for that. But his training was not a good basis for the collective responsibility and cooperative leadership the new Party was to require.

Now he acted with the suddenness and decisiveness we would come to know well. The most reluctant of us to consider splitting away from the Labour Party, he had become by October 1980 the keenest to do so. Bill and I used to worry that he might fly off the handle and make an announcement on his own.

Meanwhile, Roy's term of office as President of the European Commission was coming to an end, and he was due to meet David at his home at East Hendred in Oxfordshire on 28 November. The day before had been a painful one for me. I had gone to Stevenage to speak to my general management committee, and to tell them that I felt unable to stand again as a candidate for the constituency. I set out the reasons why in some detail. A few Party members welcomed my withdrawal as an apostate from the social- ist faith. But more pleaded with me to stay and to lead them in the fight for the Party. By this time I was convinced it could not be saved. It was, however, with some resentment that I travelled next day to East Hendred. I felt like the veteran of long and bitter wars who sees the general arrive for a flying visit. We bore the scars of the last four years, and Roy didn't. Yet I realised that he had a gravitas, a reputation as an experienced statesman that we badly needed to lend weight to our fragile enterprise. After our meeting at East Hendred, Roy publicly joined us. The media renamed us 'the Gang of Four'.

I still wasn't sure I liked this. I wanted the new party to be democratic but also socialist, committed to greater equality, redistribution of income and wealth, comprehensive schools and the National Health Service. I wasn't certain that Roy shared all those objectives. Furthermore, I didn't want our new party to be fashioned by someone, however distinguished, who had not been part of our struggle. That was one reason why I was so angry when the date of our next meeting at East Hendred, planned for 18 January 1981, was leaked to the *Observer*, almost certainly by one of Roy's entourage if not by Roy himself. I was becoming suspicious of Roy's publicity machine, and I could envisage the photographs of the three of us arriving like supplicants at the house of the great man. I flatly refused to go. The meeting was rearranged for Bill's house in Camden Town, but the media got to hear of it. So we agreed to meet at David's house in Narrow Street, Limehouse, after which our joint declaration was named.

I had failed to appreciate the media interest in the latest phase of our venture. Looking through the window of the Owens' house at the assembled journalists, I realised that my appearance at that moment was not compatible with a serious attempt to found a new political party, so I borrowed a respectable shirt from David's wife Debbie before we all sallied out. It began to dawn on me that matters were not entirely in our hands. The media would have as much to do with our success or failure as we ourselves.

Those scrutinising the Gang of Three, and now the Gang of Four, must have wearied at our various declarations, but this one was rightly seen to be the wellspring of the new party, although the party itself was not to be launched for a further two months. We read it out to the assembled media on a cold and windy street beside the warehouses that bordered the River Thames. We reprinted it in the *Guardian* a week later. It was not a document worthy of a Milton or a Paine. It had been put together by the four of us without any outside advice. But it was undoubtedly an idea whose time had come. The momentum was as much driven by the yearning of those who wanted a new party of the centre left as it was by us. Within days we had twenty-five thousand messages of support and £75,000 in donations. The post no longer came through our letter-boxes. It arrived in sackloads.

I felt the same way I was later to feel taking a raft down the Colorado River. As I approached the rapids, I was gripped by a sense of excitement linked to an awareness of being no longer in control. I couldn't know where the rocks might be, or how fast the river was flowing at that point. I was buoyed up by messages of support from my daughter, my nephews and my friends, but I didn't know whether or not we were going to come through. It was too late to turn back, and therefore pointless to worry.

The day before the Limehouse Declaration, 24 January 1981, the left had registered its further victory over the Parliamentary Labour Party at the second special conference. In the electoral college to elect the leader, the trades unions were to be the single largest component, at 40 per cent, while the constituency parties and the Parliamentary Party would each have 30 per cent. It seemed a redundant victory – the retreat had already been absolute. We felt yet further justified in what we were doing.

By now we had burned our boats and there was no way back, but we were not yet ready to launch the new party. We needed more indications of support, especially from MPs, and we also needed time to organise the launch. So we created a Council for Social Democracy, which Labour Party members were free to join – in practice, a staging-post for MPs who had not yet made up their minds to leave the old party; it attracted several who later decided not to take matters further. I formally resigned from the National Executive Committee and from the Labour Party on 2 March 1981.

In the two months between the Limehouse Declaration and the launch of the Social Democrats, thirteen Labour MPs came out in the new party's favour, and just one Conservative MP, Christopher Brocklebank-Fowler. From the beginning, the party was to be asymmetric. Only a handful of Conservative MPs and councillors ever joined, though many Conservative voters abandoned their previous loyalties to support us.

The reasons for this lay deep in the culture of the Conservative Party. It is not just a political party, but a social structure, almost a way of life. Being an active Conservative opened the way not only to political and business contacts, but to a whole range of social opportunities for the family. In the shire counties, it could mean invitations to hunt balls, debutante parties and other highly prized events. Any Conservative MP who thought of joining the Social Democrats was likely to come under pressure from his family not to do so. Mrs Thatcher's first government, which by 1981 had brought in two harsh budgets and seen unemployment and bankruptcies multiply, was nevertheless one that embraced a spectrum of Conservative opinion. Heathite Conservatives, like Lord Carrington and Jim Prior, held important offices. Willie Whitelaw exercised a calm and thoughtful influence over the headstrong Prime Minister. There seemed no irresistible reason for liberal-minded Conservatives to leave.

The launch of the new party took place on 28 March 1981. Although it started in London at the Connaught Rooms, the Gang of Four and those around them, in particular Mike Thomas, Labour and Co-op MP for Newcastle upon Tyne East, who masterminded the presentation, were determined the new party should not be seen as a London initiative. Mike and I pushed for a launch in eleven regional capitals, including Edinburgh and Cardiff, on the same day. We worked out that with four leaders and a bit of strategic planning, every region would be able to have its own launch headed by one of us, and supported by well-known people, in a few cases local MPs. In that way, each region would feel that it was part-owner of the SDP. We were also conscious of the financial implications. We had little money beyond what had been contributed by the public after the Limehouse Declaration, but we had access to lots of free publicity. By launching in every region on the same day, we were able to command the headlines in all the local television and radio stations for nothing.

The initial launch in London attracted hundreds of broadcasters and journalists from all over the world. I remember staring into a blaze of television lights in a room packed to bursting. I was also aware of the absolute need to keep to the timetable down to the last minute if I was to get to the cities to which I was assigned, Glasgow and Southampton, before the early evening television news. By plane, train and car the four of us fanned out across the country. By the end of that one day, we had fifty thousand members, many of them using credit cards to pay their subscriptions, another innovation at that time.

It was not just the emergence of a new party that attracted them, but yet another innovation, collective leadership. Collective leadership spelled friendship and a common objective, by contrast to the civil war in the Labour Party and the growing strains in the Conservative government. It enabled us to spread our message rapidly around the country. It gave us the comradeship and closeness that made it easier to withstand the taunts of betrayal that accompanied us. Until the 1983 general election, collective leadership worked well. The four of us met every week at first, then every month, over lunch at a small Italian restaurant in Westminster, L'Amico. Each of us had a particular responsibility in the new party. David Owen was the parliamentary leader (Roy Jenkins was not yet re-elected to the House of Commons), Bill Rodgers was in charge of organisation throughout the country, and I looked after communications and publicity. We took turns to chair the Party's steering committee, which met once a month. On the steering committee sat most of the MPs who had joined us from the beginning and who had a strong sense of their own crucial role in the Party's formation. There were no women MPs among them, but there were several impressive women among the early steering committee members, such as Polly Toynbee the journalist and Sue Slipman, a former President of the National Union of Students.

The steering committee had not been elected, for there was as yet no constitution for the Party. A few of its members were MPs with no apparent political future, but most had reason to believe that they would have been re-elected and seen as potential ministers if they had stayed in the Labour Party. Men like Robert Maclennan, Ian Wrigglesworth, Tom Bradley and Mike Thomas were putting their promising careers on the line.

The next big step was to work out the Party's relationship with the Liberals. Roy Jenkins had already built up a friendship of mutual trust with David Steel, but that trust did not extend to the rest of the Gang of Four. Bill and I did not know the Liberals well; David Owen had strong doubts about their cohesion and self-discipline. Yet we all realised that in these early days it was essential for us not to fight one another. Some compromise had to be reached whenever elections took place, whether for local councils or for parliamentary by-elections. David Steel was adamant that priority must be given to Roy and me in order to get us back in the Commons, for the sake of the new Party. He angered many in his own agreeably anarchistic party with his single-minded ruthlessness.

In April 1981, Bill Rodgers and I went to Königswinter on the banks of the Rhine for the annual meeting of the Anglo-German Association. I had been involved with the Königswinter conference for twenty years, and had literally sat at the feet of that most charismatic and conflicted of postwar German leaders, Willy Brandt. The German Social Democrats had been through their own Damascene conversion when, at Bad Godesberg on 15 November 1959, they had broken with their Marxist heritage. We felt at home with them. Unsure what to do in the new circumstances, our German hosts diplomatically arranged two lunches, each hosted by a senior German politician, one for the Labour MPs present, the other for the new Social Democrats. Helmut Schmidt, the powerful Social Democrat Chancellor, greeted us warmly and told Denis Healey he should consider joining us. His was the party we most admired and most wanted to emulate.

The presence at Königswinter of David Steel and his senior colleague Richard Holme, a businessman with a fine track record of public service, offered us the opportunity well away from the basilisk eye of the British media to discuss the tricky issue of our future relationship. David and I set off on a walk up the

Drachenfels, one of the range of hills above the Rhine, followed by Bill and Richard Holme. On that walk, he and I agreed that the parties would have to work together, produce an agreed policy statement and support one another on an equivalent basis when there were by-elections for Parliament. Bill and Richard reached the same conclusions, and all of us returned to Britain feeling pleased with what we had accomplished.

The ambivalence about the SDP's relations with the Liberals was, however, clear from the steering committee's reactions on our return. First, there was resentment that we had acted on our own. The steering committee was by now aware of its own importance as the executive of the Party. The days of the Gang of Four acting autonomously were over. Second, elements in the steering committee, especially those closely associated with David Owen, were grudging about relations with the Liberal Party. It was not a party they respected. At best, they conceded the necessity for some kind of working relationship.

The momentum for the Alliance was nevertheless increasing. On 16 June the two parties issued a policy statement, based on the work of a joint commission chaired by David Steel and me. The cover was adorned with a photograph of us sitting in what appeared to be an orchard but was actually Dean's Yard, the close of Westminster Abbey. The document was called 'A Fresh Start for Britain' and looked like an advertisement for vitamins for the middle-aged. But it served its purpose. We agreed on our analysis of what was wrong with Britain: adversarial politics leading to capricious changes in the boundaries between the public and private sectors; the persistence of class divisions; the centralised and secretive nature of our government; confusion about Britain's role in the world. We agreed too on the policies to deal with what was wrong: a fair voting system; constitutional reform, above all through devolution; improved economic competitiveness; the protection of the environment; continued membership of the European Community and of NATO within the context of multilateralism. In short, the two parties had found a surprising amount of common ground. But they had not yet got down to the harsh realities of combining their particular interests – of how to work together when, in the American phrase, 'the rubber hits the road'. That process was to prove hard and time-consuming.

The policy statement became the backdrop to an inspiring piece of theatre, the Liberal Party's annual assembly at Llandudno, once part of the constituency represented by that towering Liberal politician David Lloyd George. But before that happened, there was to be a huge boost to the new Party's fortunes – Roy Jenkins's victorious defeat in the Warrington by-election.

Warrington was a solid Labour seat. Many of its reasonably prosperous electors worked in manufacturing, mainly in the chemical industry. It also had a strong Catholic tradition, based on immigration from the poverty-stricken Ireland of a century before. The appointment of its MP, Thomas Williams, to the position of High Court judge led to a by-election, and the date set for the poll was 16 July. The Liberals and the SDP agreed to fight the by-election together, calling themselves the SDP/Liberal Alliance. By now the SDP was slipping from the heights of enthusiasm reached during the launch. There was talk of us being a flash in the pan. It was critical to the Party's fortunes to do well in Warrington.

I was invited to stand. If ever a constituency was made for me, this was it – moderate Labour, Catholic, a cohesive community. But I refused, probably the single biggest mistake of my political life. Why? After my divorce from Bernard in 1974 I had become a single mother and had no substantial financial resources. My mother had been a highly successful writer in the years between the wars, but her considerable savings had been devoured by the cost of intensive nursing in the three years before her death in 1970. When my father died in 1979 he had left his second wife, Delinda, in part dependent on me. I thought I would be unlikely to win Warrington, and would find myself not only without a job, but seriously damaged by another political defeat so soon after the loss of Hertford and Stevenage, also in 1979. I did not dither. I quailed. My reputation for boldness, acquired in the long fight within the Labour Party, never wholly recovered.

Roy, by contrast, seized the prospect with both hands. David Steel, who used lunches at the House of Commons with influential members of his own party very effectively at this early stage of the Alliance, persuaded the Liberal candidate in Warrington not to stand. Despite this boost to his chances, like me, Roy had a great deal to lose in the Warrington by-election, not least his role as an elder statesman. Returning to the grassroots, to party politics at a local level, was not something statesmen did. But Roy was determined to throw everything he had into this new Party. It was a gamble in which the odds were stacked heavily against him. At first Roy's campaign was tentative. It was not easy for the former President of the European Commission to adapt to the pavements of Warrington. But then, as volunteers flooded into the town, he caught the spirit of the campaign. With Bill Rodgers and me at his side, he worked the streets, addressing spontaneous meetings on street corners, answering questions and enjoying himself more and more. The centre of Warrington is a bowl-shaped marketplace, and here we kept up a semi-permanent public meeting to which anyone was free to contribute his or her comments.

A good by-election has its own rhythm. Initial enthusiasm has its counterpart in the response of the electors, which in turn reinforces the sense of excitement, culminating in the election itself. Warrington was like that, the more so because so many of the volunteers were new to the enchantment of politics at its best. The result, 42 per cent of the vote for Roy and a drop in Labour's majority from 10,000 to 1759, was a Pyrrhic victory for Doug Hoyle, the new MP. A buoyant Roy declared, 'This is my first defeat in thirty years in politics. It is by far the greatest victory that I have ever participated in.'

After Warrington, the next by-election, in Tory-held Croydon

North West, seemed a damp squib. The candidate, Bill Pitt, had fought the seat before and was determined to fight it again. Recognising my mistake over Warrington, and now optimistic the Croydon constituency could be won, I indicated my willingness to stand. But Bill Pitt was unmovable. David Steel remonstrated with him. 'She's a national figure,' he said. Bill responded: 'I am too, now.' And he was right. He went on to win Croydon North West for the Liberal/SDP Alliance, the first ever candidate to become an elected Alliance MP.

Warrington and the Croydon by-election were overtures to the magnificent performance of the assembled Liberals at Llandudno. Party activists with a strong sense of their history, they were now gathered at the heartland of liberalism. The gloom of their long decline had dissipated. They could see the glimmers of a new dawn. They were caught up in the sheer euphoria of the moment. I have rarely taken part in so inspiring and exuberant an assembly as the fringe meeting arranged by *New Outlook*, a Liberal journal, on 15 September 1981. Hundreds packed the hall, to be addressed by the spiritual leader of liberalism, Jo Grimond, and by David Steel, Roy Jenkins and me. The next day, a huge majority of the delegates voted 1600 to 112 for our policy document 'A Fresh Start for Britain', and the electoral pact implicit in it. At the end of the assembly, an exuberant David Steel, for once abandoning his usual self-restraint, told his followers to go back to their con- stituencies and prepare for government.

The SDP spurned the conventional seaside conference venues, partly out of a desire to break even minor moulds, partly because conference hotels were expensive. I proposed the idea of a rolling conference, moving by train from place to place, an echo of our original success in launching the Party from many centres almost simultaneously.

The conference train started at Perth, where it was joined by leading Scottish members. We had learned that there was going to be a by-election in September 1981 at Crosby on Merseyside, a rock-solid Conservative seat, following the death of its Member of Parliament, Sir Graham Page. The train carried a substantial complement of journalists who had every possible access, during our travels, to the politicians on board. The news of Graham Page's death led to a flood of questions and speculation. This time I knew I had to stand despite the arguments, both public and private, against it. If I refused again to stand, I knew the media would treat me as a coward, and that huge harm would be done to the new Party. I was like someone on the edge of a cliff that was crumbling beneath me. So when we reached Bradford I announced that I would stand, not taking into account the existence of a Liberal candidate in Crosby with high local standing and an excellent track record as a respected local councillor, Anthony Hill. Anthony was deeply disappointed at losing his chance to stand as the candidate for a constituency he had devoted his political life to, but he generously recognised the opportunity Crosby offered to put the Alliance firmly on the road to success. Within days he had rallied the local Liberal Party to my candidature and met with the nascent local SDP, chaired by an attractive and able young lawyer called Scott Donovan.

The Crosby constituency had always been Conservative. It was the eighth-safest Conservative seat in the country. Like other such political bastions, whether Labour or Conservative, it had been taken for granted. But beneath its placid surface were serious grievances and unaddressed issues. One end of the constituency, nearest to Liverpool's declining dockland, Seaforth and Waterloo, had wretched housing and high levels of unemployment. Nearby Thornton had one of the biggest council estates in the northwest, where problem families were dumped together. When I first visited there, I found electric cables hanging off the walls and yards ankle-deep in foul water because somebody had stolen the bottom parts of the soil pipes.

In Crosby itself, respectable middle-class families lived behind looped lace curtains in Victorian houses – it was as if they were pulling their skirts above their ankles to escape the degradation of a Liverpool that was running down and beset by riots and crime. Liverpool was Labour, had been for decades. That was one reason that Crosby was so Conservative. Beyond Crosby, alongside the wide sandy beaches of the Mersey estuary, were Blundellsands and Formby, desirable places to live. They were occasionally reminded of their great city neighbour by the detritus and lumps of sewage washed up by the tide.

The army of volunteers at Warrington moved on to Crosby, growing as it advanced. Warrington had been a sunny campaign, Crosby was cold and wet. We adapted our campaign to two facts: we didn't have much money but we had a lot of well-known faces. Bill Rodgers was almost always with me, as were familiar local figures such as Anthony Hill and Scott Donovan. Speakers at the evening meetings like Roy Jenkins, David Owen, David Steel and Jo Grimond joined us on the open lorry we had hired. The campaigners drove round the constituency day after day, through small towns and cabbage fields, blasting out the theme music of *Chariots of Fire*, David Puttnam's hugely popular and inspiring film about the 1924 Olympics.

Although we were often soaked by the heavy rain, the cold water dripping down our faces and collars, we were exhilarated by the extraordinary reception we received from the people of Crosby. They waved, shouted encouragement, and readily took the stickers and balloons we handed out from the lorry. The very fact that we were as open to the elements as they were created an atmosphere of comradeship between us. We stopped to visit pensioners' clubs, schools and colleges, old people's homes and the occasional small factory, and ended up every day at one or more public meetings, meetings attended by hundreds of people, some of them standing for an hour or more in the rain. We couldn't afford to advertise these gatherings, so we simply stuck paper arrows on the pavements pointing to the school or hall where the meeting was to be held.

The dominant local Conservatives were bewildered by what was happening. The old and hitherto reliable mantras of bringing back capital punishment and flogging, heavily relied upon by their former MP Graham Page, were not working. Their candidate, an agreeable but outgunned man called John Butcher, campaigned in the conventional manner, with leaflets and posters. His head-quarters in the centre of Crosby were festooned in the usual blue banners. But against the background of a third harsh Tory budget that was cutting expenditure and raising interest rates, he stood little chance. Local Tories were outraged by the incursion of the SDP. I remember on one occasion after a public meeting in Formby glimpsing something strange pressed against the front window of the restaurant where I was entertaining the speaker, Roy Jenkins. The something was the bare bottoms of the local rugby club.

The Conservatives fastened upon two national issues that they were confident would undermine me. One was public schools, the other abortion. Crosby was proud of its famous independent schools, Merchant Taylors' (whose distinguished alumni included the recently enthroned Archbishop of Canterbury, Robert Runcie, my friend from Oxford student days) and St Mary's College, a Roman Catholic foundation. I got asked about my views at every public meeting. I explained that parents could not be prevented from paying fees for their children's education under European law, but that I thought only schools meeting a social need, for example for boarding places, should enjoy charitable status. It was not exactly Tony Crosland at his most abrasive, but I did commend cooperation between independent schools and state schools, something he had championed. I remember flinch-ing at a big meeting in Crosby where Jo Grimond, whether artfully or artlessly – I could not decide which – extolled the virtues of public school education to an anxious questioner.

The other issue, abortion, was even more difficult. Representa-tives from SPUC (the Society for the Protection of Unborn

Children), a Roman Catholic pressure group, came to see me early in the campaign. I had voted against David Steel's Abortion Bill in 1967, so I did not find it difficult to respond. But they did not just want me to say where I stood, they wanted more – a commitment by me to accept SPUC's position on any amendment to the Abortion Act, as it now was. I told them I could never make such a commitment in advance to any pressure group or any NGO. As an MP I had to see the amendment myself, and to make my own judgement. Burke was my inspiration: 'Your representative owes you, not his industry only, but his judgement; and he betrays, instead of serving you, if he sacrifices it to your opinion.'

SPUC was outraged. They prepared and printed thousands of leaflets to say that my position on abortion was wholly unsatisfactory, and that Catholics should vote for Mr Butcher, my Conservative opponent. The leaflets were stored before delivery by SPUC volunteers in several local churches. My own supporters brought back news of this. I rang the Archbishop of Liverpool, Derek Warlock, and told him what was being planned and why. He immediately ordered the churches in the constituency to refuse to be involved.

This was the high tide of the SDP. At the count, the town hall was buzzing with my helpers leaning over the tellers and monitoring every vote. As my votes piled up on the long tables, a sense that something amazing was happening began to spread through the hall. People whispered to one another about what they could see, and anticipation built among my supporters. It was matched by the disbelief of the Conservatives. On 26 November 1981 I won Crosby with a majority of 5289 for the Alliance, overturning one of 19,727 for the Conservative candidate at the 1979 election. I was carried out of the count on the shoulders of my supporters to the cheers of the rain-soaked crowd waiting outside.

Our two parties began to believe there was no hill they could not climb – they had found one another to be good comrades in the ferocious battles they were now fighting. In the course of the

day following the poll, television pundits and political corre-
spondents called from all over the world. My photograph
appeared on the front pages of many British newspapers, and was
later to appear on the cover of *Time* magazine and other international journals.

I could not take in what had happened, nor what it meant for
me or for the new Party. After the eight months of unremitting
physical and emotional effort since I had broken away from the
Labour Party, I felt an intense need to get away from my public
life, if only for a few days. In earlier moments when I had felt
overwhelmed by the pressures on me, I had disappeared into the
hills, 'from whence cometh my help' in the words of the Book of
Common Prayer. So after a day spent thanking my new constituents for their support, I took off for the Lake District with two
of my oldest friends, John and Eileen Spencer, who long ago in
Oxford had offered me a corner of their flat on occasions when it
was so late at night, or so early in the morning, that I did not dare
to climb into college. We booked into a charming little hotel, and
early on Saturday John and I set off for the Langdale Pikes, glittering under a light swathe of snow. It took all day for the media
to find me. Some of them thought they had a sensational story,
the flight of the new MP with her unknown lover. Eileen persuaded the proprietor of the hotel to pick me up in her car and
hide me under a blanket in the back seat. By the time the media
caught up with me, I was safely back in the company of both
Eileen and John.

CHAPTER 15

Snakes and Ladders

Couples who undergo an unhappy divorce often cease to take any further interest in one another's doings. It may be just too painful. Similarly, now the Gang of Four had made the break, we had stopped watching events in the Labour Party closely. Yet even as the SDP was scaling dizzy heights in Warrington and Crosby, the Labour moderates were taking their first serious steps towards reversing the disastrous slide towards extremism. Undoubtedly they were shaken by the successful launch of the new Party and the support it attracted from former Labour activists.

They were at least as shaken by the evidence that Tony Benn and the hard left around him were not prepared to agree on a compromise leadership, a unifying ticket of Michael Foot and Denis Healey. A leadership combining these two was the best hope for those Labour men and women who were deeply troubled by the events of the past two years, but were unwilling to break with the Party. Prominent among these were the MPs Roy Hattersley, Giles Radice, Ken Weetch and Phillip Whitehead.

On 2 April 1981, Tony Benn announced his intention to run for the deputy leadership, now to be decided by the new electoral college and announced on 27 September 1981. He could expect the support of most of the constituency parties, and had successfully wooed some of the trades union leaders. If one or two of the major unions voted for him, or even if they abstained, he stood a very good chance of winning.

This was the moment when the soft left woke up. Some begged him not to stand. Others, like Joan Lestor, openly expressed their anger. A few, like Margaret Beckett, scolded the moderates for not being truly socialist. Most were scared of driving another dozen or so MPs into the arms of the SDP, as would almost certainly have happened if Tony Benn had won. Tony had carried a huge majority of the constituency vote in the electoral college, but less than 40 per cent of the trades union vote and only a third of his parliamentary colleagues. Whatever the reason, with the hair's-breadth majority of 0.8 per cent won by Denis Healey in the electoral college, a slow and stuttering fightback began.

By the early spring of 1982, the SDP had become a more conventional political party. At its constitutional convention in Kensington on 13 and 14 February, it had decided upon a single parliamentary leader to be elected by the Parliamentary Party, and a President to be elected by the party members – a dual leadership on West German lines. It was clear, however, that the parliamentary leader would be the more important of the two. The steering committee, at that time dominated by Jenkinsites, rejected one-person one-vote as the electorate for the Party leadership, an idea strongly supported by the lively Newcastle MP Mike Thomas as well as by David Owen and me. It did support measures of positive discrimination to ensure the election of more women, but that in turn was rejected by the Party's membership in a postal ballot. More radically, the membership overruled the steering committee on the issue of one-member one-vote.

By now, the Conservatives were beginning to recover some ground from the Alliance. The next by-election after Crosby was in Glasgow Hillhead, one of the Conservatives' few Scottish seats and an unlikely place for an SDP victory. Roy Jenkins was Welsh by birth and upbringing, English by style and choice. He seemed an inappropriate candidate for the Glasgow seat. But if he was to become leader of the new Party, this was likely to be his last chance. He was now the only one of the Gang of Four not back in Parliament, and the Parliamentary Party could not wait much longer. He plunged in, to prophecies of defeat from most of the media, and for much of the campaign their pessimism seemed justified.

But they underestimated Hillhead. It was a constituency of professional people, many of them academics and teachers. It liked good debate and it took itself seriously. In the last week of the election campaign, hardly a doorstep in Hillhead, hardly an apartment in the tall, handsome tenement blocks, escaped that debate as hundreds of SDP and Liberal volunteers poured in. On 25 March 1982, Roy won by just over 2000 votes in the bitterly fought campaign.

It was just one week later that an event occurred which was to confirm that, though the mould of British politics might be cracked, it was far from broken. On 2 April, Argentina, led by its military dictator General Galtieri, invaded the Falkland Islands. Argentinians went wild with delight. The British Prime Minister pondered what to do. It was not in Mrs Thatcher's nature to temporise. Whether she appreciated the huge political gamble at stake I do not know. Within a few days she had ordered the British armed services to take the islands back, come what may, an expedition that was to plough across over seven thousand miles of ocean.

If Mrs Thatcher was one main beneficiary of the Falklands war, David Owen was the other. A former junior minister for the navy as well as a former Foreign Secretary and Member for the naval town of Plymouth, he was ideally placed to make the running for the SDP on the issue. He dominated debates on the war. He managed to be at once supportive, yet to show how previous Conservative policies, like the withdrawal of the ship that guarded the channel between Argentina and the Falklands, contributed to its happening. He thrived in the contentious atmosphere that surrounded the SDP MPs, never stooping to personalities and never taking notice of the badinage from Labour, but keeping relentlessly to the argument he was making.

Roy, still assumed by most of us to be the Party's obvious choice, given his political stature and remarkable record as Home Secretary and Chancellor of the Exchequer, was duly elected leader of the SDP on 2 July by 26,300 votes against 20,900 for David Owen. I had nominated David – though I didn't expect him to win – not so much for his obvious talents as because I thought he would hold the new Party to the left of centre. I did not want to see the Jenkinsites uncontested. There had been from the beginning a slight tension between those of us who thought of the new Party as progressive liberal, and those who thought of it as social democrat. That in turn was related to perceptions of the role of the state, and the principles of redistribution and equality which for me were central.

Roy had written a major book about one of the great Liberal leaders of the twentieth century, Herbert Asquith. While I shared his admiration for Gladstone, about whom he wrote a later book, surely the most radical and far-seeing of nineteenth-century Prime Ministers, I could not forgive Asquith his hostility to women's suffrage. How the absence of votes for half the adult population was thought to be compatible with democracy I failed to understand, yet for many early-twentieth-century male politicians the issue was marginal. I had also suffered quite a lot at the hands of Roy's acolytes. Seen for many months as the main challenger to his coronation as leader, I was the target for his admirers. Whispers about my being disorganised, indecisive and incapable of leadership reached journalists and were relayed back to me. One wag made an anagram of my name: 'I whirl aimlessly.' I had to agree that it was both wounding and clever.

David had been scornful of my reluctance to run against Roy for the leadership. He acknowledged, as I did, that my high recognition and popularity among Labour voters were a crucial factor in the appeal of the new Party, more so than Roy's political eminence. What he failed to recognise was my lack of self-confidence. I readily conceded, publicly and privately, that Roy was a greater person than I was. I shared the judgement, on this, of the Jenkinsites. I was also concerned about making enemies, something that troubled David not at all and Roy much less than me. I doubt whether that would have mattered so much to me if I had then had the love and support of a spouse like Dick Neustadt, who believed in me more than I believed in myself.

It soon became obvious that Roy was not enjoying being the leader at all. To be a leader, you must at least take sheer animal pleasure from the power you wield. Roy could not get used to operating in a Chamber where he was mercilessly heckled, had no dispatch box to protect him and no Civil Service with which to prepare his elegant, inappropriate speeches. He was a brilliant fencer in a world of brutal rugby.

The general election of 1983 marked the final chapter in the early history of the Alliance. The Party had lost some goodwill during the protracted and sometimes bad-tempered negotiations over the selection of candidates, particularly for the more hopeful-looking seats, the so-called golden and silver constituencies. The idea was to sort out a broadly equivalent position for the two parties, but often the better-entrenched local Liberals would simply refuse to accept the outcome of these negotiations. Bill Rodgers, who showed remarkable persistence and patience, still had to go to David Steel from time to time to ask him to break a stalemate.

The Conservatives, meanwhile, had completely recovered their position as a result of the Falklands war, which the Prime Minister had conducted with the fabled panache of Boadicea, down to appearing, elegant scarf fanned by the wind, in a tank rather than a chariot. Because the media could not get to the Falklands without the help of the military – an early instance of the media becoming embedded – the real horrors of the Falklands did not get back to the British public. One officer who served there told me that young Argentinian soldiers were herded into trenches without adequate training or the equipment to keep out the biting cold. Killing them was like slaughtering calves in an abattoir, he said with disgust.

It was by any standards a famous victory, and won by the skin of the teeth. One more capital ship destroyed by the impressive Argentinian air force would have spelled defeat. The performance of the armed forces and the steely determination of the Prime Minister won respect at home and admiration abroad, not least from Caspar Weinberger, the American Secretary of Defense. Weinberger pulled out every stop to support Britain, defying some of his colleagues, among them Jeane Kirkpatrick, the US Ambassador to the United Nations, who quarrelled bitterly with him. As for the British public, they put the Conservatives back to the top of the polls.

As the Conservatives rose, the Alliance sank. It was now doing badly in local elections, the source of its earlier strength. It had won not a single council in the May 1982 local elections, which took place a month after the Argentinian invasion. The millions of protest voters who had flooded to the SDP in the first year of its existence were now going home – or in many cases, cleaving to a government that was fighting a patriotic war.

The Chicago Council on Foreign Relations, whose President John Rielly was a good friend of mine, had been distressed by the Falklands episode, which had set one friend of America, Argentina, against another, Great Britain. After the war and the downfall of General Galtieri, senior figures on the Chicago Council decided to invite one or two leading British politicians to a conference they were organising in Iguazu Falls, on the Argentina–Brazil border, to create an occasion in which they hoped reconciliation could be discussed. One evening, in this spectacular setting, huge waterfalls cascading in every direction, George Robertson, former Labour Spokesman on Defence, and I were smuggled into the hotel room of the Argentinian Foreign Minister Dante Caputo, to talk about ways in which our two countries, once close allies, could be brought together. We could not talk about the Falklands, since the consequences of the Argentinian defeat had to be accepted by them. But we did talk about other ways in which relations could be re-established with what was now a democratic civilian government under the upright leadership of President Raúl Alfonsín.

All, however, was not to be peace and light. When, after one of our clandestine discussions with Sr Caputo, George Robertson, John Rielly and I repaired to the small hotel bar, a desperate young barman leapt over it, threw himself at George and tried to stab him. We managed to pull him off before he had done any great damage beyond knocking George to the floor and hitting him. The hotel management was mortified, and said that the young man would be arrested. George, who had discovered that he was from Misiones, the impoverished northern province that was the recruiting ground for many of Galtieri's ill-equipped and untrained soldiers, told them not to. Within minutes George was back to his good-natured normal self.

I managed to spend a couple of weeks that summer in Cape Cod, where my brave and enchanting friend Bert Neustadt was confronting the slow and relentless advance of multiple sclerosis, cared for by a circle of devoted friends and her husband Dick. She died the following year, on 5 May 1984. I could not stay for long. The Alliance was moving towards what we all knew would be a crucial general election.

There was to be a brief return to the glory days of Warrington and Crosby when, in November 1982, Bob Mellish, a former docker who had become Labour's canny Chief Whip under Jim

Callaghan, resigned his safe Labour seat in Bermondsey. Mellish was truly representative of his constituency, a respectable working-class London borough, many of whose electors worked in the docks. It had a large and well-organised Catholic community and was, in the most favourable sense of the phrase, very Old Labour. The local Labour Party had been thoroughly infiltrated by the hard left, which chose Peter Tatchell, a man of uncompromisingly left-wing views, to be the candidate. Peter Tatchell was a brave man, who never softened his rhetoric. He was for gay rights, for easy abortion, for withdrawal from NATO, for extra-parliamentary action, if needed, to force the Thatcher government out. He was hip, provocative, all black leather jacket and tight jeans – indeed, everything calculated to outrage the conservative Labour voters of Bermondsey. And they were indeed outraged. Extremists on the right showed up to condemn Tatchell as an overt and committed homosexual. The campaign turned very nasty indeed.

Simon Hughes, the Alliance candidate, kept out of it. He did not take part in the witch-hunt against Tatchell, although he was its beneficiary. Many years later he was to admit that he himself was bisexual. He won on 24 February 1983, by over 9000 votes, having eliminated a Labour majority of nearly 12,000. It was a stupendous victory, but it was to be the last for a long time. Fortunately, Simon was to prove an outstanding MP much loved in his constituency.

A couple of weeks after the Bermondsey by-election, on 8 March 1983, yet another by-election was called, in the Labour seat of Darlington in County Durham. It looked propitious. But Darlington turned into a huge disappointment. The Alliance attracted nothing like the support from outside that had helped to win Crosby and Hillhead in such a spectacular way. The candidate, a popular local television presenter, knew very little about politics and was unable to match his Labour and Conservative opponents on matters of policy, nor to answer the increasingly hostile questions of the national media. The Alliance lost badly, managing only a third place. Liberals could not forbear to point out how different the results of the two by-elections had been. This was attributed by them to SDP inexperience. The Liberal Party went into the general election of 1983 with considerable scepticism about the political skills of its junior partner.

It had been agreed at a private meeting more than a year before at Kiddington Hall in Oxfordshire, the home of a distinguished Liberal baroness, that there should be only one person designated as leader of the Alliance in the event of a general election. But there were still two separate parties. David Steel, recognised after the experiences of the last two years to be unmatched as a campaigner and tactician, was leader of the Liberal Party. But he was not to be the leader of the Alliance. That position, it was agreed, had to be held by Roy, as the most senior and respected politician of us all. Because the phrase 'leader of the Alliance' suggested a junior position for David Steel, a new title for Roy had to be devised. It was 'Prime Minister designate', at once pompous and pretentious.

Roy was a master of both the spoken and the written word, a man who loved to conjure with phrases and to embroider the more complicated things he said with elaborate hand gestures. It was an aesthetic joy to watch him speak. His speeches belonged to the era from which the politicians he most admired had sprung, Gladstone, Lloyd George, Asquith and Churchill. He took trouble over his speeches; they were a coherent whole, often devoted to advancing an argument which developed majestically over several pages and many minutes. They bore as much relation to soundbites as Shakespeare does to slogans. Roy was not a child of the television age. On television he seemed stiff and nervous. Not for him the easy affability of the television chat-show host, nor the accusatory style of the political interviewer. The often crude medium of television, with its tendency to sacrifice complexity to the pressure of time and audience ratings, did not suit him.

As the general election campaign progressed, the Liberals,

disappointed that the Alliance's fortunes had not soared, began to look for explanations, and found one in Roy's presentational skills. Steel suggested a strategy meeting to consider how best to run the last ten days of the campaign, to be held at his remote farmhouse in Ettrick Bridge in the Scottish Lowlands. Bill and I took the invitation at face value. Such a meeting seemed sensible and could generate useful publicity. But the leading Liberals had other ideas in mind.

On the way up to Ettrick Bridge, David Owen found himself in the same plane as John Pardoe, the Liberal MP for North Cornwall from 1966 to 1979, a sharp-elbowed, quick-witted man. Pardoe was known to be highly sceptical of Jenkins's leadership. He may also have known that David Steel had sounded out the older man on the possibility of abandoning his role as leader of the Alliance, but that after careful consideration Jenkins had rejected the idea. Neither Bill nor I knew about this.

The Steels' kitchen at Ettrick Bridge is a reassuring room, with solid furniture and a view across the river valley to the green meadows beyond. It is not the setting for conspiracy, so it was not surprising that the kitchen window was open even though the press was hunkered down outside. I suggested that we should at least close the windows. The proposal that Roy step down as leader was then broached again. Most of us in the meeting took the view that any such change at this late date would be counterproductive, suggesting serious splits within the Alliance. The most we were prepared to agree was that David Steel should have a lion's share of the television appearances. We turned to other matters relevant to the campaign. And then without warning, Pardoe returned to the topic. His denunciation of Roy's role in the campaign was brutal. He told him in short order to relinquish his leadership position. Sitting across the table from Roy, I could see him gradually yielding to this extraordinary battering. I kept mouthing 'No! No! No!' at him, fixing him with an unblinking stare in an effort to attract his attention.

Pardoe looked at David Owen, but Bill interrupted before he could say anything. 'I can have nothing to do with this,' he said. I added that I would withdraw from the campaign if Roy was forced out of the leadership. I could see Roy slowly pulling himself together. The Liberals realised they could not prevail, and in a desultory way the meeting went back to other things. Amazingly, none of this came out in the media. We pulled together a rather anodyne statement on the campaign, which we fed to the journalists. We managed to field all the questions. On the leadership, none came. We had escaped, but in the pit of our stomachs was an ache of betrayal.

The general election that year was both a triumph and a gigantic defeat. The Alliance polled just 2.2 per cent fewer votes than Labour, a remarkable achievement given that the government had just won a popular war. Had the Alliance won even a percentage or two more than Labour, everything would have changed. In almost any other European country, the SDP/Liberal Alliance in 1983 would have been regarded as a phenomenal success. Its 25.4 per cent of the votes would have brought it a quarter of the seats in Parliament, around 160. In fact the Alliance won just twenty-three seats. Its vote was spread evenly across the country, and between different social and income groups. That was highly encouraging for those hoping to see a new, classless politics. In the first-past-the-post system, however, it was a huge disadvantage. It meant that we came second in lots of constituencies, but first in very few. A voting system that rewarded Labour with ten times as many parliamentary seats as the Alliance for the same number of votes would have been so discredited that it is hard to see how it could have survived. The Labour Party itself would have been thrown into a new and even worse crisis, with many MPs deciding to leave it. It was the closest we came to smashing the mould. But we failed to do so. Both Bill and I, two of the Gang of Four, were defeated.

In my case, the Crosby constituency had been substantially

altered by the Boundary Commission. The ward that had voted most heavily for me, Seaforth, had been carved out and absorbed into the neighbouring and heavily Labour constituency of Bootle. Instead, the Conservative ward of Aintree, home of the Grand National, had been removed from the safe Conservative seat of Southport and added to Crosby. There seemed no obvious reason for the changes, but they rendered Crosby virtually unwinnable. A projection done for me by a friendly psephologist indicated that I would have held Crosby had there been no boundary changes. I could not prove there had been a joint submission by the two old parties to the Boundary Commission, which is independent, but a joint submission would not be easy for it to refuse. Whether or not that was true, for the first time in my political life I suspected a conspiracy and felt very bitter about it.

In any event the Conservatives won the 1983 general election. Mrs Thatcher turned to her decisive second term. Roy, though still an MP, resigned and David Owen was elected Leader of the SDP.

CHAPTER 16

Owen Holds the Fort

The subsequent history of the SDP, and of the Alliance too, was shaped by an electoral system so unjust it makes a mockery of democracy. Governments in the United Kingdom take power, like the Blair government of 2005, on the basis of less than a quarter of the electorate and a third of those who bother to vote. The system suits the old parties so well that neither will address it as long as both agree to keep it. Neither Mrs Thatcher nor Michael Foot had any interest, whatever the electors wanted, in a reform that would give the Alliance parties much greater influence in Parliament.

The only incentive for one of the old parties to support proportional representation would be if that were the price of its obtaining, or remaining in, office. In 1996 Tony Blair, elected leader of the Labour Party in 1994, toyed with that idea in the context of a much more ambitious project – bringing the parties of the centre left together in one big tent. He was not sure he could win a majority in the forthcoming general election of 1997, but even if he did, he wanted more than that. He wanted the centre left to be paramount. He had long discussions with Roy Jenkins in which proportional representation certainly figured. He encouraged the talks between Robin Cook, a supporter of electoral reform, and

Robert Maclennan, on an agenda for constitutional change. Roy, whose elaborate manners were a shield for his shyness, warmed to the brilliant younger man who so clearly admired him. By May 1997 he saw Tony Blair as the man who had achieved what he himself had once longed to achieve, a modern classless new Labour Party in government, no longer lumbered with the obsolete statism of Clause Four. He believed that Blair was willing to reform the electoral system, and to work with the Liberal Democrats in a new administration.

And perhaps he would have done. If Blair had won a plurality rather than a decisive majority in 1997, he would have welcomed a coalition government in which the Liberal Democrats would have been the junior partner.

The first-past-the-post system was a huge handicap for the SDP to overcome. The merger with the Liberal Party in 1987 enabled both parties to survive within a new third party, the Liberal Democrats, but even then with far fewer MPs than their share of the popular vote indicated.

First-past-the-post killed 'the continuing SDP', as David Owen called his rump of the party. Against the odds, David battled to sustain his party but the task proved impossible. Immediately after the 1983 election, Steel and Owen had met at the latter's cottage in Wiltshire. I had been elected President of the SDP, but I was not invited to the meeting, an early indication that David Owen was moving sharply away from any kind of collective leadership. Steel privately proposed a merger of the two Alliance parties. Owen adamantly opposed it, conceding only that the Alliance would remain in existence at least until the European Parliament elections of 1984.

David Owen had moved quickly to stop the momentum towards a merger building up. He got Christopher Brocklebank-Fowler, the sole Conservative MP to join the SDP, to put down an anti-merger resolution for the forthcoming post-election conference of the SDP in September 1983 at Salford, near Manchester. Strongly supported by a now largely Owenite National Committee, the resolution won the support of the conference. Merger was out. For the next four years, Owen and Steel led their respective parties, cooperating only where they had to. While local parties drew steadily closer through campaigning and working together in local government elections, the leaders kept their distance.

In the 1983 general election, the SDP had been reduced to just six MPs, despite the Party's impressive contribution to the share of the vote. The Liberals had eighteen. Labour was still involved in its long civil war, with Neil Kinnock in October replacing Michael Foot as the leader. Neil was a man of the soft left, nurtured in the Aneurin Bevan tradition, but he was becoming increasingly conscious of the damage done to Labour's electoral prospects by the hard left. By now he was determined to reduce their influence. The SDP, despite the poor outcome in terms of MPs elected, continued to be a challenge to Labour. Its existence, together with the third Thatcher victory in 1987 – still four years ahead – helped Kinnock to convince his party that it had to change. He once told me that he had said to those who argued Labour voters had nowhere else to go, 'There is now!' Yet there was still a very long way to go. More of Kinnock's energy went into sorting out his Party than into fighting the Conservatives. He knew that if the Party did not return to sensible policies, it would never be able to beat them anyway.

The Conservatives were moving to the right. The Falklands war had dramatically restored their fortunes, and those of their leader. Mrs Thatcher, after two years in office, had in September 1981 weeded out of her Cabinet most of the 'wets', as they were contemptuously known, to be replaced by convinced Thatcherites.

Into the Opposition vacuum stepped David Owen. He led a tiny party. His prospects were unpromising. But by sheer force of personality and will he kept his own name and that of the SDP at the forefront of parliamentary politics for four years. He was formidable in commanding media coverage. Early every morning his office would go through all the newspapers, picking out issues and stories that deserved his attention. David had a team of loyal friends and colleagues, men and women of great ability and experience devoted to him and to the new Party. Their expertise and their reactions to the breaking news would be fed to David and his media advisers. He would then formulate his response, a press release, a soundbite, a speech, and ensure that the media had it before anyone else got round to commenting. It was a stunning performance.

David was a formidable leader but he was not a team player. He could take orders and he could give them, but he could not discuss them. Having risen in the political firmament to the dizzy height of Foreign Secretary at the age of thirty-eight, he no longer needed to take orders from anyone. He admired Mrs Thatcher who, like him, was untroubled in her self-belief and in the instant judgements that led to. Both jumped to conclusions, but Mrs Thatcher, in her early years as leader and then Prime Minister, did not disclose her conclusions as readily as David did. His forceful style commanded obeisance from the praetorian guard around him. They tended to overestimate his political judgement, which was often capricious, though not his courage, which was prodigious, sometimes amounting to recklessness. Mrs Thatcher, for her part, was underestimated for a long time, mainly because she was a woman. Her male colleagues learned to their cost her anger at being patronised. David may have been heartily detested in some quarters, but no one ever tried to patronise him.

These years were a triumph for David in Parliament, but far more controversial within the Party. On defence, he put his most experienced colleagues on a joint Liberal/SDP commission, knowing they would have to deal with the contentious issue of the UK nuclear deterrent and the eventual replacement of Trident. This was the hottest argument within the Liberal Party, which had many nuclear disarmers in its counsels. These were exactly the sort of Liberals Owen despised, living as he saw it in a world of unreality and unwilling to face the brutal facts of the Cold War.

David's SDP colleagues – among them Bill Rodgers, a former

Minister of State for Defence and former MP for Stockton-on-Tees; John Roper, the former MP for Farnworth in Lancashire and an expert on defence and disarmament; and John Cartwright, who had long taken an interest in defence matters and was still the MP for Woolwich – painstakingly talked their Liberal partners through the difficulties and dilemmas of defence policy, ending up with a responsible policy on which they could agree. Trident was not due for replacement until the end of the 1990s. The Liberal/SDP commission, reporting in June 1986, suggested that the decision on this could be postponed. Much could change within ten years, and in fact much did. The Soviet Union collapsed and most of Eastern Europe escaped from its yoke. But to David Owen, postponing the decision was once again fudging. He had declared himself passionately against any such ambiguities. So he publicly repudiated the commission's advice. It was a major mistake, born of hubris. In doing so, he not only stunned and confused the Liberal Party, which had moved a very long way to support the commission's conclusions. He also deeply offended some of his most able contemporaries, like Bill Rodgers, who had played such a large part in the creation of the new Party. David did not count the costs of his sudden judgements, but they could be very high.

Within the Alliance too, wrangling went on over the selection of candidates. David accepted that there had to be an allocation of seats between the parties at least until such time as proportional representation was introduced. But he was adamantly opposed to the joint selection of candidates, perceiving that this would pave the way to a merger of the two parties. It was still my opinion that such a merger was unavoidable if the Alliance parties were to survive. There was no room for two left-of-centre parties unless the electoral system in Britain was radically changed. The 1983 general election had dramatically demonstrated that. In the constituencies, where so much depended on the morale of volunteers to get candidates elected, there was often real anger at the National Committee's refusal to accept joint selection.

I had been selected in 1986 as prospective parliamentary candidate for Cambridge, a city now run by a Liberal and SDP council. 'We campaign together,' the activists told me. 'We deliver leaflets and knock on doors for one another. Surely we should have a voice in the selection of candidates!' Of course, that implied more than the selection of parliamentary candidates. What policies should the candidates propose, especially at local level where there would be no guidance from the national parties? The logic of campaigning together led towards merger. Joint selection, manfully fought for by Bill Rodgers in his capacity as chief negotiator for the SDP, became a big bone of contention.

At the national level, David's refusal to consider any merger of the parties only made sense on the far-fetched assumption that sooner rather than later proportional representation would be introduced. The Liberals and the SDP could then happily compete, postponing cooperation until a coalition government had to be put together. The trouble was that the assumption depended upon a hung Parliament in which the Liberals and the SDP held the balance. That might not happen for years, years in which the relations between the parties would be under huge pressure. David's position was irrational; only the charisma of his personality and the huge force of his will enabled him to override the doubts of the National Committee and of many in the Party.

The general election of June 1987 produced a more disappointing result than that of 1983. The SDP lost three of its eight seats in Parliament, among them those of Roy Jenkins in Hillhead and Ian Wrigglesworth in Stockton South, while the Liberals held on to seventeen. The Alliance's share of the vote slipped to 22.5 per cent, 2.9 points less than in 1983.

After the election, David Steel tried again to propose a merger. He was condemned by Owen's closest associates for 'bouncing' the SDP, but I felt strongly that the charge was unfair. As in 1983, David Owen had moved to pre-empt the position, announcing to a hastily convened press conference in Plymouth a few hours after the election: 'I knew that we needed a fourth party, and I think that everything that has happened since has justified that decision.' Journalists present reported Owen as strongly against merger, and unwilling to consider leading a merged party. He was later to become even more intransigent in his opposition. Seeing the Party drifting on to the rocks, I asked him repeatedly to meet me, as the Party's President, to discuss how catastrophe might be averted. He flatly refused to do so. I went to his office, and was refused entry. I rang David Sainsbury, the Party's Treasurer, an admirer of David's, and asked him to intercede. I recall his ringing me back a few hours later, to say that he had got nowhere. 'You are on your own,' he told me.

I am slow to anger, but now I was furious. I would not have my members or me treated in this cavalier way, even by this most formidable of leaders. I was made even angrier by a crude attempt to weight the questions to be put to the membership on the subject of merger, implying that the SDP would be destroyed if a merger went ahead. Faced with a National Committee which I was sure would echo David on the subject, I spent a day calling the chairs of every regional party in Great Britain and many constituency chairs as well. I knew the Party well. I had travelled from one end of the country to the other, to by-elections, local elections, constituency dinners and public meetings. I knew too that, though there were some hardened opponents, especially where local Liberals had proved difficult to deal with, most of our members were in favour of a merger.

And so it turned out. Some two-thirds of those I spoke to – and I carefully recorded their names and local parties as well as their comments – favoured a merger. At the meeting of the National Committee to discuss the issue, some members began to make claims about the views of Party activists. I interrupted, reading out name after name of those I had consulted. The Committee fell silent. They could not refute what I was telling them. So they finally agreed to a postal ballot of the members, to be conducted by the Electoral

Reform Society and based on a choice between two options: a closer constitutional framework for the Alliance, or a negotiated merger.

There was still one more hurdle, and a high one. There were five SDP MPs. The Party's constitution required that the leader be a Member of Parliament, and be nominated by at least a fifth of the Parliamentary Party. In our attenuated state, that meant just one MP. David had assumed the total loyalty of his MPs, which would mean no alternative leader could be nominated. Charles Kennedy, the youngest of the five SDP MPs, had begun to have doubts about what the first option meant. He asked David to explain it further. His response was unyielding. He would never consider a merger with the Liberal Party. That reply led Kennedy to say quietly but firmly that in that case he would be supporting the second option.

Charles Kennedy had gone to Glasgow University, like many other promising Highland youngsters. The university made special arrangements to house young men and women from the more remote parts of Scotland. It had a reputation for the brilliance of its student debates, and it had a roll of outstanding politicians among its alumni. Charles, visible in any crowd for his bright gold hair, had a gift for language, an infectious, self-mocking sense of humour and a great deal of charm. He was to become immensely popular, developing a style of politics that many people, especially young people, found attractive. He was never pompous and rarely adversarial. He seemed a leader made for a new kind of politics. I had already appreciated these qualities in him. I thought of him in terms of Sir Walter Scott's 'young Lochinvar . . . come out of the west', but I had not recognised the maturity of his political judgement until he spoke on defence at the 1986 Party Conference, introducing the conclusions of the joint defence commission. He had dealt with this highly sensitive subject by easing the tensions between the leader and the commission, patiently explaining the latter's point of view. Now he had taken up his position on the merger without any grandstanding or vituperation. It was clear he would not change his mind.

But there was still no parliamentary leader for the pro-merger case. Charles could not both stand and nominate himself, nor did he want to be leader at this early time. Yet it would be absurd for the majority of SDP members to have no one able to present their point of view to the Parliamentary Party. I felt it was my responsibility as Party President to fill the gap, and there was only one possible candidate for the post. That was Robert Maclennan, MP since 1966 for Caithness and Sutherland, and a prominent opponent of merger.

I had known Bob ever since he had been elected to Parliament. He had been my Parliamentary Secretary at the Department of Prices and Consumer Protection. He was a serious man and an extraordinarily conscientious one. He would think long and carefully before making a speech or reaching a decision, and he was often troubled about whether he had got it right. He was also thin-skinned, sensitive to criticism. Courteous in everything he did, Bob was not cut out for the sour and savage politics of the 1980s, for such politics were rare in Caithness. He used to campaign in his vast, empty constituency, making his way through the scores of little villages in his tweed suit, carrying an umbrella, and gravely greeting his electors, almost all of whom knew and respected him. At every election, I would come to campaign with him for a day or two. At election after election, regardless of his Party's fortunes, Bob was re-elected.

This was not surprising. In his quiet, determined way he fought for his remote constituency, encouraging small enterprises, befriending artists and actors to make Caithness a northern centre of the arts, helping farmers to market their beef and their sheep and to develop Caithness food products. He also learned a great deal about nuclear technology, the better to understand the work of his constituency's largest employer, the nuclear reprocessing plant at Dounreay on the north coast.

Bob and his wife Helen, herself a highly intelligent and independent-minded woman, left no one out. I remember in one campaign Bob insisted on visiting a farmer who was rumoured to be a supporter of the Scottish National Party. As the conversation proceeded, I noticed that the farmer had raised his fork-lift above Bob's head. In the fork-lift was a decayed sheep, its remains leaking on to those of us ranged below. Bob gave no indication he had noticed, and perhaps he hadn't. He parted from the farmer on the friendliest of terms.

But Bob was more than a dedicated constituency MP. In 1993 he would be asked by John Smith, then leader of the Labour Party, and Paddy Ashdown, the leader of the Liberal Democrats, to share the chairmanship of a joint constitutional committee with Robin Cook, later Foreign Secretary and an enthusiast for reform, including proportional representation. The Liberal Democrats regarded constitutional reform as a flagship issue for the Party, and had done a lot of work on it. In a significant speech in October 1993 John Smith committed the Labour Party to devolution, freedom of information, legislation on human rights and greater transparency in government. The joint committee did the spadework on these issues, and by the time of the general election of 1997 was in a position to move ahead quickly with the necessary legislation. In the meantime, in 1994, John Smith had tragically died. His successor, Tony Blair, in his first term as Prime Minister, strongly pressed by the joint committee, did adopt several of the reforms Smith had called for.

I knew that Bob was strongly committed to the survival of the SDP but recognised that without proportional representation the Party was doomed. I also knew that somehow I had to persuade him to stand for the leadership.

By late July 1987, Parliament was in recess and everyone was on holiday. Dick had invited me to stay with him in Cape Cod. Bob was staying at Helen's family home in New Hampshire (her father was a Massachusetts judge) and I invited the two of them to spend the day with Dick and me. I had arranged with Dick to take

Helen on a visit to the local sights, but during lunch I saw that I had got it wrong. Helen was going to be as much a part of the decision on the leadership issue as Bob himself. We spent a long summer afternoon discussing all the implications. There would be no contest with David, who had already indicated he would take no part in any negotiations over merger. If there was no SDP leader, there would simply be an empty chair.

Bob shared some of David's reservations about the Liberals. He thought they were anarchic and unreliable. A man of precise, lawyerly habits, he was annoyed by their lack of respect for rules and constitutional niceties. But he also believed they could be brought within a constitutional framework that might provide a solid structure for a merged third party. Furthermore, as a student of history, he appreciated the contribution the Liberal Party had made over the centuries to radical reform. So Bob agreed with me to stand as leader, but then made prodigious efforts to get David to change his mind. I shared this endeavour with him, pleading with David right up to the last minute, indeed beyond it. At the August conference in Portsmouth, when the result of the postal ballot on merger was made known, I begged him to reconsider his position. I was shouted down for my pains, and part of the National Committee pointedly marched off the platform.

The ballot revealed the pain of many members, and the depth of their attachment to the SDP, for many of them the only party they had ever joined. To this day, people speak to me with nostalgia about it, as one might about a first love. But common sense won the day. The merger was supported by 25,897 members; the first option, against merger, by 19,228. On hearing the result, David Owen immediately resigned, and that same month Bob Maclennan became the SDP's new leader. A cartoon showed me, the Fairy Godmother, with a pumpkin named Merger, and addressing a disconsolate David Owen sitting by a fireplace with his broom propped up beside him.

"WHAT DO YOU MEAN YOU DON'T WANT TO GO TO THE BALL?"

After 1983, David Owen had shaped the party in his image. In Parliament, there were none in the Alliance and few outside it to match him. He was not enamoured of the Parliamentary Liberal Party; its seventeen MPs had been elected as individuals, men and one woman all with a remarkable capacity to identify with and hold their own constituencies, most of them in the Celtic fringes, but with little sense of cohesion or Party discipline. This decentralised approach had enabled the Liberals to survive the dry years after 1922, when Asquith and Lloyd George had disastrously parted company, but thoughts of ever governing were far from their minds. The Party had developed a style of permanent opposition. David and his closest associates saw the Liberal Party through the spectrum of Parliament. What they failed to see was the way the Party in the country was changing. This owed a lot to David Steel, who was not prepared to accept permanent opposition status. He had persuaded his Party to enter the short-lived 'Lib-Lab pact' with Jim Callaghan's Labour government in 1977. A pragmatic politician, he saw no point in being marginalised in some Utopian hinterland of Liberal dreams that would never be realised.

There are few, if any, more canny politicians than David Steel, whether at Westminster or in Edinburgh. He is a good judge of people, easy to get on with, never pompous. He had excellent relations with his Borders constituency, where he has always lived, not least because of the unremitting work of his wife Judy, who often had to stoke the home fires while her husband was travelling the world or pursuing his passion for motoring over unforgiving territory such as the Sahara. Steel is also a man who understands power and is adept at dealing with those who possess it. None of that detracts from his political objectives. He has been highly successful in advancing those objectives, often unnoticed by the self-important men who think they run things. A devolved Scottish Parliament within the United Kingdom, the introduction of proportional representation for local government elections in Scotland, the commitment of the United Kingdom to African development – all owe a great deal to David Steel. He is devoted to the Africa in which his father served as a missionary of the Church of Scotland. Consistently he has travelled to sub-Saharan Africa to promote democracy and justice among his many friends and acquaintances in that continent.

Another factor for change in the Liberal Party was the opportunity offered by the rise of dogma in the two main parties in the 1980s, an opportunity seized by Liberals at the local level. Year by year, they added to their numbers. Between 1984 and 1987 they gained scores of councillors, culminating in a nationwide net gain of 249. By this time the SDP was also doing well in local elections, making almost as many net gains – 204 – in 1987 as the Liberals. Experience of local government transformed the Liberal Party. It became responsible, practical, workmanlike. Many of its members relished their ability to change things, albeit in a small compass. The Alliance was responsive to the concerns of local people, and the Liberal Party proved masterly at producing leaflets that showcased how politics could deal with problems right down to the neighbourhood level. In this, the Alliance was greatly helped by the brilliance of its chief organiser, Chris Rennard, a master of his craft. But little of this was noticed by David Owen. His visits to the local parties were necessarily fleeting, his contact with Liberal councillors limited.

Still fighting a merger, David and his close associates made a determined effort to keep the separate SDP in being. There were a few hopeful moments. The SDP seemed within striking distance of winning a by-election in Richmond, Yorkshire, solidly Conservative territory, when Leon Brittan took up the post of European Commissioner in 1989. But there never was, and never could be, any real prospect of survival for a fourth party struggling for the centre ground.

It took fourteen years and three changes of name for the new merged party, the Liberal Democrats, to exceed what the Alliance had achieved in 1983, and even then only in terms of seats, not of the share of the vote. Careful targeting of constituencies, the wise strategy of the Liberal Democrats' election organiser Chris Rennard, had gone some way to bridge the gap between the two. What the merged Party did achieve, however, was unprecedented in a first-past-the-post system: the status of a serious third party. Few other new parties in any country without proportional representation had attracted consistently over a number of years even 10 per cent of the electorate. For most of its short life, the Alliance had attracted the support of double that percentage or more. The Liberal Democrats still do.

With the benefit of hindsight, what can one say was the impact of the SDP, and of the Alliance, on the other parties? I have mentioned already the change in the Liberal Party that owed most to David Steel, but also something to the influence and example of the Social Democrats. The old Party was shaken out of a psychology of failure, in which aspiration had shrunk to little more than holding on to the sliver of political influence it had. The core tenets of its philosophy – decentralised democracy and individual liberty – would spring back into relevance after the authoritarian and centralised governments of Margaret Thatcher and Tony Blair.

The Conservatives were not much influenced by the SDP, nor by the Alliance, even though Conservative seats were much more threatened than Labour ones in the years before the merger. Mrs Thatcher refused to trim her sails to the new wind. The Falklands victory carried her through a period that would otherwise have been one of great personal unpopularity. The capacity of the Alliance to attract Tory voters was considerable, as both the 1983 and 1987 elections showed. The Alliance drew almost equally on former Conservative voters and on former Labour voters – hence there is little truth in the canard that the SDP kept the Tories in power throughout the 1980s. What did emerge was a move away from voting on class lines: the rise of the SDP/Liberal Alliance coincided with a marked weakening of class politics. Mrs Thatcher's enthusiasm for self-made entrepreneurs showed that she, at least, understood that.

The Labour Party was the most affected. The dramatic changes here owed something to the SDP as an alternative pole of attraction for Labour voters. Many of those voters were profoundly suspicious of the Labour extremists, as the fate of Bennite candidates at by-elections showed. The series of Labour defeats in every general election from 1979 to 1992 underlined the point. Polls as late as 1987 gave extremism as one of the main reasons for Labour's unpopularity; strangely enough, it played a more significant part in 1987 than in 1983. Neil Kinnock's ill-advised rally at Sheffield at the end of the 1992 campaign with fists punching the air and the spirited singing of the 'Red Flag' revived all those half-forgotten fears of Labour. Alongside a surprising prejudice against Kinnock's exuberant Welshness, it contributed to the election defeat.

New Labour was the offspring, then, of election defeats and the moderates' regained control. Its 1997 manifesto resembled that of the Alliance in 1987 more closely than coincidence alone could explain. The persistent ghosts of history, from nationalisation to neutralism, were exorcised; New Labour had nothing to do with Old Labour, not even with moderate Old Labour, and that too was deliberate. It seemed there was nothing to learn from the history of what was usually presented as Labour's failed past. Efficient, modern, centralised and managerial, New Labour professed to be a new sort of government, and in some ways it was. It was just that the values of liberal democracy and of social democracy got lost somewhere along the line.

CHAPTER 17

Private Lives

My own preoccupations in the early 1970s meant that I saw very little of the Neustadts after our first meeting in 1969, but we were brought together again both by my friendship at Aspen with Rick, their son, and by our mutual friend Anthony King. Tony, a political scientist, later Professor of Government at the University of Essex, had met Dick when Dick was on his sabbatical at Nuffield in 1961, and the two men had hugely enjoyed one another's company. Tony became a regular visitor to their cottage in Cape Cod. He and Dick were to share the fate of widowerhood, for Tony lost his wife to cancer in 1970, when he was only thirty-five. After Bernard left me in 1970, I had begun to see a good deal of Tony, whom I had met through the political broadcasts he regularly presented for the BBC. Our respective bereavements brought us together and we fell in love. Tony was strong, clear-minded, utterly trustworthy and sometimes dogmatic. He was also a caring father figure, though he had no children of his own. He and I and Rebecca spent many of our holidays together, usually in France but sometimes at Dick and Bert's cottage. It was a place of refuge for Rebecca and me.

In England, I felt hounded by the media. As a prominent politician and one who had had a very public divorce – not one I wanted – with pictures of my former husband and his new girlfriend all over the tabloid newspapers, I was obviously a target. On more than one occasion when I was in the company of a male friend I was followed by photographers, sometimes dodging in and out of the evening shadows. As someone who valued her own privacy I found it very oppressive, even though Tony and I were unlikely to be the subject of scandal, since both of us were now single. We contemplated marriage, but I did not feel free to marry without an annulment, and on this my Church was adamant. Every rule in the book had to be obeyed in full, not least because I was a public figure. My submission for annulment went through more than one ecclesiastical tribunal. I got the impression that the Church officials involved were enjoying their intricate discussions with Bernard on the finer points of what constituted a marriage vow. In any event, it was several years later that the annulment was finally granted, long after Tony and I had concluded we should go our separate ways.

It was three years after Bert's death in 1984, and eight years after Tony and I had parted, that Dick and I began to think about marriage. He loved politics, and it was fun for him that I was a politician. We both enjoyed entertaining our friends in Cape Cod – as long as it was simple and informal, bluefish or hamburgers on the barbecue washed down with Californian wine. In the long evenings, with the spectacular red and orange sunsets slowly fading into eggshell blue and then indigo, the pine branches creating a Japanese etching in the gathering darkness, we would sit on the big deck listening alternately to Ella Fitzgerald and Mozart.

Before Bert's illness, I would not have contemplated marrying Dick, for all that I enjoyed his company, nor would he have wanted to marry me. He had enjoyed a traditional marriage at its best; Bert had been a devoted and loving wife who did all she could to promote his work, an exciting career and a household in which she readily accepted responsibility for all the domestic duties. Her illness transformed him. Dick had made a conscious decision to give back to her some of the love and support she had sustained him with for so many years. Once made, his commitment was wholehearted. He became a skilled steerer of wheelchairs. Academic colleagues would see him and Bert perilously racing along the banks of the Charles River, both of them laughing their heads off. He would call in on the class she taught for non-English-speaking foreign students at Boston University, and together they would explore art galleries and exhibitions. Instead of distancing themselves from friends and visitors, he began to take over the preparation of simple meals. Guests did not expect gourmet food, because Bert had never been much of a cook. (Indeed, this was one area in which I was a more satisfactory wife than Bert, for I had learned to cook as a teenager, spurred on by my mother's similar incapacity.) They came for the conversation, the company, the laughter and the wisdom.

Those demanding years between the onset of Bert's illness and her death changed Dick radically. He was still a wonderful teacher and a brilliantly perceptive observer of political events. But his values had changed. In everything he did there was now a sensitivity to others, a concern for them that had not been so evident before. The old competitive edge had softened. He had a remarkable ability to put himself into other people's shoes – the quality known as empathy. His advice to his political masters and his students alike was to think through where the people they dealt with came from, to stand where they stood. That meant looking at their families, their early lives, the events that had shaped them. Dick investigated his subjects without prejudices or preconceptions. His inherent modesty was a key factor in his ability to understand others. He never allowed his ego to get in the way of his perceptions.

In the book about Dick jointly edited by Matt Dickinson, one of his favourite students, and his daughter Beth, *Guardian of the Presidency*,* Tony King described Dick's style of lecturing, speaking very slowly, thinking as he spoke, every sentence punctuated by long puffs on a cigarette or, later, his pipe, for he was a serial smoker. The style was never didactic. It left room for his students to contribute to what was a Socratic dialogue. Dick always assumed he could learn from them.

In some ways Dick was an old-fashioned man. He wore suits and shirts that had been carefully dry-cleaned and laundered, and were often twenty or thirty years old. He particularly liked a striped seersucker suit, yellow with age, that must have dated back to the 1950s. His summer dress, white shorts, knee socks and sandals, never varied. He hated ever-changing technology and never used a computer. His sudden incendiary temper, which flared and subsided within seconds, was largely directed at inanimate objects. 'Goddam toaster!' he would bellow from the kitchen, accompanied by an acrid smell of burning. He did not even type his books and lecture notes, but wrote them out carefully and deliberately on lined yellow pads, as he always had.

Yet the openness and directness of his discussion with his students made him fully aware of changing times. He was always abreast of what was going on. His analyses of the Clinton administration's policies and politics were as fresh, sharp and colourful as were his observations on Franklin Roosevelt, whom he admired beyond all other presidents. In 2008, his studies of presidential transitions were invoked on public radio stations by commentators on the succession of Barack Obama to the presidency.

Dick only asked me to marry him after he had decided he wanted to live. For three years he had been so deeply and privately mired in grief for Bert that he had wanted to do nothing life-affirming. Rick and Beth had taken him off on a trip to South-

---

* Dickinson and Neustadt (eds), *Guardian of the Presidency: The Legacy of Richard E. Neustadt*.

East Asia in an attempt to rekindle his interest in the outside world. Other friends introduced him to lively and attractive women, to no avail. When eventually he told his son about his hesitation in asking me to marry him, Rick responded: 'Oh go on Dad. It will be such fun!' Rick and I had bonded many years before at Aspen.'

At the end of March 1987 I got a call from Barbara, the third wife of my only brother John. John had had three sons, Daniel, Timothy and William, with his first wife Jennifer, whom he had married in 1951 when both were undergraduates at Oxford. The marriage had broken up in 1966, as I mentioned earlier, when John left Jennifer for his secretary, Elaine, whom he married the following year. Elaine and John had two children, a girl and a boy, Larissa and Alexander. She died of cancer in 1975 at the tragically early age of twenty-nine.

John, whose successful property business had collapsed into bankruptcy, devoted himself to bringing up his two younger children. He moved to a flat in a large nineteenth-century replica of an Elizabethan house, Broome Park near Canterbury. The house had once belonged to General Kitchener. Two years later, he and his family moved again, to the austere surroundings of an old farmhouse at Woolage Green in the Weald of Kent. John would walk several miles to a bus stop to avoid having to pay for a taxi. While living there, he married for a third time, to Barbara Blee, a good-looking Polish woman whom he had met in London. Theirs was a stormy marriage, but by 1987 John's bankruptcy had been discharged and his prospects were improving. He had formed a close friendship with the writer and broadcaster Malcolm Muggeridge, whose moral support meant a great deal to him. He had also found a job in London, and had moved to a basement flat in Oakley Street in Chelsea.

The call I received that day from Barbara was frantic. John had suffered a massive stroke early in the morning. He had mumbled to Larissa, now nineteen, and to fifteen-year-old Alexander that something was happening, and had then lapsed into unconsciousness. He was now in hospital.

I went there immediately. My brother, not yet sixty, lay there with tubes attached to every part of his body including his head, for he had suffered a huge cerebral haemorrhage, from which he was shortly to die. He and I had not been close in recent years, since his divorce from Jennifer of which I strongly disapproved. Yet as I looked at him, touching as only an utterly vulnerable human being can be, I remembered the childhood we had shared, the fairy stories and the invented friends, Winifred's wooden animals from South Africa and the scary writers at my parents' parties for grown-ups, and I choked with grief for the sensitive, protective, beautiful little boy who had been my brother.

Larissa, who was studying cookery on a Prue Leith course, disappeared from home. I knew she had gone to stay with a close family friend but I did not know the friend's name or address. Some time later, a gruff male voice on the telephone inquired just how long I expected him to look after his daughter's friend, my niece. Larissa now came on the phone to tell me that she did not want to live with Barbara. I immediately invited her to come and live with me and Rebecca. We had a London flat with just two bedrooms, so Larissa stayed for a month with my nephew Tim and my future son-in-law Christopher in their Hackney flat. In early June she moved in with me. By this time Rebecca had gone to work in British Columbia for a few months. Alexander was with Barbara, but Larissa made it quite clear that she wanted to live with her brother in my flat. I knew how close they were, these two parentless teenagers, and I could see that this in the end was the only satisfactory solution.

So I rang Dick in America and told him that there could be no question of us getting married. There was a short pause. 'I thought you believed in marriage,' he said, 'for richer, for poorer, in sickness

Dancing with Dick, 1987

Visiting a former Soviet Russian camp for political prisoners near Perm, Urals, 1998

With Paddy Ashdown in Kosovo, 1999

My family, Christmas 1999 at the Well House. *Back row:* Dick, Ray Honey, Roger Speirs, Rachel Neustadt, Beth Neustadt, Chris Honey, Rebecca, Margaret Honey, me. *Front row:* Phaedra and Aston Applin, Nigel, Sam, Diane and Anna-Louise Honey

With Rebecca and her son Sam Honey, aged two, 2002 *(Photo: Elaine Lockerby)*

Bill Clinton's final UK lecture as president, Warwick University,
14 December 2000, joined by Tony Blair, Dick and me

Relaxing in Italy, 2002

Rebecca with her sons Sam and Nathaniel, 2009 (Photo. Chris Honey)

The Speirs family: Larissa, Vivienne, Ishbel, John, Edward and Roger, 2008

Bill Rodgers and I receive our honorary doctorates from David Owen, the Chancellor of Liverpool University, 8 December 2008

With Timothy Brittain-Catlin outside the Senate House, Cambridge, after receiving an honorary degree, 2009 (Photo: Chris Honey)

Bicycling with Sam, 2008 (Photo: Chris Honey)

Playing chess with Nathaniel, 2008 (Photo: Chris Honey)

At the Sheikh Lotfollah Mosque in Isfahan, Iran, 2008 (Photo: Andrew Phillips)

and in health, as long as we both shall live. Doesn't that mean
that I take on board whomever you bring with you?' And so it was.
Dick became the most loving of fathers to all the disparate children
he had acquired.

There were obviously difficulties in trying to make a transatlantic
marriage work. Dick had proposed to me one summer day in 1986
of high wind and shining sky on the steep steps of his cottage
leading down to the lake. I had suddenly felt a wave of apprehension at the idea of marrying again and constraining my
· cherished freedom. I wanted time to think about what I really
wanted to do, and I asked Dick to let me postpone my decision. I
felt, too, that I had an obligation to the still slowly recovering
Liberal Democrats to fight the next election. I had lost in 1983, I
was still among the Party's few nationally known leaders, and I
was until the end of the year the Social Democrats' elected
President.

I doubted, after all the bad publicity we had had concerning
our quarrels with David Owen and his breakaway party, that
we could possibly match our 1983 share of the vote in 1987.
However, I was approached by the Liberals and Social Democrats
in Cambridge, who had established a remarkable local government bridgehead on the City Council and who had been among
the strongest advocates of the merger. Cambridge was a very
attractive constituency for anyone trying to put forward new
political ideas, and in addition it was close to the home Bernard
and I had established in north Hertfordshire some twenty years
earlier. So I agreed to stand.

The Cambridge constituency party was wonderful. Members
talked a lot, argued on policy matters, held strong and often
strongly differing opinions, and worked their socks off for
whatever election came along. We attracted hundreds to our
meetings, which were well covered by the local and sometimes
the national press. Canvassers came back with encouraging news

about electors promising their votes to us. Large fragments of the substantial Labour vote in the constituency were breaking away and floating in our direction. Furthermore, there was very little evidence of any activity on the part of the local Conservative Party, which surprised us all. But beneath the sparkling surface of the campaign something relentless but unobserved was going on. The Conservative campaign, led by the respected and well-liked MP and historian Robert Rhodes James, was quietly collecting every last potential Conservative vote. When he won by a majority of 5060 I was astonished, until I remembered the verse from Arthur Hugh Clough's 'Say Not the Struggle Naught Availeth', one of my favourite childhood poems:

> For while the tired waves, vainly breaking,
> Seem here no painful inch to gain,
> Far back through creeks and inlets making
> Comes silent, flooding in, the main.

There was to be one last political crisis and one last public appearance, which happened to coincide.

The last political crisis broke the day before my wedding to Dick on Saturday, 19 December 1987. Bob Maclennan, now the leader of the SDP, had been working on a new economic policy document with the help of two brilliant young economists whose political sensibilities in no way matched their knowledge of the dismal science. The draft paper they produced had all the hallmarks of a political disaster. Bob was keen to come up with new and radical ideas, but those ideas had to bear some relationship to the long-cherished values of the Liberal Party and to those of many, if not all, Social Democrats. The paper read like the work of a bunch of jejune neo-Thatcherites.

David Steel, astute though he is, has never been a man for detailed scrutiny and dreary homework. The paper had been left in his office, and he in turn had told his Parliamentary Party of seventeen MPs that they were free to come in and read it. He had not read it himself. Immediately, ripples of shock and horror spread out from his office. MPs who had not read it were enjoined by their colleagues to do so. Within a few days, Steel was faced with a major revolt. He read it himself, and began to understand why.

Meanwhile I had managed to get hold of a copy, and glanced at it while sorting out details of the wedding reception in my garden. Within minutes I had abandoned the reception plans for the phone. I rang David's office, and Bob's. 'You've got to withdraw this right away,' I said. I don't know whether anyone took the slightest notice, but I reinforced the message when I met my friends, in particular the Jenkinses and the Rodgerses, at the reception. The episode became known as the dead parrot, after the famous *Monty Python* sketch. By my wedding day, the parrot was still squawking, but gave up the ghost shortly afterwards.

The public event was my wedding to Dick, held in a quiet rural church in a village called Old Hall Green in Hertfordshire, with a reception in my garden at the Well House afterwards. We had invited only our families and close friends. The paparazzi, however, had got hold of the date. As we came out of the church we were faced with a mob of cameras, a mob that retreated awkwardly over the church's old gravestones, which claimed a few victims from this unseemly invasion. It was, at least, a better story for us than the dying parrot.

The 1987 election result was disappointing, though not disastrous, for the newly minted Liberal Democrats. We deserved worse. David Steel, the leader of the Liberal Party, and Robert Maclennan, the leader of the Social Democrats, remained in office to oversee the conclusion of the talks on the merger, which were completed in January 1988. Both men announced that they would not run again.

It needed self-confidence and optimism to run for office in what some believed still to be a doomed experiment, but fortunately several able men were willing to enter the competition. The election involved, under the new Party's complicated and legalistic rules, setting up election hustings around the country and a one-member one-vote election on the basis of the single transferable vote by the Party's members, now down to some hundred thousand. The election was scrupulously monitored and the votes counted by the Electoral Reform Society.

The result announced on 28 July 1988 was a solid majority for Paddy Ashdown, MP for Yeovil, over Alan Beith, MP for Berwick-on-Tweed. Paddy won 72 per cent of the 80,304 ballots issued, on a 72 per cent turnout. He was an unlikely leader for the Liberal Democrats, an athletic, commanding man whose manner owed a great deal to his distinguished military service in the Royal Marines. He had contested Yeovil for the Liberal Party in 1979 and again for the Alliance in 1983, when he was elected to Parliament with a majority of 3406. The media could not portray him in the stereotyped way they so liked, as a bearded, sandal-wearing, carrot-chewing Liberal. It was obvious that the clean-shaven Paddy wore sandals only on a beach, and would never publicly gnaw a carrot. The new cartoons of him parachuting into shabby groups of his political enemies did the Liberal Democrats a world of good.

Paddy, who could be terse and impatient but whose resolve and determination were unquestionable, set about his new Party with a will. He had strong support from the new President, Ian Wrigglesworth, another man it was hard to fit into a preordained pattern. Labour MP for Thornaby, Teesside, from 1974 to 1983 and then for Stockton South as an SDP MP from 1983 until he was defeated in 1987, Ian had brought innovation and remarkable management skills to the job of reinvigorating what had once been among the most advanced manufacturing regions of England. Tellingly, he continued as chairman of the Teesside Development Corporation long after he had ceased to be an MP.

So the new Party had been handed over to an impressive

leadership team, I had been a parliamentary candidate for the last time, the merger was now behind us and I could in good conscience depart. I had not abandoned British politics, but I imagined my future contribution would be limited to occasional television appearances and campaigning at a few by-elections. My main career, such as it might be, I supposed would now be on the other side of the Atlantic.

CHAPTER 18

The Harvard Years

In his preparations for the presidential election of 1988, George H. W. Bush had been discussing Cabinet posts with some of his colleagues. One of them was Richard Thornburgh, a successful former Governor of Pennsylvania. Thornburgh had become Director of Harvard's Institute of Politics after his two terms as Governor, in 1987. As the election approached, his aspiration to become Vice-President became increasingly apparent. But he was not what Bush needed; he was another East Coast Republican. Presidential slates are invariably heavily influenced by regional considerations, southerner with northerner, Midwest with northeast. So the attorney-generalship emerged as a more reachable ambition. Thornburgh was appointed to the job by Ronald Reagan in the election year, 1988.

There were problems, however. Reagan's optimistic, open, sweet-smelling presidency had been deeply compromised by the administration's actions in Central America. There was the nasty Iran–Contra conspiracy, where revenues from arms supplied to Iran had been recycled to the bitter opponents of the new left-wing Nicaraguan government of Daniel Ortega, known as the Contras. There were the ruthless operations of the death squads in

Guatemala and El Salvador, financed and trained by the CIA. Some of the nastiest of these operations had come to light because of the prominence of their victims. On 24 March 1980, when President Carter was still in the White House, a death squad assassinated Archbishop Romero of El Salvador while he was saying Mass in the chapel of the Divine Providence Hospital. Suspicion was directed at the Salvadorian army's death squads. The CIA-run School of the Americas based in Fort Benning, Georgia, was the centre of much of this activity.

Archbishop Romero had previously been a conservative prelate, but the murder of one of his priests, Father Rutilio Grande, a Jesuit identified with the cause of social justice, turned him into a fierce critic of the right-wing dictatorship that then ruled El Salvador. He became closely acquainted with the sufferings of the poor in his own diocese. He was not reluctant to speak out. By this time liberation theology was running like a bushfire through much of Latin America, sweeping the Christian *comunidades de base* – grassroots communities – into an ecstatic rediscovery of the revolutionary spirit of the New Testament. It was not the Christianity of the rich and well established.

Romero was to become the unofficial saint of Latin America, the man martyred for the poor. But his assassination did not bring to an end the secret policy known as 'low-intensity conflict' practised by the CIA in Latin America. Indeed, during the Reagan administration the policy was reinforced. In 1987, a secret 'Conference of the American Armies' was convened, comprising most but not all the chiefs of the armies of Latin America as well as the United States (Canada was not among the invitees). The US offered financial and training help to military forces tasked with suppressing Communism, with which, for these purposes, liberation theology was identified. The US was determined to stamp out liberation theology and in this had the support of many conservative members of the Catholic hierarchy, including within the Vatican itself. Hundreds of Jesuits and Roman Catholic priests of other orders who advocated it were killed, particularly in Central America.

On 16 November 1989, six Jesuit priests teaching at the Universidad Centroamericana in El Salvador, along with their housekeeper and her fourteen-year-old daughter, were murdered by unknown assailants. The sole eyewitness was a neighbour. There was speculation that the murders were planned by the far-right party ARENA (the National Republican Alliance), led by Roberto D'Aubuisson, and that the death squads under his command were themselves trained and armed by the CIA. This allegation was strongly denied, but I had an uneasy sense that it might be true. By this time I had learned quite a lot about extremist Central American politics. So I called a leading Jesuit in Boston. He was careful in what he said, but he told me that the Jesuits had insisted that the eyewitness, who had been spirited away to the United States 'for her own safety', be accompanied everywhere she went by a priest of their order. They feared she would be harassed and intimidated. He also told me that she had been questioned in Miami by members of the FBI.

In vain did the Latin American Council of Churches call on American Christians to recognise that profound social injustice was the real enemy in Latin America, not Communism. Such a conclusion was not acceptable to the interests that supported the Republicans and their right-wing associates in the continent. Washington's allies in the Vatican brought the appointment of reformist bishops and cardinals to an end. Some were succeeded by conservatives; others, as in the case of the Archbishop of São Paulo, Cardinal Paulo Evaristo Arns, saw their dioceses reduced in size and their influence consequently curtailed. Thus was the inspiring legacy of John XXIII reversed.

It was not an easy time for a good man to be a member of the Reagan Cabinet, least of all Attorney-General. I suspect Dick Thornburgh fought a difficult battle with his conscience. In any event, he agreed to become Attorney-General and left his post as

Director of the Institute of Politics in August 1988, leaving his deputy David Runkel in charge.

One dark night in the summer of 1988, six months after my marriage to Dick, I was swimming around Gull Pond, the lake just below Dick's house, with his friend Graham Allison. Graham had been one of Dick's favourite students and had written years before a book called *Essence of Decision: Explaining the Cuban Missile Crisis*, which was highly rated. Graham had become a professor at the Kennedy School and was now its Dean – as energetic, ambitious and enthusiastic a Dean as one could ever hope to find. As we negotiated our way around the reeds and water hyacinths at the lake's edge, he asked me if I would like to be considered for a public service professorship. This is a rare category found in only a few academic institutions. Such professors have to combine a career in public service with a high level of academic involvement in actually observing and analysing public service. The Kennedy School at any one time might have three or four such professors. They included Marvin Kalb, who had been the chief political presenter for CBS, and David Gergen, the former adviser on communications to Presidents Nixon, Ford, Reagan and Clinton. They had the same obligations to lecture and teach as did other professors, and they had to be accepted by a faculty board before they could be appointed.

I accepted with alacrity. My appointment came shortly before Thornburgh's resignation, and I was asked to step in temporarily as Acting Director of the Institute of Politics, the first non-American to take up such a position. It was a fantastic opportunity. I had a staff of seven, the enthusiastic involvement of scores of Harvard undergraduates, a well-appointed set of offices and an influential senior advisory committee chaired by Senator Edward Kennedy.

The staple fare of the Institute was the courses offered by the six Institute Fellows to undergraduates, the weekly suppers addressed by a well-known politician or campaign manager, followed by informal discussion, and a week-long annual course for newly elected Congressmen and women combining seminars on topics ranging from the customs of Congress to the mysteries of appropriations. For me, this course was an intensive immersion in the folkways of American politics, which are not much like anyone else's. For one thing, the boundaries of Congressional districts, I discovered, are drawn by the state legislature, offering tempting opportunities for the majority there to ensure the safe tenure of its Party incumbents. This process has steadily reduced the number of genuinely competitive districts to a very small proportion indeed.

I also learned a lot about the powers of lobbyists able to match their demands with substantial contributions to Party funds, whether nationally or in a specific district. The extraordinary influence of organisations like the American Association of Retired Persons (AARP), the National Rifle Association (NRA) or the American–Israeli Political Action Committee (AIPAC) was directly related to a political system that is money-driven. Ironically that system was protected by the sanctity of the First Amendment to the US Constitution, which guarantees freedom of expression. This Amendment has been called in aid against any attempts to limit spending on campaign funds – for instance, by forbidding the buying of time on television and radio for campaigning purposes. At the federal level, the United States was becoming a plutocracy where, to run for federal office, one had to be either personally very rich (a majority of Senators are dollar millionaires) or willing to limit one's freedom of debate and decision in return for financial support from one or more of the major lobbies. The discovery, originally by Howard Dean, then Governor of Vermont and a primary contender for the US presidency in 2004, of the potential for fund-raising of the Internet is now, fortunately, breaking the stranglehold of the big companies and the big lobbies.

Blessed by a wonderful staff, I decided to use the Institute of Politics for rather more than its long-established activities. Latin

America, in which I had become increasingly interested since my visits to Argentina and Brazil in 1984, was crippled by a heavy debt burden, much of it acquired owing to huge arms purchases by military dictators. Several of these dictators, as in Argentina, had been overthrown, but the consequences of their grandstanding were to be paid for by the people they had oppressed. Their financial situation was so dire that it called out for a radical approach. Harvard was a magical name in the context of Latin America. Many of the continent's political leaders, top academics and senior officials had been educated there, if not as undergraduates then as graduates in programmes tailored to their needs by the Kennedy School. It was like invoking the Holy Grail to the crusaders.

So I invited ministers of finance and bankers to a private conference to discuss how a rescue scheme might be drawn up. Some of those present had never met their opposite numbers; others revelled in the chance to speak freely. By the end of the conference the outline of what later became known as the Brady Plan had been pieced together. That plan required US banks to grant debt relief in return for the debtors underpinning future repayments by more collectable collateral and by commitments to economic reform.

In August 1990, seventeen months after the inauguration of Vice-President George Herbert Walker Bush as Ronald Reagan's successor, I was again at Aspen for its summer symposium, this time accompanied by Dick. The President was proceeding heavily through a long, dull disquisition on defence* when Mrs Thatcher, a distinguished guest of honour, hissed that Iraq had just invaded Kuwait. Had Mrs Thatcher been President, there is no doubt that she would have thrown the prepared speech to one side and announced that Saddam Hussein would be stopped and thrown out of Kuwait in short order. That was not the style of the

---

* President George H. W. Bush predicted on this occasion that the nation's armed forces could be cut by 25 per cent over the next five years.

first President Bush. At lunchtime in a large private dining area, Mrs Thatcher walked up to him and said in the tone of an exasperated headmistress, 'Don't wobble, George!' She made her reservations about the firmness of his response absolutely clear. She afterwards told me that she intended to go, uninvited, to Camp David to ensure that Bush would organise an immediate military intervention. In the event, of course, he did, putting together a large and impressive coalition supported by several Arab governments. The expulsion of Saddam Hussein from Kuwait was a textbook example of how to do it.

By 1989, the tectonic plates of geopolitics were beginning to shift. Mikhail Gorbachev was trying to move the Soviet Union towards becoming an open society. He propounded the doctrines of glasnost and perestroika, doctrines that he hoped would reform the state without destroying it. He was setting in hand work on a new constitution. On 10 April 1991, one of my most renowned Harvard colleagues, Professor Michael Sandel, together with a distinguished Canadian political scientist, Charles Taylor from McGill University, and I went at the invitation of President Gorbachev to Moscow as advisers on that new constitution. Arriving there, we were swept past the saluting sentries and through the great gates of the Kremlin to meet the chairman of the State Duma's Constitutional Commission, and to comment on the sections of the constitution it had drafted. 'Too many cooks spoil the dish,' one of the young officials told us. The draft constitution was a serious document, but parts of it read like a wish-list of rights that far outstripped the possibility of realisation – the right to shelter, to education, to a job – as if merely stating these things would bring them about.

Gorbachev was an amazing man to come out of the stifling Soviet system. He had a brightness about him, an endemic optimism, a driving vision. I had met him briefly when he visited Britain in December 1984. He was shortly to become General

Secretary of the Communist Party of the Soviet Union. He had been invited by Bernard Weatherill, the Speaker of the House of Commons, rather than by the government, so he was not a formal state visitor. Meetings had been arranged for him with the Party leaders. The SDP was a party represented in Parliament, so David Owen as its leader, and I as its President, met with Gorbachev and his small entourage of Russian officials, one of them a general almost overwhelmed by his rows of medals and his stiff military collar. It was a sunny afternoon, the Russian delegation had enjoyed a good lunch, and the elderly general began to sway within the confines of his collar. I caught Gorbachev's eye. He winked. I could not imagine Stalin winking. Things in Russia were clearly changing out of all recognition.

The Berlin Wall was dismantled soon after the Hungarians allowed the East Germans to escape to the West in September 1989. Within weeks, the elaborate structure of border guards, spies and secret police broke down. Men and women danced and demonstrated. Amazingly, the great revolution remained peaceful. After forty years, however, Communism had gone more than skin-deep. The authority of the Party lingered on in the habits of civil servants, in the loss of individualism and initiative, and in millions of drab, if secure, lives.

Back at Harvard from my Russian excursion, I wondered what we could do to help. Already the cowboy capitalists were moving into the former Soviet empire, snapping up state assets for a song, gaining control of natural resources and encouraging the disintegration of public services like health and education. The old Soviet law collapsed, but there was no other legal framework to replace it, no law of property, no law of contract, no bankruptcy provision. Debts were settled by threats of force, not by courts of law. Jungle capitalism replaced coercive Communism, and for many millions of ordinary citizens, replaced it for the worse. A small minority of business buccaneers became extremely rich. They were known as the oligarchs, and their political influence over Boris Yeltsin, first President of a post-Communist Russia, was very great indeed.

Within the Soviet Union, the Communist Party had been the source of authority and the body to whom public servants, from teachers to bureaucrats, were accountable. Now the former satellites of Central and Eastern Europe were moving towards a democratic system in which public servants were accountable to the people, who elected governments and Parliaments. To make this transformation work required a change in the attitude and culture of civil servants. The Kennedy School at Harvard offered postgraduate degrees in public administration and public policy. It prided itself on the quality of its teaching on public management and was imbued with the principles of transparency and participation. It seemed an ideal vehicle to help in the reform of these bureaucracies.

By 1990 I was no longer the Acting Director of the Institute of Politics, which I had agreed to head on a temporary basis only. I was now a Professor of Public Service, and as such had some time to devote to propagating democratic ideas and practice in the former Soviet bloc. I decided to launch an organisation that I called Project Liberty, which would offer short training courses and seminars to the former European satellites of the Soviet Union and would staff them with experts drawn from the Kennedy School and from equivalent Western European institutions.

Most American agencies at this time, the early 1990s, proposed training staffed by Americans. Project Liberty had the advantage of being multinational. I recognised that these new European democracies were unlikely to base their political institutions on the unfamiliar American model. Most of them entertained an ambition to join the European Economic Community. They wanted security, and for this purpose they planned to become members of NATO; but they also wanted to assert their historic and cultural affinity to Western Europe. Historically they had been governed by representative governments. Poland and Hungary had long parliamentary traditions: the first elected Polish Sejm dated back to 1182; Hungary's Parliament had been established in the early thirteenth century. Czechoslovakia, between the two world wars, was hailed as an ideal democracy; the Communist putsch against Edvard Beneš and Jan Masaryk in 1948 had been seen by many as the epitaph of Central European democracy. So its resurrection was likely to follow the parliamentary model, and in fact has done so.

Central Europe, and particularly those countries that had been associated with the Hapsburg Empire, also had a proud civil service tradition. The civil service was a respected profession with a strict hierarchy and strong principles. The tradition had survived the Communist era. We found in several countries, particularly Poland, a yearning to re-establish that tradition. So there was some concern about the Kennedy School's style of teaching, the 'Socratic method' involving students in dialogue with their teachers. It was a style at odds with the autocratic tradition of academics in much of Europe.

On the European continent, East and West alike, university students had been taught for centuries mainly in large lecture halls by professors whose status was rarely challenged, where there was little opportunity to question them. The Socratic method, based on the discussions of Socrates with his brilliant young companions, is a dialogue between teachers and students in which deeper understanding of the subject is discovered through questions, analysis of cases and students sometimes playing out the roles of the people involved. Lecture-based teaching had fed the dissatisfaction students displayed with their universities in the 1960s and 1970s. Case-based teaching enabled them to play a large part in their own learning, and to address contemporary issues. However, this approach, challenging long-established methods, was seen by many academics as threatening.

Project Liberty sponsored the Harvard faculty and others to

write case-studies about the transition, on subjects ranging from the environmental degradation of the Danube to the role of the secret police. We put them together under subject headings and provided notes for the teachers, as well as a description of what the case method was intended to achieve. We circulated these case-books widely. In doing so, we introduced a new approach to learning in these educationally conservative countries. We also created a contemporary archive of the transition itself.

Project Liberty got involved early on in privatisation. We were appalled by the crude asset-stripping that was going on all over Central and Eastern Europe. Sometimes the asset-strippers were Western opportunists, sometimes prominent Communist Party managers who knew exactly what assets of their former public enterprises had potential value. Communist state enterprises carried heavy social responsibilities, among them providing jobs for uneconomic workers, and where such enterprises were privatised these social services disappeared, leaving hundreds of thousands of people unsupported. What Russia was experiencing was indeed jungle capitalism, the capitalism of unrestrained greed. We in Project Liberty recognised that responsible privatisation required a structure of law on property rights, contract, bankruptcy, employment rights, health and safety. The transition state would also have to provide a social safety-net for those in poverty and rebuild the public health system. These essential requirements were not widely recognised. At the time, the advocates of 'shock therapy', moving rapidly to liberalise markets, disregarded them. Several of these advocates were associated with Harvard's Institute for International Development. Even now, there are countries in Eastern Europe and in the former Soviet Union where these requirements do not exist. But Project Liberty's first conference on privatisation went a long way towards establishing a model that would prove useful for the whole region.

The most radical reformer of all the East European leaders was the thirty-three-year-old Mart Laar, Prime Minister of Estonia. In

May 1993, he embarked on a political shock therapy of his own. He decided that the entire Cabinet of the newly democratic Estonia, and its senior civil servants, should attend a Project Liberty seminar over several days, in the capital Tallinn. Dick and I both attended, together with the most impressive team of trainers we could bring together. The Estonians were eager to discuss how to construct an open and democratic society. Their political instincts were Scandinavian rather than Russian, and we found in them highly responsive and motivated students.

My stint at the Kennedy School lasted from 1988 to 1996, punctuated by occasional visits back to England. During these years, Dick and I lived in a big apartment on Memorial Drive, the road that borders the Charles River in Cambridge, Massachusetts, with a wide view across the river to the sports field on the other side. Both of us had fairly heavy commitments to teaching courses and then to reading, discussing and critiquing the papers produced by our students. As I have mentioned, the teaching method was as far as possible interactive. Students would feel at ease in differing from their teachers, or challenging their conclusions, but almost always did so gracefully. We learned a great deal from them.

The courses I taught fell into two categories: courses about the European Community, just beginning to evolve into a single market, and courses about elective politics including one about women in politics. I had entitled my course on elective politics 'To Be a Politician', after a lively book written by an aspiring politician called Stimson Bullitt, published back in 1959. My students liked the course, but they asked me to change its title. I asked why. They told me that having attended a course with this name would do them no good in the jobs market. Furthermore, at the end of the course many decided against getting engaged in politics, mainly because of the way politicians were treated by the media.

Harvard's many centres and institutes had a high degree of autonomy; 'each tub on its own bottom' was the mantra. Thus they were responsible for raising their own funds and answerable to the university for how these were spent. The core schools like the Law School, the Medical School and the Faculty of Arts and Sciences had huge prestige, bolstered by the intense loyalty of the alumni, graduate and undergraduate alike. The Kennedy School, seen by some of the more traditional faculty as arriviste, commanded a similar intense loyalty from its much more international student body. Some of its courses, like the mid-career degree, attracted men and women with several years' experience of government administration in many parts of the world. After I returned to Britain in 1996, I found Kennedy School graduates everywhere who felt an immediate sense of comradeship with me; several remain close friends to this day.

I saw a lot of Rebecca. After leaving Oxford, she had taken a postgraduate degree at Cambridge in criminology, and then a job in New York with the Vera Institute of Justice, an NGO devoted to prison reform. She had gone on to work briefly in the US federal prison system, and then in British Columbia. From Canada, she came back to work in Massachusetts, living in the attic of an old house in which on one occasion she encountered a bat. This led to a 2 a.m. call to me and a dilemma, since I don't like bats either. The problem was ultimately resolved by me throwing a towel over the surprised creature, then casting it out of the window.

By 1995, I felt I had to spend more time in Britain, and with this Dick concurred. He relished British politics almost as much as American politics, and through Tony King had a close association with the University of Essex as well as with David and Marilyn Butler's Oxford.* He felt that we might be looking at a

---

* David Butler, the famous psephologist, is a Fellow of Nuffield College, Oxford. Marilyn, his wife, was Rector of Exeter College and former King Edward VII Professor of English Literature at Cambridge University.

new era. He was also a bit disappointed in the Clintons, fantastic communicators though they were, for their failure to understand Congress and, in Bill's case, for a lack of self-discipline. Dick was fascinated by Tony Blair and knew a good deal about New Labour through his friendship with Ed Balls, who had been an outstanding student at the Kennedy School. Watching what would happen to New Labour from a ringside seat in Britain was irresistible. So back to England we went.

CHAPTER 19

John Major: Consumer Conservatism

I was at the Kennedy School for most of the time that John Major was Prime Minister of the United Kingdom, between November 1990 and May 1997. Major was a fair-minded man – what he himself might have called 'a straight bat', to use a cricketing metaphor. He was not, however, a lucky Prime Minister. His time in that office was overshadowed by battles within his Party over the complicated Maastricht Treaty, and the break-up of Yugoslavia. John Major's personal style of politics was low-key and consensual, but in practice he took several of the policies that Mrs Thatcher had tentatively embarked upon and drove them further to the right. This was notably true in two areas I cared about, privatisation and education. He was convinced that privately owned companies competing with one another would provide better service and better value to customers than publicly owned ones. He therefore pressed on from Mrs Thatcher's privatisation of the public utilities such as the telephone service, gas and electricity, to industries that were natural monopolies in which competition was difficult, like the railways.

In education he embraced the radical changes in Kenneth Baker's 1988 Education Act. As I noted earlier, this Act removed the control of schools from local authorities and teachers to a centralised framework, with a national curriculum, a system of school inspection accountable to the Secretary of State, and a rigorous regime of tests and reports. It superseded almost everything I had tried to do when I was Education Secretary, although it did not move back to academic selection, which would have been widely unpopular.

It is hard to discover what motivated this deliberate disinheriting of the local authorities in a country that is already among the most centrally controlled of all democracies. Their administration of education had been widely approved by the public, outside a handful of inner-city areas. Local management of schools, which commanded all-party support, had given schools greater financial autonomy. School governors had, since 1978, been drawn from the local community, and included elected representatives of both parents and teachers.

The explanation lay in John Major's strongly held view, a view shared by his successor Tony Blair, that public services should be answerable to consumers, not to those involved in providing and administering these services. Major saw himself as the champion of consumers – hence his various charters on their rights. In the case of primary and secondary education, this meant parents. Many of the characteristics of English education nowadays, from league tables to regular and repeated testing, meet the demands of parents, purporting to enable them to make informed choices among schools. Schools, however, are complex organisms with aspirations and responsibilities that go far beyond what can be tested. The threat to a rounded, balanced curriculum lies in the powerful motivation for heads and teachers to concentrate on what can be measured, to the exclusion of what can only be understood.

In his massive 1988 Education Bill, Margaret Thatcher's Secretary of State for Education and Science Kenneth Baker wrested control over the curriculum away from the local authorities, and in practice even more from the schools and the teachers themselves. So extensive was Baker's national curriculum that it laid down what should be taught in over 90 per cent of school hours. Ministers devoted themselves to the content of teaching – what should be included in English or history or science – to a level unprecedented in other countries apart from what was still, at that time, the Soviet Union. Teachers felt themselves to be overcontrolled, and their professional qualities to be undervalued.

I have to admit here my own share of responsibility for the 1988 Bill. I mentioned in Chapter 12 the Green Paper I published, *Education in Schools, A Consultative Document*, advocating a core curriculum taking up about 50 per cent of the school week and dedicated to the basic subjects children needed to learn. The greater mobility of postwar generations meant that children had to know what was expected of them at a particular age (now called key stages) so that they could move from one school to another easily. The core curriculum would also set a standard in the basic subjects that most children would be expected to attain. But inhibited by the long tradition that ministers did not enter the 'secret garden' of the curriculum, I had left my intervention too late. Teachers had enjoyed a great deal of autonomy in designing their own curricula. This regime had its faults: some lacked the ability to do it, others avoided boring or difficult subjects. But what then happened was a lurch from one extreme to the other, from too much autonomy to virtually none. It is the heavy price England pays for a highly politicised system.

To Kenneth Baker's curriculum straitjacket was added by a subsequent Secretary of State for Education, John Patten, the idea of league tables, measuring each school's academic attainment. The league tables were published, with predictable results. For most schools, they reflected the intake: leafy suburbs did well, poor inner-city neighbourhoods badly. They said very little about the added value the school had brought to the children who attended it, but a great deal about their social background. The attempt in Labour's 1998 Education Act to produce more sophisticated league tables by the inclusion of what are called 'contextual value-added' criteria was well-meaning, but had only limited impact on public perceptions of 'good schools'. Teachers in the toughest areas felt that their efforts were simply not appreciated. Nor were league tables immune from manipulation, for instance by arranging admissions to ensure good examination and test results, and by teaching exactly what was in the test and nothing beyond it.

The Conservative counter-revolution, most of it happening when John Major was Prime Minister, contained a third element which has probably had the greatest impact of all: the replacing of Her Majesty's Inspectors of Schools by Ofsted, the Office for Standards in Education. HMIs saw themselves as guides and advisers to teachers, working closely with them. They conducted surveys in depth on aspects of education – for instance, the teaching of modern languages or of science. Schools would be brought into a discussion of the strengths and weaknesses the inspectors had found, with an emphasis on improvement rather than intimidation. But the government saw the HMIs as too soft, too close to the teachers, as needing to be brought to heel. Ofsted was to be a much tougher proposition. To ensure that, ministers appointed the redoubtable Chris Woodhead as head of the Office, a man accountable directly to the Prime Minister, who had no sympathy with friendly inspectors or progressive teaching methods.*

John Major could not impose his will on his warring party, which had by 1990 been in office for eleven years, but he could still appeal to the electors. His government's re-election in 1992 was a political miracle that owed much to the electors' perception of the Prime Minister as a good and likeable man. In abandoning public relations professionals for the street and the soapbox in the run-up to that election, Major had shown his own sure political instinct. The voters loved it.

*

* These paragraphs on education appeared in the Guardian on 3 March 2009, entitled 'The Winnowing Out of Happiness'.

Paddy Ashdown, the Liberal Democrats' leader, had tried on more than one occasion to get Bill Rodgers and me made peers – 'elevated to the peerage', to use the traditional expression. He had been rebuffed by Mrs Thatcher. 'But Mr Ashdown,' she had said sweetly, 'surely Mr Rodgers and Mrs Williams were *Labour* Cabinet ministers? When the Labour Chief Whip comes to me to ask for their elevation, I will certainly consider it.' It was a circumlocution Major would not have employed. So in 1993 Bill and I both became peers. We were dressed up in crimson robes and ermine collars, to the amusement of our families. Bill had preceded me, so I was able to ask him and Roy Jenkins to accompany me when I was introduced to the House of Lords. My nephew Daniel, a BBC producer and a man of mirth, presented me with a mug called 'Her Ladyship' and my husband Dick with another labelled 'Squire'.

For the next three years I split my time between the House of Lords and the Kennedy School. I lectured in the autumn semester, September to mid-December, and then came back to Britain for the other two-thirds of the year. It was a time of my life rich in personal happiness. In 1992 my daughter Rebecca had married her partner of several years, Christopher, in our local Catholic church where I had married Dick four and a half years earlier. She was given away by her father, Bernard, by now Professor of Philosophy at the University of California in Berkeley. Christopher's parents, Margaret and Ray, were devout and active Anglicans, so we also held a ceremony of celebration in our twelfth-century parish church of Saint Mary the Virgin just over the road from the home I have owned since 1967, the Well House in Furneux Pelham. The occasion was made yet more memorable when the lonely peacock that lived in a big pine tree next to the church flew down and spread out his splendid tail feathers in front of the couple.

The reception was in our house and garden. The Well House is a charming hybrid, a fifteenth-century timber-framed lath-

and-plaster house with a big L-shaped living-room, part of which was added on in the twentieth century. I had an extension built, designed by my architect nephew Timothy, adding another bedroom and bathroom above the garage, reached by a steep staircase with a rope banister. Apart from that, I made few improvements. My cleaning lady Barbara Larkin kept the place tidy, beating back the tide of books and papers that flowed in whenever I appeared. She would bicycle down from her nearby cottage if the house was menaced by floods or by birds falling down the tall chimneys. She was that rare character, a person one could absolutely count on.

What mattered to me and Rebecca was that it was a happy house, and full of light. You can tell whether a house feels happy almost immediately, and it has nothing to do with how smart or elegant it is. It also contained some of my most precious artefacts: the grand piano on which my mother had long ago accompanied my uncle Edward on his violin, and the elusive and subtle portrait of Thomas Hobbes that had belonged to my father, who wrote his doctoral thesis about the author of *Leviathan*.

In 1993 my niece Larissa married Roger, the younger son of Rosemary and Archie Speirs, a family living in Northumberland. Larissa was keen on a formal wedding, and Dick, who had always longed to give a bride away, spent a happy morning with her inspecting going-away suits and trying on morning-dress. The wedding was at St Joseph's, Bishop's Stortford, the reception in our house and garden. Roger and Larissa now have four children, Vivienne, Ishbel, John and Edward, and live in Corbridge, Northumberland. While I am in fact her children's great-aunt, as the sole surviving relative of Larissa's paternal parent's generation I have become honorary grandmother, which gives me much pleasure. I count my blessings: a son-in-law and a nephew-in-law who are marvellous fathers and share domestic responsibilities; two ebullient and joyous grandsons, Sam and Nathaniel, and five lovely honorary grandchildren, one of them Dick's granddaughter

Rachel. There is something to be said for old age – but don't overdo it; as Dick once said to me, 'Old age is not for wimps.'

Politics intruded, as ever. Bill Clinton, elected US President in 1992, was an extraordinary phenomenon, a man who not only gave the impression of loving almost everyone he encountered, but actually did. Unusually, he combined this with a restless, questioning mind. In his two terms as President, he achieved less than these formidable qualities promised, partly for personal reasons – he lacked discipline in every part of his life, from time-keeping to women – and partly because after the 1994 mid-term elections he never commanded a Democratic majority in either house of Congress.

In his first term he devoted too much of his energy to a hugely ambitious but doomed attempt to reform the American health care system. Technically outstanding, that system is also the most expensive and over-administered in the developed world, costing 15 per cent of gross domestic product in 2006,* and still leaving some forty-six million Americans without any kind of coverage.† It is administered by immensely powerful private insurance companies, which not only receive substantial premiums but compel the system to be hugely bureaucratic. The first question I was asked on the rare occasions I sought medical assistance in the USA was the name of my insurance company and the details of my policy. In the United Kingdom, I may get asked my NHS number, but often not even that.

Clinton's health-care initiative was handed over to his wife Hillary to work out in detail. Given her acute, legally trained mind, that may have seemed praiseworthy. But it was probably a mistake to put her in charge, despite her evident ability. It led to much resentment, not least among Representatives and Senators.

---

* World Health Organization, *The World Health Report 2006: Working Together for Health*.
† US Census Bureau.

She was the First Lady, the chatelaine of the White House, a ceremonial position. The First Lady was not meant to be a policy
wonk. Furthermore, to get this policy through Congress the legis-
lators needed to feel a sense of ownership. That ambitious
politicians would swallow even the most brilliant and detailed
policy on a highly controversial topic like health was to expect too
much. The insurance companies waged a devastating campaign
against the scheme, suggesting it would pave the way to 'socialised
medicine', the nightmare fantasy conservative American politicians try to identify with the NHS. With a deeply divided and
partly hostile Congress, the imaginative proposal of the President
and his wife crumbled.

Whatever Congress felt about the First Lady, Hillary Clinton
was far more than a chatelaine of the White House. She had rapidly become a formidable global figure. In 1995, the United
Nations organised its Fourth World Conference on Women. I
was invited by the UN Secretary-General, Boutros Boutros-
Ghali, to serve on the international steering committee, and we
agreed to ask Hillary Clinton to be one of the key speakers. It was
there, in Beijing, that she delivered her lecture on the human
rights of women. The lecture was bold and unusual. It managed
to bridge the East–West divide by the global appeal of its theme.
Her fine lawyer's mind was evident in her awareness of the rights
of women. But what impressed me more was her readiness to
breach conventional diplomatic constraints. To the consternation of her country's leading Asian ally, Japan, she marched while
in Beijing with the 'comfort women' of South Korea, women
who had been prostituted during the Second World War to the
sexual requirements of the Japanese army. She defended the
unwelcome delegates from Tibetan communities overseas against
police harassment, to the irritation of the host country, China.
Her commitment to human rights overrode diplomatic niceties.
Here was a woman who was truly a global leader. That was why
I was disappointed when the grubby exigencies of national

politics, and her own huge personal ambition, led her later to compromise on critical international issues like the invasion of Iraq and the building of illegal Israeli settlements on the West Bank.

The first two years of a re-elected President's second term mark the apogee of his influence, the time when he is in the strongest position to bargain with the other actors with whom he shares power. There was a lot on Clinton's plate in 1996, from education reform and social security to the chaotic aftermath of the break-up of Yugoslavia. Clinton, instead of addressing them, frittered his time away, enchanted by Monica Lewinsky, an attractive student intern working for Leon Panetta, his chief of staff.

In Britain, the last year or two of the Major government was given over to bitter quarrels within the government Party, mainly about Europe, and specifically, as already mentioned, about the Maastricht Treaty, a complex document that extended qualified majority voting to new areas of activity. The Conservative Party had never been of one mind on Europe. Mrs Thatcher had paradoxically taken the longest step forward on the path to European integration of any Prime Minister since Edward Heath, by agreeing to the implementation of the single market in 1986. This was the mortar that held the Union together, that brought benefit to every member. But many Conservatives wanted the momentum towards closer union to stop right there. They admired Mrs Thatcher's battle for a rebate; they opposed any increase in the powers of the Commission, or any move towards a single currency or common defence. So deep did emotions on Europe run that the Party came close to breaking up and to jeopardising its own future.

Major's government had to deal with the aftermath of the Cold War as well. What at first seemed beneficial, promising the possibility of a 'peace dividend' from which everyone would benefit, carried with it two contentious consequences: the uniting of Germany and the break-up of Yugoslavia. Despite Mrs Thatcher's sourly expressed fears, the unification was conducted by Helmut Kohl without triumphalism, but it soon got bogged down in the difficult details of compatibility between the prosperous West and the austere statist East.

If the unification of Germany proved less difficult than feared, the disintegration of Yugoslavia after the collapse of the Soviet Union in 1991 was the opposite. Slovenia, culturally and historically very much part of the old Hapsburg Empire, slipped away quickly and with minimum trouble, its de facto independence being conceded in the Brioni Accords of 7 July that year. But by the time Croatia began to agitate for independence, the President of Yugoslavia, Slobodan Milošević, now firmly in the saddle, was determined that no further secessions should be allowed. In June 1991, the Croatian leaders nonetheless declared their intention to secede from Yugoslavia. In this they were ferociously opposed by the large Serb minority living in Slavonia and the Krajina, people already aroused by Milošević's fierce Serbian nationalism. Civil war broke out. That autumn, Croatia's loveliest historic town, Dubrovnik, was shelled by the Yugoslav navy and bombed by the Yugoslav air force. It would have taken very little to stop the assault, and two far more powerful navies, the American and the British, were not far away – in the Mediterranean – at the time. In the east, the medieval Danubian town of Vukovar was subjected to a Stalingrad-like siege and in November 1991 was captured by Yugoslav Federal troops. Many atrocities were committed. But Croatia had not been fully recognised by the international community, and neither the Americans nor the British had the stomach for a fight. Steeled by Thatcher, earlier that year the two countries' governments had turned back Saddam Hussein's invasion of Kuwait, a clear breach of international law. But the disintegration of Yugoslavia fell into the black hole of the UN system, the lack of any international law obliging governments to protect their own citizens. Throughout the whole terrible story of Milošević's attacks on his country's citizens, this absence of a clear

legal ruling hampered and haunted everything Western governments did, or more often failed to do.

On 23 December 1991, the German government, strongly lobbied by its own Croatian minority and much influenced by the
Foreign Minister Hans-Dietrich Genscher, recognised the independence of Croatia, overruling the misgivings of the British and
the French, who had appointed Lord Carrington to broker a compromise with the Yugoslav government. Bonn's unilateral action
was the spark that ignited the civil war. Serbs were driven out of
Slavonia and the Krajina where they had settled in substantial
numbers. The Serbs retaliated. Old hatreds were re-ignited, for
the Serbs had never forgotten Croatia's past as an ally of Nazi
Germany, nor forgiven the savage repression of their countrymen
by the Ustaše between the two world wars. But the Federal
Republic was unable to contribute to bringing the civil war to an
end: Article 26 of its own constitution forbade military action
outside its territory. Belgrade succeeded in re-establishing control
over the Krajina and most of Slavonia. Fighting subsided and in
February 1992 the UN sent a peacekeeping mission, UNPRO-
FOR, to keep the warring parties apart.

The recognition of Croatia as an independent entity on 15
January 1992, far from ending the rolling conflict in the former
Yugoslavia, fuelled it. The next significant province to resist
Milošević's efforts to impose a greater Serbia on the diverse former
state of Yugoslavia was Bosnia-Herzegovina. Once, like Slovenia,
part of the multicultural Hapsburg Empire, Bosnia-Herzegovina
had a reputation as a tolerant province in which large Serbian,
Bosnian-Muslim and Croatian communities had long lived
together in reasonable harmony. But the secession of Croatia,
coupled with the conflict between Serbs and Croats there, had
alarmed Bosnians.

In April 1992, following a referendum boycotted by the Serb
population, Bosnia's President Alija Izetbegović declared independence. For Milošević, this was the last straw. He ordered the

army, now overwhelmingly Serbian, to break Bosnia's resistance. Within weeks, his heavily armed troops had overrun a crescent running from the Krajina in Croatia along the Sava River, down the Drina and south to Montenegro. Non-Serbs were viciously expelled through a campaign of ethnic cleansing. The Bosnian Serbs set up siege around the capital, Sarajevo, a city previously famed as an example of tolerance and culture. The brutal war was to go on for over three years.

The United States government regarded the Balkans, with some justice, as Europe's problem. Indeed Europe, in the form of the European Council of Ministers' President, Jacques Poos, had loudly announced in 1991, 'The hour of Europe has dawned.' The US had heard the European Union congratulating itself on its successful integration of the long-established dictatorships of Spain and Portugal into a democratic community. They knew that Europe, economically, was doing pretty well, and that some of the poorest new members, like Ireland, Greece and Portugal, had experienced impressive improvements in their standards of living. Surely this stable, wealthy European Union could sort out the conflicts within the small, angry south-eastern tatters of the continent?

It couldn't. The damage done to American assessments of Europe's potential by the wars of the Yugoslav secession was immense. The French and British governments, the two big member states of the European Union with trained and experienced military establishments and a certain historical enthusiasm for intervention, duly sent in troops in February 1992, as did the Netherlands and some twenty others, twelve of them EU member states. They were under a vague UN mandate 'to create the conditions of peace and security', and to protect UN convoys carrying humanitarian aid. The outcome could have been predicted: civilians begging the soldiers to intervene and protect them, the soldiers under orders not to do so.

In addition, UNPROFOR was hobbled by a dual key command

under which it could use lethal force only if its commander asked for the authority to do so and the UN Secretary-General's special representative, Yasushi Akashi, agreed. He almost never did. Meanwhile the shelling, the bombing, the ethnic cleansing of minorities paraded across our television screens, leaving in its trail frustration, anger and contempt. In the United States, the impotence of the Europeans aroused scorn. That scorn was shared by the former British Prime Minister most admired in the United States, Margaret Thatcher.

Because there was a United Nations boycott of arms sales to the former Yugoslavia, the lightly armed Bosnians needed protection. They were no match for the heavily armed Serbs under Milošević's command. The Americans did have a policy, one constructed on the basis of one absolute prohibition – they would not intervene on the ground. The policy was called 'lift and strike' – lift the embargo so that the Bosnians could buy arms to defend themselves, strike by air against the military bases and heavy artillery concentrations besieging Bosnian towns, above all, Sarajevo. Margaret Thatcher and I made contact when she was on a tour of the United States to promote her autobiography. We agreed to lobby together for the 'lift and strike' policy. The British and French governments believed this US policy would only escalate the fighting and cut off the supplies of humanitarian aid that were getting through. To the Americans that response seemed a typically craven instance of European appeasement. Bosnians might be hungry, but they were being killed by mortar fire, not by starvation.

One evening at the Institute of Politics I had met and talked with Lynn Martin, a feisty lady who had been George H. W. Bush's Secretary of Labor (1991–3), a loyal Republican from Illinois. She told me how upset she was about Bosnia. I shared her feelings. I had twice been to see Douglas Hurd, Major's Foreign Secretary, in London. He had indicated to me that the government opposed 'lift and strike', and was also unlikely to take on the

Serbs militarily. I learned later that military estimates of the numbers of troops needed to defeat the Yugoslav army on the ground were around 400,000 – far beyond the capacity of France and Britain.*

Lynn and I agreed to go to Sarajevo together. We wanted to make our own assessment. We also knew that as two women former Cabinet ministers from different governments, we would be able to command at least some media interest. We flew to Zagreb, and were taken to the huge refugee camp at Karaula. We listened to harrowing tales of expulsion and ethnic cleansing from the refugees camped there, many of them women with young children who had turned their bunks into pathetic outposts of home. There was enough to eat, but nothing to do. A few half-hearted attempts had been made to teach the children or organise games for them, but the camp had the same sense of hopelessness I had encountered before and would encounter again, born of having no idea what the future might hold.

The next day we were handed helmets and flak jackets for our UNPROFOR flight to Sarajevo. We were in a troop plane, long benches with belts to hold on to. Our companions were men of the French Foreign Legion under the command of the formidable General Morillon, who sat in the front, his face furrowed by deep lines as if he never stopped thinking harsh thoughts. He bore an air of authority that was somehow reassuring. When the plane got above Sarajevo, we could see occasional flashes from the Serbian artillery ringing the besieged capital. We were told that the minute we landed we must run from the aircraft to a line of sandbags at the edge of the runway, because the passengers were likely to be targeted by Serb snipers. The plane corkscrewed down to the little airport so as to make it a difficult target for the shells and machine-guns whooshing around us.

Having arrived in one piece, we were taken off in an armed

* John Major, *The Autobiography*, HarperCollins, 1999.

jeep for a look at Sarajevo. It was a ghost city, rather like those devastated German cities I had seen way back in 1948. The houses were pockmarked by shells, or partly ruined. There were no lights. People did not leave their houses unless their need was desperate, for the streets were sniper alleys, targeted by Serbian sharpshooters. We went off to have supper with a Bosnian family who described to us what it was like to live in a besieged city. They were sensitive, cultivated people, longing to hear something about the outside world. They gave us each a slice of quiche, made of flour and young stinging nettles, actually quite good to eat, like spinach. They explained how the children had made a risky expedition to pick them. The children were still at school; they did their homework in a small room in the middle of the house, lit by one or two candles. There was no electricity, but even if there had been it would have been dangerous to show lights. Books were the family's main comfort, books read by candlelight as their ancestors would have done.

Lynn and I spent the night on the floor of a battered flat that trembled occasionally when a shell landed nearby, sporadically illuminated by the flash of gunfire. It wasn't easy to sleep, but it was a catalyst for conversation. Most of our fellow squatters were UN workers or from the more adventurous NGOs. We aired our despair at the impotence and vacillation of our respective governments.

There was, I believe, another factor in the equation. Britain and France were queasy about German reunification. It seemed that a Titan might appear in the European Community, a country dominant economically and eventually politically too. Both the Foreign Office and the Quai d'Orsay were past masters at the game of balance-of-power politics. They had been playing it for centuries. Vis-à-vis Germany, in Central and Eastern Europe Serbia was a countervailing force, with a powerful army and close relations with Russia. It was surely not sensible to offend her unnecessarily. In the Foreign Office, there is a majestic mural dating from 1902, the height of the British imperialist era. It shows Britannia, one arm protectively around Belgium, the other around Serbia. The unnamed menace is, of course, Germany. The image burns deep. The Foreign Office and the Quai d'Orsay have long been friendly to Serbia. Sir Ivor Roberts, appointed as Chargé d'Affaires to Belgrade in 1994, had warm relations with the Serb leaders, including General Ratko Mladić and Radovan Karadžić. Karadžić was captured and sent to the International Criminal Court at The Hague, but Mladić still successfully avoids arrest for war crimes.

In 1993, the US managed to bring about an alliance between the Croats and Bosniaks, the Bosnian Muslims, by bribing them with financial support and arms supplies. The alliance was uneasy, because the parties were mutually suspicious, but it began to work. The alliance gained some remarkable victories in Croatia, pushing Serb militias out of the Krajina and western Slavonia. But there was to be a vicious retaliation in Bosnia. The United Nations had established six 'safe-haven' towns for Bosniak civilians to be protected by UNPROFOR. On 12 July 1995 one of those havens, Srebrenica, was overrun by the Serb army; its eight thousand male inhabitants, men and boys, were slaughtered in cold blood. The Dutch UN peacekeepers were overwhelmed and abandoned their mission, after calling for air strikes, a call that was not responded to.

Srebrenica ignited such outrage in the US that President Clinton sent Richard Holbrooke, a man with a reputation for toughness, to end the Serb atrocities. Holbrooke told the Serb government to lift the siege of Sarajevo immediately. They took no more notice than they had of UN resolutions and threats made by Britain and France, directed at them so often before. But Holbrooke was not a man given to idle threats. From 30 August that year NATO began bombing Serb mortar positions around Sarajevo, and kept the raids going for ten days. The Serbs offered to negotiate a compromise, but discussions gridlocked. After four more days of NATO bombing, and an intervention by President Yeltsin of Russia indicating that he would not use his veto to protect Serbia, the Serb government abandoned the siege, which had lasted forty-six months, from April 1992 until February 1996.

I shared American frustration with the Europeans. Although I felt very strongly about the weak and indecisive position on the break-up of the former Yugoslavia taken by the British and French governments, it wasn't clear how that could be changed other than by American intervention, as I have just described, and that happened only in 1995, after the Serb massacre of unarmed Bosniak men and boys at Srebrenica. When the US did intervene, Serb aggression stopped in relatively short order. The crudely constructed Dayton settlement included independence for Bosnia, the third state to be carved out of the former Yugoslavia. It was imposed in December 1995 on the warring parties by air power and sixty thousand NATO troops. It seemed a lot better than what had gone before. But the wars had not ended. Within four years they would break out again in Kosovo, the historic cradle of Serb nationalism.

CHAPTER 20

The Blair Phenomenon

John Major's astonishing election victory in 1992 benefited from the emergence of considerable prejudice towards the idea of a Welsh Prime Minister. Neil Kinnock was proudly Welsh; he spoke with a Welsh lilt, and had the loquaciousness for which his countrymen are famed. The ruder tabloids dubbed him 'the Welsh windbag'. His red hair, enthusiasm and vitality marked him out from the crowd, and from other politicians. Unlike the Scots, who at least until recently were viewed by the English with favour, the Welsh were treated with condescension and suspicion. It seems to have gone back a long time. During the campaign, some electors reminded me of the old nursery rhyme:

> Taffy was a Welshman,
> Taffy was a thief,
> Taffy came to my house
> And stole a leg of beef!

I was surprised and, having had a grandmother born in Wales, displeased. The vague prejudice solidified after Labour's final, and very unwise, election rally in Sheffield, a city whose council was once led by David Blunkett and whose town hall flew the Red Flag. As Labour Party activists punched the air and sang the revolutionary song of the same name, you could almost feel the public in their millions sliding back towards safe, reliable Mr Major. The last thing they wanted was the Labour left back.

The 1992 election had lessons for Tony Blair and Peter Mandelson, his strategist and comrade, even more than for Kinnock's successor, the popular and canny John Smith. Had he been leader already, Smith might well have won the election for Labour. His unexpected and much mourned death in May 1994 left the leadership open to new people and new ideas. It also left Labour MPs desperate for someone who could win, after the Party's four lost elections and fifteen years in Opposition.

Tony Blair emerged from relative obscurity. He had not been active in the old Labour Party, apart from standing at a by-election in solidly Conservative Beaconsfield in May 1982, when he famously wore a CND pin in his lapel. When he was elected in 1983 for the safe Labour seat of Sedgefield in County Durham, he joined the Tribune group, the largest left-wing group in the Labour Party at the time. He was seen early on as an attractive and articulate candidate for the leadership, but he did not begin to have the kind of political record that Gordon Brown could claim, decades of devoted and distinguished work for the Labour Party from schooldays on. Nor was Blair a political star at university, as Brown had been – the youngest student to enter Edinburgh University in the postwar period, one of the most brilliant, and at the age of twenty-one, elected as the university's Rector. Given the contrast in their youthful political commitment, it is not surprising that Brown felt cheated, and cheated partly because he considered that it was his proper behaviour towards his dead leader, John Smith – behaviour instilled by his upbringing in a manse – that allowed his fast-footed colleague to pass him in the race for the succession. Brown has never recovered from that episode. The notorious deal made between him and Blair at the

Granita restaurant in Islington in 1994, the subject of different interpretations, failed to heal the breach.

Brown may have been held back from engaging in a radical transformation of the old Labour Party by the depth of his own roots. Tony Blair, elected its leader that year, was much more easily able to adapt to the desires and prejudices of the post-Thatcher electorate, which had moved on from socialism to a more materialist, pragmatic and less class-bound set of attitudes. John Major, in his autobiography, said of Blair that he 'looked and sounded like a middle-of-the-road Tory'. It is true that his good manners and smart but unassertive clothes were reassuring to Conservative voters. What John Major left out of the picture were Blair's mastery with words, his dazzling charm, his blending of apparent personal modesty with stunning hubris, his capacity to sum up people and to recognise instinctively their strengths and their weaknesses. He could also accurately assess how much use they could be to him. When they no longer were, sentiment rarely stayed his hand. A complex man, Blair is above all else an actor, an actor whose preferred roles in the real world range from Coriolanus to Henry V, men struggling with the challenges and difficulties of power.

In Peter Mandelson, Blair had a brilliant, ambitious, quicksilver friend and ally, as committed to winning power as he was himself. Together with Alastair Campbell, Anji Hunter and others, Blair and Mandelson managed to transform the Labour Party into a modern, centrist organisation with little ideological baggage to get in the way. The dropping of the obsolescent Clause Four in 1995 was only a beginning, albeit a courageous and necessary one. Blair and his companions quietly adopted much of Mrs Thatcher's legacy, from trades union law to the public services – notably education, Blair's vaunted top priority. I was amazed that this breathtaking exercise in putting new wine into old bottles, retaining the Labour label for its millions of traditional loyalists while abandoning many of the principles and policies with which

those loyalties were associated, worked so well. It brought a remarkable reward: victories in three general elections with convincing
majorities, and the establishment of New Labour as the natural
party of government.

My own association with New Labour was brief. Peter
Mandelson and I knew each other from our common membership
of organisations devoted to Europe. I admired his sharp intelligence, wit and openness to new ideas. He invited me to lunch at
the Tate Gallery and it emerged that this was all about wooing me
back to the Labour Party, or more precisely to New Labour. I was
popular among Labour voters and often appeared on radio and television; as such I could be useful to the new Party. But neither
Peter nor I imagined that would mean New Labour changing
direction. I was devoted to the Liberal Democrats, despite the
long ordeal of the Party's creation. I was critical of the line Blair
took on crime and punishment, however brilliant his exposition;
and I doubted his commitment to comprehensive schools. So
Peter and I parted politely. No senior member of New Labour ever
approached me again until Gordon Brown became Prime
Minister in 2007.

In 1994, when Blair became leader of the Labour Party (not
until 1995 was it widely known as the *New* Labour Party), his
vision of big-tent politics dazzled many of my contemporaries on
the moderate left and for a while attracted me too. It was a vision
of inclusive politics in which a broad centre-left majority in the
country would deliver social democratic governments as the norm
in most political circumstances. For his mentor Roy Jenkins, the
vision was one of healing the great divide between Liberal and
Labour that dated back to the First World War. For Blair, no historian, the vision was of a compromise between the Labour and
Liberal traditions. The 'Third Way' was sufficiently attractive and
sufficiently vague for many to be able to sign on. Blair himself
attempted to define it in a speech made in Malmö, Sweden, on 6
June 1997, shortly after his momentous victory. 'Our task today,'

he declared, 'is not to fight old battles, but to show that there is a Third Way, a way of combining an open, successful and competitive economy with a just and decent human society.' The Third Way was symbolic of Blair's inclusive style of leadership. However, it needed the complement of Gordon Brown's unflinching austerity in economic matters to be convincing. The combination, though hardly harmonious, worked well.

Several leading Liberal Democrats were excited by the prospect of influencing, perhaps even serving in, such a government. A reformed and moderate Labour Party might not win a majority, and would need Liberal Democrat support. In such a situation, might not Labour abandon its long-held opposition to voting reform? Proportional representation of any kind would transform the composition of the House of Commons, and the Liberal Democrats would almost certainly be the main beneficiaries. Indeed, with proportional representation the prospects for electing governments of the centre-left would improve dramatically. Prominent Liberal Democrats, not least Roy Jenkins and Paddy Ashdown, began to believe we might be on the edge of a breakthrough. I thought that would only happen if Labour gained a plurality but no majority after the next election, or a tiny majority like those I had lived with as a minister in Jim Callaghan's 1976–9 government. It would be hard, even impossible, to get Labour MPs to accept proportional representation, which would lose the Party seats, unless it was essential to keeping a Labour government in power. The greater the majority a government gets, the more unfettered is its power to do as it pleases – an observation Francis Pym, a former Conservative Foreign Secretary, unwisely made, and paid for with his ministerial post.

I made my reservations plain to Paddy Ashdown in a note I sent him in July 1996, warning him to be careful of Blair. On 26 September, at our annual Brighton Conference, I went further, saying that we should not sacrifice our ideas and principles for a few seats in the Cabinet. In a later discussion with Paddy, I told him that being a member of the Cabinet, unless one was in one of the three or four top jobs, was not as influential as it might appear. I added that he would have far more influence with Blair if he was not, and did not seem to be, burning with ambition to get into government.

I considered Blair to be a brilliant fixer, who could turn promises and people to his own advantage. So it proved, for the tempting words on voting reform yielded nothing once New Labour had got a convincing majority. It took Scottish and Welsh devolution and proportional representation in both devolved Parliaments, which the Maclennan–Cook joint constitutional committee had championed, and pressure from the European Parliament for MEPs to be elected not appointed, to begin the erosion of the ludicrously unfair British voting system. And even then, it was only a start. The Westminster Parliament remained, and remains, resolutely unreformed.

In all Tony Blair's political dealings, retaining power was the imperative; it took precedence over everything else. Even his most deeply held convictions, like being at the heart of Europe and therefore part of the Eurozone, were sacrificed in the interest of being certain to win elections. When confronted by power greater than his own, whether that of Rupert Murdoch or of President George Bush, he yielded to it so as to maintain his own influence. Asked the question, 'Did Blair ever publicly confront President George W. Bush Junior on any significant issue?', the answer is 'No, never.' As with so many other senior British politicians, especially in the Labour Party, American might, military and economic, dazzled him. The last British politician publicly to confront an American President was Mrs Thatcher, first over the Falklands and then over the response to Saddam Hussein's invasion of Kuwait. Yet far from harming the special relationship, her strongly held positions won her, and Britain, respect, and rightly so.

In foreign policy matters generally, Blair showed the self-confidence and boldness that made him initially so attractive to the British public. This was an area where, apart from affairs concerning the European Union, he could operate without having to deal with Gordon Brown, his Chancellor of the Exchequer. In European matters, particularly the question of the single currency, Blair's aspirations were curbed and eventually blocked by the Chancellor. But on foreign policy, other than economic matters, Brown had surprisingly little to say.

The wars of secession over the break-up of the Yugoslav Federation in Croatia and then in Bosnia-Herzegovina were a source of frustration for many of us who championed the idea of a closer European Union – and that included Tony Blair as well as Roy Jenkins and me. The divided and timorous government of John Major proved unable to deal with Milošević's brutal tactics. Neither the siege of Sarajevo nor the massacre of Srebrenica ignited British indignation to the point of supporting military action beyond protecting humanitarian aid.

Reluctance to get involved militarily was not limited to the European Union. As I mentioned earlier, the US government, under strong pressure from an outraged public opinion, adopted the policy called 'lift and strike'. It lifted the sanctions on sending arms to Bosnia, and compelled Croatia and Bosnia-Herzegovina to 'strike' by forming an alliance against the Serb army, despite their dislike for one another – an alliance that managed to win back much of the territory occupied by the Serbs. Peter Galbraith, son of the great economist Kenneth Galbraith and ambassador to Croatia, played a major part in selling the policy. The military help the allies received from the United States was limited to the supply of arms. It was only after the massacre at Srebrenica in 1995 that President Clinton agreed to US military intervention, and that was limited to air attacks. There were to be no 'boots on the ground'.

During the Bosnian war I was approached by Nicholas Hinton, the head of Save the Children and before that for eight years Director of the National Council for Voluntary Organisations (NCVO). Hinton had come up with the innovative idea of sending small teams of well-informed people to troublespots, places where crises with potentially serious repercussions were germinating. The organisation he envisioned would be politically independent, truthful in its analyses, thoughtful in its policy prescriptions and resistant to pressure from governments and private interests alike. With little money but strong support from me and others, he launched what he called the International Crisis Group, and became its first President in 1995. I served on its board for ten years. Its first area of operation was Bosnia-Herzegovina. The ICG rapidly became respected for its clear-sightedness and objectivity. Heedless of his own safety, Nicholas Hinton was killed in a road accident in Split, Croatia, on 20 January 1997, while on a peacekeeping mission. His legacy survived and flourished. The ICG, later headed by the robust and blunt-speaking Gareth Evans, former Foreign Minister of Australia, became what one might call the think-tank for the global community.

Eventually, under relentless US pressure, Milošević accepted the Dayton Agreement, extending independence to Bosnia-Herzegovina as well as Croatia. But his lust for an 'ethnically pure' Yugoslavia was not yet slaked. In March 1998 he turned his attention to Kosovo, the province historically and even mythically associated with Serb nationalism. He ignited sectarianism and its vicious sequel, ethnic cleansing, in yet another fragment of Tito's once united Yugoslav Federation.

Milošević's actions in Kosovo were in part a response to attacks on his government by the Kosovo Liberation Army, an insurgent force dedicated to Kosovar independence in a province that was 80 per cent Albanian and only 20 per cent Serb. Ethnic antagonism, as ever, carried its own antibodies. Public anger grew as television coverage of burned villages and hapless refugee families filled their screens.

The response that Milošević's latest offensive against his own citizens drew from Tony Blair was not one of compromise or appeasement. Blair had been outraged, and in addition frustrated by the weak reaction of the British government to Milošević's attempt to suppress Croatia and Bosnia-Herzegovina. Whatever his readiness to compromise in policy matters to obtain or retain power, it did not extend to the brutalities of dictators. The lessons of Croatia and Bosnia-Herzegovina were lessons about responses that were at once late and inadequate. Blair was determined that this should not be repeated in Kosovo. He wanted to discover all he could about what was going on.

An important source of information for him was Paddy Ashdown, with whom he had established a relationship of trust in the three years leading up to the 1997 election. Although heavy demands were made on him as leader of the Liberal Democrat Party, Paddy had kept closely in touch with events in the former Yugoslavia, and knew many of the protagonists on both sides. He decided to visit Kosovo shortly before Christmas 1998, and invited me to accompany him and his personal assistant, Roger Lowry. Blair asked Paddy to report directly to him on the situation.

The three of us travelled from Skopje in Macedonia, where the UN-appointed monitors were based, to Pristina, the capital of Kosovo, and then to Prizren, close to where ethnic cleansing had been reported. The countryside was as lovely and as deceptive as that of Northern Ireland, and I would observe with pleasure the bucolic-looking scene. Then Paddy would scan the same places, and point out the mortars hidden behind trees, the machine-gun nests in the rocks, the occasional sniper close to a village. I soon became aware that we were in menacing territory. On at least one occasion, as I was about to get out of the personnel carrier, Paddy warned me to step carefully because there was a mine beside the road. Here was a man who understood war and understood also how to survive. I did not protest when he announced that we would leave at dawn to accompany staff of the United Nations High Commission for Refugees on a tour of ethnically cleansed villages, though I did disobey his command to eat two cold fried eggs that looked like the eyes of a dead monster. Paddy was unmoved. 'It's all you'll get to eat all day,' he said unsympathetically.

When we got there, we found that the villages had been sacked and burned. In many houses there were sticks of furniture and abandoned animals, left behind in the desperate flight of the inhabitants. One house, I remember, had a child's burned sandal in the middle of the disparate meaningless remnants that are the detritus of war. The few villagers who were visible said that a child going to school or a farmer trying to milk a cow to provide some sustenance for his family would be targeted and shot by snipers – the technique I had seen four years before in Sarajevo.

I noticed, as we went round the villages, that all the people we talked to were men. In a traditional Muslim society, the women would be hidden at home. So I left Paddy and Roger behind to do my own investigating; I knew that Kosovar countrywomen brought up in the Muslim tradition would be unlikely to talk freely to strange men. Talking to the women, I found out much more about the systematic rape and abuse of women by the Serb army, a weapon of war used in Bosnia and identified by Anne Warburton in her January 1993 report.* Rape was a weapon of war because traditional Muslims would not accept a woman who had been raped as a potential wife. She had been dishonoured, however unwillingly on her part. So rape became a form of subtle genocide, the destruction of a race or a people.

We concluded our visit with a series of meetings, some with

---

* EC Investigative Mission into the Treatment of Muslim Women in the Former Yugoslavia: Report to EC Foreign Ministers, Warburton II Report, 1993.

Kosovar leaders, some with senior Serbian officials. The Kosovar leaders ranged from Ibrahsim Rugova, the gentle, donnish leader of the Kosovo independence movement, a man inspired by Mahatma Gandhi, to the fiercely militant Hashim Thaqi, who led the Liberation Army. The senior Serb officials, the regional governor Zoran Andjelković and the deputy Prime Minister Nikola Šainović, whom we met in Belgrade, veered from denial ('There is no ethnic cleansing in Kosovo') to defiance ('It's our country'). Their behaviour reflected their master's confidence that NATO would do nothing, because if it tried to do something it would split. But Milošević underestimated President Yeltsin's desire to maintain friendly relations with the West, and in particular with the United States.

Blair's frustration over the European Union's unwillingness to intervene in Kosovo was now extended to his beloved United States, in the person of its reluctant President. Bill Clinton felt a sense of shame for his avoidance of military service in the hell of Vietnam. That shame took the form of unwillingness to be responsible for any US military casualties. He had been further shaken by the US intervention in lawless Somalia, where an American soldier had been dragged through the streets of Mogadishu. War in far-away Yugoslavia would be very hard to justify back home. So he dragged his feet, agreeing, as after Srebrenica, only to air strikes. In addition, he insisted that bombing should take place from relatively safe heights above the clouds, to limit US casualties.

Bombing of what remained of Yugoslavia after the Dayton Agreement began on 24 March 1999. The trouble was that bombing from very high up could not be precise. As NATO air forces attacked Yugoslav military and logistic targets day after day, inevitably many civilians were killed. Far from being seen as saviours, the United States and its allies began to be perceived as bullies. Distraught over these unintended consequences of the military intervention, Tony Blair began to press his case in

Washington. Air power on its own could not break the will of Slobodan Milošević, he argued. There had to be the threat of 'boots on the ground' as well.

Blair stuck with his campaign, sometimes clashing painfully, though privately, with Clinton. While the air raids continued, the first intimations that NATO might be considering an invasion reached Belgrade. They also reached Moscow, where Yeltsin was put under intense pressure to intervene with Milošević. The Russian President made it clear that he would not use his UN veto to stop such an action. In June 1999, Milošević decided to withdraw his troops. Yeltsin's influence was conclusive, but Blair's persistence had been crucial in shifting NATO's stance.

Kosovo was not Blair's only attempt at what he later called 'liberal intervention'. In the same year, 1999, United Nations troops were dispatched to Sierra Leone in West Africa, faced with an attempted coup by a nasty mixture of criminal groups and Liberian militia whose object was to take over the country's valuable diamond mines. The UN troops were not winning, and some Britons were taken hostage. In May 2000, Tony Blair sent a substantial number of British troops to Sierra Leone, to rescue the hostages and secure the airport for UN peacekeepers. The mission soon extended to frustrating the attempted coup, and in that it easily succeeded. Years after, I asked Martti Ahtisaari, the former Finnish President and a statesman renowned for his record of brokering peace, why the intervention had been so successful. He answered that in Sierra Leone there had been a core of men and women dedicated to the values of democracy. On that foundation it had proved possible to rebuild the country.

In pursuit of his campaign for military intervention in Kosovo, Blair advocated what he called 'a new doctrine of international community'. It was the centrepiece of his famous speech to the Economic Club of Chicago on 24 April 1999. Like other Blair speeches, it was at once inspiring and vague. The heart of the argument was that there are some situations so awful that they justify intervention by others. He mentioned genocide; he also referred to the expulsion of Albanians from Kosovo.

Blair's two interventions, in Sierra Leone and in Kosovo, were eventually successful. This built up his confidence in his own judgement. It also satisfied a deep moral conviction that, as he said in that speech, 'values and interests merge'. These were factors that would influence his decision to share in the invasion of Iraq. But there was also an intensely political factor – his fear that the United States might drift into isolationism. He had seen some signs of this in the Clinton administration, and feared, rightly, that it might go much further under George W. Bush, elected President in November 2000. Standing with the United States, even with an administration perceived to be both dogmatic and hubristic, would become a leitmotif of Blair's foreign policy once Robin Cook had gone in March 2003.

In 2001, soon after the 9/11 terrorist attacks, I was elected leader of the Liberal Democrat peers. I succeeded my old friend Bill Rodgers, who had followed Roy Jenkins as leader in the Lords, serving from 1998 until 2001. In that year, he suffered a stroke which led him to resign his office. For me, it was an extraordinary time to be elected as leader, for my three-year term of office coincided with the run-up to the invasion of Iraq, the largest public demonstration against a war ever seen in Britain, the military victory and the dreadful postwar story of misjudgement, exploitation and brutality.

Blair believed in the rightness of the war. He was so convinced that Iraq had weapons of mass destruction that he dismissed doubts and reservations from well-informed people and allowed the presentation of sketchy and sometimes questionable intelligence to convey much more certainty than was justified. My own Party, the only national party that opposed the Iraq War, argued that there had been no second UN resolution confirming the UN Security Council's commitment to invading Iraq and hence the war could not be called legitimate. The point was not just a dry legal one. The UN inspectors, led by the Swedish diplomat Hans Blix, had not been allowed time to finish their job, and therefore could not confirm that to the best of their knowledge no weapons of mass destruction had been found in Iraq. The timetable of war forbade that.

Worse still were the illusions of the war's advocates, men like Vice-President Cheney and Donald Rumsfeld, the US Defense Secretary. Heedless of the State Department's warnings, these men persuaded themselves that victory would be easy and the postwar confusion could be left to sort itself out. And here there is a real question about Tony Blair. Let us assume he thought the war justified, and did believe Iraq had weapons of mass destruction. Was he not troubled by the rosy scenarios of the Pentagon? Did his advisers warn him? And why did he ask so few questions, as far as one can tell, about the plans for the occupation and postwar reconstruction of such a key country in the Middle East? In his readiness to adopt Bush's strategy, Blair bitterly disappointed his American admirers. I suspect he was too credulous about American efficiency and American wisdom.

The most brilliant political communicator of all British politicians in the twentieth century, with the exceptions only of David Lloyd George and Winston Churchill, Blair was more complex and more conflicted than my description of him as a successful power-broker implies. He was and is a man of strong moral convictions, with a messianic streak. He did not spend much time reading history; if he had, he might have anticipated the long shadow Kosovo would cast over relations with Russia. To use a colloquial expression, it was the combination of conviction with the power to act that turned him on. I sometimes think of him as a Faustian figure, an angel on each shoulder battling for his soul: Alastair Campbell, the hard-nosed, highly professional, cynical friend; Cherie Blair, the passionate, highly-strung – and also conflicted – spouse with her own Christian convictions and unflinching commitment to human rights and international law.

While she was 'first lady', Cherie Blair was invited to lecture on human rights at the prestigious Harvard Law School. Her lecture spared no government, not even the one led by her husband. She was uncompromising in her condemnation of human rights abuses, including Guantánamo and the procedure known as extraordinary rendition. Her gesture to marital loyalty was to insist that the lecture be private, and that there should be no publicity associated with it. The communication of her core beliefs was not compromised.

I am still puzzled by Tony Blair's insouciance towards these pillars of a good world society, especially given Cherie's championing of them. His three Parliaments, when he was in office, did little to strengthen them. In his relations with the Bush administration he failed to oppose Guantánamo Bay and the detention without trial of so-called 'enemy combatants'. He slid lightly over extraordinary rendition, the secret transportation of terrorist suspects to countries untroubled by the protection afforded by international treaties against torture. Britain's cooperation in extraordinary rendition went, we now know, far beyond just keeping silent. British-owned territories, like Diego Garcia, were unquestionably implicated. So were members of Britain's security services.

Since Blair's departure as Prime Minister, more troubling evidence about his willingness to go along with Bush's policies has emerged, however contrary to Britain's judgements or even her principles they may have been. Ministers responding to parliamentary questions or to debates repeatedly denied that the government had condoned or assisted in the ugliest manifestations of the abuse of power, extraordinary rendition, and torture which often accompanied it. The United Kingdom has signed every international document that unreservedly condemns its use. Yet returning detainees and even US government sources allege that the United Kingdom assisted in procedures that were illegal under international law.

At home, one Terrorist Act after another was pushed through

Parliament with little regard to such civil liberties as a fair trial, privacy or access to legal advice. The right to asylum, theoretically guaranteed by the Geneva Conventions, was mocked by successive laws which pruned away the support asylum seekers were entitled to while their cases were considered. By the end of Tony Blair's government, they were neither provided with basic benefits nor allowed to work. This lack of compassion was compounded by the setting of targets for deportation, putting huge pressure on immigration officials to comply. The targets were personally advocated by the Prime Minister, aware as ever of the avidity of the right-wing media and of the public on this issue.

Yet on overseas aid, which appealed to public sympathy without any discomfort or inconvenience for our own way of life, the Prime Minister was eloquence itself, not least with regard to Africa – 'a scar on the conscience of the world', as he told delegates at the Labour Party Conference in October 2001. Where his own political power was not at risk, Blair could be the most moral of politicians. The irony of Iraq, the invasion of which originally commanded public support especially among Conservative voters, was that the scale of civilian deaths and the chaos and horror of victory's aftermath undermined New Labour's hold on the electorate, and damaged, irremediably, the moral case for its continuation in power.

EPILOGUE

The View from Here

I was born at a time of political and economic misery. The Great Crash in the world's financial markets had occurred a year earlier, in 1929. The real economy was drifting into depression. The dole queues were lengthening. In the United States the administration of Herbert Hoover had no idea what to do. In Europe weak governments were challenged, and in some cases superseded, by nationalist dictators.

Eighty years later, from where I am now, it looks as if history may be repeating itself. We are living, so the pundits tell us, through the worst economic crisis since the Great Crash. Banks have collapsed, or have been rescued only through huge injections of taxpayers' money. Unemployment is heading towards levels not seen since before the Second World War. Lenders are foreclosing on thousands of mortgaged homes. I was too young then to remember much about the 1930s, and I could not have understood the trenchant analysis of John Kenneth Galbraith's *The Great Crash*. But my senses did understand poverty, the smell of unwashed people in unwashed clothes, the sight of men queuing for jobs, the feeling of despair.

In Britain, and perhaps more widely, there is a serious loss of trust in representative democracy. That has been fuelled by fears about the personal consequences of the economic crisis and by newspaper revelations about the abuse of expenses by a substantial number of parliamentarians.

The big and important difference from the 1930s depression is that this current crisis has been accompanied by a massive shift of power in the world from West to East. It took the old European imperial countries, the United Kingdom and France, a long time to come to terms with their loss of power. I saw during the Suez crisis of 1956 the incomprehension they felt at being abandoned by their strongest ally, the United States. I saw too the resistance Harold Wilson put up to the withdrawal of the United Kingdom from most of its bases east of Suez in 1967, a withdrawal forced on us by the weakness of sterling and the consequent devaluation. Rapid economic growth, coupled with a rising share of world exports, have transformed the prospects of the great Asian powers like China and India, as well as those of a host of smaller countries ranging from Indonesia to Malaysia. Alarmed by the Asian banking crisis of the 1990s, which was driven by uncontrolled liberalisation of the financial markets, several of these countries maintained controls over the movement of capital. Those that did survived that banking crisis much better than those such as Thailand that let the markets rip. They will also survive this latest crisis better, and will therefore come out of it relatively stronger than the Western economies, which are once again learning painfully that there is such a thing as market failure. Expectations of sustained growth and ever-expanding prosperity, the twin promises of global liberalisation, have been shattered. Central and Eastern European countries, the newest recruits to the European Union, are seeing factories close and emigrant workers returning. People are beginning to ask if the ecstatic escape from Communism in the 1990s was quite as good as it seemed at the time. The Washington Consensus, the rarely challenged dogma of the past twenty years, no longer commands the respect it did.

Few people know what to do now. The old gods hang around because there is no new religion on offer. Many of them were figures of authority in a previous disposition; they still seek to be, but offer subtly different nostrums now. Their instinct is to shore up the glittering economic system they constructed. They are reluctant to admit that it cannot, and should not, be maintained.

The sense of injustice in wider society is palpable. The historic evidence is clear. Deeply unequal societies are far less committed to democracy and the rule of law than are fairer ones. The most stable and happy societies, according to much international research, have moderate differences in wealth and in incomes both within and between the public and private sectors. They enjoy high standards of education; they support and admire public service; they understand that a good society requires as its foundation a sense of the common good. The G20 summit of 2009 was something of a triumph. The measures to stimulate the global economy, to limit the rise in unemployment and to strengthen the regulation of banks and finance hold the promise of a better-balanced system. It is, however, only half a transformation. The second part requires the abandonment of short-term profit as our motivation, and a much longer vision than 'the bottom line'.

The future Western leaders are trying to construct rests upon the recovery of steady and sustained growth and rising prosperity based on consumption. Absent a miracle, it cannot be done. The resources to keep the growth economy going worldwide are simply not adequate in a world short of clean water, fertile soil and energy. The present global economic system is intrinsically wasteful, unjust and unsustainable. Arable land diminishes as desertification spreads. In many parts of the globe, water is already a scarce commodity, and will become more so as the world's forests are cut down. In our oceans, fish stocks are collapsing past the point of recovery. The world economy is nearing the limits of the planet's capacity.

The more intensive globalisation that advances in communications, transport and finance have produced has also brought
much closer interconnections among people, opportunities for
trade, investment and travel. Millions in the rich countries of the
West have discovered through trade and tourism the cultures and
values of the East. Millions more in the emerging economies have
moved up into a middle class that enjoys for the first time the
everyday artefacts of the West: cars, televisions, mobile telephones, computers, washing machines. They have escaped from
the relentless toil of subsistence farming. Many of them have
benefited from schooling up to secondary level and beyond. These
are big advances on the world of eighty years ago.

Globalisation has brought with it not only a new middle class,
but also a new elite. I taught many members of this global elite in
my decade of lecturing at the John F. Kennedy School of
Government at Harvard. It is an international elite that shares
information and understanding across national and cultural
boundaries, connections that are stronger than those to fellow citizens, from whom it becomes increasingly alienated. It is an elite
that wields great power, and knows it. Representative political
institutions such as national legislatures and parliaments, bypassed
by globalisation, begin to look anachronistic. They flay at their
governments on behalf of their electors, but often their governments lack the capacity and the power to respond.

So the world financial crisis cannot be cured by national governments alone, however powerful; yet the mechanisms for
international political cooperation exist in only the most rudimentary form, and this mainly at leadership level, the periodic
meetings of the 'G' government leaders, G8, G20, G77. The most
radical experiment in cooperation between nation states, the
European Union, has been crippled by national jealousies and
limited to economic supranationalism, the single market. It is still
unable to move forward to political or military interdependence,
or even to agree on the Lisbon Treaty, a collection of modest steps

towards greater integration. Consequently Europe, in political matters, punches far below its weight.

Given that elected political institutions remain almost entirely national, they cannot, by the nature of their mandate, deal with such urgent global issues as climate change. They can only try to bring pressure on their own governments. So there is a profound asymmetry. As globalisation proceeds, democracy is bypassed. The exception is, of course, the European Parliament. It has incrementally added to its influence, but has a long way to go, notably in the field of foreign affairs where Britain and France cling to their ancient prerogatives.

Democracy is undermined not only by its inability to connect with the biggest issues of the times, which are global. Paradoxically, it is also undermined by excessive concentration of power at the national level. Britain is a notable example. Over the past thirty years, starting with Margaret Thatcher's election in 1979, local government in Britain has been denuded of its effective powers and responsibilities, which have passed to quangos and government agencies. Today Britain is the most centralised democracy in the world, rescued from dull uniformity only by devolved governments in Scotland and Wales, both of which show a vitality unknown to Westminster. Yet the desire of citizens to be involved in the wider society is clear. There are still hundreds of nongovernmental organisations, national and local, contributing their ideas and energies on every issue of significance. In addition, there are thousands upon thousands of bloggers expounding their views on every available Internet channel.

As a schoolgirl I watched with delight the construction of the welfare state, the great achievement of social democracy. Sixty years later, the social security system and the National Health Service still stand as the fundamental safeguards for the citizen. Much else has gone. Tony Crosland's vision of equality has been most nearly realised, ironically, in the areas he was least engaged in, race and gender equality. Greater equality in incomes, wealth and educational opportunity remains elusive; the differentials in personal wealth and incomes are much wider than they have been for over a century. Ludicrously over-rewarded senior managers are now paid fifty to a hundred times more than the average pay of their employees, whereas in 1964, when I was first elected an MP, the ratio was around nine to one. Furthermore, the highly paid employ clever accountants to ensure they do not pay taxes equivalent to their earnings.

In the last decade I have lost two of the people who have shaped my life: Bernard, who was at the centre of my early adult years from the age of twenty to forty, and Dick, my second husband, who illuminated my later years. I miss Dick – his wisdom, his laughter and his ebullience – hugely. Both died in 2003, Bernard after a long illness confronted with great courage, Dick shortly after a fall in his early eighties. Both had touched the lives of hundreds of students who were devoted to them, and through their writings had influenced thousands more. They were very different personalities, but their deaths each evoked an intense sense of loss among those who had known them.

I now belong to the generation that every year sees its ranks reduced. In the same year that Dick and Bernard died, Roy Jenkins, who had inspired so many of my contemporaries, died too. He and I had not been close during the Wilson administrations, but it was then that I learned to admire his unflinching commitment to liberalism and his fastidiousness when it came to the corruption of language and ideas in modern public life. He was unquestionably a great man, and his biographies, as much as his political record, ensure that he will be remembered. Uncompromising, clear-eyed and fiercely demanding of the best performance and the highest principle was another friend, also unquestionably a great person, Helen Suzman of South Africa, with whom I stayed in her cottage overlooking the great silver

expanse of Plettenberg Bay. There were others there too, including Margaret Legum, poet, economist and champion of the poor,
who lived with her husband Colin, the distinguished journalist, in
Fischhoek, one of the few racially mixed towns in the Western
Cape. Margaret died on 1 November 2007.

Recalling this great gathering of the recently dead, it would be
tempting to claim that we shall not see their like again. I don't
believe it. Each challenge and each crisis evokes new ideas and
new heroes. I can only say how blessed I have been to have
known men and women of such courage and vision.

'All political careers end in failure.' Like other portentous remarks
by the late Enoch Powell, this doesn't bear examination. In one
sense, of course, all careers end in failure. We all die, and what we
leave behind, like our own bodies, either disappears or gradually
decays. Only a very few of us leave behind something that lasts, or
that can be built upon by posterity. In a more specific sense,
though, did Mr Powell mean that political careers aim at power,
but that few achieve it, and that the legacy even of those who do
so is often disappointing? That may say more about him and his
attitude to the prevailing climate of society at the time, the
Zeitgeist, than about political careers. For as a way of life politics
can be richly fulfilling.

Several things attracted me to politics when I was young. I was
a competitive child. I liked risk, matching myself against challenges. Climbing my father's bookshelves to the very top was one
such challenge. So was amateurishly climbing mountains, breaking
fingernails as I clung on to wet rock. I was drawn to some obvious
causes, poverty and inequality, lives limited by the accident of
birthplace, gender or colour. Like many other would-be political
activists, I wanted to make the world a better place. The deep satisfaction of growing up in the cold, austere, wonderful world of the
Attlee government, the first-ever Labour majority government, was
to watch that happening, to be part of that revolution by consent.

Then there was the sheer excitement of politics – like being in the front row at the theatre – seeing in real time what was going on around the world. I remember once asking an elderly friend who had lost her husband and her daughter within a few months of one another, what kept her going. 'Not knowing what is going to happen tomorrow,' she replied. That is my feeling too. Sixty years ago, Parliament was more influential and more significant than it is today, and the country it represented cut a bigger swathe in the world. Today my front row is in a multiplex theatre showing performances from all over the globe. I am aware that from my seat I can see only one part of the vast multifarious panorama. But the performances remain stimulating, feed my limitless curiosity about the people and places around me. I do not think a great deal about the past, unless prompted to do so, but I find the future fascinating.

Dedication, idealism, enthusiasm, excitement; these are not words most people today associate with politics. The loss of trust in politicians has been as dramatic as the more recent loss of trust in bankers. The words 'public service', so proudly pronounced by my great-uncle Leigh in Westmorland over ninety years ago, by many I knew in the postwar Labour movement and by my parents, too often evoke nowadays cynicism or disbelief. Yet without it society fragments. And politicians must bear some of the blame. They have learned how to spin the truth so as to leave a misleading impression. They have used the media, through leaks and unattributable briefing, to defend themselves against the media. When their popularity declines, like hungry wolves they turn upon each other. In the thirty years since the election of Margaret Thatcher's first government, Britain has had three Prime Ministers of remarkable ability, courage and ambition, not only for themselves but for the country – Thatcher, Blair and Brown. These have been Prime Ministers operating on the same phenomenal level as the challenges they have had to face. Yet all of them have belittled themselves by their behaviour towards colleagues, friends and rivals. Systematic briefing against colleagues and opportunistic distortion of facts can be effective political weapons. But they destroy the foundations of democratic civic life. Extremist parties of both right and left are strengthened by them. Citizens yearn for integrity. We should remind ourselves of the tragedy of the Weimar Republic after the First World War, when Germany's political leaders were denigrated and ridiculed to the point where they were destroyed along with the infant democracy they were trying to build.

Being an MP is like being a member of an extended family. You learn to love your family in all its knobbliness, perversity, courage and complexity. You learn respect and you build up trust. That is why every poll shows that people think more highly of their own Member of Parliament than of politicians as a whole. You belong to them. The fruit of long service in politics ripens into a harvest of men and women, most of whom you do not know, but who feel they are friends and who trust you. It is a huge responsibility and a huge privilege.

To be a good politician in a democracy, you have to care for people and to be fascinated by what makes them tick. You will interact with all sorts of people in your constituency or your district, and in the streets where you campaign. A few will berate you or curse you, but most people, once they grow up, are basically courteous. Many of them, too, will want to be heard. The politician whose eyes shift constantly to his watch, or to the apparently most important person in the room, feeds the distrust felt by the electorate. It is a distrust born of being manipulated, conned, even deceived, and it is fed by a relentlessly cynical national press.

Of all the comments I have encountered when campaigning, the one that infuriates me most is 'You're all in it for what you can get out of it.' It is a view fed by the extensive coverage of a small minority of greedy and corrupt politicians. That minority does not disappear. It has been the source of stories about corrupt politicians all my life. But the incidence was rare when I started out, and still is. Only once in my political life has anyone tried to bribe me, and he was a slippery fellow called Emil Savundra who left a crumpled £5 note in my hand when we shook hands in farewell. I returned it to him, saying, 'Mr Savundra, I don't come that cheap.' My friends and I found it laughable then, but we don't now. Every case of corruption, albeit exaggerated by the media, makes one cringe. It's true that politicians seek to be elected. What such comments imply, however, is that we are all in it for our own financial or personal self-interest.

There has been, in the past half-century, a shift away from 'legacy politics' to career politics. The great political figures of the eighteenth and early nineteenth centuries, in particular, often came from wealthy landowning families with a tradition of public service. They did not need money because they already had it. They did not need to hold on to office because they could always return to the influential circles from which they came. So resigning on a point of principle was a fairly cheap option for them.

The career politician, on the other hand, is a product of democracy, the opening up of politics to everybody. Being an MP has become a respectably paid job, though not one that begins to compare financially with being a top lawyer or the chief executive of a large company. Chief executives of the top hundred FTSE companies nowadays earn ten or more times as much as the Prime Minister. Getting selected, whether by a primary election as in the United States, or by a party choice as in the United Kingdom, is often more important than getting elected, because so many constituencies are safe for one party or another. This has brought with it the professionalisation not just of elective politics, but also of the preparation to be a politician. Hence more and more young people start by becoming an MP's political aide, rise to become an adviser to an influential politician, and finally get elected, usually for a safe seat. This process means that more and more MPs know no life outside politics, have never run a business or been responsible for a public service, or have worked abroad long enough to understand the culture and values of another country. They have little experience of what their constituents persist in calling 'real life'.

Councillors come from a much wider background than do parliamentary politicians. They are not part of the incestuous culture of the 'Westminster village'. Yet there is little attraction now in local government service. It is a tragedy for politics that local government has been emasculated by Conservative and Labour administrations alike. Local councils have seen almost all their functions, from education to planning, subjected to rigorous regulation and direction, and their discretion constrained. The work is less fulfilling than it used to be. Given the intensity and long hours of many modern jobs, getting time off from paid work is difficult and will put promotion at risk. Local government has become the province of the retired. It is impoverished by the disappearance of younger people.

Yet politicians, even career politicians, are not all 'in it for what they can get out of it'. Had that been the case, the Liberal Democrats would not exist. What career advantage could this new high-risk party offer to an ambitious young politician hungry for office? What about the politicians, some of them among the most able we have, who resigned over the invasion of Iraq, or in an earlier era, over that of the Suez Canal Zone? What about the patient delving by MPs on parliamentary Select Committees, often coming up with findings that embarrass their own government and may not be well received by their Party superiors?

Most of the politicians I have known, over three generations, are honourable and honest men and women who came into public life to make society better or to represent the concerns of their own community. They deal with the heavy responsibilities of their constituents' needs, devoting hours and hours every week to their problems and complaints. The grand detachment of the past, MPs making occasional visits to their constituencies to greet and be greeted, has long since gone, replaced by weekly 'surgeries' to which people bring their problems, and by endless meetings with organisers of local charities or protest groups. Everywhere, in this more demanding and less deferential time, the demands on MPs have increased, often to the detriment of parliamentary debate and scrutiny.

Many are drawn into politics by some core conviction. Mine is very simple. As I said earlier, I have never understood or accepted that some people, through the accident of birth, should be so much richer, have so much greater opportunities and better access to education, health care and good housing than others. This goes back to what I saw at Christ Church Elementary School in the 1930s, reinforced at the international level by what I witnessed of the horrors of war and the deprivations of poverty, and what my mother taught me about them. It was natural for me to be a social-ist, and I was confirmed in that by the bold vision of the postwar Attlee government. But I also learned in the postwar decades, as I mentioned in Chapter 13, the way power was monopolised and abused by the *nomenklatura*, the Communist elite. It was not only the destruction of the kulaks in the 1930s, the killing or impris-oning of prisoners of war returning home from the West; it was also the special trains and hotels, the health resorts and best schools reserved for the rulers and their associates. When I trav-elled around Russia and Eastern Europe for Project Liberty soon after the Berlin Wall had been breached, my well-meaning hosts often put me up in what had been Communist Party hotels. The big, heavily furnished rooms all boasted an empty refrigerator, usu-ally unconnected to any electricity supply, standing in the middle, a pointless icon of privilege. The cars and special carriages in the trains had thick curtains or blinds to screen one from the prying eyes of the populace. This was a ruling class insulated from those it ruled.

So I was always a democratic socialist, trying to hammer out a compromise between capitalism and social justice, a compromise that might attract enough public support to be viable. I was also a Christian socialist because Christ loved the poor, lived among them and spoke the Gospel to them. Over sixty years, my convictions have not changed. I have seen the pendulum swing from democratic socialism to the almost complete hegemony of capitalism, disregarding market failure, massive and growing inequality, and the misery of millions deprived of even the most basic services. Public health and education in China and Russia after 'market liberalisation' were starved of resources in the 1990s, and now are having to be painfully rebuilt. Worldwide, the rich are again in the saddle. Yet I have a strong sense that things have gone too far, and that the pendulum is swinging back again. Climate change, the biggest challenge of all, demands international action, state intervention and community response. It will compel us to construct an international regime that is motivated by mutual survival, not by institutional selfishness; one that recognises the world must live by sharing fairly its limited resources.

That is true, too, of the other challenge to our survival, the proliferation of nuclear weapons, an issue that now absorbs much of my remaining energy and sense of purpose. There is likely to be a burgeoning of nuclear power installations worldwide in the next twenty years: civil nuclear energy is seen by many governments as the most effective response to climate change. Technically, enriching nuclear materials to generate electricity follows the same path as enriching them to make weapons of mass destruction. So everything depends on the framework of international regulation and inspection within which the development of nuclear power takes place. So acute is the need for this framework that national sovereignty itself in this area will have to be superseded. The fuel cycle, from the supply of nuclear materials to the processing of waste, can be controlled effectively only by making it multinational. That in turn will require more powerful international institutions, such as a better-resourced International Atomic Energy Authority.

Politicians seek the power to realise their visions, their core convictions. Some feel at ease with power, even though the responsibility that comes with it can be awesome – like deaths in a war, for instance, or lives wrecked by ill-conceived domestic policies. Leaders can shield themselves from the consequences of their decisions by creating around themselves circles of friends and sycophants. Some modern regimes resemble medieval courts, a monarch dispensing patronage and surrounded by advisers, none of them accountable to the citizens nor elected by them. Small wonder that these same citizens feel alienated.

Like many women of my generation and of the generation before mine, I thought of myself as not quite good enough for the very highest positions in politics. I ran for deputy leader of the Labour Party in 1976 against Michael Foot, but never for leader. I was President of the Social Democratic Party and the first SDP MP to be elected, but I conceded the Party leadership to Roy Jenkins without a fight, to the disgust of my colleague David Owen. To me the leading figures in politics were giants, until I got to know them and discovered that they were flawed and sometimes self-doubting, like me. I accepted the criticisms made of me, that I was disorganised and lacked a ruthless killer instinct. Throughout most of my life in politics, after Bernard left, I had no partner who believed in me and supported me – though I had wonderful friends – until I married Dick in December 1987. Few people write about the partners of political leaders, but they are indispensable. It is still easier for an able male politician to find such a person than for a woman, though thankfully that is beginning to alter.

I have seen over my lifetime changes so radical they amount to a transformation – in the lives of women, in the advent of multi-racial and multicultural societies, and in the strains these changes have brought to our communities. These changes have provided the themes of this book and, being part of it all, not 'monitoring' them but being actively involved, has been more exciting and indeed more encouraging than I could ever have anticipated.

The near future offers even more challenge and even more change, not least trying to resolve the ethical questions that shadow the rapid development of the life sciences. As a grand-parent now, I rejoice in my grandchildren, my grandnephews and nieces, and pray they may be generous, understanding and wise. I recently revisited my childhood home in the New Forest with my older grandson, Sam, who found it as magical as I do. That day, the gnarled and ancient trees had been reborn in puckered emerald-green leaves, the grass scattered with violets and primroses in the annual miracle of spring.

'Look thy last on all things lovely,' wrote Walter de la Mare. I hope it will not be the last for our endangered species. That depends on whether the next generation and the one after that resolve the dilemma of how to get the balance right between progress and human values, between growth and the stewardship of a fragile planet that needs to be cherished if it is to survive. The answer to the dilemma was put most succinctly by another poet, one who knew about Hiroshima and Nagasaki, W. H. Auden: 'We must love one another or die.'

ACKNOWLEDGEMENTS

I want to thank the scores of people who have contributed to this autobiography by being an important part of my life, too many to list here. A long life is a bit like a jigsaw puzzle, incomplete without each piece being in place. Many will find themselves mentioned in the text. In these acknowledgements, I single out those who have read and commented on early drafts, and whose comments and corrections have helped to shape the final version.

Mark Bostridge, David McKie, Peter Metcalfe and Paul Twinn read all, or almost all, the book in draft; their help was generously offered and thankfully received. In my office, Josh Harris and Ruth Brock managed to make sense of lots of drafts, as well as handling a flood of contributions. Others read those parts of the book they had been personally involved in; their memories of those years proved invaluable. Among them were Marian Clark and Helen Green, John and Eileen Spencer, Val Arnold-Forster and Phyllis Cook. Rodney Donald and Guido Declercq, companions on my car journey across the United States, provided their own memories of the trip. The descriptions of my time in the House of Commons owe much to Roy Hattersley, Frank Judd, David Owen, Bill Rodgers, and my personal secretary Carol

Bracken, now Carol Savage. John Burgh and Robert Maclennan recalled the Department of Prices and Consumer Protection for me, and in both cases their help went well beyond that.

My former personal assistant Ed Flood worked mightily to recollect with me the Harvard years, as did Kathy Eckroad, Sally Mackycynus, Dick's secretary, and Kalypso Nicolaidis, my fellow professor on courses dealing with the European Union. Both Kathy and Ed, key collaborators in Project Liberty, reminded me of what we had achieved in the 1990s. Graham Allison, Dean of the Kennedy School of Government for much of my time there, and Michael Sandel, the 2009 Reith lecturer with whom I went to Russia, provided useful information and thoughtful insights. Ted Sorensen, John F. Kennedy's speechwriter, generously allowed me to use a long interview with him on the Cuban Missile Crisis. I am also grateful to Robert Skidelsky for many conversations about Russia.

On the House of Lords, in addition to my predecessor Bill Rodgers and my successor Tom McNally, for whose support I am very grateful, I would like to acknowledge the help of Paddy Ashdown, especially on Kosovo, Navnit and Ann Dholakia, especially on India, Andrew Phillips, especially on Iran, Jane Bonham-Carter on John Lyttle, Celia Thomas and Carolyn Rampton, successive heads of the Liberal Democrat Whips' office, and my colleagues on the Liberal Democrat front benches in the Parliamentary opposition to the Iraq war, Charles Kennedy, Menzies Campbell and William Wallace. John Roper as my Chief Whip ensured well-considered judgements and an enthusiastically united Lords Parliamentary Party.

Peter and Barbara Metcalfe, Jim Caldwell, my constituency agent, Bill and Hilda Lawrence, and Brian Hall shared with me our experiences of the growth and development of Stevenage. Many of those I was closest to in the Hitchin constituency are sadly no longer alive. My debt to them, particularly Stanley and Helen Grant of Letchworth, is immense.

Lennie Goodings, my editor at Virago, and her colleague Zoë Gullen have shown remarkable forbearance, and a sympathetic capacity for improving the text. Sue Wedlake, from the US Embassy, managed to find the photograph of Bill Clinton's last lecture in the UK as President, and Linda Silverman managed to marry the captions to the photographs.

My friends Hilary and Helge contributed their recollections of life in our shared home. So did my daughter Rebecca. My son-in-law Christopher, my niece Larissa and her husband Roger, my sister-in-law Jennifer, her son Tim and her daughter Ishbel have all provided helpful comments and Christopher is responsible for several of the photographs. Their support has been indispensable in what has been a long and sometimes frustrating project, which all started with my late husband Dick's inspiration and encouragement. His daughter Elizabeth sensitively evokes Dick's personality in the book she and Matt Dickinson co-edited, *Guardian of the Presidency*. All of us miss him still.

INDEX

INDEX

Williams, Tom 111